Arts & Crafts for Children

THE WORLD BOOK OF

Arts & Crafts for Children

Arnold Arnold

M

ISBN 0 333 21295 9

First published in Great Britain 1976 by
Macmillan London Limited
London and Basingstoke
Associated companies in New York, Toronto,
Dublin, Melbourne, Johannesburg and Delhi

Reprinted 1977

First published in the U.S.A. 1975 by
Thomas Y. Crowell Company
Published simultaneously in Canada by
Fitzhenry and Whiteside Limited

Printed in Great Britain by Billing & Sons Ltd.
British Library Cataloguing in Publication Data
Arnold, Arnold
    The world book of arts and crafts for
    children.
    Index.
    ISBN 0-333-21295-9
    1. Title
    745.5'02'4054 TT157
    Handicraft

To all children and especially to my own:
Geoffrey, Marguerite and Francis;
To the child within me;
To Gail;
And to the future

Contents

Foreword

Children learn best through play. They develop and hone skills by experimenting with materials, tools and their own unfolding capacities. But they also need guidance. They don't acquire good learning habits by being drilled, by being forced to copy or learn by rote, or by being shown how to 'produce'. These principles have long been accepted by enlightened British educators, and they have recently been reaffirmed by both Plowden and Bullock Reports.

Many secondary schools do offer art, craft and design courses. But they are optional and, above infant-school levels, reserved for the non-academic student. Indeed, it is possible to take 'O' and 'A' levels in ceramics and art, though it is patently absurd to test a fifteen- or eighteen-year-old's performance in art or craft. While these tests seem to lend a spurious respectability to the arts, they also turn them into yet another credentials-acquisition ploy.

This book is intended for all children and not just for those who demonstrate special aptitude for or interest in art or craft. Moreover, I hope to influence parents and teachers to encourage the children in their charge to use tools and materials in an inventive manner. All children need some of these experiences, at home and in school.

Historically, craftsmanship declines in proportion to industrialization. This is true for all cultures. Esquimaux who live in Quonset huts lose their igloo-building skills. They also lose an important part of their cultural heritage. This is unavoidable to some extent. But the decultured Esquimaux lose out on other scores. They become confused, neurotic and dissatisfied, without knowing why. They lose their will to work and survive. Many become perpetual welfare clients. Eventually they become extinct.

Signs of cultural decline and disorientation are visible throughout the technologically developed world. More than the current economic crisis, Britain, like other industrialized nations, suffers a psychological one that is linked to a loss in skills and craftsmanship. Until very recently, Britain was one of the most craft-conscious countries in the world. British craftsmanship was legendary, even in industry. British goods were sought everywhere. British craftsmanship extended to the factory floor, the office and even to the retail shop. Pride of craft may seem like an absurdity now, but it enhances the self-esteem and work satisfaction of everyone. The quality of and demand for British goods have declined correspondingly. The effect on individuals is not merely economic. Most Britons no longer take pride in acquiring and practising skills, and the products of their labour fail to satisfy them and their customers. No amount of North Sea oil will restore this loss.

A return to craft-consciousness offers Britain one avenue of national, cultural and spiritual revival. Britain can only compete with countries more lavishly endowed with raw materials, space and automation by a return to craftsmanship. Such a revival requires an education of present-day and future generations in all walks of life – managers, factory workers, individual creators, government bureaucrats, teachers and students – who are experienced in and have respect for artistry and craftsmanship. The industries of the future that will allow Britain to thrive once again can find their beginnings only in a revival of creative craftsmanship.

A return to craft-consciousness, especially in the education of children, will pay rich dividends in the quality of individual, family and community life. It builds character, endurance and self-reliance among young and old. The traditions of such craftsmanship have deep roots in Britain. They need merely be reinterpreted to serve modern requirements. The British eighteenth-century family relied largely on crafts practised by all its members. Victorian homes of all classes were partially handmade. John Ruskin and William Morris a hundred years ago, and Sir Herbert Read in this century, foresaw the consequences of the decline in British craftsmanship. These men may seem dated and romantic dreamers today, but they were prophetic. I should like this book to make the educational and creative opportunities that were once the privilege of the few available to all children. They need and deserve them.

Arnold Arnold, London, 1976

1 Approaches and attitudes

... They have no pleasure in the work by which they make their bread ... for they feel that the kind of labour to which they are condemned is verily a degrading one, and makes them less than men. *John Ruskin*

'Evidence of non-involvement and the disinclination to exert effort are appearing in homes and classrooms ... What does this behaviour mean? ... What is today's environment feeding back to children? All around, children see adults place greater reliance on mechanical aids than on their own capacities and resources.'* Written by an astute teacher and observer of children, this is a terrible indictment of our times and attitudes. But what can we expect? We plonk children before the TV set at earliest ages from three to seven hours

each day. Here processes, skills and achievements are necessarily telescoped. Anything portrayed on TV looks as if it could be done by anyone without experience and with a very small expenditure of time, effort and devotion. Small wonder that children's endurance and respect for excellence are eroded.

This book offers concerned parents, teachers, recreation workers and therapists the means to counteract these trends.

Children need values and ethics. Our society fails them in these respects more than in any other. Art and craft provide opportunities for awakening practical senses of right and wrong, what works and what doesn't, what is permissible and possible and what isn't, and an ability to savour success and cope with momentary failure and frustration. They foster

* Dorothy H. Cohen, 'Children of Technology: Images or The Real Thing' in *Childhood Education*, J. of The Association for Childhood Education International, Washington, DC, 48:6:3.72, 298–300

making judgements. Every stroke of hammer or brush is a decision. The child learns in art and craft activities to consider each such decision in advance and to live with the result. We can't afford to allow our children's creative abilities and endowments to atrophy in expectation that they won't need these in an expected technological future. Its promised benefits have proven elusive. The earth cannot support ever-expanding population growth. The technologies have polluted the environment, concentrated non-absorbable wastes on land and in the sea and air, and are making life hazardous and unhealthy. 'Only madmen and economists believe growth can go on for ever in a finite world.'*

Nature inevitably redresses such imbalances if it can. And so the choice is a return to a labour-intensive husbandry of resources, or disaster. Implicit in either course is the exercise of craft by those who wish to prosper and survive – the change in life style or a possible ecological debacle. It is with hope for the former rather than fear of calamity that this book has been written. Genuine craft attitudes are a vital necessity if our children are to have the means to thrive during the difficult

* Jeremy Swift, *The Other Eden*: Dent, 1974

decades ahead. Art can endow them with beauty and purpose. The practice of both will assure that essential human qualities will be preserved and enhanced, come what may.

The background material that precedes each of the following chapters suggests attitudes for introducing art and craft techniques to children and young people. One without the other has no value. I therefore hope that these introductions are read with as much care and attention as the recipes.

There are two reasons for educating children. The first is, or should be, to elicit and develop their humanity. The second is to make them economically independent and useful. In automating production, and training young people for work in such an economy, we tend to lose sight of the first, essential object of learning: the exercise of species specific skills, irrespective of their economic usefulness.

Many of our schools neglect manual education at primary

and secondary levels as the demand for genuine craft declines. This has caused a deterioration in general competence and also in the consumer's judgement. It creates 'a mechanization of responsibility as well, taking judgement farther and farther away from the minds, and therefore the ethics, of men'.*

Education in essential human skills is likely to decline further as it has already in fields in which automation has taken command – in printing and tool- and die-making trades, for example. Humanness may die piecemeal. And unless this trend is reversed at least in so far as the education of young people is concerned, we may need a redefinition of what it means to be human.

Significantly, there has been a strong revival of arts and crafts, especially among the disaffected young. Unfortunately, many who engage in craft occupations as young adults or who practise them for the first time as hobbies in middle or old age suffer a distorted creative sense imposed by miseducation and misinformation. Even when they use tools, they don't exercise craft. 'The housewife who bakes her own bread according to a recipe, sews a dress from a pattern [that she did not design] . . . is doing useful, satisfying, but contrary to the women's magazines, uncreative work . . . To do by hand what a machine ordinarily does is not a creative act.'†

Most art and craft manuals, instruction books, periodicals, kits and even teachers stress production, following or tracing patterns, plans and recipes. This is a denial of the very essence of creative tool use. It is essential that children should be sheltered from such production in early as much as in later years. They need exposure to the creative processes of art and craft.

* Ward Just, *Military Men*: Avon Books, 1970
† Judith Groch, *The Right to Create*: Little, Brown & Co, 1969

1 Art and craft education

Where schools, museums and other institutions fail children, it is up to parents to make up the deficit. Proper introduction to the arts and crafts affects a child's personality, outlook, achievement and future, regardless of his individual bent or eventual career. It refines abilities, no matter which stream of higher education, vocation or avocation he or she enters later. A young man or woman who enjoys a background and interest in any of the arts or crafts will be more sensitive to people, ideas and the material world. He or she will be able to choose, care for, value and use the tools of his or her calling and those required for daily existence with discretion and imagination. And he or she will certainly be more likely to survive successfully in a declining world economy than those who cannot use their hands.

The increase in leisure and the nature of employment today make art and craft education a necessity. For the moment at least a large part of the population in technologically developed countries spends more time in leisure than on life-supporting labour. Our children need skills that will sustain their interests in adulthood during their hours and years away from work. Those lacking avocational interests tend to become passive; their abilities atrophy; they lack lustre and curiosity; they are frustrated and dissatisfied; and their life expectancy is shortened. Genuine craft – and not do-it-yourself projects – could engage and satisfy them. But this requires an education in childhood and youth that stresses creative development.

The art and craft education of children requires more than mere exposure to tools and materials. Children need direct contacts with active artists and craftsmen. They need to see them work in the flesh and be able to touch their work. They need a familiarity with different styles and forms created in former times and in different cultures, as well as in their own, not to imitate, but to be inspired by them.

2 Ages and stages

Young children can be introduced to a great variety of tools and materials, provided elementary safety precautions and what the child can and cannot yet do are kept in mind. For example, any five-year-old, who has built with blocks, drawn, painted and finger-painted, can handle a coping saw or jigsaw into which a spiral safety blade has been inserted. But first the child needs direction. He must be provided with a proper workspace, with tools and materials. He needs incentives and to have the nature of the work pointed out to him. This is true at all stages of development. It is equally important to shelter today's child from the temptation to imitate TV, comic book, cartoon and other pervasive stereotypes, encouraging him to invent his own symbols.

3 Individual differences

Not every child is equally inventive or inclined to identical interests. Some prefer to draw, others to sculpt; still others enjoy work with wood, leather, fibres, fabric or film. A child can learn identical skills from any art and equal satisfaction in craft. All provide opportunities for expression and development of self, provided they are introduced in a proper manner.

Every child enjoys working with his or her hands. His or her inclinations are most readily observable at early ages before they are overlaid by outside influences. But you can only discover and nurture them by exposure to direct experience with tools and materials. A child's interest in any art or craft can also serve as a focal point for other learning, including academic skills. One who doesn't read with interest or skill may suddenly become passionately immersed in books dealing with a craft subject that engages him. Another, who may be uninterested in numbers, will discover that mathematics has practical uses in making plans, or measuring or weighing the materials with which he enjoys working.

4 Special children

Conventional definitions of intelligence are extremely limited and inexact. Children are quite often classified as mentally retarded, hyperactive, autistic, slow learners or even brain-damaged when their abilities lie outside what is usually taught and tested. Art and craft education offers parents, teachers and therapists alternative opportunities for reaching many children and young people who are otherwise neglected or left behind in the classroom.

5 Process versus production

A misunderstanding of the difference between learning and performance has created confusion in the art and craft education of children as in most other aspects of education. *Production* is not, and should not be, the object of manual skill development and self-expression. Instead, it can and should lead to the discovery of *processes*.

Creative work involves a progressive discovery of tools, materials, processes and self, and how they can be transformed imaginatively. Such creation may be frustrating or exhilarating or both. It may lead to messes or masterpieces. None of this is important to the child, except in so far as it leads to exercise, experience, new insights, competence, independence, co-ordination, wonder, curiosity, intuition, spontaneity, whimsy, discovery, self-discipline and endurance. Most of these qualities are not measured or measurable. They are especially important because few schools stimulate and none can test them.

A child given colouring books and 'paint-by-number' kits can turn out Mona Lisas or Last Suppers on an assembly line.

One who is reared on 'hobby kits' can produce a stream of miniature ballistic missiles and detailed facsimile space capsules merely by gluing bits of prefabricated plastic together. This kind of mass production is mesmerizing and habit-forming. It fosters an illusion of craft and creativity. Such activities are only unskilled, menial and soul-destroying labour.

But a child who slowly builds competence by daubing clumsily with a paintbrush discovers how to bend materials to his will. A child who is experienced in such craft becomes progressively critical of his own efforts.

Ultimately the child's creation does turn into a product of some sort. 'What shall I make?' is not an unreasonable question for a child to ask once he has mastered new tools and skills. Or he may be inspired to learn because he wants to make or invent something, draw, paint or sculpt what he experiences or feels, or build an object he wants to use in play or give as a present. Or he may simply wish to make his surroundings more beautiful. Especially then his work should not evade the creative processes of art and craft. It should be self-generated and not depend on prefabricated parts, patterns or plans.

6 Play, self-expression and creativity

Play, self-expression, creativity and art are usually inexactly and loosely defined. The following describes what is meant by these terms for the purposes of this book.

Child's play differs from that of most adults because personality, abilities and intellect are in formative stages during childhood. The child literally 'forms' himself through play.* It is his work and means to growth. The adult 're-forms'

* Judy Ann Spitler, 'Changing View of Play in the Education of Young Children': Teachers College, Columbia University. 1971 (PhD thesis, unpublished)

himself by the same process. For most it is recreation. But the quality of *playfulness* is common to both adult and child. Such playfulness is the essence of *self-expression* and *creativity* and it serves as the most useful definition of these hackneyed terms.

Craft describes the exercise of skills. It is the hallmark of competence. An artist practises craft when he paints or sculpts. A scientist practises craft when he prepares a slide for his microscope. A mechanic practises craft when he repairs a car. None of these acts is creative unless an element of inventive playfulness enters into the manipulation of tools and materials. The degree to which a child may depart from prescribed paths in his self-expressive play decides the extent to which he can create himself.

Art involves the playful use of self. This is why children are creative by definition. But by definition they also lack experience, competence and craft. Children need tools and materials presented to them in a way that allows them to discover their disciplined uses. Craft can accomplish this only if it is introduced as a process rather than as a means of production. Without playfulness the child turns into a mindless producer. Without craft he lacks the means to achieve mature playfulness. And he can only acquire the former through the exercise of the latter.

7 What to teach and when

The judgement of what to teach – and when not to teach – emerges when art and craft are viewed as educational processes. The decision of what to do, make or express must be left to the child once he sets to work. First, however, work space, tools and materials must be provided. The desirable balance between direction and freedom can be achieved only 'if the teacher [or parent] is one who inspires rather than dictates, where the discoveries about the nature of materials are discussed so that children learn through [their own and] each other's experience as well as from the teacher. A group of ten-year-olds, for example, might discover that wax crayons resist water-based ink. From this starting point [simple wax-resist] the gifted teacher will try to create situations in which the process of using wax to repel water is examined in as many contrasting ways as possible.'*

A child can learn the limits of safety and behaviour in art and craft as in all other activities. He needs to discover how to arrange, control and care for his tools. He must understand that he may not paint on the wall or decorate baby brother's hair with clay. He needs to be shown the disciplines of craft, while the playful and experimental aspects of art must be left in his hands.

Every beginner in art and craft – adult, teenager or child – tends to lose control over his medium. The materials spread as if they had a will of their own, from the centre of the table to its edges and beyond. Things are spilled, surfaces marred, and an object that is the product of hours of thoughtful labour is shattered in the confusion.

You can show the child that things work better if he keeps materials in bins and boxes, hangs up his tools in prearranged places when they aren't in use, and keeps them in good working order. He needs clothing, table and floor spaces that are washable. How hammer or coping saw must be held and how to nail or drill to best effect and in safety must be demonstrated. The child needs properly organized material and tool storage places. He needs help with cleaning up messes until he can be expected to do this unaided. But don't expect too much, too soon, from a child. Ceaseless demand for self-discipline and neatness can be as discouraging as constant disorder.

* Henry Pluckrose, quoted in *The Fourth R: A Commentary on Youth, Education, and the Arts* by Joseph Featherstone: Associated Council of the Arts, 1972

The visual, auditory and tactile qualities of materials must be pointed out to the child. He needs to learn how to recognize and identify them and how to express them verbally and in his creative work. Experience and familiarity with the origins of material will increase his interest in them. Eventually he will want to know how to weigh and measure, plan and design when projects demand precision. But even these skills

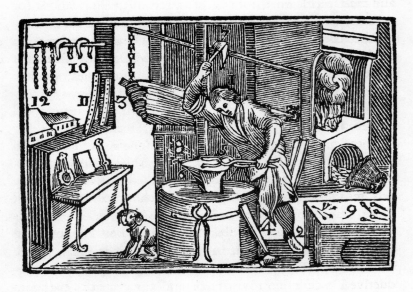

evolve from spontaneous experiences that lead from non-numerical to geometric and eventually to numerical judgements.

Parents and teachers should work with craft materials themselves and become familiar with the opportunities they offer. But in presenting the same materials to children, parents and teachers must remember the developmental level of each child and of his or her previous experiences. In any event don't show the child tricks – how to draw in perspective, in proportion, or a 'stick' man. Children can only see and express things one-dimensionally until they reach quite advanced

stages of development.* But this can never be accelerated.
Interference can short-circuit it.

8 Tools, materials and judgement

Children and young people can only discover the allowable
limits of the technologies through an education in manual arts
and crafts. This does not suggest a return to hand labour for
the sake of misplaced nostalgia.

Since the advent of industrialization and with the explosion
of the technologies, tools have proliferated to an extent that
most have escaped ethical governance. As a result, we lack
principles required to guide us in their use, from steam to
internal combustion engine, from chemicals, drugs and
plastics to nuclear energy.

These are persuasive reasons for educating children and
young people in handicrafts. A wooden plank cut up with a ·
handsaw teaches a child more than the gift of a factory-made
box, ready for decoration. A fabric remnant that the child cuts,
glues, staples or sews to form an abstract design or an ill-
fitting doll's apron provides more valuable experiences than
a gift of patterns that assure a perfect result, or a whole
wardrobe of Barbie-doll dresses. It is infinitely more productive if a child improvises a paper, cardboard or twig loom
than if he weaves on a miniature, prefabricated and prestrung
one. These suggestions are not made for the sake of economy
but for the sake of the child.

9 Mixed media, skills and scrap materials

Once a child has learned how to handle a hand drill and how
to choose the right bit for making a hole in a particular
material, he can apply the same skill and knowledge to wood,

* Arnold Arnold, *Teaching Your Child to Learn from Birth to School Age*:
Prentice-Hall, 1971

metal, brick or seashells for that matter. He should be encouraged to look for and find a variety of materials on which to exercise his skills, tools, and imagination, rather than limiting himself to one application. Experience with and especially the discovery of a variety of raw, manufactured and scrap materials enable the young craftsman to draw on and choose from a large reservoir of different media. He'll use the proper tool required for each different material because he is sensitive to their differences in texture, density and weight. He can shape any material to achieve a desired effect. These abilities are necessary for life in a world rich with diverse materials and experiences.

The search for diversity in effect and for possible combinations of different materials is a creative act in itself. It brings harmony to what, on the surface, may seem like clashing or divergent characteristics. A large part of the art consists of discovering how each can support, complement or counteract all others. This is why collages and assemblages are stressed in many of the following chapters. They are not 'modern' art; they are essential experiences. Abstraction underlies the work of even traditional and realistic artists and craftsmen. It is also the structure that underlies a child's later outlook, as in creation. He learns to see, recognize and create structure, instead of being confused by surface detail. And so the assemblage the child makes out of scraps of paper and wood enables him eventually to get greater satisfaction out of his still or movie camera than if he lacked this experience.

10 Work spaces, lighting and clothing
(See also 81, 113 and 138.)

A child does not need a carpenter's bench for work with wood any more than he needs an easel for painting. He does need a solid worktable for either, large and low enough so that he can work in comfort, sitting or standing. A well-built trestle table can serve the purpose (see diagram). It should consist of a 2-cm (¾-inch) plywood top, with all surfaces carefully sanded and coated with several light applications of varnish or shellac. Sawhorses make practical legs provided the tabletop is attached to them firmly. A child outgrows other worktables rapidly. Metal sawhorse angle brackets can be bought inexpensively in any hardware shop. 2·5cm × 5cm (1″ × 2″) wooden legs can be inserted into these and replaced with

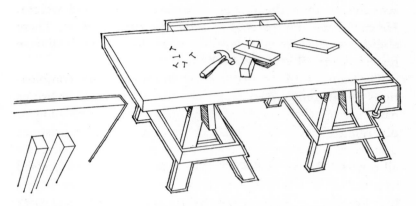

longer ones as the child grows taller. 2·5cm × 5cm (1″ × 2″) strips should be glued and screwed also to the underside of the tabletop so that it cannot slide off the sawhorses as the child works (see diagram).

Either trestle table or tabletop carpenter's workbench can be used for any kind of art or craft work. A woodworking vice (see 91) can be attached. Wooden rails can be nailed or screwed in place to secure small parts, bins, tools and paint jars. A pegboard, hung within reach, can become a tool storage centre.

Shelves and receptacles are required for materials storage. The floor under and around the worktable should be protected.

The worktable or bench should be placed next to a window so that the light falls on the work from the side opposite the child's handedness (from the left for a right-handed child, and from the right for a left-handed child). He should not face, nor should his back be turned to, the window while he works. An overhead light is needed for work after dark or on overcast days, so that work spaces are relatively shadow-free. Keep extension cords out of the way, out from underfoot, and out of the child's reach.

A smock or old clothing will protect the child from spills that are bound to occur. Sleeves should be buttoned at the wrist or rolled up above the elbows. Shirts should be tucked into belts or skirts and buttoned. When heat-producing or power tools are used, smocks should be belted. These suggestions allow for safe, unhampered limb and manual movements.

11 Safety

Only you can tell whether your child can use a tool safely at his or her stage of development. A child needs experience before he can appreciate and remember the logic of caution. A totally protected and inexperienced child is far more likely to injure himself and others than one who is gradually exposed to experiences, including those that pose minor hazards, provided he receives guidance and supervision. Children usually confine themselves to working with tools on appropriate materials *if these are furnished*. A hammer given without tacks or wood invariably invites inappropriate use. Insisting that a child follows given patterns and plans also leads to potentially damaging experimentation when no one is looking. The gift of new tools must coincide with a time at which the child understands what he may and may not do with them. You must become aware of hazards, and foresee and point them out as often and as patiently as necessary. Do not expect a child, even at ages when he or she can read, to study and heed the cautions on labels or packages. You must do this yourself and then make appropriate judgements about the possible dangers.

Proper arrangement of the child's work spaces (see 10), when and how materials are introduced, and foresight will prevent accidents. All tools and materials suggested in this book are safe if given as and when recommended, with some exceptions for which special cautions are listed in every case. Your attention is drawn to those tools and materials that are sharp, pointed or potentially toxic in the hands of children too immature to use them with caution.

Two materials – plastics and glass – are largely excluded from this book for safety reasons. Plastic scrap, like vinyl, can be glued to collages and assemblages without danger, provided organic glues are used, but such scraps will not adhere permanently.

Virtually all synthetic paints and glues, except acrylics, and all aerosol spray paints and adhesives are highly toxic and potentially carcinogenic. Some synthetic glues bond so effectively that any of the material that dries on the skin, or a part accidentally glued to a finger, may require surgery for removal. Many tar- and cellulose-derived finishes and glues, as well as paints, dyes and ceramic glazes that contain lead, are dangerous and inappropriate for use by young people. (See also 165.)

12 Organization of contents

Each of the chapters in this book deals with one major craft, art or materials subject, and is subdivided into parts in an ascending order of skill and difficulty. General background or cautionary information is given within these subdivisions. The number of art and craft projects themselves, and the amount of subject matter included, are possible only because duplication is avoided through cross-references. For example, cutting with scissors requires the same basic instructions and cautions whether the material is paper, foil, cloth or thin, split leather. Overlapping skills are described only once, in appropriate places, and cross-referenced by section-number whenever the same technique applies elsewhere.

2 Paper and foil

We need craftsmanship in education, in a machine age as much, if not more than any other, because it is a fundamental *mode of education*, through which the child explores, discovers the qualities of, and comes to terms with the world in which he lives. *Mairi Seonaid Robertson*

13 Background

Paper was first invented in China by Ts'ai Lun in the year AD105. It was made of the bark of the mulberry bush, similar to tapa cloth still used by Pacific islanders. By the time of Marco Polo paper was made in the Far East by pressing vegetable fibres into sheets in a manner not very different from modern techniques. Paper objects and miniatures were also used in religious ceremonies. Foil-covered paper money was a part of Chinese funerary rites as early as AD739.

The ancient Egyptians used the leaves of the papyrus tree – hence our word 'paper' – pasted into sheets for record-keeping. The Romans discovered how to make parchment – sheepskin sliced very thin. This remained the sole writing surface throughout Europe for many centuries. England's first paper

making factory was established in 1495 but failed almost immediately due to a lack of demand. A second, similar venture was started in 1586. It thrived as a result of Gutenberg's invention of movable type some fifty years earlier (see 202). Paper making remained a laborious process until the nineteenth century and the invention of power-driven machinery. The basic raw materials and processes – vegetable and cloth fibres; wood pulp; clay and chemicals added for different weights, textures and colours, laid on to a variety of screens and then dried and pressed, washed and bleached – remained virtually the same. More recently plastics have been introduced to paper and paperboard making. Yet a few craftsmen still produce handmade papers for special purposes.

In China, Japan, Korea and India children have enjoyed a profusion of paper and papier mâché toys and paper folding, pasting and related craft for centuries. Many, like origami, are traditional by now and children develop skill, patience and a quality of mind peculiar to the culture of childhood in the Orient. Until the late eighteenth century paper did not fall into the hands of European children, save for occasional waste scraps. But from about 1800 onwards it became an important raw material of play and for the production of kites, balloons, toy soldiers and doll and structural cutouts, among other playthings.

First projects
14 Crumpling, twisting and tearing

Tools and materials: coloured tissue paper; bond paper; newspaper

Crumpling paper, rolling it into balls, twisting it into sausages, or simply tearing it to shreds can be extremely satisfying to a young child. It calls different sensations and muscles into play. The child discovers textures and other properties of the material. Tissue and other paper balls can be strung, taped or pasted together; or, tied to twine, can be dragged by a toddler behind him.

Place the child before a table at which he can work in comfort (see 10) or in his highchair. Give him an assortment of paper and a large, empty box. Then show him how to crumple, twist and tear and put the pieces into the box. (See also 207.)

15 Sorting

Tools and materials: same as 14; empty egg carton or assortment of small boxes

Once a child enjoys crumpling, twisting and tearing paper, he can be shown how to sort the different pieces. Set him up with an empty egg carton or a number of small boxes or containers.

Demonstrate how he can distribute the shapes he creates, sorting them by relative size, shape or colour. Aside from sheer play value, this sets the stage for size, shape and colour recognition, and sorting and labelling skills and controls that are necessary for other learning.

16 Wrapping

Tools and materials: tissue paper; newspaper; small paper bags; small empty boxes; toys and other objects; 1·25cm ($\frac{1}{2}''$) masking tape cut into 2·5cm (1″) strips, each taped to the edge of the tabletop by one corner

Unwrapping presents is one of the joys of childhood. Wrapping things up can give a child similar pleasure. Wrapping a box and making it 'disappear' is a kind of magic. Quite incidentally the child discovers how to fold paper and tape down corners, edges and folds.

NOTE Do not give young children plastic bags or cellophane tape. The first can be hazardous and the second frustrating.

Lacing
17 Making a threader

Tools and materials: drinking straws cut into 2·5cm (1″) lengths; white paste (see 21 and 23–5); strands of coloured-wool yarn

Before a child learns to lace he can be shown how to make his own threader. Choose lengths of yarn long enough for whatever is to be laced or strung.

It takes nearly 130cm (50″) of yarn to lace round the edges of a perforated piece of 21·6cm × 27·9cm ($8\frac{1}{2}'' \times 11''$) bond paper. Dip about 1cm ($\frac{1}{2}''$) of one end of the yarn into the paste and twirl it between thumb and forefinger to point the tip. Insert this end into one of the straw cut-offs while the paste is still wet and let it dry thoroughly. Tie a thick knot into the other end of the yarn, and the child is ready to string beads and macaroni shapes, or to lace punched paper (see 18). A blunt lacing needle, used in leather craft (see 127), is also a good, safe tool for young children. Plastic- or metal-tipped shoe laces are usually too short and not nearly as colourful.

18 Punching holes

Tools and materials: paper hole punch (see 126 for revolving punch); assorted white and coloured construction and bond papers; foil; paper cups and plates; threader (see 17)

A child old enough to thread and lace may not have the strength to use a hole punch. This may have to be done for him at first. Punch holes at regular or irregular intervals around the edges of the paper. Holes can be punched into inside areas by folding the paper one or more times (see

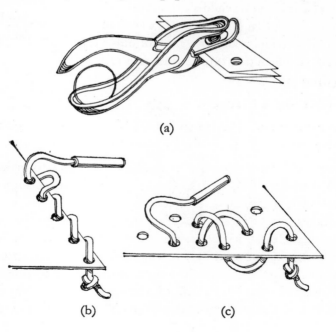

(a)

(b)   (c)

diagram a). Show the child how to insert his threader at whichever hole he chooses, pulling the yarn all the way through to the knotted end. Demonstrate how he can lace over and under (see diagram b) or bind the edges (see diagram c), always pulling the spare yarn all the way through each hole at every turn. He'll discover the variety of patterns he can create going from one hole to the next, skipping some and criss-crossing in every direction. Prepare several straw-tipped threaders in advance so that he can work with concentration until he tires.

Eventually the child will be able to punch his or her own holes. Save the punched-out paper discs for use in pasting (see 21), collages (see 29) and paper mosaics (see 31).

19 Grommet lacing

Tools and materials: grommet and die set (available in needlework shops) (see also 130); child-size hammer (see 84);
30cm × 30cm × 2cm (12″ × 12″ × ¾″) well-sanded pine board, plywood or scrap wood, or a sheet of heavy cardboard;
paper hole punch (see 18); threader (see 17);
paper products (see 18)

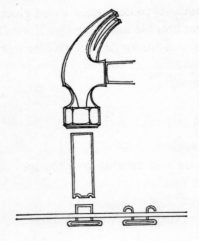

After the holes have been punched as in 18 above, tape one edge of the paper to the wooden board and show the child how to push one grommet up through one of the holes. Use the grommet die and hammer to demonstrate how to bend the rim of the grommet so that it is securely fastened to the paper (see diagram). Make sure that the threader fits through the grommet. When the child has finished attaching all the grommets, he can lace and unlace his designs since the grommets strengthen the paper holes so that they won't tear.

20 Lacing cut paper shapes together

Tools and materials: same as 17 and 18; scissors (see 38)

Small paper shapes – circles, squares, triangles, rectangles and irregularly shaped pieces – can be laced, one to all others, if holes have been punched into each. Once a child is able to handle child-size scissors (see 38–40), he can cut out his own paper shapes for lacing.

Pasting and gluing
21 First steps in pasting

Ordinary white school paste, casein-based glues, mucilage and acrylics are water soluble and harmless if swallowed. Do not give pre-school and junior-school children other adhesives, cow gum or epoxy (see 11 and 165). (See 23–7 for homemade paste and glue recipes.)

22 Adhesives for older children

Use organic and acrylic adhesives only, until the child is sufficiently mature and reliable to heed and follow cautions and instructions (see 11 and 165). Children have accidents, even at older ages. They are not likely to wash their hands as often or as well as they should after handling glues that might be toxic. Cow gum, like aeroplane dope and other adhesives commonly used by young people, is toxic and inflammable.

23 Making your own adhesives

The following glues can be made easily and require only materials that are found in any home or local shops. They keep well in the refrigerator or other cool place in closed, screw-top jars. If the glue becomes too stiff to use or dries out, it can be restored by the addition of a little water. All except one of the recipes (see 26) are entirely non-toxic, and many are useful for paper as well as for bonding other materials, as detailed in each instance.

24 Flour paste (short-term adhesion)

Tools and materials: flour; water; mixing bowl

Mixed to a consistency of double cream, this is a useful adhesive for paper, cloth and other materials. It is not permanent but the adhesion will last long enough for most pre-schoolers' and infants' purposes.

25 Flour paste (long-term adhesion)

Tools and materials: flour; water; muslin or cheesecloth; glass dish

Wrap a handful of flour in the muslin. Wash and knead the flour inside the muslin bag under cold, running water until the water is no longer milky as it runs off and most of the starch is removed. The remainder is almost pure gluten. Allow to dry in a glass dish. The dry gluten will store indefinitely without refrigeration.

To use, chip flakes off the gluten cake, add a few drops of cold water, and allow to stand for a few minutes. Then knead the flakes until they become soft and pliant. Add more cold water to thin out to the required consistency.

26 Transparent glue

Tools and materials: 25 g (2oz) white gelatine;
150 g (5oz) acetic acid (available at chemist's); 175 g (6oz) water;
cooking pot

Soak gelatine in water for twelve hours. Then heat the softened gelatine in the same water until it dissolves. Stir in acetic acid and add cold water until the mixture comes to about half a litre (one pint).

This glue is slightly toxic, but strong enough to cement glass. It can be made stronger or weaker by using more or less gelatine. An older child can use it to mount photographs, pictures cut from magazines, or his own drawings on paper, wood or glass. By brushing the adhesive on top of the pictures as well as coating them on the reverse side, they will adhere and be protected at the same time. Wipe off any excess before the glue sets with a cloth soaked in warm water.

27 Cornflour paste

Tools and materials: 2 tablespoons cornflour; ¼ teaspoon alum;
1 cup water; oil of cloves; cooking pot

Mix flour, alum and part of the water to form a smooth cream. Add the balance of the water, stir, and cook over low heat until the mixture becomes translucent. The longer it cooks, the greater the adhesive power. Add a few drops of oil of cloves after the mixture is taken off the stove. Keep in closed jar in the refrigerator and stir thoroughly before using. This is a useful adhesive for paper, cloth, wood and thin leather especially.

28 Acrylic adhesives

Acrylic media are a relatively recent development. They are available from art supply stores and school material suppliers. The painting medium itself is water soluble and non-toxic and can be used as an adhesive and, at the same time, as an opaque or transparent varnish and protective coating. When totally dry, it waterproofs whatever it covers. Acrylics are therefore ideal adhesives for collages (see 29) and assemblages (see 30), and as varnish for papier mâché (see 47–57), painting (see 148–71) and sculpting (see 195–9).

29 Collages

Tools and materials: paste or glue (see 21–8);
empty egg cartons or small boxes; scrap materials;
sheets of white card; drawing paper; brown wrapping paper;
cardboard; bowl with wide base, filled with water; sponge or rags

Keep glue, water and other materials to one side of a newspaper-covered table, depending on the child's 'handedness' (see 10). Let the child sort the different scrap materials by kind, shape or colour in the egg cartons or other small containers. Then suggest that he arranges and pastes the materials down on the paper or cardboard. Once started, a child will think of ingenious and original ways of combining the materials.

Demonstrate working methods – how to apply a little glue at a time; how to brush it on; and how to keep the jar closed to prevent the glue drying out. Point out the contrasting qualities and textures of the materials. Name colours and shapes and assist – but don't do all the work – in cleaning up. Don't show the child how to make pictures or designs.

Praise inventiveness, good work habits, and endurance. Don't compare his creations with those produced by other children or by adults, or with reality. Display the child's work.

Comment on unique features of his conceptions. Restrict your suggestions to those that will help him achieve what he wants to make in an effective, organized manner.

Ordinary newspaper can be similarly cut up and pasted together again so that different patterns of type and portions of photographs are re-formed into unique designs. A child can draw or paint into his collage, cut up and use his own drawings, and combine them with scrap and other materials in decorative ways.

30 Assemblages

Tools and materials: scrap materials; paste or glue (see 21–8); wire (see 116–18); wood, plywood or heavy cardboard base

Assemblages are three-dimensional collages. They can be constructed on or around a wood or cardboard base or free-standing wood, wire or cardboard forms or frames to which other materials are adhered. These can be pasted, nailed, screwed, bolted or worked on, depending on the availability of materials and tools and the child's level of skill development. Portions can be painted, shellacked or varnished, and the finished assemblage may stand free, or hang on a wall or from an overhead fixture.

31 Paper mosaics

Tools and materials: shallow jewellery or shoebox lid; or picture frame or moulding nailed or glued to a wood or cardboard base; paste (see 21–8); seeds; beans; peas; macaroni shapes; seashells; snippets of white or coloured paper; punched-out paper (see 18) and other small or cut-apart scrap materials

A mosaic can be a kind of collage of small, more or less uniform or dissimilar, multicoloured or monochromatic snippets of material, pasted or glued within a given area. The box lid or frame helps the child to confine his work area. Within it he can arrange and paste the materials. The area to be covered should be small. Show the child how to start pasting on one side or corner of the frame, adhering one small fragment to the tray, placing another next to it, and working towards opposite sides until the whole is covered.

Point out to the child that he can design forms, textures, shadings and shapes through contrast of colour and material as he pastes. The object, in this as in all other such activities, is to allow the child to create his own raw materials. Here the importance of sequence is demonstrably important. The child can tear paper into small, irregular shapes and use them to make mosaics before he can cut with scissors. Later he can cut geometric and other shapes out of coloured paper for similar assembly.

Folding and shaping paper
32 Paper folding

Tools and materials: sheets of bond writing or typing paper; or coloured card; burnisher; or letter-opener with a rounded point; or spoon handle

The ability to fold a square of paper neatly, corner to corner and edge to edge, should be second nature by the time a child goes to school. Demonstrate how to line up one paper edge with another, corner to corner, folding the paper in half neatly and running a finger along the fold once edges and corners meet exactly. The crease should then be burnished with the tool. Unfold the paper to show the crease. Refold and halve the paper a second time, quartering it. Unfold it again.

Most paper folding requires a square piece of paper for a start. With writing and other square-cut papers no measurement is required to turn a rectangle into a square. Take one corner of the paper and bend it over without creasing until one of the two short sides lies directly on top of and parallel to one of the long sides. Holding the parallel edges in position, make a sharp crease first with a finger and then with the burnisher. A section of the paper will extend beyond the folded triangle. Bend this up and over the side of the triangle so that this new crease is parallel to the paper edge. Burnish the crease, open this flap, and tear or cut it off carefully along the crease. When the triangle is opened it will form a perfect square.

Suggest that the child makes several such squares. Let him then fold and refold the square and subsequent triangles corner to corner, burnishing each crease, until the bulk of the paper prevents further folding. Unfold and point out the diagonal and triangular patterns of creases.

33 Accordion folds and pleats

Tools and materials: same as 32

Once a child's arm, hand and finger coordination becomes more refined as a result of simple paper folding, he'll be more adept and deliberate in everything he touches and does. He is now ready for pleating.

Start by folding the paper in half – the long way if it is rectangular. Fold one half of this rectangle in half again and again, each crease parallel to the last (see diagram a) until the first strip is about 1·25cm ($\frac{1}{2}''$) wide. Unfold. Now, using the first two folded strips as a guide, refold the paper, alternately in one direction and then in the other, to make an accordion pleat (see diagram b).

By using paper clips and rubber bands to hold different portions in place, the pleated paper can be formed and pasted into various shapes (see diagram c).

Lightweight coloured papers offer many design possibilities. Foils can also be used by older children who are sufficiently mature and cautious so as not to cut themselves on sharp corners and edges. Once the principle of accordion pleating is

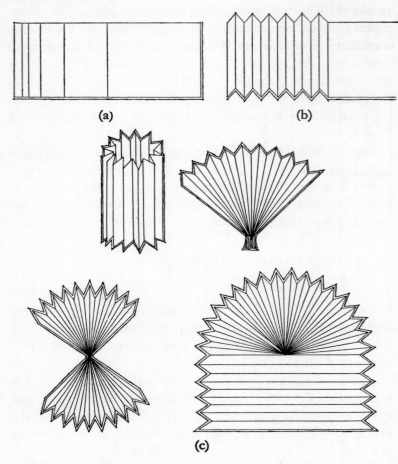

(a)

(b)

(c)

understood, it can be combined with other forms of paper craft and construction (see 39, 40, 42–6, 58–65).

34 Origami for beginners

Tools and materials: square, coloured, lightweight paper (see 32); burnisher (see 32)

No one, regardless of age, can tackle origami with any degree of success until he has perfected the skills described in 32 and

33 above. The following examples are not intended to be copied. Encourage the child to invent his own folds and combinations of folds, and to improvise. He will find delight

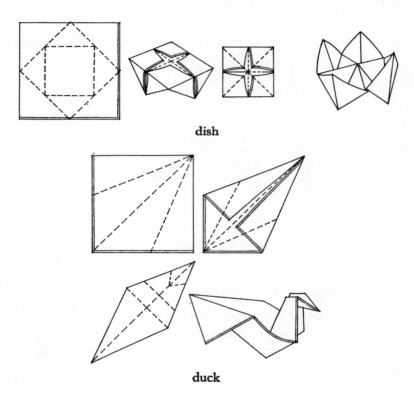

dish

duck

in the shapes he creates. He'll 'see' things, animals and people.

35 Advanced origami

Tools and materials: same as 34

The following are additional and more complex origami folds and constructions that demonstrate some of the possibilities:

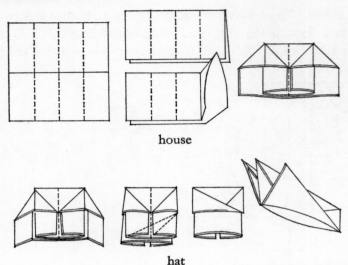

house

hat

36 Paper curling and curving

Tools and materials: card or writing paper; dowel;
unsharpened pencil; rolling pin; or burnisher

A child can curve sheets and strips of paper by winding each
around a dowel, pencil, bottle or rolling pin (see diagram a).
He can achieve a similar effect by pulling a paper strip with
one hand out from under his other hand or thumb, over a
table edge (see diagram b). To make curled paper strips or
shapes, pull the paper over one edge of the burnishing tool,

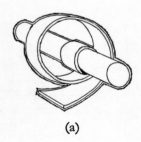

(a)

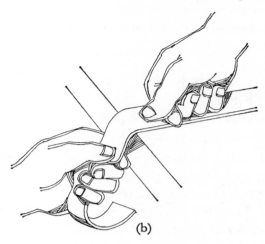

(b)

wedging the strip between the tool's edge and thumb while pulling.

Embossing and cutting

37 Embossing on paper and foil

Tools and materials: any dull, pointed instrument; a used-up ballpoint pen; a scriber; or the end of a pointed paint brush handle; several sheets of blotting paper; masking tape; writing or any other soft paper; or foil

A pre-schooler can run a scriber across paper or foil taped to blotting paper. Show him how to make impressions deep enough to be visible, but sufficiently light so that the paper does not tear. He can make scribbles, designs, patterns, dots and dashes. When he turns paper or foil over, he'll discover his designs raised on the other side. He can deepen the impressions by scribing along all edges of the raised designs on the 'wrong' side of the paper. Wooden blocks or letters, wire or plastic netting, and other raised designs like pastry-cutters can also be pressed into foil placed on top of several sheets of blotting paper or a rubber pad. The aim should be to make embossed designs with a combination of created effects, rather than copying or reproducing existing shapes. (See also 137.)

38 Cutting paper

Tools and materials: school scissors (with rounded points); newspaper; bond paper or card

Don't give your child battery or electrically-operated scissors. Buy good, school-grade scissors with rounded points. Once he matures the child can be trusted with small pointed scissors. Make sure that the scissor grip loops are twisted at an angle so that they fit flat against the skin of thumb and forefinger. Inexpensive scissors do not have twisted grips and they cut into the flesh during extended use. Attach the scissors to your child's worktable or workbench with a long ribbon or string.

The child's cutting will be ragged at first but it will improve in time. He'll acquire greater control faster if he is left without patterns to follow than when these are imposed on him. Encourage pre-schoolers to cut sheets of news- and other paper into snippets at random. Holes can be punched into the cut paper shapes (see 18). They can be laced together (see 20), or used for pasting (see 21–8), collages (see 29) and assemblages (see 30). Later, strips can be cut for paper weaving (see 42–6).

39 Folded-paper cutting

Tools and materials: same as 38

A child can cut along the burnished lines of paper he has learned to fold (see 32–5). Folded and accordion-pleated papers allow the child to make 'interior' cuts in the paper with scissors (see diagram).

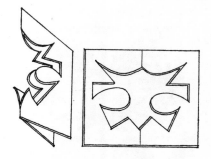

40 Cutting out paper shapes

Tools and materials: scissors; coloured card; drawings and paintings made by the child; photographs and pictures cut from magazines; semi-stiff, starched fabric and felt; ribbons

At this stage of proficiency a child can begin to cut out shapes that interest him from some of the above-listed materials, among others. He can use these cuttings in his collages (see 29) or mount them. Do not show the child how to cut paper flowers, dolls, and other clichés. Let him discover and invent his own forms. Limit what you show the child to basic principles, working method, tool and material use, neat work habits and safety measures appropriate to his or her maturity.

41 Polish paper cuts

Tools and materials: same as 38

Poland has produced its own unique paper folk art. A child can learn to adapt these to his collages and assemblages and to make decorations and paper objects. He will need all or most of the skills described previously in this chapter before he can be expected to manipulate paper in the required manner.

The following diagrams show two of the standard folds and cuts that can be varied, adapted and combined.

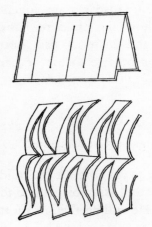

Winding and weaving

42 Paper winding

Tools and materials: rolls of coloured-paper party streamers;
or 1·25cm ($\frac{1}{2}$″) strips of paper pasted together to form long
ribbons; transparent glue (see 26); or paste; or water glass
(sodium silicate), available from chemist's shop

Coil the end of the streamer or ribbon to form a solid core
(see 36). Keep winding, pasting the beginning of the next
strip to the end of the last until a firm and solid round, square
or triangular disc of the desired dimension has been wound
(see diagram a). Paste down the end of the last strip and soak
the whole coil thoroughly in transparent glue, paste or water
glass. Gently press into the centre of the saturated coil to form
a hollow shape (see diagram b), or leave the coil in its original

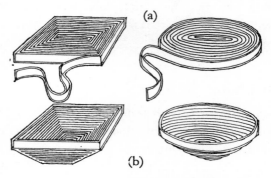

(a)

(b)

state. Such coils can be combined with others to make
mosaics (see 31 and 201), wall hangings and decorations.

43 Paper strips and streamers

Tools and materials: same as 42; small cardboard boxes;
empty, washed glass or plastic bottles

Paper streamers and strips can be wound and pasted around
containers, bins and boxes. Coat one side or part of the

object to be decorated with glue or paste. Wind paper strips or ribbons on to the glued portion. Coat the next section a small area at a time so that it does not dry before it is covered with paper. The child can paste snippets, strips or ribbons of paper side by side, overlapping or criss-crossing one another in any pattern of his or her choice. When the container has been totally covered, paste down all loose paper ends and coat the whole with transparent glue, paste or water glass.

44 Paper weaving

The principles of paper weaving are similar to those required for caning and weaving with fibres, yarn and thread (see Chapter 10). A child can discover the basic processes by first experimenting in paper. They are more understandable when first tried on a loom that the child makes himself (see 45 and 46), weaving with strips that are less flexible than spun fibres and more manageable than reeds.

45 Constructing the loom

Tools and materials: sheets of 21·6cm × 27·9cm (8½″ × 11″) bond paper or coloured card; scissors; sheet of 22·5cm × 30cm (9″ × 12″) cardboard; masking tape

Fold one sheet of paper in half and cut slots into it at right angles to the fold at more or less regular intervals without cutting all the way to the ends of the paper (see diagram). Later,

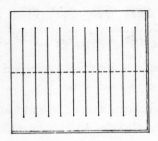

when able to use ruler and triangle, the child can lay out the slots with a pencil, each about 6mm to 12mm ($\frac{1}{4}''$ to $\frac{1}{2}''$) apart. Once the principle is understood, various paper shapes – round, triangular, square, and those used in Polish paper cuts (see 41) or scrolls (cut from adding-machine tape) – can be used to make looms for different paper weaves.

Tape one end of this 'loom' to a sheet of cardboard and it is ready for use.

46 Paper weaves

Tools and materials: paper loom (see 45); coloured card or other papers; scissors; paste (see 21–8)

Cut the paper into strips, each 6mm to 12mm ($\frac{1}{4}''$ to $\frac{1}{2}''$) wide and longer than the loom is wide by at least 2·5cm (1"). Show the child how to start the weave by feeding the first strip over

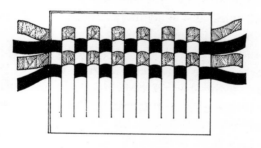

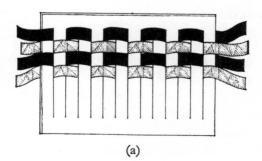

(a)

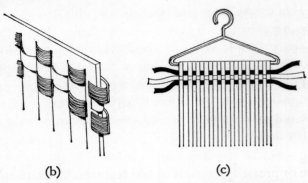

(b)   (c)

and under successive strips of the loom, and the second over and under alternate strips, and so on (see diagram a). Different coloured strips can be used in a variety of ways, or different-coloured strips can be pasted together to achieve different patterns.

When the loom is filled, cut off all but about 6mm ($\frac{1}{4}''$) from each end of the protruding horizontal paper strips that extend beyond both sides, and bend and paste them under the outside vertical strips (see diagram b).

Longer and larger weaves are possible by cutting or pasting long strips of paper together, hanging them, side by side, from a wire clothes-hanger to which they are fastened with tape or clothespegs (see diagram c). Twist the hook of the clothes-hanger so that it can be hung from the back of a chair.

Papier mâché
47 The process

Modelling, building and forming with papier mâché are a favoured craft in Japan, China, India and Mexico. Papier mâché consists of shredded paper soaked in a flour paste or glue, formed as a mash or laid in strips over an armature (see 50–53). The objects that can be formed range from abstract and decorative sculpture, landscapes and panoramas, to play figures, toys, masks, jewellery, pottery and household articles and utensils.

The two basic papier mâché techniques can be used singly or in combination. The mash is useful for forming and moulding small objects, or for sculpting or adding detail to larger constructions. The paper strip technique works best when used in combination with armatures (see 51–3). Other materials – string, twine, tinsel, cloth scraps, ribbon, mesh or netting – can be embedded in or adhered to the papier mâché surface or pressed against it to add textures. When thoroughly dry, papier mâché can be painted (see 56) or waterproofed (see 57).

48 Mash

Tools and materials: newspaper; egg cartons; card and tissue paper, shredded and torn into small pieces; large mixing bowl; flour; water; flour paste (see 24); oil of cloves

Soak the torn and shredded paper for a day and a half in warm water until it turns to pulp. Drain off excess water and squeeze whatever surplus water you can out of the remainder. Mix flour and water to the consistency of double cream. Stir and knead in the pulped paper. The mash should be the consistency of clay for use as a modelling compound. It must be thinned with water until it can be poured if it is to be used as a moulding compound or for adding detail to or decorating papier mâché strip constructions (see 49). Finally, add a few drops of oil of cloves as a preservative.

49 Papier mâché strip construction

Tools and materials: same as 48, except that the paper is torn into strips of different widths

Prepare the same paste mixture detailed in 48. Add a small handful of paper strips to the mixture, letting them soak for ten to fifteen minutes before use. Run each strip through between the second and third finger of one hand to remove excess moisture and paste, before laying it over the armature (see 50–53).

Papier mâché strip construction requires ample working space, arranged so that the child can reach and use all the required materials without confusion (see 10). A wide-based bowl filled with paste is less likely to spill than one that has a narrow base.

50 Armatures

Armatures are essential for working with papier mâché strips and for large modelling and sculpting projects involving mash. An armature is a three-dimensional skeleton of the object to be formed, over which the papier mâché strips (or other modelling compounds) are laid. Armatures can be made out of a large variety of materials (see 51–3).

51 Armatures made out of paper

Tools and materials: newspaper; masking tape; string or twine; scissors

Show the child how to fold, twist, and bundle newspaper into skeleton shapes. Each individual bundle should be taped or tied and then attached to others until the shape of the wanted figure is roughly constructed (see diagram). The armature need only be solid enough so that it can be worked with while the papier mâché strips are laid over it. Once dry, the papier mâché will add strength to the armature and become rigid. When the child is satisfied that the armature approximates the contours of the intended object, show him how to cover it with individual strips of paper soaked in paste (see 49), fleshing out shapes and adding detail with wadded, soaked strips or mash (see 48), adhered with other strips to the main body of the work.

The paste-soaked strips should overlap. Several layers are required until the wall thickness is built up, to withstand usage. When the armature has been covered with one layer,

the next should be applied at right angles to the first wherever possible. The width and length of the strips depend on which fit the contours of the object being formed: 5cm × 30cm (2″ × 12″) strips can be used for gently curved or relatively flat surfaces, 2cm × 15cm ($\frac{3}{4}$″ × 6″) strips are required for more acute curves.

52 Armatures made out of cardboard

Tools and materials: light cardboard; shoe or jewellery boxes; corrugated cardboard and boxes; coping saw, jigsaw or keyhole saw (see 92 and 97); sharp mounting or craft knife for more experienced young people (see 69); masking tape

The age, maturity, experience and strength of the child determine which materials and tools he can use. Light cardboard can be cut with large scissors, but heavier cardboard and corrugated cardboard must be cut with a coping saw, keyhole saw or sharp knife. Young children can bend, twist and tape cardboard into desired shapes and, in combination with bundles of newspaper (see 51) and scraps of wood, form armatures. Suggest that, wherever possible, existing shapes are used and combined with others.

53 Armatures made out of other materials

Tools and materials: balloons; sand-filled plastic bags; empty plastic bottles; wire; pipecleaners; wood scraps; pebbles; clay; modelling compounds, among other materials

Virtually any expendable, easily worked material can be used by itself or in combination with others to form papier mâché armatures. A blown-up balloon, approximately the same size as a child's head, can be a useful armature for a papier mâché mask, bowl or other container. Puncture or deflate the balloon and remove it when the papier mâché has dried completely. Paper- or sand-filled plastic bags can be used similarly as armatures for different shapes that need to be hollow when completed. Coat any material that must be separated from the dried papier mâché with a thin layer of Vaseline or vegetable oil before covering it, or the papier mâché may adhere to it.

Pipecleaners (see 114), plastic-covered wire (see 116 and 117), and coat-hanger wire (see 120–22) are useful for armatures that will be totally enclosed with papier mâché. Wire or plastic mesh or netting fastened to the wire armature will cut down on weight and the amount of papier mâché required to cover these armatures.

Wood scraps can be taped or nailed together (see 85–9) and combined with other materials to make larger and more substantial armatures when required.

54 Adding detail to sculptures and objects

Tools and materials: twigs; dowels; paperclips; string; twine; buttons; ribbon; discarded ping-pong, tennis, and other balls; whole and cut-apart egg boxes; bottle tops; and other scrap or discarded parts and materials

Any of these can be embedded in or covered with papier mâché, and added and adhered to armatures or partially completed papier mâché constructions to add detail and texture. Make the child conscious of the possibility of such improvisation whenever possible.

55 Moulding with papier mâché

Moulding is a process with which the child should be familiar. The moulds should consist of household items or they can be improvised or made by the child. A child may wish to duplicate his own work or make multiples – like wheels for a toy he builds.

Show the child how to make the original object. In the case of a wheel, for instance, he will only need to press a dowel end or some other circular object into modelling compound, clay or plaster of Paris (see 197–8). When the mould has dried thoroughly, it must be coated with Vaseline or vegetable oil. Papier mâché mash or strips (see 48 and 49) can then be laid into the open mould. Remove the moulded object after it has dried completely, coat the mould with more Vaseline, and repeat the process for additional identical castings.

Papier mâché shrinks considerably as it dries. Hence there is likely to be some variation between successively cast papier mâché shapes. Do not apply heat or place papier mâché into an oven. It is inflammable, and the slower it dries, the less shrinkage and distortion there will be.

Plastic ice-cube trays and other existing shapes and cavities can be used to mould components for child-originated constructions. They differ from commercially produced toy moulds in so far as they make a demand on the child to discover them, their possibilities, and the uses to which they can be put as a part of his own creations.

56 Painting papier mâché
(See below for required materials.)

When thoroughly dry, papier mâché modelled, sculpted or moulded objects can be painted with any medium. Poster paints (see 149) and acrylics (see 167) are recommended. More mature children who can be relied on to wash hands and brushes with the required solvents and with soap and water after they have completed their work, can use oil paints, japan colours, lacquers and enamels applied in thin, successive layers (see 165–170). Water glass (see 42) or wood sealer (see 107), which closes the pores of the material, is a useful undercoating for these finishes. Or several coats of white poster paint when overpainted with other poster colours or acrylics will bring out their brilliance.

57 Preserving papier mâché objects

Several thin coats of shellac, clear varnish (see 109), water glass (see 42) or transparent glue (see 26), brushed on lightly over fully dry, unpainted or painted papier mâché objects, will strengthen, protect, waterproof and preserve them indefinitely. Wait until each coat is completely dry before applying the next. Never allow a child to use spray cans and, preferably, do not use them yourself (see 11 and 165).

Paper construction
58 Building with paper

Paper construction as a craft for children became popular in Europe around the end of the eighteenth century. At about that time large sheets of paper imprinted with cut-out designs appeared in France, Germany, Holland and England. They included toy houses; dress-up dolls; toy soldiers; theatres and puppets; and panoramas of towns, farms, castles and battle-fields, some printed in black and white, other hand- or stencil-coloured.

Many of these same cut-outs were still available in France twenty years ago, by which time they included three-dimensional railway train, ship, early dirigible, balloon and aeroplane models, similar to those now only available in plastics. The original woodblocks, the stencils by which these early cut-outs were coloured, and the paper construc-tions of the past can now be seen only in museums. More recent published paper constructions include a working model of a pendulum clock, every gear and part made out of paper, that can still be bought in France today.

During the past seventy-five years paper and cardboard construction became a craft employed by architects, engineers, artists and designers. As a craft medium for children it requires experience in some of the more fundamental skills detailed in earlier portions of this chapter.

59 Slot construction

Tools and materials: a deck of old playing cards;
or rectangular file cards; or cardboard or heavy card;
scissors

Demonstrate how cuts can be made into the sides of cards so that each can be slotted to the next, slot to slot (see diagram a). Cards with cuts made at right angles to their sides up to and slightly beyond the centre can be slotted together so that they will stand on a more or less level surface. Four square or rectangular cards with two such slots cut into one side each will form a free-standing box that needs only top and bottom pasted or taped to it to enclose it fully. Show the child the dividers in corrugated food and beverage cartons that are joined in just such a manner. A child can use this principle for a great variety of paper and cardboard construction. Paper plates and cups and lightweight cardboard tubes can be jointed in the same way (see diagram b and diagrams a and b on page 73).

To stimulate the use of this principle in children's paper and cardboard craft, I originated a toy, The Builder, first shown in New York's Museum of Modern Art in 1953. That year Charles Eames, the furniture designer, created his House of Cards, coincidentally employing the same principle although in a slightly varied form. Both toys, enjoyed by several generations of children, have since been copied widely. Regrettably, such playthings are given to children as substitutes rather than as inspirations for craft activities.

When slotting material thicker than card, and especially when using cardboard (see 67), the slots should be cut a

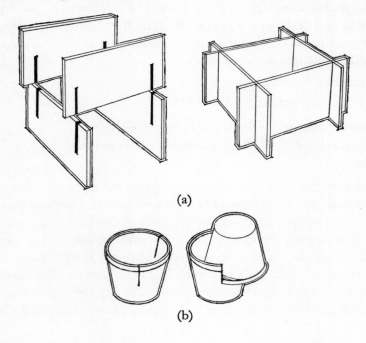

(a)

(b)

shade wider than the thickness of the material or else it will buckle and fray at the joints when pieces are slotted together.

60 Paper joints and levers

Tools and materials: light cardboard; old playing cards; file cards; scissors; hole punch (see 18); paperclips; or grommet set (see 19) and hammer; string or twine; heavy sheet of cardboard, plywood, or scrap wood for working surface

Jointed paper dolls and jumping jacks were among the first European paper toys produced during the late seventeen hundreds. They were children's favourites, then as now. In Europe, jointed paper dolls were printed on lightweight paper and sold as penny sheets. They needed to be mounted on stiffer paper or cardboard, cut out, and assembled with string. Any child can use these principles of paper jointing to create a great variety of playthings, mobile constructions and lever-operated toys.

Cut the paper or card stock into strips 2·5cm × 12·7cm (1″ × 5″) or longer, punch a hole at both ends of each (see 18), insert grommets, and join one to the next with string or paperclips (see diagram a). The same principle, using paper

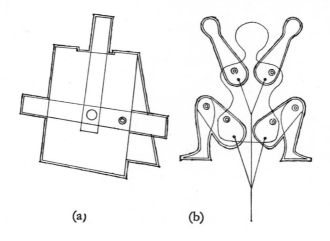

(a)   (b)

strips as levers, can be employed to make mobile and animated toys, mechanisms, and designs (see diagram b).

61 Scoring paper with a scriber

Tools and materials: soft pencil; ruler; card; scriber; used-up ballpoint pen, or other dull, pointed instrument

Paper construction often requires sharp folds (see 32–5 and 41) and creases. Sometimes the texture and weight of the paper cause ordinary folds to be uneven or wavy, or to crack. Heavy or textured papers should always be crease-scored with a scriber before they are folded.

Draw a line with pencil and ruler from one side of the paper to the other, or wherever the paper is to be folded. Then place the ruler so that the line is just visible. Next, run the scriber along the ruler's edge, pressing on the point sufficiently hard to emboss the paper without breaking its surface. It will then fold easily along the scored line.

Wavy, round and semi-circular scores can be made freehand or along templates (see 65). Such scores are especially effective in paper sculpture (see 73). When combined with straight scores and cuts, curved scores lend dimension and texture to paper design (see diagram).

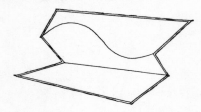

62 Scoring with a knife

Tools and materials: same as 61; metal-edge ruler; Stanley knife

Heavy paper and cardboard require cut-scores before they can be folded. Obviously this is not to be done by young children. Instead of using the scriber (see 61), run the knife blade along the marked line and the metal edge of the ruler, cutting no deeper than halfway through the material. It will then bend without cracking. Needless to say, the material is substantially weakened at such a fold and may require tape or other interior support in some constructions. (Observe the safety cautions suggested in 69 when making such cuts.)

63 Planning and layout

At early stages all paper construction should be spontaneous and improvised. When the design has reached its ultimate pleasing shape, it may be a mass of small pieces joined to one another. Component forms can then be disassembled, laid out flat, and used as templates. Reconstruction from these templates requires some use of draughting instruments in many cases. Even before he can count, add and subtract, a child can learn to use a compass, triangles and a ruler for simple geometric designing.

The following describes some of the designing skills that are useful in paper construction. Be sure to encourage the child to develop a form spontaneously as a paper mock-up (see 64) before he details his design and works it out more precisely. Placement of folds, scores, glue laps and tabs must first be established by trial and error and by improvisation before they can be placed with precision.

64 Paper mock-ups

Tools and materials: card or heavy bond paper; scissors; scriber (see 61) or scoring board; masking tape, paperclips, stapler and paste

There are many ways of constructing an ordinary paper cube or box. Teaching a child one or all of the various methods is futile. He must experiment spontaneously before he can understand construction principles. Let him cut out pieces of paper and join them with tape, paperclips or a stapler to form solid shapes. They may not be neat and square, but he'll discover methods of construction – what works and what doesn't.

This technique is useful for discovering and inventing geometric as well as non-geometric organic forms. In working in this manner, it soon becomes obvious that different weights of paper and other supplementary materials can be useful or are essential in various portions of a complex structure.

A young child will be perfectly satisfied with such a relatively crude mock-up. Rough construction details can be covered with coloured paper or poster paints. At later stages young people may wish to execute more-finished versions after working out construction details on their paper mock-ups.

65 Paper templates

A paper or any other template is simply a shape worked out so that it can be reproduced or traced on to another piece of material. For example, it is easier to design a single equilateral triangle and, having made a template of it, to repeat it as often as necessary, than to construct a whole figure geometrically throughout.

The paper mock-up (see 64), cut apart and unfolded, can become a rough model for a more-finished and precise template made with ruler, compass, triangle and other draughting instruments. A final template can then be constructed to be copied, reproduced or repeated as many times as required.

66 Glue laps

Tools and materials: same as 64 and 65

The mock-up may contain one or more sides that need to be fastened to other edges. One method of making such joints neatly requires the addition of a glue lap to one of each set of two sides that are to be fastened (see diagram a). Each such glue lap should be slightly shorter than the length of the side to which it is to be attached so that the corners don't bulk and buckle when the two matching edges are pasted together.

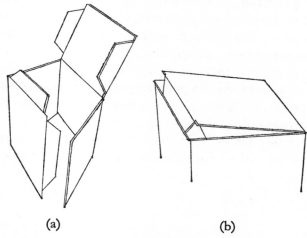

(a)   (b)

Each glue lap should be pasted to the underside of the paper edge to which it is to be attached.

When making geometric constructions like a cube or a box, the side to which a glue lap is attached should be shorter by the thickness of the material used than the other sides (see diagram b). Add each required glue lap to the template or layout, score the line where glue lap and side are joined, bend the glue lap down, and paste it to the underside of the matching edge.

Cardboard construction
67 Building with cardboard

Collages, assemblages, designs, models, toys, usable child- and adult-size furniture and storage spaces can be made entirely out of cardboard or corrugated cardboard or with these materials in combination with others. Cardboard 'carpentry' has become something of a separate craft. It is a useful preparation for working in wood. Most of the methods employed can be used for both wood and paper.

Cardboard is a mixture of raw wood pulp, scrap paper and cloth fibres, cooked and pressed, like paper (see 13), into un-bleached sheets of varying thickness. First used as a packaging material in the nineteenth century, cardboard has become increasingly important as construction material as well.

Cardboard is available in a large variety of grades, ranging from soft, pulpy board used for egg cartons, to heavier boards lined on one or both sides with paper. The latter are used for folding and set-up boxes and posters. Still better grades include poster board, illustration board, backing boards for pads of drawing and writing paper, and binder's board used for library bindings of books. Fluted, corrugated cardboard is now available in several plies also. In addition, there exists a range of composition boards consisting of paper or cardboard laminated to thin sheets of plywood, foam-core plastics and asbestos, used mostly for packaging and building insulation. Finally, there are cardboard tubes that are available in a range of wall thicknesses, diameters, lengths and strengths. All of them, with the exception of asbestos board, make excellent craft materials for young people. Asbestos board tends to crumble, and the dust, if inhaled, is a health hazard.

Raw or lined cardboard and corrugated board can be used as it is or painted (see 149 and 165–9). Raw cardboard can be primed before painting with other than poster paints (see 107). It can also be lined with white or coloured paper or foil (see 22–8 and 68).

68 Laminating paper and foil to cardboard

Tools and materials: cardboard or corrugated board;
white or coloured papers and foils; paste or glue (see 22–8)

It is easier and quicker to laminate large sheets of paper to
cardboard before cutting it up into small pieces. When covering
large areas of paper and cardboard with paste, use a square of
cardboard as a spreader instead of a brush.

69 Using sharp tools and knives
(See also 11 and 82.)

Until he is sufficiently experienced and reliable, even an older
child should not work with sharp tools except under close
adult supervision. Anyone is bound to cut himself at some
time while using them. The relative severity or harmlessness
of such cuts depends on observance of simple but imperative
safety rules. To deprive children of developing the necessary

self-discipline and caution means to invite possibly serious
injury later. My five-year-old daughter and four-year-old son,
practised in craft since earliest ages, have learned to cut
linoleum blocks with sharp gouges, under supervision,
without harming themselves.

Set the stage for eventual careful use of potentially dangerous tools by introducing children to simple and safe ones at early ages and by insisting on the same precautions and disciplines in their use as for those they will need later. The following precautions are worth observing:

a. Never walk about holding a pair of scissors or a knife, unless absolutely necessary. Then carry the tool by the handle, blade pointing ahead and towards the ground.

b. Provide only finely sharpened and honed, rust-free tools inserted into an appropriate holder. The handle should be long enough to fit the child's hand, allowing him to hold the tool without touching the blade itself. Dull, ragged or rusty tools cause serious and infected injuries.

c. Check before use the locking device that holds a knife blade in its holder and assure that there is no 'play' in the blade.

d. When not in use store the tool, metal parts lightly coated with oil or Vaseline, wrapped in wax paper, in a cloth or leather sheath or in a tool rack, out of reach of young children.

e. To cut paper foil or cardboard with a knife blade: Draw the line along which the cut is to be made with a pencil and a ruler or T-square. Cut only along the edge of a metal T-square (see diagram); never use a straight-edge (it can slip), or a plastic or wooden edge, along which to run a knife. Hold

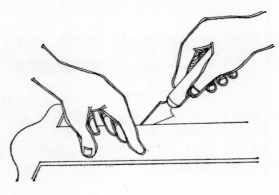

the knife in one hand and the T-square down on to the paper or board with the fingers of the other hand spread apart. Check the position of the fingers on the T-square before cutting, to make sure that no fingertip projects beyond the metal edge along which the cut is to be made. Make several passes with the knife blade along the pencil line using the metal edge as the guide. Never attempt to cut through heavy paper or even lightweight cardboard with a single pass of the blade.

f. Teach young people to keep their eyes on the blade while cutting: never to look away, even for a moment, and to stop cutting if their attention is required elsewhere.

g. Demonstrate how to keep the hand holding the T-square or the material *behind* the knife blade and never ahead of it. This is especially important when whittling or carving wood, cutting wood and linoleum blocks, and using chisels and gouges. Always make cuts or gouge material in a direction away from the hand holding the material.

h. Sharp knives and tools momentarily laid aside on the worktable should be embedded in a kneaded eraser.

i. Teach young people how to hold sharp and pointed tools.

j. Keep a first-aid kit near work areas. The kit should include Band-Aids, bandage, surgical tape, mild disinfectant, a rubber band to use as a temporary tourniquet, and a tube of Vaseline.

70 Flexible, fluted cardboard strips

Flexible, fluted cardboard, more malleable than the corrugated kind, can be bought in rolls or found, used as protective wadding and as buffers in containers for large appliances. It can be cut into strips with scissors or a knife, bent parallel with the fluting (cut-scored for folds at right angles to the fluting), rolled, curved and coiled, glued, taped or stapled to itself and to other materials. It is especially useful for making armatures (see 50–53 and 195) and as a base for papier mâché, clay, or plaster panoramas or landscapes.

71 Corrugated cardboard

Cut-apart grocery cartons or sheets of corrugated board can be cut into various shapes with a sharp knife blade or with a coping saw, keyhole saw or back saw. It can be bent parallel to the fluting without scoring. Bends at right angles to the fluting require cut scores (see 62). Several layers of corrugated board, laminated to each other, are sufficiently strong for large collages, assemblages and life-size, usable tables, chairs, storage shelves and other furniture, as well as play material, building blocks and toy vehicles on which the child can ride, and life-size dolls' houses and play shops.

Slot construction (see 59) provides greatest strength and flexibility. Tape the edges of finished corrugated board constructions with packaging tape to prevent fraying and separation of the cover papers from the fluting. Corrugated cardboard can be painted like any other paper or cardboard (see 67).

72 Cardboard tubes

Cardboard tubes, cut into different lengths with a sharp knife blade, coping saw, keyhole saw or back saw, are useful in three-dimensional design, in assemblages, or as components like table and chair legs in combination with other materials. They can be pasted, tied, taped or jointed.

Semi-circular cross-laps can be cut into the ends of cardboard tubes with a saw. Use one such cut-off as a template for marking identical joints into other tube ends. Several tubes, notched in this manner, will fit together like logs used to build a cabin (see diagram b). Slot jointed tube ends can fit to slot jointed flat cardboard shapes (see diagram a).

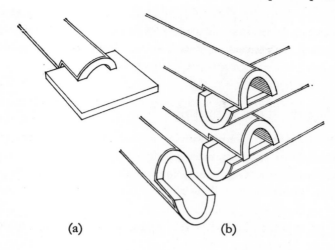

(a)   (b)

Paper sculpture
73 Formed paper relief

Tools and materials: white and coloured card; fluted cardboard;
scissors; sharp knife blade (see 62 and 69); scriber;
scoring board; Cellophane tape; masking tape; stapler;
paste (see 22–8); heavy cardboard base

Paper can be sculpted in relief by cutting, scoring and folding
(see 32–6, 41–3 and 58–66). Such sculpture should not be
attempted until the different methods of paper folding, cutting
and scoring have been explored.

For spontaneous paper sculpture a wood or heavy cardboard base is essential. Paper shapes can be curved and curled
and attached to it with tape, paste or staples. These shapes can
be given three-dimensional detail and texture (see 61).

Making decorative papers
74 Techniques and methods

Paper making is beyond the scope of this book (see 13). But a
child can create interesting and decorative papers by pasting

(see 21–9), printing (see Chapter 8), drawing, and the techniques described below (see 75–6). Such decorative papers can be used in paper constructions, collages, assemblages, sculpting and making useful objects.

75 Spatter and stippling

Tools and materials: white drawing or bond paper; sponge;
toothbrush or stippling brush; bowl of clean water;
poster paints (see 149); clean, empty baby food jars;
tongue depressors or lolly sticks

Prepare thick poster paint mixtures, each colour in its own jar. Show the child how to dip sponge or brush into the paint and then dab it lightly on to the paper. The lighter the touch, the more interesting and varied the effects will be. After stippling one sheet with a single colour, wash out the sponge or brush, squeeze it dry, and use a second colour, as before. A third colour and more can be added in turn, either while previous coatings are still wet or after they have dried. A great many different effects and colour mixtures can be achieved in this way. (See also 156 for another spatter effect.)

76 Ink-patterned paper

Tools and materials: white drawing or bond paper;
India ink in various colours; eyedropper, one for each colour;
sponge; bowl of clear water; sheets of newspaper or blotting
paper; coloured felt markers (optional)

Place the drawing paper on top of several layers of newspaper or on to heavy blotting paper. Moisten the drawing paper with water and sponge. Drop blots of coloured ink on to the moistened paper, using the eyedropper. The inks will crawl and bleed, creating a variety of patterns and designs. Several different colours can be used in succession. Additional variation can be achieved by dropping small amounts of soapy water into the design, again using an eyedropper. Do not disturb or move the paper until the water and inks have dried thoroughly.

Such moistened paper can also be flooded with watercolour applied with a brush, which is then drawn into with coloured felt marker and drawing pens dipped into India ink. These and other 'resist' methods (see 159 and 166) can be combined with each other.

3 Carpentry

Life without industry is guilt, industry without art is brutality.
John Ruskin

77 Background

Carpentry invokes the smell, feel and texture of wood and wood shavings and of hand-held tools. Wood is a vanishing resource. Today's farming, printing, building, packaging, plastics and chemical industries eat into the surviving and replanted reservoir of forests at a rate faster than they can regenerate. But trees are not only a source of prime raw materials. They are the major converters of carbon dioxide into breathable oxygen. For all these reasons wood will certainly become a treasured commodity once again, used discreetly as a craft material. This will also stimulate a revival of interest in its unique properties, care in its use, and preservation.

As a first introduction to carpentry, cardboard – corrugated

and chip – and the various wall and composition boards are as useful as wood and sometimes more so. They are softer and easier to saw, joint and work and they are usually less expensive. Therefore many of the projects described in this chapter apply equally to materials other than wood on which carpentry tools can be used (see 58–72).

78 Carpentry tools

Today's production and hobby carpentry involves the use of a profusion of power tools. But the judgement demanded for working in wood requires training in and use of simple hand tools, not only as a learning process for young people but also as preparation for an eventual use of machinery. Sawing, hammering, drilling, jointing and other operations in wood-working require a familiarity with the characteristics of the raw material that can only be gained from working with hand tools.

There's a knack to driving a nail with a hammer that, if it becomes second nature, frees a child or young person so that he can concentrate on the creative aspects of crafts. There are efficient ways of using a screwdriver, a hand drill or a saw, setting up work, preparing jigs or making a mortise, so that the process of creation can take precedence over production (see 5). These operations require experience that, cumulatively, lays the foundation on which more advanced skills can be built.

But it's not enough to give a child a hand-tool kit or a workbench. He needs experiences and an outlook that make it possible for him to use carpentry tools imaginatively and with a purpose. He needs to be given raw materials on which to exercise tools, skills and his own ideas. He needs guidance to enable him to understand that the purpose of the exercise of his skills is expression and not mere production.

It is important to give a child only one or two tools at a time, together with materials on which they can be used. They should be presented so that he is encouraged to explore them and be inventive. He also needs to be shown basic craft disciplines and have some of the possible effects of violating them explained to him.

Some parents and teachers are afraid to give carpentry tools to young children. They worry that a child might hurt himself, misuse the tools, or create havoc among siblings or furniture. Yet children to whom materials are properly introduced, who are fired with enthusiasm for creating self-originated ideas and objects, and who are given guidance, are not likely to misuse tools. As pointed out earlier, anything is

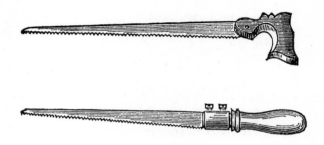

dangerous in the hands of an undisciplined or inexperienced child.

Tools for children are best bought from educational, jeweller's, art supply and hardware shops, rather than in toy shops. Most professional tools come in a variety of sizes and weights, some sufficiently small and light that they fit the hands of children mature enough to use them. An upholsterer's tack hammer, of which the handle has been shortened, makes an excellent child's carpentry hammer. Model makers' and jewellers' coping saws fit the hands of any five-year-old. A regular compass, keyhole, wallboard, dovetail saw or back saw is far more useful and workable than the miniature cross-cut saws usually found in children's toy tool chests. And they are much less dangerous. The least expensive, lightweight carpenter's hand drill is preferable to its shoddy toy counterpart and is no more expensive.

79 When to provide tools

Give the child a new tool only when he can hold it properly. If the smallest or lightest-weight professional tool is too heavy or difficult to hold and guide, then the child should not be expected to work with it. The same principle applies to the material. A child mature enough to handle a coping saw may not have the strength and endurance to saw through 3mm ($\frac{1}{8}''$) plywood. Give him balsa, wallboard or soft cardboard instead. The chronology in which tools are given is important. Before a child can learn how to use a hand drill, he must know how to clamp the wood to the table so that it does not slip when drilled, and how to place scrap wood under it so that the bottom edges of the holes don't fray and splinter and the table surface is not damaged.

80 Spontaneity and planning

The more advanced forms of carpentry, like all other craft, require planning, measurement, marking, and transfer of designs for parts that are to be sawed, drilled or jointed. But don't teach a child how to mark or saw along a straight line, or how to joint or make objects that require numerical or geometric measurement, until he has experienced spontaneous craft. The meaning and purpose of numbers, measures, weights and proportions can become clear only when the child has the maturity, skills and desire to apply them to creative ends.

81 Work spaces

Carpentry involves work that can ruin household or school furniture. Most commercially made children's worktables and benches (other than those made for school use) are inadequate, expensive and last for only a short time. As an alternative to the trestle worktable (see 10) that is adjustable as the child grows, a tabletop workbench can be made in any home or school workshop. It can be stored when not in use.

82 Safety

Carpentry requires some special precautions, which are detailed for each tool and project to which they apply. (See also 11 and 69.) Teach the child to be especially conscious of the hand and fingers that hold the material while wood is sawed, drilled, gouged or chiselled, or a nail driven. Insist that a vice or clamp holds the material to the table whenever possible, instead of holding in the hand. Whenever the child uses sharp tools, chisels, knives, gouges or even a screwdriver, the hand resting on or holding the material should always be well away from, behind, and out of the way of the stroke of the tool.

First projects
83 Preparation for play

Tools and materials: large wooden building blocks;
peg and hole toys; wooden or plastic nuts, bolts, and slats;
wrench; workbench; wooden mallet and wooden screwdriver

These toys are essential preparation for later craft skills and interests. Piling building blocks on top of one another and fitting pegs to matching holes are not only exercises in coordination; they stimulate understanding of which shapes fit and which don't, and of relative sizes. Large plastic or wooden nuts and bolts and sanded wooden slats with holes drilled through them so that they can be bolted together, with a large wooden or small metal wrench to tighten the bolts, and similar toys, prepare the child for insights and skills he will need for carpentry as for other craft and learning.

A workbench is the most useful first tool kit for children one and a half to three years old. Remove all tools but the mallet at the start. Teach the child to hold it near the end of the handle and not near the head, as young children are wont to do. Suggest that he or she keeps eyes fixed on the peg to be hammered and the other hand well out of harm's way.

84 Tack hammering

Tools and materials: splinter-free, well-sanded, short lengths of
5cm × 5cm (2″ × 2″) wood; several boxes of long-stemmed
drawing pins or carpet tacks; tack hammer with shortened
handle; G-clamp (see 90)

At nursery school or kindergarten age a child who has enjoyed preparatory experiences (see 83) should possess sufficient
coordination to use a small hammer to drive tacks into planks.
Show him how to start the tack by holding and tapping it
gently into wood clamped to the worktable. He can hammer
designs with coloured tacks.

85 Nailing

Tools and materials: splinter-free, well-sanded 5cm (2″) thick
wood scraps; lath; tongue depressors; carpet tacks or roofing
nails; tack hammer with shortened handle;
25 × 25 × 2cm (10″ × 10″ × ¾″) plywood as a work surface

Do not give young children small-headed brads or common or
finishing nails to hammer. They are difficult to strike. Roofing
nails have extra-large heads and are therefore especially useful
at early ages.

Set the child up at his or her worktable or workbench (see
10 and 81) or, if the work is to be done at a regular table, make
sure that a wooden workboard is provided. Then show the
child how to nail lath and tongue depressors to scrap wood
shapes. Demonstrate how a single nail only hinges the lath
to the wood; a second and third nail will hold it firmly. Teach
the child to check the length of the nail against the depth of
layers of wood he plans to join before nailing them together
so that the nail ends do not protrude beyond the material
(see diagram a).

You may have to show the child repeatedly how the nail
must be started at a slight angle away from the carpenter, and

held between fingers only until the point has penetrated the wood and the nail can stand up by itself; and how the hammer should be held (see diagram b). Point out that the hammer's head will strike the nail squarely if he keeps his eyes fixed on

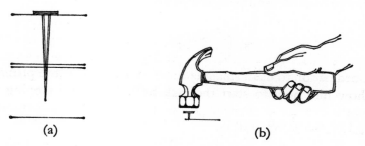

(a)   (b)

the nail's head. Teach him how to tap the nail rather than hit it hard. Then let him work on his own and discover the different ways of nailing pieces of wood to each other.

86 The nail set

Tools and materials: same as 85; common nails; nail set

Once the child is adept at nailing with large-headed roofing nails and tacks, he can be given common nails of various lengths. A nail set can now be added to his tool kit. It will enable him to drive common nailheads slightly below the surface of the wood for a better and safer finish.

87 Sandpapering

Tools and materials: bag of wood scraps and cut-offs, obtainable from timber yard or woodworking shop;
two blocks of wood, each 5cm × 7·5cm × 2·5cm (2″ × 3″ × 1″) (more or less); two sheets of medium sandpaper;
two sheets of fine sandpaper

Cut the sheets of sandpaper with scissors so that they fit round the wooden blocks. Tape or staple one sheet of each grade of sandpaper to the blocks, sandpaper side facing out (see diagram). Then let the child sand scrap wood until it is splinter-free and smooth, using the coarser paper first and then the finer one to obtain a good finish. The child must be shown how to sand with the grain of the wood.

This is a good opportunity to point out the different grains of various woods and the difference between the texture and appearance of end grain and that running lengthwise on the board. Show the child how the wood is marred when sanded against the grain.

88 Gluing

(See 21–8 for tools and materials.)

For use by children and young people, most of the recommended pastes and adhesives serve wood as well as paper, with only a few exceptions. Wallpaper and flour pastes and cow gum do not bond wood effectively.

Commercially available casein glues, mucilage and acrylics are recommended for children's carpentry projects. Show the child how to apply a minimum of adhesive and yet cover one or both surfaces with an even coating of glue. Have him wipe away excess glue around joints with a damp cloth before the glue begins to set. Later he can use clamps to hold pieces of wood together while the glue dries (see 90). The child must learn to be patient and not to disturb glued joints and surfaces until the adhesive has set completely.

89 Collages and assemblages

Tools and materials: sanded scrap wood (see 87); lath;
tongue depressors; scrap and waste wood turnings and moulding;
tack hammer (see 85); assortment of common nails, each size
kept in its own screw-top glass jar or in separate compartments
of an egg carton; paste (see 21–8);
30cm × 30cm × 2cm (12″ × 12″ × ¾″) pine or plywood board, to
be used as a base or working surface

The child can nail different shapes of wood on top of and next
to one another on to the board, or make an open or partially
enclosed hollow framework (see diagram), or combine both
techniques. When completed, they can be painted (see 106–10
and Chapter 6). (See also 29 and 30.)

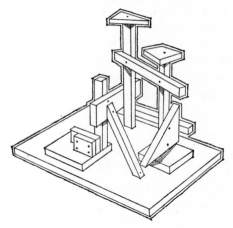

Carpentry for beginners
90 Clamping

Tools and materials: two G-clamps; two corner clamps;
two model maker's or wood hand-screw clamps

Once a child enjoys woodworking, clamping will expedite
gluing and other operations. He can then attempt more
ambitious projects.

It doesn't matter if the wood is marred or scratched during a child's early carpentry efforts. Nevertheless it is important to instil care and good work habits as early as possible. Teach the child to keep a scrap of wood or lath between the jaws of any metal clamp he may use and the outside surfaces of the wood that is held. When the wood is protected in this manner, G-clamps can be useful for nailing and gluing. Corner clamps enable the child to join wooden pieces at perfect right angles (see 97). The model maker's and wood hand-screw clamps are designed for more delicate work.

91 The vice

Tools and materials: carpenter's vice

Once a child understands the purpose of clamps, he'll benefit from being given a carpenter's vice. It is available at any hardware shop and can be attached to a trestle table (see 10), tabletop workbench (see 81) or any other worktable. A combination of clamps and vice is the equivalent of several extra pairs of hands.

92 The coping saw or jigsaw

Tools and materials: jeweller's or other coping saw;
coping saw workbench attachment (see diagram b)
package of spiral coping saw blades; box lids;
or 10cm × 15cm × 3mm (4″ × 6″ × $\frac{1}{8}$″) cardboard;
gummed white paper sheets, each about 6mm ($\frac{1}{4}$″) larger all around than the cardboard or balsa (if no pre-gummed paper is available, white drawing paper or bond paper and paste will serve the same ends); box of wax crayons; scissors;
15cm × 22cm (6″ × 9″) manilla envelopes

The diagram shows how the coping saw workbench attachment can be made if none is available in local hardware or craft shops. Without it a child will find it difficult to use a coping saw effectively.

Let the child draw a picture or design on to the paper. Make

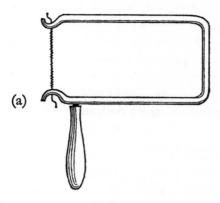

(a)

sure that the whole paper surface is covered with colour. Paste the drawing to the cardboard and trim off any excess paper. Clamp the workbench attachment to the table. Insert

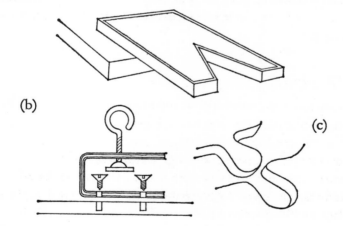

(b)

(c)

a spiral saw blade into the jaws of the coping saw. A child cannot cut himself with such a blade while working with it. Show him how to hold the saw by the handle after he is seated before the table. Saw cuts should be made inside the V-shaped notch of the workbench attachment. Then suggest that the child cuts the picture into as many small pieces as he chooses. He'll make his own jigsaw puzzle.

Demonstrate how to start the first cut (and all future cuts) by moving the saw blade up and down gently against the edge of the material, keeping the blade as perpendicular as possible. Any five- or six-year-old can make such a puzzle without difficulty at one or more work sessions. He can put the cut-apart pieces of his puzzle into an envelope as a gift. Once he becomes proficient in the use of the coping saw, he can be shown how to cut interlocking puzzle pieces (see diagram c) and other shapes.

Note: For other work with a coping saw involving interior cuts, it is necessary to drill a hole inside the area to be cut away (see 93), large enough so that the coping saw blade can be inserted through it before it is fitted to the saw itself. Then attach the blade to the saw handle and cut away the interior portion. If any blade other than a spiral blade is used, be sure that the teeth of the blade face *down* when inserted into the coping saw.

93 Drilling

Tools and materials: hand drill with 6mm ($\frac{1}{4}$″) chuck;
assorted drill bits, including 6mm ($\frac{1}{4}$″) bit;
coping saw (see 92); mallet; 6mm ($\frac{1}{4}$″) dowel;
sandpaper (see 87); carpenter's vice or G-clamps (see 90 and 91);
sheets of 15cm × 15cm × 2cm (6″ × 6″ × $\frac{3}{4}$″) pine or plywood (to
be drilled); one sheet of 20cm × 20cm × 2cm (8″ × 8″ × $\frac{3}{4}$″) pine
or plywood (to be placed under the wood to be drilled);
set square (see 99); pencil

Let the child sand the wood to be drilled until it is splinter-free and smooth. Then show him how to clamp it into the vice for horizontal drilling of the surface (see diagram a) or vertical drilling of the edge (see diagram b), or flat to the table with G-clamps for vertical drilling. Place the larger piece of scrap wood behind or underneath the wood to be drilled. It will assure a clean hole and it protects the table or other surface from being penetrated by the drill bit. Insert the 6mm ($\frac{1}{4}$″) bit into the chuck of the drill and tighten it firmly. Then

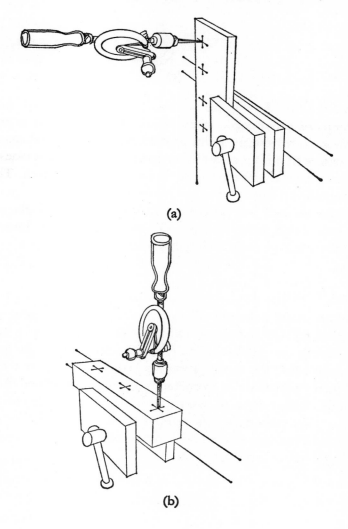

(a)

(b)

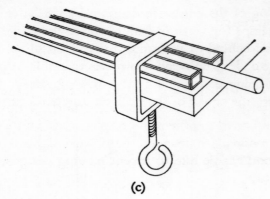

(c)

show the child how to mark a small cross on the wood, using set square and pencil, wherever he wishes to drill a hole. Demonstrate how the point of the bit must be placed against the centre of this cross, and how to turn the handle of the drill to keep it at a right angle to the wood and assure a clean, perpendicular hole.

After the drill has penetrated all the way through the first layer of wood, give it a couple of extra turns to assure total penetration and a clean hole. Remove the wood from vice or clamp and let the child inspect it. Then allow him to drill as many holes as he wishes.

When he has finished, place the length of dowel into the vice or secure it to the edge of the table with a clamp (see diagram c). Let the child saw off several short lengths with his coping saw. He can then drive these dowels into the holes he drilled into the wood, using his mallet.

Due to variations in diameter and possible swelling of the wood, he may have to sand the dowels before they fit the holes. Once the child has learned these operations, he can drill different scraps of wood and lath and peg them together to build, model and construct.

94 The wrench

Tools and materials: same as 93; nuts and 6mm ($\frac{1}{4}''$) bolts in different lengths; small adjustable wrench

Once the child has learned to drill holes into the wood and lath, he can join them with nuts and bolts. Strips of lath, drilled and bolted to others and to pieces of scrap wood, will familiarize him with levers. Empty cotton reels bolted to drilled wood enable him to invent moving designs, mechanisms and toys.

95 The screwdriver

Tools and materials: small screwdriver; small flat-headed screws; hand drill and bits (see 93); 2cm ($\frac{3}{4}''$) soft pine scrap wood; lath; tongue depressors; 20cm × 20cm × 2cm ($8'' \times 8'' \times \frac{3}{4}''$) pine board or plywood (to be placed under the wood as it is drilled and screwed together)

There is no point in giving a child a screwdriver until he has learned how to use a drill. Unless holes are pre-drilled slightly smaller than the diameter of the shank of the screws, a screwdriver is extremely hazardous and difficult to use. Unlike nails, screws should never be held in the hand while a screwdriver is used; the tool can slip and inflict a deep and painful wound. Insert the pointed end of the screw into the hole and turn it hand-tight before using the screwdriver.

Clamp two pieces of wood, one quarter again as thick, when clamped, as the screws are long, to the table or into the vice, together with the 2cm ($\frac{3}{4}''$)-thick backing board. Select a bit slightly smaller in diameter than the screw to be used. Insert it into the chuck of the drill and drill a hole through the two pieces of wood that are to be joined, no deeper than three-quarters of the way through the second piece. Show the child how to check the screw length against the thickness of the two pieces of wood to assure that the sharp point of the screw will not penetrate the far side after it is screwed into the wood (see diagram). Then screw the two pieces of wood together.

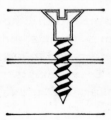

Once the child has observed and understood these various operations, he needs ample opportunity to practise on his own.

96 Countersink

Tools and materials: same as 95; countersink

The top of the shank of any screw is slightly larger than the threaded part. Hence the head is likely to protrude above the surface of the wood unless it is forced into it. Show the child how to insert the countersink into the chuck of the hand drill to enlarge the hole he first drilled into the wood, so that the screw, once fully driven into the wood with the screwdriver, lies flush with the surface of the wood or slightly below it.

97 Mitre box and back saw

Tools and materials: back saw (for younger children provide a keyhole, wallboard or compass saw); mitre box;
set square (see 99); pencil; two G-clamps and two corner clamps (see 90); 5cm × 25cm × 1·25cm (2″ × 10″ × ½″) pine board

Clamp the mitre box to the table edge firmly. Place the pine board inside it (see diagram). Demonstrate the different cuts that can be made by placing the saw into the different slots cut into the mitre box. Show the child how 90° and 45° cut pieces can be joined for gluing, nailing and screwing. Corner clamps are useful for demonstrating some of the possible joints, as well as for holding the cut wood in place for jointing.

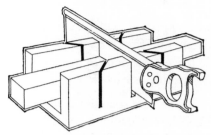

It is important that the child learns how to hold the saw properly from the very start, using the 'pistol grip' with index finger extended as a guide. This assures the most effective control of any hand saw. The mitre box is the best introduction to sawing since it teaches the importance of maintaining the proper angle of the saw to achieve the desired cut. Once the child understands these operations and requirements, he is ready to saw. Later he can learn to mark the lines (see 98–102). He must then line up the marked line with the appropriate mitre box slot.

Starting the cut without fraying the wood is a matter of practice and experience. Start at one edge of the wood with short, quick strokes of the saw blade until the teeth make a small notch within which they remain. Then, using longer, even strokes of the saw, the wood can be cut all the way through. When the child nears the end of his cut, he must shorten the strokes of the saw once more so that the further edges of the board do not splinter at the finish.

If the saw blade frays the wood, either the saw is not held perpendicular to the cut already made, or it may require a little soap applied to the teeth. If the ease of sawing does not improve, the teeth of the saw may require setting and sharpening. Any hardware shop will have this done at nominal cost. Keep the saw blade covered with a thin film of oil while it is not in use.

98 Planning and measurement without numbers

Identical rudiments apply to all crafts in making plans, drawings and measurements. Some of the tools used in carpentry make it possible for young people to plan and duplicate parts without using numerical measurements.

Tools: set square; right-angle triangle; compass; dividers; marking gauge; pencil; mitre box

A simple six-sided box can be made by a child who is not yet familiar with mathematical operations.

Materials: 60cm × 7·5cm × 2cm (24″ × 3″ × ¾″) wood; 30cm × 30cm × 6mm (12″ × 12″ × ¼″) plywood

The child marks off a short length of 7·5cm (3″) wide wood. He then places it inside his mitre box and cuts along this mark (see 97). He places the short, sawed-off piece on top of another, longer piece of 7·5cm (3″) wood, with ends lined up, and runs a sharp pencil point along the other end of the top piece, marking another of the same size on to the bottom one (see diagram). After this second piece is cut, he will have two identical pieces for opposite sides of the box. When the same operation is repeated a second time, the four pieces required for the frame of the box will be complete. He can glue, nail or screw these sides together, using corner clamps (see 90). This frame can then be traced on to the 30cm (12″) plywood

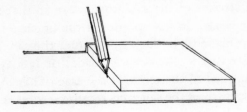

to form the bottom and lid of the box. After being cut with a saw, they can be glued, nailed, screwed or hinged to the frame. Use the marking gauge to indicate the line on the top and bottom pieces along which nails or screws are to be driven (see 100). The box will be reasonably square and a satisfying piece of work.

99 The set square

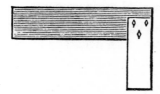

This tool is of value only if at least one side of the wood is perfectly straight. For younger children all sides of the wood should be trimmed square before it is given to them.

100 The marking gauge

This tool is especially useful at a stage at which the child cannot as yet make numerical measurements with precision.

He can set it to any desired width and duplicate this measurement elsewhere. For example, he can set the gauge to approximately half the width of the edge of a piece of wood and mark this distance on the top side of any other wood to which it is to be nailed or screwed. Nails or screws driven along such a line, unless they are driven crooked, are unlikely to protrude through the outside surface of the wood beneath.

101 Templates

Templates are useful in any craft, especially at an age when the child cannot measure with accuracy or where organic shapes defy measurement (see 65). Once a child knows how to make

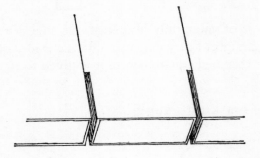

templates, he can duplicate or transfer any shape he wishes. Insist that the child invents his own templates. Point out that when a template is used, a pencil line drawn around the outside produces a slightly larger (and one drawn around an interior shape a slightly smaller) duplicate of the original. In sawing or otherwise cutting out such a shape an allowance must be made for the difference by cutting either slightly inside or outside the marked line, as appropriate, or redrawing it beforehand (see diagram).

102 Using tools to make tools

Braces, struts, temporary supports for pieces that are to be jointed, strips of wood fastened to the workbench to hold a board that is being worked on, and other temporary aids devised by the young craftsman are a sign of mature craftsmanship. Encourage the invention of tools that aid or speed

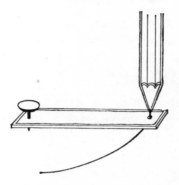

the work. For example, a strip of 1·25cm × 2·5cm × 30cm ($\frac{1}{2}$" × 1" × 12") wood into which holes, small enough to hold a pencil snugly, are drilled at intervals, and a nail driven through one end, can be turned into a useful beam compass (see diagram).

103 Jointing

Use of the mitre box (see 97) and corner clamps (see 90) gives the young craftsman ideas about jointing wood. Other, more complex and durable joints will enable him to use his craft with greater versatility.

104 Bracing

Wooden strips and right-angle and other braces can be glued, nailed or screwed to a wooden base to provide temporary or permanent support for other pieces that are attached to them and each other.

105 The plane

The plane is a sharp tool, and as such demands of the user considerable experience, coordination and self-discipline (see also 69).

Tools and materials: block or trimming plane; workbench (see 81); 5cm × 15cm × 35cm (2″ × 6″ × 14″) pine; 2·5cm × 5cm × 25cm (1″ × 2″ × 10″) pine

A block or trimming plane is best to teach young carpenters how to shave warped, uneven wood; to trim wood too thick to fit; or to round edges. Nail a strip of 2·5cm × 5cm (1″ × 2″) wood to the worktable against which to brace the wood for planing (see diagram). Demonstrate how and why the wood

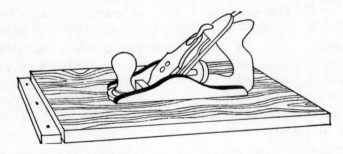

must always be planed with the grain, and how to adjust the blade setting at the knurled knob attached to the handle of the plane.

Check the depth of the cut by inspecting the knife edge on the bottom of the plane and try it out on scrap wood. A thin, level, even sliver, and no more, should be removed with each pass of the plane. Too deep a bite or a blade set crooked will nick and crease the surface so that it requires endless planing and sanding before it is smooth and level again.

106 Wood finishing

After a construction or an object has been made, the young carpenter may choose to preserve the wood – paint, varnish, shellac or stain it. Younger age groups will find it sufficiently satisfying to paint wood with poster colours (see 149). If they wish, they can protect the painted surfaces with water glass (see 42), transparent glue (see 26) or a light coat of varnish or shellac. Bear in mind that the last two are volatile and toxic, and constitute a serious fire hazard. They also ruin paint brushes unless these are thoroughly rinsed in a proper solvent after use and then washed in warm water and soap (see 110 and 165).

107 Sanding and sealing wood

Tools and materials: sandpaper (in two or three different grades, ranging from medium-coarse to fine); steel wool; sealer; flat 2·5 cm (1″) paint brush (or wider if the work is large); rags

Wood should be sanded and sealed before it is painted, or most of the paint will sink in, giving it an uneven coating. Sealing compounds for wood are best bought in hardware and paint shops. The wood should be thoroughly sanded, first using a coarse paper and then finer grades, always with the grain, until it is perfectly smooth to the touch. For a high finish it should then be polished with fine steel wool. Two light coats of sealer, each evenly applied with a brush, will close the pores of the wood. The second coat is applied only after the first has dried completely. Wipe away any excess with a cloth or rag after each application. After the final coat has dried, rub it down gently with steel wool once more.

108 Painting the wood

The variety of water- and oil-base and synthetic paints, enamels, and other finishes is so great that it would be futile to try to list and describe them. Dress the child in old and protective clothing. (See 11 and 165 for essential general safety precautions.)

If the construction or object is to be painted in a single colour, it is best to do so after final assembly of all parts. However, if small sections or parts are to be painted in several different colours or shades, it is best to paint them before assembly, provided no edges that are to be glued are covered with paint. Painted surfaces give poor adhesion.

109 Natural wood finish

Tools and materials: linseed oil; white (clear) vinegar; turpentine; rags

Mix all three liquid ingredients in equal proportion. Keep in a closed jar and shake well before using. After the wood has been sanded (see 107) but not sealed, apply this mixture to the surface with a cloth; wipe off any excess. Repeat this process two or three times, rubbing with steel wool after each application has dried, until the wood is thoroughly penetrated and the pores are sealed. This provides a matte finish that is resistant to water, alcohol and other stains.

110 Brushes

Use bristle brushes, 1·25cm ($\frac{1}{2}$″) wide or wider, for painting wood, depending on the size of the object or the delicacy of the design. Use long-haired, narrow brushes for stripes, and round ones for painting detail. Instruct the young craftsman never to leave paint-filled brushes lying about but to rinse them at once after use, in the appropriate solvent.

Brushes on which paint has dried are difficult to restore, and may be totally ruined. Wipe the brush on newspaper or rags and rinse it in thinner poured into a jar. Then wash it in

mild soap and warm water. Brushes should never be stored standing on their hair. Keep them lying flat or standing on the wood handle in a jar, or, preferably, hang them by the handle so that none of the hair touches any surface. If paint has dried on a brush, it should be hung in solvent. Make a brush holder out of wire that allows the brush to soak without its hair touching the bottom or sides of the jar (see diagram).

4 Wire and metal

... This is an art
Which does mend nature – change it rather: but
The art itself is nature. *William Shakespeare*

111 Background

In early cultures that discovered the material and the means
to refine and work metal, the tribal smith or metal craftsman
was a man set apart from the rest. His secrets were sanctified

by ritual and custom. The metal smiths of Benin in Africa, who wrought magnificent bronzes, the artisans of ancient China, Mesopotamia, Greece, Rome and South America, were versed in metal craft even while the people of central and northern Europe and those east and west of the Ural Mountains had barely become aware of the existence and possibilities of these materials. North American Indians were still in the Stone Age at the time of the arrival of Europeans, despite rich mineral deposits close to the surface on their continent. Yet today there is hardly any tribe or group of human beings, no matter how isolated, that does not possess some idea of how to work and use metals.

Some of the common metals we take for granted, like aluminium, were discovered less than two hundred years ago. The French emperor Napoleon treasured aluminium more than gold and ordered a special set of tableware to be cast from this metal for his court. But many metals will soon become scarce once again at the present rate of wasteful consumption. Even scrap metals, many of them essential in the smelting of alloys, are now in short supply. Huge quantities of discarded metal are heaped daily on to rubbish dumps to rust and be irretrievably dissipated.

112 Work spaces
(See 10 and 81.)

113 Safety and developmental education

The development of metal craft skills should begin at early ages. Working with metal is actually less dangerous than many other crafts that are regarded as safe. At earliest ages a child needs no tools other than his or her fingers to bend and twist pipecleaners or plastic-covered wire. The sharp ends of such wire are easily covered with masking tape.

Metal foil has edges that are not much sharper than those

of paper. The young child must learn that they should be treated with care and that the foil can be folded or rolled to be perfectly safe. Metal and the required tools can't be worked by a child in whose hands they are unsafe – he just doesn't have the strength. Coat-hanger wire, for example, is very difficult to model. Ordinary pliers require relatively large hands and a firm grip.

First projects
114 Pipecleaners

Tools and materials: pipecleaners;
modelling clay or modelling dough (see 53, 117, 175 and 195)

As in all craft, the young beginner needs ample opportunities to play with the materials. It is sufficiently difficult and intriguing to discover how to bend pipecleaners into curves and angles; how to twist two or more strands together; how

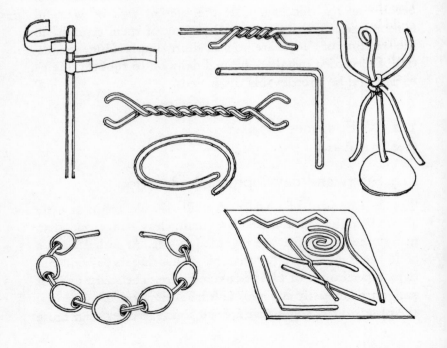

to splice several lengths; or how to insert one end of a pipe-cleaner into a lump of clay to make it stand up.

Other possibilities include gluing paper or ribbon to a pipe-cleaner; using pipecleaners as armatures for clay or modelling-compound objects, figures and shapes; stringing wood or clay beads on to pipecleaners; and pasting formed pipecleaners to card (see diagram).

115 Foil projects
(See 21–46.)

Wirework for beginners
116 Covered wire construction

Tools and materials: diagonal cutting pliers; combination nose pliers; single-strand plastic-covered wire; roll of masking tape; scissors

Use the same techniques as those described in 114. Show the child how to snip off required lengths of wire with the cutting pliers; how to bend, model and twist the strands by hand and with pliers. Dowels, cardboard tubes and other pre-formed shapes can be used as jigs (see diagram). As a precaution

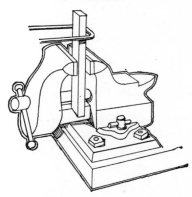

suggest that the child covers any wire that protrudes beyond the plastic-covered ends with small pieces of masking tape.

117 Making armatures

(See 53, 114, 116 and 195 for tools and materials.)

Any available wire that the child can work will do. For younger children pipecleaners are best as armatures for modelling with clay and dough. Older and stronger children can use coat-hanger wire (see 120–22). Sculptor's armature wire is available from art supply shops. It is fairly large in diameter but is made of soft, flexible, lightweight alloy that is easily cut with pliers.

Provide a 1·25–2cm ($\frac{1}{2}''$–$\frac{3}{4}''$) plywood base in which holes have been drilled (see 93), into which the armature wire ends can be inserted and secured. Or nail, screw and brace a dowel on the base to which the wire can be attached (see diagram).

Once the wire armature is made, the child can cover it with clay or other modelling compound (see Chapter 7).

118 The metalworking vice

There are substantial differences between a woodworking vice and one used for metalwork. For young people's craft purposes a metal vice can be adapted to woodwork (see 91), but not vice versa. For the beginner's wire modelling, a lightweight vice that can be clamped to any table is sufficient. For later, heavier work a vice, preferably one that swivels at least 180°, that can be bolted to a worktable is needed.

The vice is a practical, essential tool for safety. Materials held in the hand can slip and cause injury. Wire can be bent safely by hand or with a mallet when it is firmly locked into the jaws of a vice. Besides, most vices include a small anvil on the side away from the jaws that can serve as a wire modelling surface.

119 Wirework

Once the first metalworking skills, tools and experiences have been acquired, a child is ready for more advanced work. Wire modelling, apart from being an art form in itself, has many practical applications, from electric circuit wiring and repair to jewellery making.

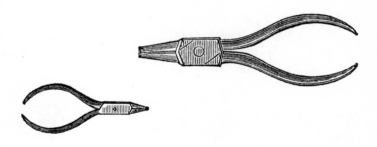

120 Wire cutting

Tools and materials: ordinary pliers;
diagonal cutting pliers (for cutting up to 22-gauge wire);
combination nose pliers;
hacksaw or jigsaw (for cutting 20-gauge or heavier wire);
metalworking vice (see 118)

Copper, steel and brass wire is available in different thicknesses, varying from 26-gauge (fine) to 12-gauge (heavy). It can be bought round, half-round and square.

Ordinary pliers can be used to cut wire, but they are not

very efficient, especially in the hands of young people. Even diagonal cutting pliers will not cut heavy wire, like a coat-hanger. Wire that cannot be cut easily with pliers must be locked into the vice so that the place where the cut is to be made protrudes slightly from the jaws. A half-round or tri-angular file (see 122), a hacksaw or a coping saw should be used to cut heavy wire.

121 Twisting and jointing

Tools and materials: same as 120;
copper, brass or other soft alloy wire

The same basic twists, bends and joints apply as in 114. Wire that is too difficult to model in the hand should be locked into a vice and bent with a mallet or a ball peen hammer. To make a sharp angle, lock the wire into the vice just below the place where the bend is to be made and tap it with the hammer until the required angle is formed (see diagram a). Curve the wire

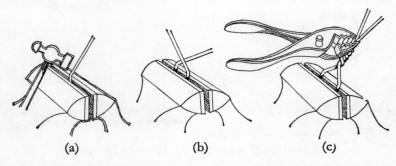

(a)   (b)   (c)

around pipe or dowel for round and oval shapes. To twist heavy wires into a double strand, bend each at the centre into a 45° angle and lock both pieces into the vice side by side (see diagram b). Twist the protruding ends with ordinary pliers, starting near the jaws of the vice (see diagram c), or use a wrench if the wire is very heavy.

With these techniques wire can be bent and twisted into

interesting shapes. Start with copper wire that can be easily formed in the hand, twisted around itself or paper, cardboard or wood armatures (see 51–3 and 117).

122 Filing and finishing

Tools and materials: round metal file; half-round metal file; triangular file; needle file; steel wool; emery cloth or paper; buffing compound and cloth; metalworking vice (see 118)

Pliers (see 120) or files (see diagram) leave sharp, ragged ends on wire when used for cutting. Ends and edges must be blunted and rounded before the metal is worked. Heavy wire can be locked into the vice to file ends smooth and finish them with emery cloth or paper. Wire can be cleaned, polished or given texture or a high finish by rubbing with steel wool, emery paper, or buffing compound and cloth.

5 Leather

Never forget the material you are working with, and always try to use it for what it can do best. *William Morris*

123 Background

American Indian tribes cured animal skins by salting and burying them in wood-chip-and-water filled holes dug into the ground, and then drying and working them until they became pliable. Eskimo women still scrape and chew reindeer skins with their teeth to make them durable and soft enough for wearing. Tanning and tooling of leather were known among the Egyptians more than 1,300 years before Christ; in China this craft was perfected even earlier. The ancient Jews discovered how to preserve hides with oak bark, and they used leather for making ritual articles, sandals, leggings, and shields and armour, as did the Greeks and Romans.

Some of the first craft guilds were formed by British and European leatherworkers in the fourteenth century. Two different guilds became responsible for the preparation of animal skins – the tanners for leather and the skinners for furs.

Cutting, working and tooling leather take time and patience even when done by machine. But the ancient ways of working are still practised in Morocco, India and Mexico, and to a lesser extent by a few remaining European and American craftsmen.

Leather from various animal species has different thickness, texture and other characteristics. No leather made from other than domestic breeds should ever be used for craft. Split cowhide can be cut easily with scissors and worked by young children. Calfskin, sheepskin, pigskin and goatskin in various grades are obtainable from tanneries and craft suppliers. Suede is the flesh side of the leather regardless of its source.

Leather can be bought in whole and half skins, in sides, and as remnants. The back side of the skin is the most valuable, fault-free grade. It should be stored flat, grain side up, on an open shelf. Leather thong – thin strips of leather used for lacing and binding – is expensive. Vinyl lacing, while lacking the quality of the organic material, is a useful substitute, available from craft material suppliers.

The first efforts in leatherwork by children should be spontaneous and involve activities that familiarize them with the characteristics of the material and with the techniques and tools required to work it successfully. More mature young people should be encouraged to make paper templates and mock-ups (see 64 and 65) before working with the leather itself. Many of the paper and foil craft techniques – punching (see 18), lacing (see 20), weaving (see 42–6), scoring, scribing and cutting (see 37–41) – are essential preparations for leather craft. They involve similar, and in many cases identical, procedures, in less expensive, more easily worked, and expendable materials.

Beginning with leather
124 Scissors – cutting and gluing

Tools and materials: split leather (see 123); scissors;
sheets of heavy cardboard; leather glue; wax or tracing paper;
mallet

Leather is usually cut with a sharp knife. However, young
children can cut split leather with ordinary scissors. Split
leather scraps can often be obtained free or inexpensively from
manufacturers of wallets, purses and gloves.

Scissors-cut split leather can be glued to itself or to cardboard, wood, metal, felt and other materials. Cow gum is the
most commonly used and effective adhesive.

White vegetable, casein and acrylic glues are also used.
Cornflour paste (see 27) adheres leather especially well. Suggest that a minimum of glue is used for such pasting so that it
does not stain the leather. Brush two or three light coats of
the cornflour glue on both surfaces. Press the leather together
before the glue dries. Wipe off any excess with a damp cloth,
then place the leather between two pieces of wood larger than
the glued surfaces and hold them together with G-clamps (see
90) for half an hour or more, until the glue is completely dry.

125 Collage and appliqué

Tools and materials: same as 124; leather remnants;
scrap material

Split leather from different hides, or dyed in a variety of stains,
can be used for collages and assemblages (see 29, 30 and 89).
Cut into very small pieces, leather can be used as mosaic
modules (see 31 and 201); use the adhesives suggested in 124.
Appliqué consists of pasting smaller pieces of leather to a
larger piece.

126 Stamping and punching

Tools and materials: round drive punch; revolving punch;
one-pronged chisel; multiple-pronged chisel; dividers;
rawhide mallet;
25cm × 30cm × 2cm (10″ × 12″ × ¾″) wooden workboard;
leather remnants

The listed punches and chisels are required for basic leatherwork, though one of each suffices for beginners. Punching
holes into leather is the first step for all lacing (see 127), sewing (see 131), and studding and grommeting (see 130).
Demonstrate how a line is marked with a ruler and soft pencil
wherever the leather is to be laced, sewn or grommeted. After
marking with a pair of dividers the places on the line where
the holes are to be made (see diagram a), use a punch or chisel
of a size that matches the lace, thread or grommet to perforate
the leather (see diagram b). All punching dies, including the
revolving punch, can be hammered with a mallet.

Two different hole patterns are generally used for lacing
around the edges of leather. The first consists of holes punched
in a straight line (see diagram c, and diagrams b–d on pages
115–16). The second consists of alternate, staggered holes for

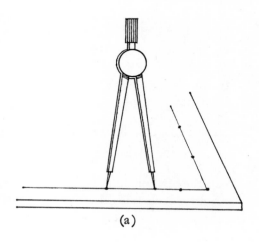

(a)

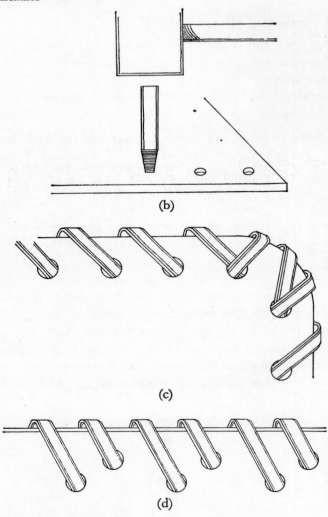

(b)

(c)

(d)

a different lacing effect (see diagram d). The punched-out circles of leather can be saved and used for collages and mosaics (see 31 and 124).

Be sure to keep the leather on a wooden workboard when driving punches and chisels with the mallet so as not to mar furniture surfaces.

127 Lacing

Tools and materials: leather or vinyl thong; lacing needle;
hole or die punched leather shapes

Old leather belts can be cut into thin strips to provide thong.
After holes have been punched into the leather (see 126),
secure one end of the thong in the lacing needle (see diagram
a). Push the needle into the first hole and pull the thong
through, leaving about 2·5cm (1″) protruding from it. This
end can be knotted and trimmed with scissors and then
pulled up close to the first hole, or it can be tucked under the
first few stitches. Then show the child how to lace around the
edge of the leather, from hole to hole, using the whipstitch
(see diagram b). If the holes are staggered, a more decorative
version of the whipstitch can be laced (see diagram d).

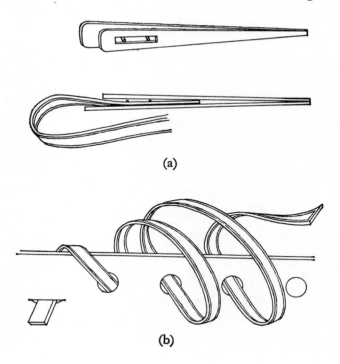

(a)

(b)

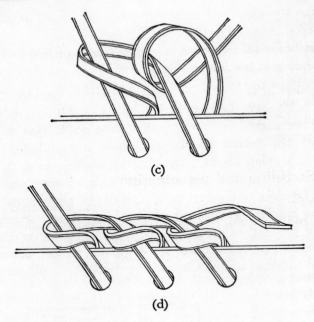

(c)

(d)

Diagrams (c) and (d) show additional simple, common lacing methods that can be adapted and varied.

128 Braiding and plaiting

Tools and materials: leather or vinyl thong

Thong can be braided and plaited like fibres (see 252–6); the same techniques apply and can be adapted.

129 Shaping and fastening

Tools and materials: leather; rags or sponge;
bowl of clear water and soap; towel; straight edge

Leather can be creased or folded without cracking the surface, provided it is first moistened slowly until it becomes pliable. It can then be folded over a wooden or metal straight edge.

Moisten the flesh side until the water begins to darken the finished side of the leather.

Very heavy leather, especially if it is to be carved or folded, should always be cased. This means scrubbing it clean with mild soap and water. Rinse off all soap and then let the leather soak in water for about five minutes. Wrap the wet leather in a towel and leave it overnight. Next day it will be soft enough to be worked.

130 Studding and grommeting

Tools and materials: same as 126; grommets and grommet die; eyelets and eyelet die; rivets and rivet set; rawhide mallet; 25cm × 30cm × 2cm (10″ × 12″ × ¾″) wooden workboard

Holes must be pre-punched for all of the above-listed fasteners and attachments (see 126), each the exact same size as or a shade larger than the diameter of the shank of the attachment. A variety of each kind is available, together with the required die or set, in craft supply shops. The metal piece is inserted into the hole and spread with the die and mallet (see 19).

131 Sewing

Tools and materials: leather; space marker wheel; or dividers; harness needle (for younger age groups or for heavy thread); 'sharps' (for older age groups or for finer thread); revolving leather punch; rawhide mallet; reel of saddler's or bookbinder's linen thread; or coarse nylon thread or twine

The harness needle is ideal for young children since it is blunt. 'Sharps' are available in various sizes. The line where the leather is to be sewn must first be marked (see 126), and spaces for stitch holes marked with the space marker wheel (see diagram a) or dividers (see 126) and then punched (see 126), before it can be sewn. Heavy leather to be sewn at the edges should be skived (the edge bevelled with a sharp knife) and if possible glued before marking, punching and sewing. The following stitches are those most commonly used in sewing leather:

Running stitch (diagram b)
Back stitch (diagram c)
Saddler's stitch (diagrams d and e)
Locked saddler's stitch (diagram f)

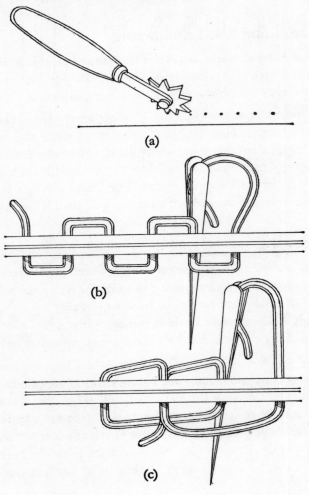

(a)

(b)

(c)

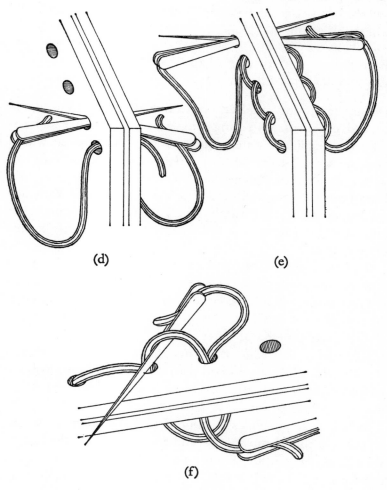

(d)

(e)

(f)

Awls for more advanced leather sewing are also available from craft supply shops and instructions are supplied.

132 Care of tools

Leatherworking tools, like all sharp tools, require frequent honing and occasional sharpening. They need to be kept rust-free and covered with a thin film of light oil, especially when not in use.

Finishing and decorating
133 Dyeing and colouring

Do not let young children use leather dyes; they are highly corrosive and toxic. Young people can dye leather successfully with ordinary waterproof or India inks, applied with a sable or camel's-hair brush or, if large areas are to be tinted, with a sponge. The leather will take the ink only if it has not been polished or waxed and if it has been sanded with fine sandpaper. First wash the leather with mild soap and water and let dry before it is tinted. Dilute the inks if subtle tints are required.

Wax-free, unpolished and sanded leather can be painted with oil and acrylic paints (see 167 and 168). All dyeing, tinting or painting should be done after the leather has been cut, embossed or carved, but before it is glued, laced, plaited, studded, grommeted or sewn.

Exposed leather edges that are not laced can be sanded and stained with ink or burnished with a bone burnisher. Rub the burnisher back and forth over the leather edge until it develops a glossy patina.

Saddle soap provides a good finish for stained leather. Apply it with a damp sponge and rub it well into the leather with a circular motion. Do not rub too hard over ink-stained portions. Polish with a soft, dry cloth after the saddle soap has dried.

134 Stamping and embossing

Tools and materials: leather; stamping dies;
embossing ball end modeller; rawhide mallet;
25cm × 30cm × 2cm (10″ × 12″ × ¾″) wooden workboard

Stamping, punching and embossing dies for leather are available in a great variety of designs. Provide only those that make simple geometric shapes – a circle, square, triangle, bar, or the like. A child can combine these to make designs.

Tape a scrap of leather to the wooden workboard, polished side facing up. Demonstrate how to hold the die in one hand and the mallet in the other, striking the flat, solid end of the punch to stamp the shape into the leather. Show how the different-shaped dies can be punched into the leather next to one another to form various designs. Embossing – engraving by pressing into the leather with a rounded modeller – is usually done on the flesh side of the leather.

135 Combining leather with other materials

The different leatherworking methods can be combined and used for work in other materials. For example, metal or wooden shapes can be covered with leather; leather shapes can be embedded into wood; and leather, fibres and fabrics can be combined in a number of creative ways.

6 Drawing and painting

Art is a natural discipline. *Sir Herbert Edward Read*

136 Background

Drawing and painting are developmental necessities for children, just as speaking, reading, dancing, etc., are. A child needs art experiences, not to become an artist, but to exercise essential human qualities – coordination, vision, craft, imagination, thought and expression. A child who is given no free rein in the use of art materials, who is restricted to colouring books that speak for him or clay moulds that are preformed, who is told what to draw, paint, sculpt or mould, may never realize his graphic and plastic self-expressive faculties.

These are self-evident truths recognized in every branch of education – save in the art education of children or young people. Often they are violated at every turn. When the child uses art materials at home or in the classroom, he is usually given little opportunity to play with them or discover their properties. Instead he is often shown how to draw cliché clouds, ocean waves or people, smiling moons and suns, or the stereotype houses, trees, flowers and animals found in comic strips and TV cartoons. Or the child is given moulds to fill with modelling dough, or pre-drawn pictures to colour and trace. Once he can count, numbered outline pictures are provided that he is required to fill in with matching numbered pencils or paints.

Every child and every adult possesses a sense that is not generally recognized – a *sense of aesthetic necessity*. It dictates a preference, shared by our whole species, for a particular balance and order, symmetry and asymmetry, that, when experienced or created, evoke a deep sense of satisfaction. This sense of aesthetic necessity imbues human thought, language, music, science, mythology and art with a universality. At its highest cultivation it allows people from any culture to understand and appreciate all others. It embraces faith, belief and religious experience. In children this commonality lies closest to the surface of consciousness; it is not yet overlaid with cultural prejudice.

It is the dual responsibility of parent and teacher to introduce the child to his own culture and, at the same time, to nurture his universal sense of aesthetic necessity to protect him from cultural parochialism. The arts are one of the avenues by which these goals can be reached.

One cause of confusion in art education stems from a misunderstanding of the processes involved in learning how to write. Here the child must eventually draw symbols with accuracy. Yet early free drawing is an essential preparation for writing skills. The child can only learn to control his writing instrument by scribbling at random until his coordination increases to a point at which the pencil follows his dictates. Thereafter the child still needs freedom in his art, though for different reasons. The real purpose of writing is expression; but this exercise is denied the child while he learns his letters. Especially then, he needs free rein in his artistic activities.

Art should be a creative challenge, providing great satisfaction when it is met with whatever skill, ability, imagination and capacity for involvement the child possesses. Art activities create values. They educate the emotions and foster an ethical viewpoint. Forms and feelings can be tried out and their ethical implications explored without consequence. Art education provides a beneficial release of physical and psychological energy.

137 Chronology of development

No child should ever be made or expected to draw, paint or sculpt. Some children prefer other arts and crafts. But the materials should be made available and attractive to all children. The particulars suggested in this chapter match materials and techniques children can handle to a chronology of skill and perceptual development. Art interests and skills require encouragement. But even more than that, they require opportunity.

Some basics are worth observing. For example, crayons are easier to control than chalks; yet chalks are a more satisfactory medium. A compass is fun, but it should not be given to young children until they have enjoyed several years of free-hand drawing, or else the use of mechanical drawing instruments may become so attractive that they may preclude the development of other, more important skills.

As with all materials of play, the child's first efforts centre around an exploration of what the materials can be made to do and how he can affect and transform them. He must *play* with them. He increases his control through play. His abilities unfold in the act of discovery. The crayon scribbles turn bolder, into long, sweeping, involute lines, and then are converted into random dots and dashes. (By all means show the child that he can also lay the crayon on its side and, after peeling off the paper, make broad strokes and textured masses of colour.) The same principles hold true for chalk or paint, for squeezing, pressing and rolling clay into beads, sausages and flat sheets, or for scratching into dried slabs of modelling compound or plaster (see Chapter 7).

When he has exhausted the possibilities of spontaneous exploration, he may discover by accident that what he has drawn, painted or formed reminds him of a figure, animal, object or plant he has seen. The similarity between what he sees in his art and reality may be remote or nonexistent. 'Look! I've made a fire engine,' means no more than seeing a man in the moon. The child merely imagines or wishes that his creation is what he wants it to be. It is quite enough. It's a big step forward, but it's one that cannot be forced or accelerated.

Teach control of the material: 'Let's arrange all the paints over here, each jar with its tongue depressor to spoon out the paint into the bun tin. Dip out a little of each as you need it. But keep the paint jar lids closed so that the paint doesn't dry out. Also don't dip a tongue depressor or brush loaded with blue paint into the yellow by accident. It'll turn all the yellow paint green.' Suggest free experimentation: 'Make whatever you like. Try some big, long lines and then some very little ones.' Appreciate the result: 'That looks very good' (or happy, or sad, or rough, or smooth). Encourage discovery of the different effects possible with different materials. Suggest to the child that he tries out what happens when he rubs the paint with his fingers, or other tools that he chooses. Some techniques must first be demonstrated before a child can experiment with them on his own.

Ultimately the child begins to be able to predict what he is going to do with increasing certainty and sureness. The results may still seem unreal or abstract to adults, but they are very real to him. His main satisfaction stems from his ability to make tools and materials obey him.

Art teaches the child how to cope with failure. If something is messed up, it's easy enough to start over again, and improve with practice. Fear of failure (and refusal to try repeatedly once they have failed) is one of the major learning handicaps suffered by children in our success-driven time.

The child may suffer occasional frustration, especially at times when his understanding is ahead of his ability to express himself – as it usually is at all stages of development. But coming to grips with these frustrations and coping with them, instead of being frozen into passivity, is an essential lesson for every art and craft and for all of life. 'It is only fear that prevents the child from becoming an artist – fear that his private world of fantasy will seem ridiculous to the adult. . . . Cast out fear from the child, and you have then released all its potentialities for emotional growth and maturation.'*

As stated earlier, the child needs exposure to working artists and to the art of his own and other cultures and times. He can then become aware of the variety of forms and styles that is available. Reality and fantasy, filtered through his perceptions and limited only by the discipline imposed by physical circumstances, allow the child to create a *new* reality. This is what art is all about. Through his art the child participates in the real world – and at the same time he can invent his own, in which anything is possible, anything can be invoked or imagined.

* Herbert Read, *The Grass Roots of Art: Problems of Contemporary Art*, No 2, New York: Wittenborn & Co, 1947

138 Materials and work spaces

Every child needs his own private work space or, at the very least, room at a table low enough so that he can work comfortably, sitting or standing. He needs space to lay out his materials within reach. Preferably the working surface should be spillproof – Formica, linoleum, plastic, glass or oilcloth; or covered with protective material – a heavy sheet of cardboard, or layers of newspaper firmly taped down.

Children don't need an easel for painting. Most children's easels are too flimsy to be of any use. As an alternative work surface, layers of newspaper, a large sheet of cardboard or corrugated board, or a bulletin board, blackboard or wallboard can be tacked to, nailed to, or hung on a wall. The child then needs a tray hung below the wall work surface to hold paint jars, brushes, crayons or chalks, or a small table placed to his left or right, depending on his handedness. (See also 10.)

139 Surfaces

For drawing: newsprint; brown or white wrapping paper; greaseproof paper; white or coloured card; different strengths of cardboard; panels cut from corrugated cartons
For painting: all the above; sheets of printed newspaper; wallboard or plasterboard panels

Drawing and painting papers and surfaces should be large enough so that the child can make bold strokes with crayon or brush. This may seem wasteful, especially at early ages, when children tend to make a few scribbles on a sheet and then claim they have finished. But a pre-schooler can be encouraged to work all over the paper with some endurance if the paper is large enough and the supply limited.

Impress on the child that he must not draw or paint beyond

the paper surface on to wall, table or floor. Freedom has its limitations. It carries with it the responsibility to confine the work and to exercise essential restraints. Insist that the child helps to clean up after he has finished, until he or she is old enough to do this unaided. These are the right kind of controls – more beneficial than those imposed by staying within the lines of a colouring book.

Drawing
140 Crayon scribbling

Tools and materials: school grade crayons (see 139 for surfaces)

Children's wax crayons are available in a variety of grades. Provide only 'school grade' crayons. They are less brittle, larger, and more easily handled by young children than those usually found in toy, chain and stationery stores. Let the child experiment. (See 137 and 138 for additional suggestions on how to introduce him.)

At first, give the child a small assortment of primary colours only – red, yellow, blue, black, white. Add others later. Provide a box into which he can tumble them out of their packages; in the package they are too closely packed to be handled with ease. Keep each drawing session short, ending it as soon as the child tires. Keep paper and crayons on open shelves where he can reach them unaided. Don't set particular hours or days aside as drawing times. Rather suggest, from time to time, that he or she uses the materials in between other play activities.

Crayons are not an ideal drawing material. Chalks are much better. But the younger age groups can handle crayons more easily at first, without breaking or crumbling them as they work.

141 Chalk drawing on paper

Tools and materials: lecturer's coloured chalks
(see 139 for surfaces)

Large, fat lecturer's chalks are best. Show the child how to
smudge colours chalked on the paper, with a rag, fingers or
hand. Demonstrate some of the basic colour mixtures – blue
and yellow, red and yellow, red and blue. Make the child
aware of the three basic qualities of form – line, mass and
texture (see 153); explain that 'texture' means both roughness
and smoothness. (See 140 for other suggestions that apply to
both the crayon and chalk media.)

142 Chalk drawing on a blackboard

Tools and materials: same as 141;
blackboard (see below for making your own);
felt blackboard wiper

Large slate blackboards are expensive. A satisfactory blackboard can be made by painting 'blackboard paint' on to well-
sanded and sealed plywood (see 107). Apply several coats of
the paint, each after the last has dried, using brush strokes at
right angles to the preceding coating.

The advantage of a blackboard is that it is always in view
once it has been hung. The picture can be wiped out and
another started, without ever running out of drawing surfaces.
But this is also a disadvantage: you cannot keep the result
and hang it on a wall permanently. Children need to have their
art admired and respected. They thrive on praise – it is an
incentive for future work. Yet be discriminating. Once you
have hung and admired some of the child's work, let him
know that you prefer some of his drawings to others. Such
criticism can be a spur to his future efforts.

143 Felt marker drawing

Tools and materials: small assortment of felt markers
(see 139 for surfaces)

Many felt markers are indelible. They contain dyes that, while non-toxic, discolour fabric and wood surfaces. Provide protective clothing and cover table and floor for beginners. Teach the child to replace the cap of each marker when he has finished using it for the moment, otherwise they dry out quickly.

Felt markers are available in a variety of nib sizes. Provide the child not only with a small variety of colours but also with different-size nibs, ranging from fine to broad. Suggest combinations of felt marker drawing with chalks and crayons. This increases variety of possible effects. (See 140 for other suggestions that apply to felt markers as well.)

144 Action drawing

Tools and materials: same as 140, 141 and 143;
large drawing surfaces (see 139)

Encourage movement with crayon, chalk and felt markers – broad sweeps made more or less at random across the paper. The child will then not get bogged down working in one small area of paper; he'll become aware of effects that might not otherwise occur to him. Suggest that he covers the whole paper or board with a single line that curves or zig-zags in and out and doubles back on itself, without lifting the drawing instrument off the paper.

145 Crayon transfer

Tools and materials: school grade crayons;
two or more sheets of bond (writing) paper;
large sheet of heavy cardboard (for working surface);
stylus; used-up ball point pen

Show the child how to cover one section of a sheet of paper with heavily applied wax crayon of one colour. Turn this coloured paper over on top of a second sheet. When the child draws on to the back of the heavily coloured area with a stylus, crayon lines will be transferred on to the second sheet.

Eventually the child may wish to draw several adjacent areas of colour on a new sheet of clean paper. When the paper is turned over and used as before, he will achieve surprising effects wherever one colour area changes to another. The position of the top sheet can also be varied so that different colours are superimposed in successive drawings with the stylus.

146 Crayon engraving

Tools and materials: same as 145

Show the child how to make a solid, thick area of a single light-toned crayon colour on one sheet of paper taped to the cardboard. Then cover this area with black crayon so that hardly any trace of the first colour shows through. Use the stylus to draw into the black area. As the child works, his design will show through the black in the colour that was applied first.

Two or more different light colours can be laid on top of one another and then covered with black crayon as before. Multicoloured lines will appear, depending on the amount of pressure applied to the stylus.

147 Mural drawing

Tools and materials: large sheet of wrapping paper tacked to a wall;
crayons; chalks; felt markers

One child or a group of children will enjoy drawing a mural.
Don't expect it to be completed in a single day – let this be a
continuing project. Suggest that, in addition to drawing on
to the paper, the children adhere cut paper (see 37–41), fabrics
(see 272–4), and other scrap materials. Don't insist that the
mural should be representational or assume any particular
form.

First painting
148 Water painting

Tools and materials: large sheet of white or brown paper;
bowl of clear water; long-handled, flat bristle brush

Young children need and enjoy water play. Painting with
clear water, without colour, confines the mess and introduces
the child to painting materials and techniques. A two- or
three-year-old will get great satisfaction out of painting with
water. No directions or safety precautions are required, save
for a mop and a towel.

149 Poster paints

Tools and materials: red, yellow, blue and black powdered
tempera pigment (available in packages from school and art
supply shops); or the same assortment of ready-mixed poster
paints in screw-top jars; long-handled, flat bristle brush;
225g (8 oz) glass screw-top jars; bun tin or paper cups;
bucket, bowl or pail of clear water;
tongue depressors or lolly sticks (to stir the paints);
painting paper (see 139); newspaper or blotting paper;
rags or sponge (for wiping hands and paint brush handle)

Powdered poster pigments are more economical than ready-
mixed paints. Besides, they can be used for making finger

paints (see 150) and other purposes. For brush painting, mix the pigments with water to the consistency of double cream, a sufficient quantity of each to fill one of the jars. Keep the lids tightly closed when the paints are not in use or else they'll dry out and cake. Distribute the different colours in the cups of the bun tin or paper cups for the child's painting, so that the whole batch is not ruined if he fails to rinse a brush loaded with one colour before dipping it into another.

Pre-mixed poster colours are equally useful, though more expensive. Do not buy fluorescent poster colours; they are toxic, though this fact is not marked on the label.

Dress the child in a plastic or other apron and roll up his sleeves before painting begins. Set up the paint and water containers within easy reach next to the paper or other work surface. Be sure to change the water when it gets muddy from repeated brush rinsing. Secure the paper firmly to the table or wall surface with masking tape.

Start the child at his first painting session with a single colour. When he has some experience in applying it to the paper, a second colour, a third, and more can be added to his palette. Once a second colour is provided, teach the child to rinse his brush thoroughly in water before dipping it into the different paint, or else he'll mix the colours inadvertently. Suggest that he mixes paints on his painting or in unfilled portions of the bun tin. Show him that, in addition to painting over other colours he has painted, he can paint one colour next to another. These are the first and essential disciplines required for painting. Accidents will happen; overlook them. You can guard against them by placing ample newspaper under and around the work.

Teach the child to thin out his paints whenever they get too thick (as they may). If he thins them too much you can always add a little more powder pigment.

Encourage the child to experiment – to try his brush in different ways, including the wooden end; to make lines, dots and solid shapes; even to use his fingers. Suggest large, bold strokes with the brush, as well as small, delicate ones. Then let him paint to his heart's content for as long as he enjoys daubing away.

When the painting is finished, help the child to remove it. Let it dry on newspaper or blotting paper, flat on the floor or table, before hanging it for display. Ask the child if he wants to paint another picture. Let him make the necessary preparations to whatever extent he is able and help him with the rest. At the end of a painting session, insist that he helps to clean up, screw the lids to the jars, wash out his brush and water container, and remove the protective newspaper from table and floor. The paint brush should be rinsed and then washed with mild soap and warm water. (See also 29, 30, 56, 153–5, 158, 159 and 160–64.)

150 Finger painting

Tools and materials: red, yellow, blue and black finger paints (see 152 for recipe to make your own); roll or sheets of finger painting paper (see 151 for alternative finger painting surfaces); four tongue depressors or lolly sticks; two large bowls or buckets of fresh water; sponge or rags; masking tape; newspaper or blotting paper; plastic-, metal- or formica-topped table

Finger paints are more difficult to use than poster paints – a fact not generally appreciated. Finger painting should follow, rather than precede, a child's introduction to painting with a brush (see 148 and 149). Separate one sheet of finger painting paper and tape it to the table surface. Set out the open paint jars, each with its own tongue depressor; the two bowls of water; and rags or sponge to one side and within easy reach, depending on the child's handedness. Spill a small quantity of fresh water on to the paper and distribute it with the palm of the hand or with the sponge until the paper is evenly moistened. Sponge away any excess moisture. Then dip out a small blob of paint from one of the paint jars, using a tongue depressor. Spread the blob of paint on the paper with the palm of a hand. Then draw into the paint with a finger. Let the child work into the paint with his or her hands and fingers.

Provide the child with a single colour at first. Later a second, third and fourth colour can be added, each dipped out of its jar and dropped on to the paper as before. Show the child how to spread each colour *next to* the others on the paper, before mixing them in portions of the painting. This is important, or else each painting will turn out the same muddy purple or brown.

The disciplines of not mixing paints in their jars and not painting beyond the work surface (see 149) apply here as well, as do the guidelines concerning line, mass and texture effects (see 153). However, in finger painting some application beyond the paper is unavoidable as the child works up to and along the paper edge; this is why a washable table surface is essential.

Encourage experimentation with different effects the child can create, using his or her hands and fingers only. Suggest frequent washing of hands in one of the fresh water buckets or bowls to help keep the colours fresh. One of the advantages of finger painting is that, as long as paper and paints remain moist, a design can be wiped out and started again or changed. A few drops of water added when necessary will keep the paint and paper workable.

Once some of the hand and finger effects that are possible have been thoroughly explored in succeeding sessions, add a comb, dowels, wooden blocks and other materials to the child's inventory of work tools. He can draw these through the wet paint or press them into it, creating many different effects.

Let a finished painting dry on several layers of newspaper or sheets of blotting paper. If the painting buckles as it dries, it can be ironed between layers of newspaper or blotting paper. In succeeding painting sessions encourage the child to do as much of the preparatory work, paper wetting, and dipping out of paint as possible.

151 Alternative finger painting surfaces

If finger painting paper is not available, the following materials will take the paint adequately enough to permit the child to work in this medium:

Any slick, glossy paper, including the covers of magazines; a glass or enamel tray; a sheet of metal or foil; oilcloth

152 Making your own finger paints

Tools and materials: powdered poster pigments (see 149) – ½ tablespoon each of four colours; 1½ cups laundry starch 1 litre (2 pints) boiling water; ½ cup talc (optional); four screw-top glass jars; 1½ cups soap flakes; tongue depressors, one for each colour

Mix the laundry starch with cold water to the consistency of a creamy paste. Add the boiling water and cook until the mixture becomes transparent and glassy. Stir constantly. Let the mixture cool somewhat before stirring in the soap flakes. Once these are completely dissolved, add the talc. Let the mixture cool and then pour it equally into the four jars, filling each to about an inch (2·5 cm) below the lip at most. Stir half a spoonful of each powder colour into its respective jar.

Soap flakes, liquid cornstarch, or wheat paste mixed with water to a creamy consistency can also be added to powdered pigments to make finger paints, depending on availability of materials.

153 Dot mass and line painting

Ask the child to paint with brush or finger (see 149 and 150) using dots or short dashes only. They can be placed closely next to one another or farther apart, or they can overlap. The same colour or different colours used in this manner will produce a great variety of effects when the finished painting is viewed from a distance. French pointillist painters at the turn of this century explored this technique with great imagination. Show your child black-and-white and colour reproductions of photographs, illustrations and paintings through a magnifying glass. He'll discover that all the different colours and shadings in printing are achieved through the use of small dots of only four colours, each printed next to the others. He can achieve similar effects with his dot paintings. The same can be done in drawings or paintings executed exclusively in line and/or in large masses of colour.

154 Line and blob blowing

Tools and materials: drinking straws;
liquid watercolours or inks; eyedroppers, one for each colour;
sheets of white drawing or bond paper

Many effects in drawing and painting are accidental. Once discovered, an artist can re-create them at will. This quality of art makes it playful and, therefore, of special value to children and young people.

Tape the drawing paper to a newspaper- or cardboard-covered tabletop. Use one of the eyedroppers to drop a small amount of ink or watercolour on to the paper. Show the child how he can 'chase' the colour across the paper by blowing at it with a drinking straw. Hold the straw while blowing so that it comes close to, but does not touch, the paint or ink. Different colours when blown in this manner can be used to create delightful effects and designs.

155 Blot pictures

Tools and materials: same as 154, omitting drinking straws

Fold a sheet of bond paper in half and then unfold it. Drop a small amount of ink or watercolour into the crease with an eyedropper. Now refold the paper and rub a finger along the crease without exerting pressure. When the paper is unfolded, a complex blot design will appear. Some control can be exercised, depending on where the ink is placed and how much pressure is exerted after the paper is folded. The variety of designs is as infinite as cloud formations.

156 Spatter painting

Tools and materials: old, discarded toothbrush, or stipple brush;
poster colours (see 149);
watercolour paints or India ink in different colours (optional);
drawing or bond paper

Poster paints should be diluted to the consistency of single cream; liquid watercolours or India inks can be used undiluted.

Attach the paper to a wall (see 139). Load the toothbrush or stipple brush with paint. Then, holding the brush as shown (see diagram a), run a thumb over the tops of the bristles so that the paint spatters on to the paper. Different colours spattered next to or over one another, or one or more suc-

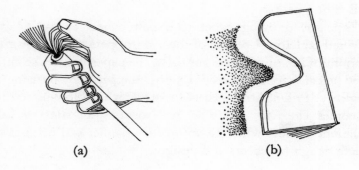

(a)   (b)

cessive colours spattered past a straight or shaped piece of paper or cardboard (see diagram b), will create a variety of effects. The various colour effects and mixtures will be similar in some respects to those possible with pointillist painting (see 153). The spatter technique, used by itself or in combination with others, can suggest forms, textures and designs that are limited in their variety only by the child's inventiveness and imagination.

157 Comb painting

Tools and materials: same as 149 and 150; an old comb

A comb drawn across wet poster or finger paint can create different line patterns. Parallel straight, wavy and crossed lines, and stipples (dots) made by moving the comb's teeth rapidly up and down on the paint, supply textures and increase the child's arsenal of possible effects. But more than this, such use of materials can stimulate the child to discover and create other, different effects.

158 String painting

Tools and materials: poster colours (see 149);
transparent watercolours or inks;
different lengths of string, twine or thread; sheets of bond paper;
newspaper-covered or washable table surface

Dip one length of string into one of the paint jars or ink bottles. Then lay the wet coloured string on to one of the sheets of paper and pull the string to form coloured lines and smeared areas of colour. When the first colour has dried, or even while it is still wet, draw another, differently coloured piece of string across the page, and a third if desired.

Or, the paper can be folded in half as for blot painting (see 155). Place and draw the coloured string through the folded paper.

159 Painting on wet paper

Tools and materials: same as 149; India inks or watercolours

When paper is thoroughly moistened and the excess water wiped off prior to painting on to it with poster paints, the colour, once applied, will run and spread in surprising ways. It will seep across the paper surface and blend into any other colour applied subsequently if the paper remains moist. The paper should be placed on a flat, level surface. If the child picks the paper up while the paint is still wet, he can make the paint run in whatever direction he chooses, and exercise some control over its spread and mixture. India ink, black and in colours, or watercolours, can also be dropped on to the wet paper and paint (see 154). These don't mix readily with poster paint; hence they will run over and around the poster paint and will dry in interesting patterns.

160 Action painting

Tools and materials: same as 149 or 150

See 144 for a discussion of purpose. Some caution is required so that the child does not splash paint, helter-skelter, beyond the painting surface. But it is important to encourage sweeping brush strokes.

161 Scrap materials painting

Tools and materials: same as 149; scrap materials

Natural and fabricated materials – egg cartons, cardboard, wood scraps, feathers, pebbles, paper cups and plates, egg shells, boxes – can be painted, decorated or used as the basis for a variety of art experiences. Suggest that the child designs with the materials, rather than just coating them with paint. The shapes and divisions of sundry packaging materials can in themselves suggest patterns and colour areas. (See also 29, 30 and 56.)

162 Mixed-media painting

After a child has had some experience with different drawing and painting media, he can combine some of these for a variety of effects. As discussed in 159 and in the various sections that deal with 'resist' techniques (see 166), even and sometimes especially those media that do not mix naturally offer opportunities for creating interesting effects when they are combined. Encourage the child to experiment – to invent techniques and to apply them imaginatively. He will eventually transfer the versatility of approach he learns in art to all his other activities.

163 Communal painting

Tools and materials: large sheet of brown wrapping or white paper taped to the wall; poster colours and brushes (see 149); one brush per child; bun tins, one per child; buckets of clean water

Several children can be encouraged to paint a communal design or picture. Each child can be assigned his own area in which to paint whatever he or she pleases. Or all children can agree to one common theme, each assuming responsibility for particular portions, shapes, colours or subjects (see 147).

164 Painting on dry clay, modelling dough or plaster

Tools and materials: same as 174–6, 189 and 192; poster colours (see 149); round bristle brush; shellac and solvent (see 165)

Clay, modelling dough or plaster, when dry, can be painted with poster colours by pre-school and older children. The painted shapes will not be waterproof and the paint is likely to flake off or stain fingers when handled. Do not bake or fire water-base-painted clay shapes – the paint will blister and discolour. To preserve such shapes after they have been painted, cover them with several light coats of shellac, each applied after the last has dried completely.

Shellac coatings should be applied only by adults and by mature young people able to observe the required precautions.

Advanced drawing and painting
165 A note of caution

The media and techniques detailed in the following sections are suggested for young people nine years old or older, depending on their experience, maturity, dexterity and interests. Some of these media require considerable caution (see also 11, 108, 133 and 164). Paints, other than water-based, casein and acrylic, and their solvents, are often highly toxic and in-flammable chemicals. Some contain high concentrations of lead that can cause brain damage if inhaled or ingested even in small quantities over a period of time. All the solvents for oil-base paints, japan colours, varnish, shellac, and model-making and plastic paints – turpentine, alcohol and acetone – can injure eyes and cause severe lung and skin irritation, especially when they come into contact with broken or sensitive areas. If that should happen by accident, or if any of these paints, or flakes of dried paint, or solvents are swallowed by a baby or child, contact your local hospital immediately for information about instant antidotes and remedies. As these paints and solvents are inflammable, they should only be used in well-ventilated rooms or workshops.

All such volatile, inflammable and toxic substances require great care in handling, protective clothing, gloves, and, if used over long periods of time, inhalator face masks. They should be stored in their proper closed containers, well away from other inflammable materials – preferably in a paint shed outside and away from living quarters or work areas. Read and heed the instructions and warnings on paint can labels before buying and allowing young people to use them. Some, like fluorescent colours, are toxic even though their manufacturers are not required by law to state this fact on the label.

Never allow children and young people to use aerosol spray paints, fixatives or, for that matter, any pressurized spray product. All chemicals inhaled as fragmented particles, and especially paints, are damaging since they coat the lungs. Never permit an empty spray can to be tossed into a fire or furnace – it will explode.

Transparent watercolours, though perfectly harmless, and pastel chalks, are unsuitable art media for children and young people. Paintboxes, usually sold as children's art materials, which contain small, dried cakes of paint that must be moistened with a brush are especially frustrating and useless, except to professional artists.

166 Wax crayon resist

Tools and materials: coloured wax crayons (see 140);
poster colours and bristle brush (see 149); or India inks;
bun tin (to hold paints); white drawing paper

Draw lines, masses, dots, textures and designs or pictures on to the paper with coloured wax crayons. Then, using poster paint thinned so that it flows like watercolour, or India ink, paint over the whole sheet of paper in one or several colours. The water-base ink or paint will flow into all the areas that have not been covered with wax crayons and in some places will be separated from the crayon designs by a fine white line. This combination of media that resist one another can be varied. For example, use only white crayon to make the drawings and paint over them with different-coloured paints or inks. The white drawings and textures will show up in sharp contrast to the paint.

167 Painting with acrylics

Acrylics are a relatively recently developed synthetic painting medium. They are non-toxic, water soluble, but they dry as a waterproof film. They can be applied thick, like oil paints; or in flat tones, like oil, tempera, or casein colours; or transparent, like oil tints; or in washes, like watercolours, depending on the degree of dilution. Acrylics are available that give a matte or a glossy finish, which does not yellow with time and requires no varnish or other protective coating. In addition to a standard assortment of colours, colourless acrylic preparations are available that can be mixed with paint pigments to increase or retard drying time, to make them more or less glossy, to give them more body or texture, as waterproofing over any other surface or paint, or as an adhesive (see 28, 57 and 164).

168 Oil painting

Oil painting is relatively slow, difficult to control, and painstaking, especially for younger children. It should not be attempted except by young people who have a great deal of experience in water-base media and acrylics, which are much more immediate since they dry within minutes.

169 Inlay cardboard painting

Tools and materials: poster colours (see 149);
sheets of heavy and light cardboard;
backing or drawing or writing pads; or corrugated board;
cardboard cutting and pasting materials (see 23–30 and 67–72)

Design and build a cardboard collage or assemblage and paint different portions to enhance the design and the three-dimensional effect. Contrast of dark against light tones, such as painting two adjacent sides or edges a light shade and the other or others a darker shade of the same colour, will give the construction greater depth and interest.

170 Sand painting

Tools and materials: sifted fine sand;
vegetable colouring or poster paints (see 149);
screw-top jars, one for each colour;
paper cones, one for each colour; scissors; masking tape;
white paste or glue (see 25–6); 2·5cm (1″) house painter's brush;
sheet of cardboard or brown wrapping paper; newspaper

Fill each jar about three-quarters full of sand. Then add sufficient colouring to stain the grains of sand thoroughly, using a different colour for each jar. Close and shake each container to assure even penetration of the colour. Then pour

the coloured sand from each container on to a separate sheet of newspaper; spread the sand and let it dry. Rinse and clean all jars and let them dry. Pour each batch of coloured sand back into its jar as soon as it has dried.

One painting cone is required for each separate colour. Cut a small hole into the end of each cone, tape it closed, and fill the cone with the sand. (If necessary, enlarge the hole until the sand can flow freely; see diagram.) Fold over the top of each cone and arrange all on the table, ready for painting.

Now brush the cardboard or wrapping paper with a thick coating of glue. Pick up one of the painting cones loaded with coloured sand, being sure to keep the tape adhered to the hole to prevent the sand from running out prematurely. Remove the tape and let the sand run out of the cone on to the paste-covered board or paper, moving the cone to make different shapes, lines, patterns and designs. Use the different painting cones to achieve a variety of effects, bearing in mind that the sand will adhere only as long as the paste remains moist. For this reason, it is important to use a good deal of very moist paste at the start and to paint rapidly with the sand cones.

To form solid areas of colour, outline the area with sand and then move the cone back and forth to cover the area evenly. Keep in mind that the sand will not adhere to itself but only to the exposed glue-covered area. When the design is finished or the glue has dried so that no more sand will adhere, let the painting stand and dry thoroughly for a while. Then, holding the painting over a waste basket or sheet of newspaper, shake off the excess sand that is bound to have accumulated but not adhered in some portions.

171 Painting on plastics

Water-base and oil-base paints, enamels and other conventional paints, inks and dyes do not adhere well to any of the common varieties except foamed plastics like polystyrene. They require special paints and solvents, all of which are toxic. (See 11 and 165 before providing young people with any of these.)

7 Pottery and modelling

Art is both a form for communication and a means of expression of feeling which ought to permeate the whole curriculum and the whole life of the school. A society which neglects or despises it is dangerously sick. It affects or should affect, all aspects of our life from the design of commonplace articles of everyday life to the highest form of individual expression. *The Plowden Report*

172 Background

The craft of pottery is more than seven thousand years old. Decorated pot sherds have been unearthed in Iran that date back more than five thousand years. The earliest potters formed clay found next to river banks and in swamps. Using the same methods described in 184–8, they worked the material, which, when dried for a period in the shade, provided them with storage vessels for grain and other dry solids.

Air-dried and unfired natural clay pots are easily broken; they cannot be used for cooking since they crack when heated over an open fire. Liquids can seep through the pores of the clay. Prehistoric craftsmen discovered that slow heating and cooling hardens clay that is free of air bubbles, and makes it impervious. Some of the impurities left in the clay, like fine silica sand or even soot from the fire, provided accidental, primitive glazes that strengthened and waterproofed the vessels further. By about 1500 BC the Egyptians and the Chinese had independently produced highly colourful and successful glazes. Those used by the Egyptians were eventually adopted by the Greeks and Romans. A great variety of glazes have been developed since, most of them lead-based, that provide durable and decorative finishes for different ceramics.

In ancient Crete, Egypt and Greece, as in China and South America, succeeding generations of potters contributed innovative techniques and styles, leaving distinctive marks on their pottery. Classic earthenware forms evolved, based on utility and convenience but also on what was pleasing to eye and hand, and these were eventually sanctified by ritual and custom. Bands of colour made of tinted 'slip' – watered-down clay – and glazes coloured with earth and vegetable dyes were added. Later artists drew designs and pictures on vessels with these colouring materials. Still others built up designs in relief, using slip as a modelling compound or adhesive.

Incising into clay led to the development of the alphabet. At first pictures were drawn on moist slabs of clay. In time these turned into a kind of shorthand that evolved into cuneiform, the early writing of Mesopotamian civilizations. Writing in cuneiform meant pressing wedge-shaped tools into moist clay, each wedge or combination of wedges standing for a different word or idea. Early in the first century AD the Chinese discovered that incised clay tablets could be inked and the design or picture transferred to paper by rubbing to make multiple copies (see 13 and 202). Thus ceramics played a crucial role in the discovery of printing.

Sculpting and carving in stone are related to forming with clay as well as to the bone and flint chipping of Stone Age civilizations. Prehistoric societies like those of the North American Indians learned how to flake chips off flint, using other stones as tools. Animal bones, soapstone, soft sandstone, limestone and alabaster were eventually worked in different cultures for utilitarian, decorative, architectural and ritual purposes. Once iron was mined and formed (see 111), harder and more durable stone like marble could be worked with metal tools. And with the discovery of casting techniques and materials, clay came into wide use in sculpture again since clay-formed objects could be duplicated in plaster of Paris – a form of powdered alabaster – and in bronze and other metals.

Mosaic craft is included in this chapter, though mosaic tiles are traditionally made of glass. Glass mosaic tiles are too difficult and hazardous for young craftsmen to make and cut. Commercial glass tiles are available, but it seems more productive to encourage young people to make their own tiles out of clay or plaster. (See also 31.)

173 Pottery and modelling for beginners

In pottery and modelling, more than in other arts and crafts, it is useful for young children and even older ones to gain experience in a particular chronological order. First they need experience in forming with clay or modelling compounds spontaneously so that they can discover their qualities.

Clay is delicate. Learning to wedge clay as a matter of course (see 178 and 191) will assure the young craftsman that his creations will not crack while drying or being fired. Attaching components of pottery or sculptures with slip (see 179 and 193) assures that they won't drop off as the clay dries.

Evading these simple disciplines leads to disappointment. The work becomes increasingly satisfying and productive if these and other operations become second nature.

174 Commercial modelling compounds

There are any number of modelling compounds other than natural clay available from art and craft supplies and toy shops. Some are claylike or clay derivatives that dry impervious without firing. Many of these can be painted with poster paints (see 149), acrylics (see 167) and other media. Many are useful for children and young people.

Some modelling compounds, like Plasticine, retain their malleability indefinitely and never dry out. They are not recommended for use by children. Other synthetic modelling compounds, like plastic wood and metal, are highly toxic.

Commercially available modelling 'dough' is a good working material for young children, though expensive, considering that it can be made at home or in the classroom at practically no expense.

175 Homemade modelling compounds

(a) *Modelling dough (I)*

Tools and materials: 2 cups plain flour; 2 tablespoons olive oil; small plastic bags and string; cold water; 1 cup salt; vegetable colours

Mix flour, olive oil and salt until they are uniformly distributed. Add water until the dough is stiff without being sticky. Divide the dough into as many parts as the number of different vegetable colours that are available. Press a thumb into each lump of dough and pour a few drops of vegetable colour into the dent made. Then work the colour evenly into each lump and place it in its own plastic bag. If the bag is kept closed in the refrigerator, the dough remains usable for three to four days. Periodic moistening and working of the dough will keep it fresh and workable for a longer time. The dough can be made without olive oil, using equal proportions of flour and salt, diluted with water only.

(b) Modelling dough (II)

Tools and materials: 1 cup salt; saucepan; vegetable colours; ½ cup boiling water; ½ cup cornstarch; plastic bags and string

Stir salt, cornstarch and water over low flame until stiff. When cool, knead until the dough reaches a pliable, even consistency. Add vegetable colours and store as described in 175a.

(c) Wood dough

Tools and materials: 1 cup sawdust; ½ cup flour paste (see 25); cold water; plastic bags and string

Mix ingredients and knead dough until it becomes uniformly pliable. Store as in 175a.

176 Clay and clay storage

There are three basic types of clay: earthenware clay bodies, stoneware clay bodies and porcelain clay bodies. All are found in different colours, each containing different minerals. Stoneware clay is best for young craftsmen. It is available in grey and in a reddish-brick colour (terracotta). Other clays vary in colour, ranging from black or white to various shades of grey and brown.

Clay is best kept in a metal can with a tight-fitting cover, like a rubbish bin. Place three bricks in the bottom and cover them with a wooden board. Add clear water up to just below the level of the board. Then place lumps of moist clay on the board and cover them with canvas or other rags, leaving an end hanging in the water to act as a wick, drawing up water as needed to keep cloths and clay moist (see diagram). Add another layer of lumps of clay, wrap the cloth over them, and so on until the can is filled to a level where the cover fits snugly. As long as water is kept in the bottom of the can and

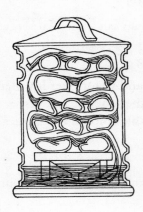

the cloth is kept moist the clay will remain soft and workable indefinitely.

Clay that has been permitted to become too dry to be workable can be reconditioned; wait until it is completely dry and hard. Then place large chunks in a canvas bag and break them up with a hammer or mallet. Sift out the powdered clay and keep hammering the large lumps until they are reduced to very small pieces, granules and powder. Place the dry clay particles in a metal can and cover them with several inches of water. Let stand for a week or longer, until the clay has turned uniformly mushy and no granules remain. Pour off excess water. Let the clay stand for several more days and then pour off whatever water has settled on top. The clay is now reconditioned though still too moist to be workable. Remove portions as needed and set them on to a plaster bat (see 192). The excess moisture will be absorbed by the plaster within one half to one hour; then the clay is ready for wedging (see 178 and 191) and use.

Clay should be soft, yet firm for pottery, and somewhat stiffer for modelling and sculpting.

177 Work spaces

For work with clay and modelling compounds, a child should be dressed in old clothes, in a smock or an apron. Sleeves should be rolled above the elbows.

Provide a table at which the child can work in comfort, standing or sitting (see 10). He or she also needs a sheet of heavy cardboard or plywood, approximately 35 cm × 42 cm × 3 mm (14″ × 17″ × ⅛″), as a work surface. Cover the rest of the table with oilcloth or newspaper. A bowl of slip (see 179), a bucket of water, and a towel or rags should be available to wash and dry hands periodically.

178 Working up and drying clay

Get the child used to wedging clay before using it for pottery or modelling. It is unlikely that he or she can do this properly at an early age, since it requires a good deal of strength and perseverance. (For more craftsmanlike wedging, see 191.) Until the child is more mature, encourage him to break the amount of clay needed for a project in half repeatedly and press and beat both portions together again to work out as many air bubbles as possible. Clay that contains air bubbles may crack even while drying in air and especially when fired in a kiln.

Allow the finished work to dry thoroughly at room temperature for at least two to three days. If this 'greenware' suffers any flaw – air bubbles; walls too thin; clay or dough too dry while it was worked so that it cracks; or added parts fall off because they were improperly adhered to the main body (see 182) – it can be repaired with slip (see 179). Discuss possible reasons for these flaws with the child and encourage him to avoid them in future work. Works that dry more or less properly deserve ample praise and prominent display.

Pinched, coiled and slab-built pottery or sculpture can be bisque-fired in a kiln (see 194) and glazed (see 194) if: the proper clay was used; it was properly wedged; coils and slabs were properly joined with slip; and the pottery or sculpture was thoroughly air-dried. It is unlikely that young children can keep all this in mind, even under supervision. Their work is therefore best left unfired, though it can be painted once it is thoroughly dry (see 164).

Modelling doughs cannot be fired, of course. When dry they can also be painted (see 175), preserved, and waterproofed to some extent with several coats of acrylic medium (see 167), transparent glue (see 26), shellac, clear varnish or nail polish (see 165). The same is true for self-setting clays.

179 Slip

Slip is required for successful clay or pottery work. It consists of clay thinned with water to the consistency of double cream so that it can be applied with a brush. Slip can be used to smooth out rough or jointed portions of clay, cement coils and slabs (see 185, 186 and 188), or fill cracks that appear as the clay is worked into shape. (Filling cracks is not recommended for clay that is to be fired.) Slip is also the required adhesive for attaching small parts to the main body of the work – arms to a clay figure, a handle to a cup, or other formed details and decorations.

Keep the bowl of slip next to the child and get him used to working with it as with the regular clay.

180 Drying finished work

Unfinished work can be kept workable as long as required by covering it with a damp cloth. Be sure to keep moistening the cloth periodically. Once the object is completed it must be air-dried, whether or not it is to be glazed or fired. It is important that the object dries as evenly as possible. Cover small extensions or additions to the main body of the work with dry cloths or rags to retard the rate of drying out of these portions. Due to the usually thinner wall thickness of handles, spouts and other small added parts, they tend to dry more rapidly than the rest and may crack, especially at slip-jointed edges. Once the rest of the vessel or shape has dried partially, the small additions should be uncovered so that they will dry along with the rest.

Keep a drying clay shape on a sheltered shelf, indoors, in the shade. Do not move it while drying and do not try to speed up the drying process. Clay shapes of average wall thickness take at least a week to dry out.

181 Basic forms

Sections 1–7 and 137 explain why a child should be encouraged to discover his or her own forms and shapes. But children also need to learn some of the basic processes to which the material lends itself and through which they can develop their own forms. In work with clay or modelling compounds these introductions are essential. Then let the child pinch, pull or pound the material to see what happens, combine and attach them to each other with slip or toothpicks and develop an endless variety of adaptations.

(a) Rolling beads

Break off a small lump of clay, about the size of an adult's fingernail or larger. Show the child how to roll it between his palms to shape it into a roughly formed sphere and to continue rolling it with a circular motion of his palm on the table or other work surface until it turns into a ball. Thread finished balls on to toothpicks or a threader (see 17) and let them dry completely. Perfectly round or slightly flattened beads can then be painted, strung or used for mosaics (see 31 and 201).

(b) Rolling coils and strips

Break off as much clay or dough as fits comfortably into a child's hand. Show him how to squeeze and then roll it between his palms to form a sausage. Break off a small section of the sausage and roll it between palm and table or workboard surface until it reaches the desired thickness. Keep breaking off lengths for easier handling. The rest can be rolled into coils later, and the coils can be flattened with a small strip of wood if so desired. Keep the coils covered with a damp cloth so they will stay moist until they are used.

(c) Forming a flat slab

Break off as much clay or dough as the child can hold comfortably in his or her hand. Place it on the working surface and pound it more or less flat by hand. Place this roughly formed slab between two strips of 6mm or 12mm ($\frac{1}{4}$″ or $\frac{1}{2}$″) lath, depending on the thickness of clay slab required, and roll out the clay or dough between the pieces of lath with a rolling pin

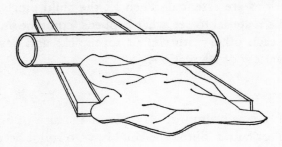

or bottle (see diagram). Be sure to keep the rolling pin or bottle on the lath. When the clay is rolled out to a uniform thickness, it can be cut into strips or other shapes with a dull knife edge or with cutters made out of strip metal. Such a slab can be used for pottery (see 188), sculpture and building. Patterns and textures can be drawn, etched or pressed into it.

182 Combining basic forms

The three basic clay modelling techniques can be modified and combined. The spherical beads (see 181a) can be rolled into ovals or, pinched in the centre, turned into bar-bell shapes, among others. The coil strips can be twisted into spirals or other curves (see diagram a), or the slabs can be folded back and forth to form accordion shapes (see diagram b). These and other variations can be combined, stuck to each other with slip or toothpicks while still moist, or used as decorative devices on pottery and other objects.

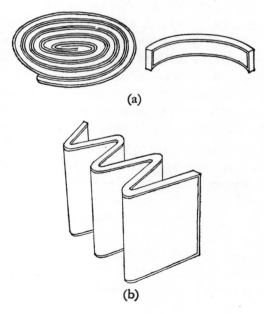

(a)

(b)

183 Textures

The moist clay can be scratched into with toothpick, wire or pointed tool. Short lengths of wooden dowel, children's wooden blocks, sanded scrap wood shapes (see 87), and bottle caps can be pressed into clay slabs to form patterns and designs. Plastic or wire mesh, rope, twine, embossed wallpaper scraps and any other textured material can be used. Don't neglect to point out that smoothness is a texture too. Show the child how to make slabs or shapes velvet smooth by brushing over the surface with slip (see 179). When dry, the smooth clay shapes can be polished with wax to heighten the effect. Textured clay slabs can be painted after they have dried (see 149 and 167).

184 Thumb pots

Give the child a small lump of clay, no more than fits comfortably in his hand. Suggest that he wedges it (see 178) as well as he can. Let him form it into a more or less round or oval shape. Then demonstrate how he can press his thumb into the centre of the ball and smooth the inside and outside with slip (see 179). He's made his first thumb pot.

Once he has made several thumb pots, show the child how he can work on his next one with thumb and fingers to extend and thin the wall of the pot. Demonstrate how he must work all around, pressing the clay, a little at a time, so that the pot remains more or less round and the wall thins out evenly. He can smooth the inside and outside of his pot with slip, incise textures or designs on the outside, or add handles made from coil strips (see 181b) or slabs cut into strips (see 181c), using slip as an adhesive.

Other variations and refinements consist of squeezing a finished thumb pot into a number of pinched shapes; pressing a pouring lip into the rim; and adding a coil or slab-built rim or base. Don't insist on perfection, and do admire the result of the child's work.

185 Coil pots

Let the child make a number of coil strips and cover them with a damp cloth (see 181b). The base should be made out of a tightly wound coil (see 182) or out of a slab cut with the rim of a glass (see diagram a). Curl up the edge of the base all round and smooth it with slip. This is essential whether or not the coils of the pot are to remain visible, since the slip makes the coil strips adhere to each other and fills in small gaps that may not be visible.

Place the next coil all around the inside of the curled up base. Pinch off any extra length and pinch both ends of the formed coil so that they fit together to form a joint no thicker than the coil itself (see diagram b). Professional potters cut each end at matching 45° angles and fit them together with slip (see diagram c). Now add coil after coil, adhering each to the last with slip. To make the pot belly outward, attach each succeeding coil layer on top but towards the outside of the last, overlapping it by about one-half the thickness (see diagram d). To make the vessel narrower, attach coils to the inside of the previous strip in the same manner. It is better not to make the walls of a coiled vessel perfectly perpendicular. The coils work best when they overlap. After adhesion of three or four strips, go over all of them with slip: either smooth them out by working both clay and slip into an even wall, or, if the coil texture is to remain visible, use slip to provide an additional bond for the coils. In working the coil walls they can be thinned, flattened and given additional shape; they are then less likely to separate when drying.

Coil pots can have wide, narrow or multiple necks. If dressed with slip and smoothed on the outside, they can be incised and lined, and decorations can be added with beads,

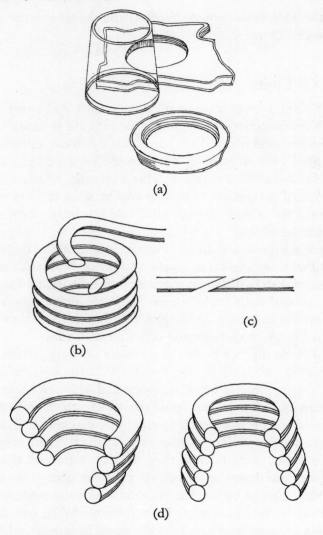

(a)

(b)

(c)

(d)

coil strips or slab strips adhered with slip. Handles, lips and stoppers can be added. There is no limit to the size of pots built with coils. Early Egyptian, Incan and African pottery was mostly coil-built and some of their vessels reached enormous size.

Slip-smoothed coil pots, when fully dry, can be decorated with coloured slip (see 193).

186 Coil sculpture

The technique described in 185 can be applied to sculpture. Simple and complex shapes can be built up with coils of clay. It's like building with logs, except that the clay coils can be bent and formed in any way desired. More experienced young people may need a basic assortment of sculpting tools to enable them to realize the possibilities offered by this method of modelling and building with clay.

Tools and materials: wedging wire (to cut off large chunks of clay); wedging board (see 191); knife (for cutting clay);
sharp-pointed tool (for incising); modelling sticks;
wire hook tools; sponge (for smoothing clay with water);
brushes (for applying slip); syringe (for wetting clay surfaces);
wet rags (for keeping clay moist); pail or bowl of fresh water

187 Hollowed-out pottery and sculpture

Solid clay forms take a long time to dry completely. It is therefore best to remove as much excess clay as possible from the interior of any formed shape without weakening the structure to the point that it collapses. Large, free-standing objects can be easily hollowed out through their bases, leaving at least a 1·25 cm ($\frac{1}{2}$″) wall. Some solid shapes, an egg for example, must be cut in half with the wedging wire. Scoop out the excess clay, leaving 1·25 cm ($\frac{1}{2}$″) wall, being careful not to squeeze or distort the outside shape while hollowing it. Fit the halves together and seal with slip. Correct any external distortion with clay and slip and let the hollowed-out egg air-dry on the shelf.

188 Slab-built pottery and sculpture

Using the technique described in 181c have the child form a 6mm- ($\frac{1}{4}''$-) thick slab of clay. Use a knife, wire or pointed tool to cut as large a square or rectangle of clay as possible out of the slab. Use a paper or cardboard template (see 65) or a right-angle triangle to assure that the slab is reasonably square. Now show the child how to lift the clay slab and form it into a cylinder, sealing the joint with slip (see diagram a). Stand this cylinder on another slab that is larger than the circumference of the opening and that has been thoroughly moistened with slip. Trim around the base of the cylinder with a sharp tool. Brush more slip into and around the joint, inside the vessel and out, to make sure of a good bond. A simple slab-built vessel has been formed.

Once the principle of slab-built pottery is understood, any number of shapes, vessels and constructions can be designed and modelled. Make a cardboard mock-up first; cut it apart and use the flattened cardboard as a template for the clay slab (see 65). Slab walls can also be set on a slab base and jointed by scooping out a small channel along the joint (see diagram b) and filling it in with slip and coil strips to form a good bond.

Slab-built pottery and sculptures can be built and draped around various forms or pressed into moulds (see 197). Fill a plastic bag with sand and drape a large slab of clay around it, joining the edges with slip. Use additional slabs to form the bottom and top, leaving a small opening. When the vessel or sculpture is almost a closed figure, puncture the plastic bag, let the sand run out, and pull out the plastic bag slowly through the opening (see diagrams c, d and e). Paper tubes, egg-carton bases, a blown-up balloon, a cigar box, a clay shape wrapped in newspaper, or any other object can be used, provided one end of the slab-built structure is left open enough so that whatever is used as the form can be with-

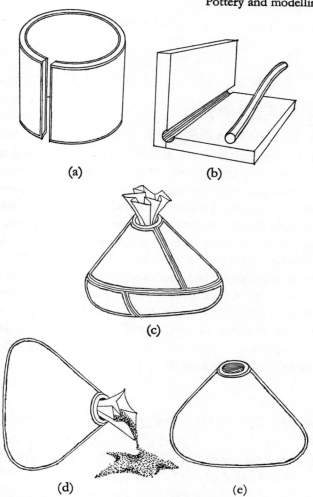

(a)

(b)

(c)

(d)

(e)

drawn. This opening can be sealed partially or entirely with an additional slab and with slip.

189 Engraving into dry clay slabs

Using the techniques described in 181c and 188, have the child prepare a number of clay slabs. He can cut them into whatever shapes he chooses and then set them on the shelf to dry for several days. When the slabs are fully air-dried, he can etch into them with pointed tools – a scriber, pointed wire or engraving tool, or the point of a compass or dividers.

Advanced pottery
190 Digging and preparing clay

Clay is found near streams, rivers and swamps. It can usually be recognized by its smooth, dense texture and the pattern of cracks that appear on the surface when it begins to dry out. Dig up a sample and let it dry in the air. Break it up and crush it, sift it through a sifter to remove grit, sand, and other impurities, and condition it as described in 176. Wedge the conditioned clay (see 178 and 191) and then model it by any of the methods described in 184–9. Let the completed object dry on an open shelf and, if a kiln is available, test-fire it to see whether the clay is suitable. More should be dug only if, having been properly sifted and conditioned, wedged, worked, formed and dried, it does not crumble or crack after air-drying or develop similar serious flaws in firing.

191 Wedging board

Before working with clay, either for pottery or for sculpture, it must be wedged (see 178). For wedging, the clay should be moister than for modelling. A wedging board should be built if clay is used regularly in fair amounts.

A wedging board consists of a shallow wooden tray to the rear of which a wooden post is attached; from the post wire is strung to one corner of the board. Clay is cut on the wire and wedged in the tray.

Tools and materials: 45cm × 60cm × 1cm (18″ × 24″ × ¾″) plywood; two strips of 43cm × 7·5cm × 1cm (17¼″ × 3″ × ¾″) pine; two strips of 60cm × 7·5cm × 1cm (24″ × 3″ × ¾″) pine; twenty-two 2cm (¾″) screws;

one strip of 60cm × 2·5cm × 1·25cm (24″ × 1″ × ½″) pine;
one 75cm (30″) length of wire;
hand drill and bits; screwdriver; pliers

Assemble as shown in this diagram.

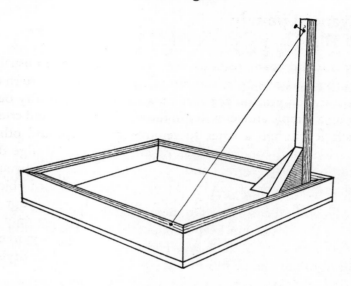

Scrape or break clay out of the storage bin (see 176), add
water if required, and work it into a solid lump. Then use the
wedging board wire to cut the lump of clay in half. Rejoin the
halves; turn one at right angles to the other and pound
together by beating and squeezing the clay by hand on the
wedging board. Repeat several times to be sure that all air
bubbles have been worked out of the clay and that it has a
uniform, moist and workable consistency. It will in all
likelihood be too moist and sticky for pottery or sculpture.
Place the clay on a plaster bat to remove excess moisture
quickly (see 192).

192 Making a plaster bat

Plaster that has set absorbs moisture. If you place wedged or other clay on a plaster bat – a slab of plaster – it loses moisture within thirty minutes to an hour, by which time it should be ready for pottery or sculpture (see 176). To make a plaster bat:

Tools and materials: plaster bat mould – a 15cm × 25cm × 5cm (6″ × 10″ × 2″) open box built of wood or a foil metal pie plate with about 5cm (2″) high rim;
2·5cm × 30cm × 6mm (1″ × 12″ × ¼″) sanded board;
2 litres (4 pints) plaster of Paris; 1 litre (2 pints) water (clear and cold); mixing bowl; large metal spoon

Sift the plaster slowly through your fingers into the water-filled bowl. Do not mix the plaster and water until all the plaster has been sifted and has formed a small mound about 5cm (2″) above the level of the water. Then stir the plaster slowly with the spoon. Do not remove the spoon while mixing the plaster but keep it immersed until the mixture has turned into a smooth, lump-free, creamy paste, ready for pouring. Pour the plaster into the plaster bat mould at once. Smooth the top surface of the plaster bat with the sanded board, if required. The plaster itself will set and be sufficiently hard to use within fifteen to thirty minutes. After it has set, tap the plaster bat out of its mould. Several bats should be made at one time. Each can be used repeatedly.

Place each lump of well-wedged but too moist clay on a plaster bat until it has lost enough moisture to be workable.

After work with plaster of Paris is completed, wait until the plaster has set and hardened in the bowl or on hands. Add water to the bowl, then rinse your hands in the bowl. The dried plaster will flake off easily. Drain the excess water through a sieve, collect the flaked plaster, wrap it in a newspaper, and burn. Plaster blocks drains.

193 Decorating clay with slip

Tools and materials: prepared slip (see 179);
poster paints (see 149); vegetable colours;
acrylic pigments (see 167); India inks; pottery or sculpture

Slip can be used to decorate sculpture or pottery that is to be air-dried, with or without kiln firing. If the clay is not to be fired in a kiln, coloured slip can be made by adding one of the pigments listed above to the slip.

If the clay product is to be fired, it is best to buy coloured slip of the same clay that was used to make the object, available in a variety of tints from art and craft supply shops.

Homemade or purchased slip can be painted on pottery or sculpture with water colour brushes. To paint even strips on a pot or vase, tie a flat lettering brush of the desired width to an upright stake (see diagram). Load it with slip, using another brush. The bowl, placed against the brush and turned slowly on the table, will receive an even stripe.

194 Firing in a homemade kiln

Before clay sculpture or pottery can be considered for firing it must be thoroughly air-dried (see 180). This takes a week or longer. Then, if it has not developed any flaws, the 'green-ware' is ready for its first, 'bisque' firing.

Kiln-firing is essential for any clay vessel that is expected to be durable and impervious to liquids, unless it is made of self-setting clay (see 174). A vessel can be glazed and fired at a first and only firing. Professional potters fire the unglazed clay during the bisque firing and then glaze it with a second 'glaze' firing. A single bisque firing, glazed or unglazed, is enough for young people's work.

Commercially available electric kilns, small or large, are expensive. The smallest ones severely limit the size of objects that can be made and fired. But it is possible to build and use a simple homemade kiln for unglazed bisque firing of pottery and hollowed-out sculpture.

Tools and materials: large metal rubbish bin with tight-fitting cover; spike or cold chisel and hammer;
enough sawdust to fill the rubbish bin;
sufficient coal or coke to line the bottom of the rubbish bin about 5cm (2″) deep; newspaper; air-dried pottery or sculpture

Use the hammer and spike (or cold chisel) to punch holes into the sides and lid of the rubbish bin, each 6mm to 1cm ($\frac{1}{4}$″ to $\frac{3}{8}$″) wide and about 7·5cm (3″) from the next. Line the bottom of the bin with coal or coke and place the largest air-dried pottery or sculpture on this layer (see diagram). Fill all spaces in and around the object and coal with tamped-down sawdust. Add a layer of 10cm or 12cm (4″ or 5″) of sawdust on top of the object or objects and place the next assortment of dry clay objects on top of this layer. Fill the places in and around these with sawdust, add a further 10cm or 12cm (4″ or 5″) layer of sawdust, and so on until the whole bin is filled with alternating layers of sawdust and clay-formed objects. The top layer of sawdust, at least 10cm (4″) deep, should be level with the rim of the bin.

Light the sawdust from the top with newspaper tapers. When the top layer of sawdust smoulders evenly, replace the lid of the bin and let the fire work all the way down through the sawdust, coal and clay product filled bin. This should take twenty-four hours or more. If sudden winds increase the burning rate, use moist clay to close some of the holes punched into the rubbish bin.

After the fire has burned out in the bin, let the earthenware cool until it can be handled. Then remove the fired objects and

let them cool completely before further handling. They may be slightly sooty. Some of the soot will wash off and the rest will have partially glazed the clay.

Glaze-firing is impractical in such a kiln, first because there is no way to protect the wet, glaze-covered surfaces from sawdust and soot; and second because there is not enough heat generated (the heat is not even enough for successful glazing). For glaze-firing you need access to professional help and a large kiln. It is possible to get objects fired at professional potteries, art schools etc. Ask around in your neighbourhood if you do not want to go to the trouble of making a kiln.

Sculpting, carving and moulding
195 Sculpting with clay

The techniques and tools described in 174–83 and 186–93 apply. Sculpture can be coil- or slab-built (see 186 and 188) or hollowed (see 187) after it has been worked into the desired

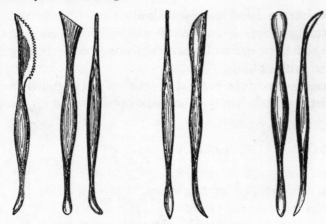

shape. Use fingers and clay-working tools to add and shape the clay. Larger sculptures should be draped over armatures (see 50–53 and 117). Hollow clay shapes, whether hollowed or worked over an armature, dry more quickly and evenly and are less likely to develop cracks and flaws than solid ones.

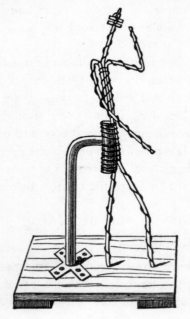

After having dried completely in the air, clay sculptures can be fired if a large enough kiln is available (see 194), or they can be cast in plaster of Paris and other materials (see 197–9).

When sculpting in clay requires more than one session, it is necessary to cover the unfinished work with a damp cloth and to moisten it periodically to keep the clay pliant and workable.

196 Soap and wax carving

Tools and materials: dull, small, long-handled knife;
pointed etching and engraving tools;
small files (see 122) and rasps;
bar of soap; beeswax; dental moulding or casting wax;
or paraffin wax; 15cm × 15cm × 2cm (6″ × 6″ × ¾″) wooden work
base; candle in holder (optional);
forged steel modelling tools

Soap, beeswax, and paraffin wax are easily carved with blunt tools. They lend themselves to being worked by children in the young age groups. Show the child how to carve and re-move slivers, incise and engrave lines and shapes, smooth or create sharp edges, and form the material to create desired shapes.

When the young craftsman has practised basic carving skills and when he can be trusted to be careful, light a candle and show him how to warm his tools for carving, cutting, whittling and shaving the material. Beeswax can be formed in the hand; candle wax or paraffin wax can be melted in a double boiler. Half-fill a large cooking pot with water. Break up candles or paraffin slabs into a second, smaller pot and place it inside the larger, water-filled pot. Bring the water to the boil until the wax liquefies. When it has cooled so that it is warm to the touch, let the child scoop it out and form it in his hand. He can carve and engrave on the wax and give it detail and texture with cold or warmed tools.

197 Making an open plaster mould

Children should be discouraged from filling prepared and manufactured moulds with clay or modelling compounds and dough (see 1–8 and 137). Materials in which papier mâché, clay, modelling compounds or plaster are cast for creative purposes, and moulds made by the child from models he has sculpted or formed, are something else entirely. There are two good reasons for making and using such moulds: to cast an object made of clay and to reproduce it in more durable material, and to make multiple duplicates of the child's creation. For example, he may wish to duplicate a modelled or incised plaque to make a necklace of identical modules.

An open mould is sufficient for any small clay object that has a flat base or back. The following steps are required to make such an open mould out of plaster of Paris for duplicating and casting models in clay.

Make sure that no undercuts exist on the original clay model as shown in the diagram. They would prevent the separation of the mould from the model once the plaster has set.

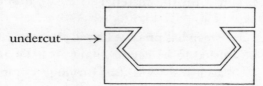

undercut──→

Place the air-dried clay model, right side up, into a cardboard or wooden box about 2·5cm (1″) wider than the model on all four sides and 2·5cm higher than the object itself. Mix enough plaster to fill the whole box. Follow the directions and proportions given in 192 for mixing plaster of Paris. As soon as it is mixed, pour the plaster slowly all around and over the object inside the box until the box is completely filled with plaster. Tap the box with a finger all around to allow any air bubbles trapped in the plaster to rise to the surface.

The plaster will set and harden in fifteen to thirty minutes. Remove the plaster cast and clay model from the box. Tap the cast to release the clay model. If it does not come free easily, attach a small piece of fresh clay to the bottom of the model and pull it gently away from the mould. The mould should now consist of a nearly perfect, reverse replica of the original. Use plaster-modelling tools to correct or smooth irregularities in the mould and to clean out any clay that may adhere. See 198 for directions on how to make clay duplicates from such a mould.

198 Casting in clay from an open plaster mould

Tools and materials: slip (see 179), mixed to the consistency of treacle; clay-modelling tools (see 186 and 195); spatula or lath, longer than the open mould is wide

Pour slip into the open mould until it is filled completely and the clay bellies up slightly. Tap the outside of the mould gently to remove air bubbles. Scrape off excess slip with the spatula or lath and level the top of the mould. After a day or two the clay will have dried enough so that it can be separated from the mould. Tap the plaster mould to release the casting. If it does not come free, press a wad of fresh clay to the casting and pull. It should then come loose from the mould without difficulty, unless there are undercuts in the mould. The mould can be used for casting additional duplicates after it has been cleaned. Any small irregularities in the casting can be corrected with modelling tools and slip. The casting can then be air-dried and eventually fired, if a kiln is available.

199 Other mould-making and casting materials

A greased plaster of Paris or rubber mould can be used for casting hollow papier mâché shapes (see 48) or ones of modelling dough. Coat an open mould or mould parts with mâché mash or modelling dough about 3mm to 6mm ($\frac{1}{8}$″ to $\frac{1}{4}$″) thick. Let it air-dry in the mould.

Synthetic and plastic mould-making and casting resins, including and especially epoxy, are toxic and carcinogenic. Do not allow children and young people to use these materials.

200 Mosaics

Tile- and mosaic-making are closely related. The ancient Babylonians, Egyptians, Greeks and Romans cut slabs of clay into small tiles and dried, painted and glazed them for assembly into decorative wall and floor designs and murals. True mosaics were made by cutting and breaking up coloured glass into fragments and composing complex designs and pictures with these pieces embedded in chalk mortar.

Glass mosaic tiles and plastic mosaic modules are available but children and young people should make their own materials whenever possible instead of working with prefabricated parts. Very young children can make paper mosaic modules (see 31); older ones can make them out of cloth snippets, leather (see 126), clay and plaster of Paris. Scrap materials such as pebbles and seeds, can also be used.

201 Clay and plaster mosaic tiles

A 3mm to 6mm ($\frac{1}{8}$″ to $\frac{1}{4}$″) clay slab (see 188) or plaster bat (see 192) can be incised with a dull knife and divided into small mosaic modules. Do not cut all the way through the slab or bat. Geometric and non-geometric shapes can be cut and, after the clay or plaster has dried, broken apart and sorted by shape and size (see diagram a). Shaped metal strips, metal tubes and pipes can also be used to embed shapes in plaster or clay. Or a bottle or rolling pin can be covered with strips of cardboard, wire or string, outlining a latticework of shapes (see diagram b). This can be rolled over the wet clay slab or plaster bat to incise shapes.

After the clay has dried or the plaster has set, either can be painted (see 164 and 167–9). If water-base paints are used, the colours can be made more or less waterproof if the painted

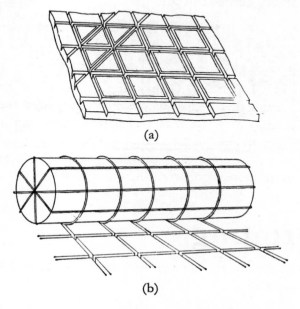

(a)

(b)

tiles are covered with several successive coatings of clear varnish or shellac (see 165), transparent glue (see 26), water glass (see 42), or acrylic medium (see 28 and 167), after the paints have dried.

Mosaic tiles can be set into chalk mortar, a sand and paste mixture, plaster of Paris or cement. Younger children will find it more convenient to work inside a cardboard box lid or wood tray whose sides are no higher than the tiles are thick. Show the child how to cover a small area with mortar or adhesive, set the tiles, and when the coated area is filled prepare the next section until the whole tray is covered with mosaic tiles.

8 Printing

Let the children make their own equipment as far as they can.
Jean-Jacques Rousseau

202 Background

If writing gave permanence to the word and allowed the
events of history to become known to scholars of future
generations, printing brought information within reach of all.
The printed picture and word have special value in this age.
The reader can re-examine what he read earlier and refresh his
memory as quickly and often as he chooses. Film and TV in
their present form, except for microfilm, cannot be used in
this manner. Audiovisual media invite a different kind of
participation from that of print (see Chapter 9) if they are to
be thought-provoking and educative.

Printing as a craft can be enormously satisfying, especially for young people. It enables them to leave their mark, to experiment with combinations of forms, shapes, textures, colours and type that they can create, design and duplicate. Even pre-scholars can achieve interesting and satisfying results with a wide range of simple printing materials.

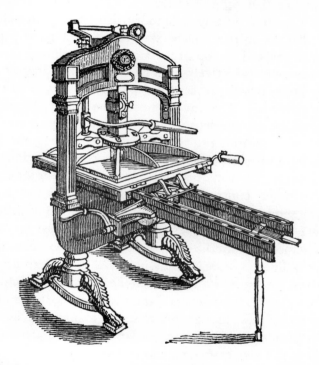

Printing was first practised in China, about AD800 – six hundred years after paper was invented there (see 13). Between AD841 and 846 the great 'stone classics' were printed in China by carving and inking stones and rubbing on paper laid over them. Twenty-two years afterwards, the first book was printed from wood blocks, and this technique for reproducing pictures and text has since developed into a fine art in China.

Printing from movable type, known to the Chinese for over six centuries, was independently invented by Johann Gutenberg in the fifteenth century in the German city of Mainz.

From Gutenberg's time to the late eighteenth century, letterpress printing remained nearly unchanged. Lithography, invented by accident in 1796, is a printing method based on the principle that oil and water don't mix. Alois Senefelder discovered, after writing a laundry list on a grease-coated stone, that its mirror image was transferred to paper inadvertently placed on top of the stone. This printing method did not compete effectively with letterpress and intaglio until photographic transfer of screened pictures and type to metal became possible. The invention of the linotype machine permitted rapid type-setting and -casting. Electrotyping, a method of duplicating printing plates for letterpress, and other innovations turned printing from a craft into an industry. More recently, phototype setting, electronic colour separation and computer controlled processes have automated and brought about a further technological revolution in printing.

These crafts, in their present-day techno-industrial forms, are far removed from the experience of children. There is just no way children can be actively involved in modern printing processes. Instead, they must practise earlier, labour-intensive methods in order to understand and use these media creatively. These techniques, though unprofitable to industry, are still required for really fine work. Today they are practised only by artists and rare craftsmen and craftswomen.

First prints
203 Blotting paper monoprints

Tools and materials: poster paints; brushes;
drawing paper (see 149); sheets of blotting paper

Suggest to the child that he paints a design on the drawing paper, using brushes and very moist poster paints. Place a sheet of blotting paper over the painting before it has a chance to dry. Rub the blotting paper without shifting it. The painting will transfer to the blotting paper. Place the original and the blotted monoprint next to one another. Point out that the monoprint is a mirror image of the original. Let the child look at the monoprint in a mirror if one is handy. He'll discover that the design appears there as in the original. This recognition is important for future print-making, in which the design cut into the block must be a mirror image of the expected print.

204 Carbon paper duplicating

Tools and materials: bond writing or typing paper; carbon paper; pencil or ballpoint pen

Slip one sheet of carbon paper between two sheets of bond writing or typing paper and suggest that the child draws on the top sheet with a pencil or ballpoint pen. By interleaving five or six sheets of writing paper with carbon paper, he can make several copies at a time. Point out that direct 'duplicating' is not the same as printing, in which the original is always reversed.

205 Potato and other vegetable prints

Tools and materials: stamp pads impregnated with stamp pad ink or vegetable dyes, or with linoleum block water-base or oil-base ink; bun tin filled with very thick poster colours;
brush (see 149); dull knife blade; newspaper;
potatoes; carrots; cabbage stalks; white radishes; turnips;
onions; corn cobs; any other close-fibred vegetable or stalks

Any of the vegetables, if cut in half, into sections or into different shapes, and inked or coated with poster paint will print. Do not encourage the child to carve a design into the top of a halved potato. It is easier and better to carve the whole potato half into whatever printing shape has been chosen (see diagram).

It is best to make different shapes for each colour or to duplicate the same shape if the child wishes to print each in

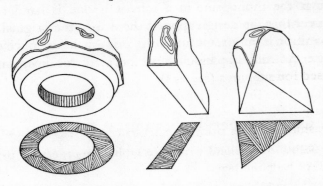

several colours. The ink is difficult to wipe off vegetable stamps, and if the child presses one that still contains one colour into other colours, all will soon turn muddy. The poster colours can be painted on to the stamping surface with a brush. Homemade stamp pads can be improvised by placing a piece of felt in a tin lid, and coating it liberally with bottled stamp-pad ink or vegetable dye; the ink or dye can be replenished when it dries out.

206 Printing with a brayer

Tools and materials: brayer (see below);
sheet of plate glass, perspex, or plastic to roll out ink;
water-base or oil-base linoleum printing inks in red, yellow, blue, black and white (and turpentine if oil-base inks are used);
spatula or palette knife; newspapers or other absorbent papers;
spoon; clothesline and clothespegs

A brayer is an ink roller attached to a handle. Inexpensive brayers are made of hard rubber and are good enough for beginners. Be sure to keep the brayer clean and hung on a nail when it is not in use. Caked printing inks ruin a brayer. Also, if left sitting on its rubber surface, the brayer will flatten and become useless.

A brayer can be used in two ways: to coat a printing block or surface with ink; and to roll over the paper that is placed on top of an inked printing block to make an impression. However, the curved surface of a soup spoon usually obtains a better printing impression than a brayer. A brayer can also be used for rubbings (see 218).

Water-base linoleum printing ink, while not as brilliant as oil-base ink, is the preferred medium for beginners. Besides, all washing up after printing can be done with water. Oil-base inks require turpentine as a solvent and cleaner.

Squeeze about 5cm (2″) of ink out of the tube on to the plastic sheet. Use a flexible knife – a spatula or palette knife – to spread the ink ribbon. Then roll the brayer over the ink, moving it back and forth until it covers a portion of the plastic or glass surface with a smooth, tacky film. If ripples and waves appear on the ink surface, it has not been spread sufficiently or it may be too thin. Let the ink dry in the air for ten to fifteen minutes and roll it out again. When the brayer is well covered with ink, roll it over the printing block. If the block has not been printed before, several coats may be needed before it is cured and the ink has penetrated the pores of the material. Move the brayer over the block from several directions. Once cured, a couple of passes with the well-inked brayer over the block, each at right angles to the other, should suffice to ink the surface for a good impression.

Once the block is inked, gently drop a sheet of absorbent paper on top of it. Do not move the paper once it is in contact with the block or it will smear. Rub the curved side of a spoon over the paper to get a good impression. The first few prints may be unsatisfactory. But these proofs let you know how much pressure to apply; whether the ink is too wet, too dry or just right; and whether the block needs heavier or lighter inking or deeper cutting in places.

Hang finished prints until they are completely dry before stacking them.

207 Scrap material prints

Tools and materials: same as 206

Any material with a deep and well-defined grain or texture can be used as a printing surface. The following is a partial listing of improvised printing surfaces.

Coarse linen or canvas cloth
Cardboard shapes
Plant leaves, whole or with the flesh
    stripped from the skeleton
Bottle corks or shapes cut out of flat
    cork sheets
Crumpled tissue paper
Straw matting
Raffia or string pasted to cardboard

Embossed wallpaper
Bottlecaps
Bulrushes and moss
Pebbles
Sponge
Coins
Bark
Egg-carton tray
Woodgrain and wood
    scraps

Ink and print any of these on to newsprint or other absorbent paper surfaces, using the techniques described in 206.

For best results with whole plant leaves, coat one side with a thin layer of paste (see 23–7). When it has dried, paint poster colour on the paste-covered surface or ink it with a brayer and print as in 206. Several such paste-covered leaves or any of the other materials suggested above, each inked with a different colour or tint, can be overprinted to form interesting designs and patterns.

Advanced printing with and without a press
208 Modular shape printing

Tools and materials: same as 205 and 206;
modular wood, cardboard, linoleum or rubber shapes

Sanded woodblock shapes, small pieces of linoleum glued to
wood, dowel ends, rubber scraps and even the edges of thick
cardboard strips attached to dowels or stamp handles can be
printed next to and overlapping each other in one or more
colours. If transparent inks are used, a third colour will appear

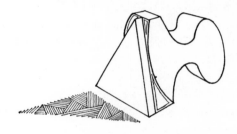

wherever two or more colours are 'trapped' by overprinting.
Anyone can make printing modules him- or herself. The
shapes, if they cannot be held comfortably in the hand, can be
glued to a wooden board or to cardboard, provided all are the
same height. Others can be attached to moulding or stamp
handles (see diagram) and printed like rubber stamps. Make
sure the stamp handle closely fits the shape to be printed so
that the edges of the wooden base do not print accidentally
along with the design (see diagram).

209 Ink engraving

Tools and materials: same as 206; sheet of heavy cardboard;
drawing paper or newspapers;
stylus or used-up ballpoint pen

Use the brayer to coat the cardboard with a thick layer of ink.
Cover the cardboard with a sheet of drawing paper or news-

print and draw on to it with the stylus or ballpoint pen. Be careful not to lean on the paper, or to press a hand or finger on it. When the drawing is done, lift the paper off the ink-covered cardboard. The lines and textures engraved on the paper with the stylus will be printed on the side of the paper that rested on the ink.

210 Cylinder printing

Tools and materials: same as 206; large bottle or rolling pin; thick card; scissors (see 38); paste (see 22–8)

Cut paper strips and shapes with scissors, and paste them on the thick portion of a bottle or a rolling pin. The paper must all be of the same thickness and none of the shapes can overlap or cross. Ink the glass or perspex surface as in 206. Roll the bottle or rolling pin over the inked area, inking the raised paper surfaces pasted to it. Then roll the inked cylinder on a sheet of newspaper or other absorbent paper. The raised and inked paper design pasted to the bottle will print. With careful marking on the end of the bottle or tube where the print ends, either can be re-inked and a continous repeat pattern printed (see 214).

Similar prints can be made with twine, string, or thread pasted to the cylindrical surface, provided material of the same thickness is used in each case and none of it crosses or over-laps.

211 Linoleum block cutting

Tools and materials: unmounted battleship-grey linoleum; black India ink; or felt markers (see 143); inexpensive watercolour brush; set of linoleum cutting tools; oilstone

Unmounted linoleum is easier for young people to control while cutting. Suggest that the young craftsman designs directly on linoleum with brush and India ink or black felt marker. Explain that everything not painted black will have to be cut away and that the black-painted portions are the ones that will print.

The linoleum should be fresh, soft and not brittle. Properly instructed, children as young as five can design and cut linoleum blocks successfully. Use an oilstone to keep the cutting tools sharp at all times. The sharper they are, the less likelihood that a blade will skip out of a cut and injure the user. Instruct the child that the hand holding down the linoleum must be behind the tool at all times (see diagram on page 70). The cut should be made in a direction away from the hand holding the material. If a young person cannot be depended on to observe caution, he is too immature to work with linoleum.

Provide the child with scraps of linoleum on which to try the different cutting blades and to discover the possible variety of effects. Small cuts, dots and fine lines spaced closely or farther apart create tones and textures. The depth of the cut should be no deeper than half the thickness of the linoleum; it should never be so deep that the fabric backing shows through. To assure a large edition of prints and that the block won't crumble, bevel each cut and never undercut the linoleum (see diagram). Point out that if the child decides to

cut letters of the alphabet or sign his name, the letters must be drawn and cut in reverse or they won't read when printed (see 203).

The block is ready for printing only after all uninked areas have been cut away. Wash the block in mild soap and warm water to remove ink and grease and then let it dry thoroughly on a flat surface.

212 Linoleum block printing in one colour

Tools and materials: same as 206;
newspaper; Japanese rice paper; or tissue paper

Ink and print the block as described in 206. Cure the linoleum with repeated inking. Drop the newsprint or rice paper gently on the block. Don't move the paper once it is placed or it will smear. The first few impressions, whether printed with a brayer or spoon or on a press, will probably be poor. Compare each proof with the next. They will show where additional cutting, greater or less pressure, or more or less ink may be needed to make the best possible print.

After printing, wash the block with solvent (turpentine, if oil-base inks were used; water, if water-base inks were used) and then in mild soap and warm water. Clean ink off brayer and glass or perspex plate and hang up brayer and prints (see 206). If quite a lot of ink is left on the glass plate, the ink can be scraped off with a spatula and wrapped in plastic for future use.

A properly cared-for block is good for many editions and prints.

213 Linoleum block printing in more than one colour

Tools and materials: same as 211 and 212;
sheets or roll of wax paper

A two-colour print – red and black, for example – requires that two blocks be designed, cut, and printed, one for each colour (see 220). Design and print the black plate as in 212. Pull several good proofs. Then wash, dry, and apply a heavy coating of orange ink to the same block and print it on a sheet of wax paper. Place the printed wax paper sheet upside down on a second, uncut linoleum block the same size as the first.

Rub the back of the wax paper to transfer the design to the second linoleum block. Peel off the wax paper. Let the ink dry thoroughly on the second block if the impression is a good one. If the print is poor, wash the ink off the block and try again, as before.

This transfer of the design from the first block to the second is essential so that the second colour cut can be registered more or less exactly with the first. Precise registration is difficult without a printing press, but you can come close. Once the orange ink is dry on the second, uncut block, paint in whatever areas you have chosen to print in the second (red) colour with black ink or felt marker. Be sure to 'trap' (overlap) colour areas that are supposed to meet and have adjoining edges. Paint the black ink about 3mm ($\frac{1}{8}$") over the orange ink in these places. Then cut away all but the black-painted areas.

Pull a number of proofs of the second block until it is cured. Then ink the block with the chosen second colour and lay one of the black proofs on the second block. If both linoleum blocks and the paper are cut to exactly the same size, registration will not be too difficult. Print the second colour and check the proof for any additional cutting or inking that may be needed. Then print a whole edition of the red, second block.

In printing, the lightest colour is always printed first and the black last. After the red edition has been printed and has dried, ink the black block again. Place one of the red prints as squarely as possible on the black block, face down, and print. A fairly high percentage of the prints will be sufficiently well registered to be considered good if reasonable care is exercised in printing.

A third, fourth, or more colours can be cut and printed in the same way. Each requires its own block; transfer of the other colours to wax paper and then to the next block that is to be cut; painting in of the desired colour area; cutting and printing, as before.

Close registration is possible only on a press on which corner stops can be attached so that, once a block is positioned, the paper can be registered and laid in exactly the same place for each colour. Such paper stops can be taped to a linoleum block cut much larger than the picture that is to be cut and printed, even when no press is available.

Another way to make colour prints is to cut and print the black block and hand-stamp it with modular shapes, each inked with different colours (see 208).

214 Repeat-pattern making and printing

Tools and materials: same as 205–13

Potato, vegetable, scrap materials, cardboard, clay, slab, plaster and cylinders, as well as linoleum blocks, can be designed to repeat themselves in all directions. Repeat patterns can be used for fabric and decorative paper printing. The simpler the design, the easier it is to repeat it so that the top and each side of one print fit other sides of the same design, when printed adjacent to each other. Cylinder printing assures a continuous repeat design in one direction, though the ends of the cylinder must be designed carefully so that prints match edge to edge.

215 Fabric printing

Tools and materials: same as 214; rawhide mallet; white or plain coloured cotton or silk

Because of the size of the material required even for a scarf, fabric is usually printed with repeat patterns (see 214). All the detailed techniques apply. Oil-base printing inks or fabric colours, available from art and craft material suppliers, are used to print on fabrics that, when thoroughly dried after printing, are to be washable.

Cover a large table with thick layers of newspaper. Keep the unprinted fabric rolled up at one end. Unroll enough of the fabric to cover the table and tape it to the table edges so that it is slightly stretched and wrinkle free. Place the inked block, face down, on the fabric, starting at one corner of the cut end.

Beat the block with the mallet for a good impression. Re-ink the block and make a second impression next to the first one, and so on until the whole fabric surface, taped to the table, is printed.

Stretch several lengths of twine across the room beyond the far end of the table and drape the printed fabric over it (see diagram). Tape the next length of fabric to the table and

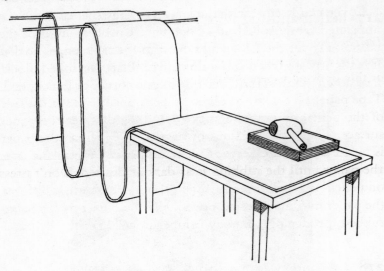

continue printing as before. Cease printing when you run out of drying space. After the printed fabric has dried it can be rolled up and the printing process continued as before.

216 Rubbings

Historically, as pointed out in 202, rubbings from stone preceded the invention of printing. Finding surfaces from which interesting rubbings can be made is a worthwhile quest. It can help make children and young people aware of their surroundings. The following are common surfaces that lend themselves to rubbings, in addition to those listed in 207:

Coins; pebbled and cut glass; plastic or wire mesh;
vegetable grater; brick and cement blocks;
weathered wooden boards; metal manhole covers; tombstones;
stone, metal, or plastic plaques and reliefs

217 Pencil and graphite stick rubbings

Tools and materials: No 6B pencil or graphite stick;
soft, lightweight paper: tissue paper; rice paper;
or thin drawing paper; masking tape

Tape paper on top of the object to be rubbed. Use the flat side
of the pencil or graphite stick to rub gently over the paper
surface. The raised portions of the design to which the paper
is taped will soon emerge. Rub more pencil or graphite over
the paper until the rubbing is as dark as desired. Don't press
on pencil or graphite stick while rubbing. Pressure will force
the paper into the recessed portions of the object that is being
rubbed, producing a muddy print that lacks detail.

218 Ink and brayer rubbings

Tools and materials: same as 206; masking tape

Ink the object to be rubbed with the brayer, gently lay the
paper on the inked surface, and tape it. Print with spoon or
clean brayer as in 206. Valuable objects, wood, clay or stone
carvings should never be inked directly since it may not be
possible to clean them perfectly. To rub them, use the technique described in 217.

219 Stencil printing

Stencil printing has value only if the child makes his or her
own stencils; prepared stencils may seem like an amusing
pastime but undermine a child's creative drive (see 1–7 and
137).

220 Scissors-cut stencil printing

Tools and materials: brown wrapping paper; waxpaper;
or wrapping paper soaked in vegetable oil; scissors (see 38);
masking tape; drawing paper or card (for printing);
poster colours (see 149); large, stiff stipple brush

Paper folding and cutting techniques (see 32–41) can be
applied to stencil cutting with scissors. Very young children
can create interesting and unique stencils that they can print
in one or more colours.

After the child has cut the design of the stencil, tape one
edge to the drawing paper or card on which it is to be printed.

Mix the poster colours to a stiff paste. Provide only one colour
of the child's choice as a start. Others can be added later. Then
show him or her how to dip the tip of the stipple brush into
the colour, deep enough to cover only the end of the bristles.
Apply the paint around the edges of the cut-out portions of the
stencil with a rapid up and down motion of the brush. The
brush will require frequent dipping in the paint. After the
edges have been given a coat of colour, work the brush
towards the centre of each opening in the stencil, until all

are coloured. There is no need to cover the whole paper with a thick layer of paint. A stippled, light coating will give the print texture.

Do not remove the stencil from the paper until the paint has dried completely. Then unfasten the tape and lift off the stencil, and the design will be revealed underneath. If the paint crawls under the stencil edges it means the paint mixture was too watery. Two (or more) colour stencils can be designed in the same way as multicolour linoleum blocks (see illustration).

Various colour effects and designs can be created by printing the same stencil a second time, turned to a different position on the paper after the first printing, and using a different colour for a subsequent impression. Different stencils can be printed in sequence, one after the other, each in different colours or tones, but only when the preceding coat of paint has dried. Care must be exercised when stencilling one poster colour over another. Do not press hard on the stipple brush or the preceding layer of paint may be moistened and dissolved.

Repeat-patterns on paper and fabric (see 214 and 215) can be printed with stencils. Once each impression has dried, move the stencil to the next position and print.

9 Photography, films and sound recording

Choosing is creating. *Friedrich Wilhelm Nietzsche*

221 Background

TV sets, still- and motion-picture cameras and projectors, TV and sound tape equipment are now found in nearly every school and in most homes. Yet few young people know how to use any of these media creatively. Nineteenth-century craft and activity books for children invariably explained how to make a pinhole camera, blueprints of leaves and flowers, and flip-book and zoetrope animations. Recently developed photographic and sound-recording processes and techniques offer even more stimulating challenges to young people who know how to use them. Creative work in these media involves inexpensive materials and equipment that is readily available, and sharpens a child's judgement.

One of the by-products of such experiences is that they 'provide children with critical skills for becoming active, intelligent, appreciative and selective consumers of the moving image'.* With the proliferation of audiovisual media beamed at children at home, in the classroom and at the

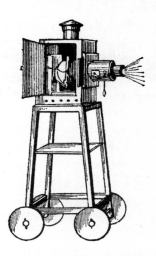

cinema, and the amount of time today's child spends just watching and listening to them, he or she had best learn to become selective and critical or he or she will be swamped by them. Active involvement in these techniques allows children to become participants where now they are too often spectators.

This chapter describes how media can be used in a variety of ways and on many levels as means of expression. Children need little equipment and much stimulation if they are to use them inventively. They need guided experiences that allow them to acquire background and skills; that lead them to-

* Lewis Mumford, *Art and Technics*, New York: Columbia University Press, 1952

wards a craft approach in using the materials and making discriminating choices of what they wish to state and how to state it. Used for these purposes rather than as instant magic, the media can be excellent learning tools. The child, who is impatient by nature, receives the rewarding results of his or her creations almost at once. But do not allow this instant quality of the materials to be the sole source of satisfaction.

Few of today's children realize that most of these processes are of recent vintage. It is virtually impossible for a modern child to comprehend that his parents or grandparents knew a time without TV, for example. And with rapid technological change, new processes descend on us before we have explored, used, understood or formed any opinion about the potential of those we already possess.

Photography, still in its infancy during the latter half of the nineteenth century and the beginning of this one, was used primarily to portray people and places, and to imitate painting. The unique, creative properties of film were not realized until the 1920s, when the possibilities of still- and motion-picture film were explored by artists and early filmmakers. The propaganda demands of World War II and the popularity of picture magazines before the advent of TV caused the flourishing of documentary still photography and the picture story, now largely a thing of the past. The Polaroid camera and Land's new colour process, among other instant picture-taking features of today's still- and motion-picture equipment, enable anyone to snap a picture or to immortalize baby's first steps.

The instant quality of many of these processes tends to foster the delusion that the mere possession of the equipment and its casual use enable anyone to be creative. It's not so. According to records kept by processors of amateur film, the repertoire of what is photographed is extremely limited and deadly dull. And most tape recorders are used primarily for business, professional and surveillance purposes and to lift radio and TV shows or records. This chapter is intended to help young people make better use of the technologies, to be creative producers rather than passive consumers.

222 Photography without a camera

A camera is not needed to take pictures. A variety of photographic papers and easily available and quite harmless chemicals exist that make many photographic experiences possible for young children at little expense. The processes are simple; the greatest emphasis can be placed on originality and invention, looking for and discovering materials and subjects for image-making, and arranging them in new and surprising ways. Once the initial technique of picture-taking and print-making are mastered, suggest to the child that he or she experiments with exposures of negatives and prints and discovers variations on conventional techniques.

223 Lenses, prisms and kaleidoscopes

Plastic and glass lenses and mirrors that enlarge, reduce and invert images; prisms that break up light; and a kaleidoscope that creates optical repeat-pattern illusions in motion can be stimulating and diverting toys for children. They also teach. A hair or a leaf seen through a magnifying glass opens up a new world to which the child might otherwise remain blind. The changing patterns of form, colour, texture and light, created by paperclips, glass fragments, snippets of paper, or grains of sand seen through a kaleidoscope, awaken the child to patterns, motion and visual surprise. It's no coincidence that David Brewster, the inventor of the kaleidoscope, should also have given birth to the stereoscope in 1844, by which two pictures of the same scene, each viewed from a slightly different angle through a stereopticon, create a three-dimensional illusion. The stereoscope became a favourite Victorian amusement for children and adults and is still used to help children discover the startling world of optics. All these are essential preparations for an interest in and an understanding of what we know today as 'the media' – photography, film, animation, sound and videotape, and holography.

224 Shadow pictures

Tools and materials: cut paper shapes;
darkened room and a single, strong light source: lamp, candle or
flashlight

Shadows thrown on the wall in the shape of faces, animals and
other figures made entirely with the fingers of two hands have
long amused small children. The wiggling ears of the shadow
rabbit were children's movies and TV, long before the
invention of the latter. Shapes cut from black paper can add to
the illusion of moving shadow pictures (see diagram).

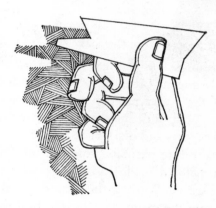

Appreciating and eventually imitating the creation of shadow
and silhouette shapes and how they can be combined and
projected helps children learn to see and compose images.
These are essential disciplines in photography and especially
in making photograms (see 227).

225 Photocollage

Tools and materials: black and white and colour photographs cut
from magazines and travel folders; card; scissors (see 38);
paste (see 21–8)

Encourage the child to cut out photographs and parts of
photographs and paste them next to, over, and partially under

each other on card to make decorative pictures or to tell a story. A photograph of a standing man can be pasted upside down so that he stands on his head.

226 Blueprints

Tools and materials: blueprint paper; dilute peroxide;
sheet of plate glass or perspex; large sheet of heavy cardboard;
two enamel, rubber or plastic trays, larger than the cut sheets of blueprint paper to be used;
two sheets of heavy blotting paper; or clothesline and clothespegs (to dry prints); pitcher of clear cold water;
scrap materials; choose those that have well-defined silhouettes

Design and arrange the scrap materials on the blueprint paper sandwiched between cardboard and glass plate. Follow directions on the paper package label for light source and exposure time. Wait until the exposed paper turns light blue. Then remove objects and glass plate and soak the paper in the tray filled with dilute peroxide solution until the unexposed portions turn brilliant white and the exposed portions of the paper turn dark blue. Wash in the second tray filled with clear water and hang the print on the clothesline or place it between two sheets of blotting paper to dry. Double-exposures are not possible.

227 Direct photograms

Tools and materials: package of No 2 photographic contact paper;
paper developer (either powder or in solution); hypo;
fresh water;
three enamel, rubber or plastic trays, each larger than the photographic paper size; red darkroom safety light;
100-watt lightbulb and shade;
two-socket overhead light fixture with separate switch for each socket; large sheet of heavy cardboard;
sheet of plate glass or perspex;

rubber or plastic apron (to protect against chemicals); rags;
scrap materials; choose those that have well-defined silhouettes
Here a wide range of grey tones, as well as sharp black and
whites, and multiple-exposures are possible. Start by letting
the child print silhouettes of his or her own hands.

It is important that the child learns to remove the photographic paper from the package one sheet at a time only, when
the red safety light is switched on and the 100-watt bulb is
switched off, using the two-socket fixture. Make sure he closes
the paper package carefully so that the paper is not light-
struck later. Place the paper, emulsion (shiny) side up, on the
cardboard and arrange scrap materials on it. Cover both with
perspex. Mix all chemicals in advance, each in its own tray,
according to the instructions given on the package labels.

Arrange the package of photographic paper to the right of
the actual exposure surface and the three trays to the left –
developer tray first, hypo tray next, and clear water tray last,
in that order. The cardboard and glass exposure surface
should be directly under the light source. Switch on the
100-watt light bulb only during the exposure period. Keep
the red safety light switched on during development and
fixing of the print.

Teach the child to count: 'One thousand and one, one
thousand and two . . .' for controlled timing of each exposure.
On completion of the exposure time, switch off the white
light and switch on the red safety light. Remove the glass
covering and objects from the paper and dip the paper face
down in the developer. Agitate the print, grasping it by one
corner and moving it rapidly back and forth. Keep the paper
fully immersed in developer. Turn it over for inspection once
in a while. When the image comes up, leave the paper face
side up in the developer until it reaches the desired intensity
of tone. Then let the developer run off the paper as it is lifted
out of the tray and immerse the print in the hypo tray to fix the
image. Follow the timing directions on the paper and hypo

package labels. Agitate as before. On completion of the fixative bath, let the hypo run off the paper and immerse the print in clear water. The longer the print washes in clear water, the less likely it is to stain in time. Dry the print between sheets of blotting paper. Weight the blotting paper to keep the print from curling.

The developer is good for many prints as long as the image comes up on the exposed paper with sufficient intensity of tone. However, each print will need longer time in the developer, which weakens with use. Change the hypo after each dozen or so prints and the water after each three or four.

After several prints have been made, suggest that the child tries to make a double exposure. Arrange the objects on the paper as before, but expose them for only half the previous time. Then rearrange the objects on the paper for a second exposure a little shorter than the first. When developed, fixed and washed, the print, if properly exposed, will contain overlapping images in tones of grey as well as in black and white. Encourage the child to play with double-, triple-, and multi-exposures of silhouettes for different designs, effects and gradations of tones.

228 Slide-making

Tools and materials: slide projector;
slide binders (available in photographic supply shops);
clear acetate or plastic film cut to size;
black and white (and coloured) acetate inks and solvent;
inexpensive brush; drawing pens and holder;
transparent, coloured, pressure-adhesive acetate

Let the child draw and paint on the clear acetate or design with snippets of pressure adhesive, transparent coloured acetate, or a combination of both. Each completed slide can be inserted in a slide binder and projected. A light show can be given with a series of these prepared slides.

229 Cameras

In making photograms the child learns the relationship between negative and positive image making. The child becomes involved in printing and development, in preparing handmade negatives and processing them. All that remains to be learned is the optical photo-negative making and developing process, for which a camera is essential. It is important that the child plays with these materials as much as with his perceptions. This is why a pinhole camera is a useful first camera.

230 The pinhole camera

The first camera – before the invention of photosensitive materials – the camera obscura, was used by artists to project and reduce real-life scenes on a screen for copying. The pinhole camera is its direct descendant. As shown, it projects the image on to photosensitive film or paper to produce a negative which, after it has been developed, can be printed like the photograms in 227.

How to build a pinhole camera:

Tools and materials: same as 227;
matte black poster board; or cardboard 6·25cm (2½″) square;
sheet of aluminium foil; No 10 sewing needle; black card;
sharp knife blade; triangle and T-square;
black poster paint, or blackboard paint and solvent (to paint cardboard if no black poster board is available);
small, inexpensive paint brush;
100mm × 125mm (4″ × 5″) film or photographic paper (see below for details)

Read 61, 62 and 66 for details on how to design, cut, score and build the 11·25cm × 13·75cm × 12·5cm (4½″ × 5½″ × 5″) box shown in diagram (a). Cut out the square in the front of the box

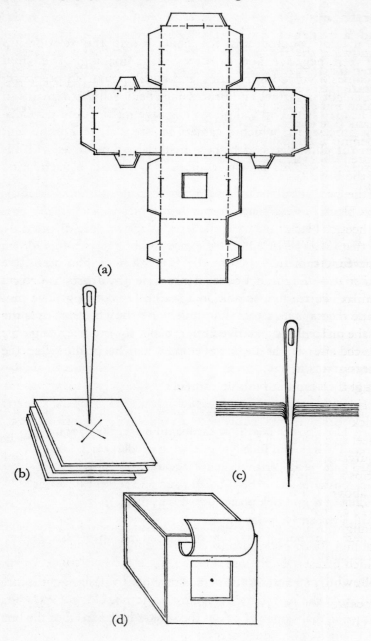

(a)

(b)

(c)

(d)

for the 'lens'. Cut out two pieces of poster board or cardboard and a piece of foil, $6·25$ cm $\times$ $6·25$ cm ($2\frac{1}{2}'' \times 2\frac{1}{2}''$) square. Sandwich the foil between the boards and tape the edges, after marking diagonals on one of the boards to find the centre (see diagram b). Push the needle through the centre point, but no deeper than about halfway from the point to the shank (see diagram c). Centre the foil on the inside of the lens opening and tape it down firmly. Now fold the box along the scored lines and lock or paste all tabs except those on the back of the box. Tape all exterior edges, except those on the back of the box, with black tape. Paint the inside and outside of the box black (unless black poster board was used). Finally, tape a sheet of black card over the lens, as shown (see diagram d), so that it can be lifted up for exposure, but stays folded down between exposures.

For paper negatives: Use Kodabromide paper F.1 or F.2 or a similar substitute available in 100mm $\times$ 125mm ($4'' \times 5''$) size. Tape the paper, emulsion (shiny) side facing the lens opening to the inside back flap of the camera in a dark room, using only the red safety light as illumination. Close the back flap and, if necessary, tape the edges. Make sure that the camera lens flap is tightly closed and take the camera into sunlight for exposure.

For film negatives: Use Kodak Royal Pan Film 4141, extra thick base, or its equivalent in 100mm $\times$ 125mm ($4'' \times 5''$) sheet size. Or a roll of 120 or 620 Kodak Tri-X Pan Film or its equivalent can be cut, in a dark room, into $7·5$ cm- ($3''$-) long strips and taped on the back flap of the camera – one at a time, as above.

To expose the film: Place the camera on a firm base with the sunlight behind it. The required exposure is too long for hand holding. It's a good idea to tape the camera to the surface on which it rests. To expose the film, raise the lens cover for the following exposure times:

Kodabromide Paper	bright sun:	cloudy bright:
F.1 or F.2	2 mins;	8 mins

Tri-X or Royal Pan Film	bright sun: 1–2 secs;	cloudy bright: 4–8 secs

Film processing: Use Kodak Tri-chem pack and follow the instructions on the package, or whichever chemicals are recommended for any other film that is used.

Printing the negative: Follow the directions given in 227, except that the paper negative is placed emulsion (shiny) side up on the bottom and the photographic paper on which it is to be printed, emulsion side down on top of it. Hold the sheets together in close contact with the perspex plate. Experiment with exposures, starting with fifteen seconds. For film negatives, place the photographic paper on the bottom, emulsion side up and the film negative directly on top of it. Start with a ten-second exposure. Develop the print as directed in 227.

Obviously a pinhole camera is a crude instrument; yet remarkably good photographs can be taken with it. Double-exposures can be made, although this requires a good deal of experimentation with exposure times, negative development, and printing. The benefit of the camera lies precisely in that. The young photographer learns by trial and error and gets the feel of the material far better than with an instant camera.

231 The low-cost camera

Any number of very low-cost cameras are available, excellent for children and young people. It is much wiser to economize on equipment and be lavish with film than vice versa. Tripods, exposure meters, flash and strobe units, fancy camera bags and the host of gadgets that are the supposed essentials of photography just get in the way of learning how to use camera and film. Today's high-speed films make flash equipment virtually unnecessary, and the rest is useful only to the most advanced amateur or professional and for special purposes.

232 Hints on picture taking

Photography is a creative medium only if the child is highly selective about what he shoots, chooses the portion of subject or scene that is most significant, and the precise moment of the peak of action. Get the child used to looking through the viewfinder, scanning the scene, object, or person, and deciding which segment is most significant and representative of the whole. Suggest that he moves closer or farther away, to shoot from a selected angle at eye level, from above or below, and at different exposures. Suggest to the child that he photographs the puddle instead of the whole street, the leaf instead of the forest.

Most cameras include two lens controls: the 'f' stop and the shutter speed control. The 'f' stop determines how large a shutter opening is to be used; and the shutter speed control determines how long the shutter remains open when the picture is taken. Before placing film in the camera, open the back of the camera and let the child look through the lens at all the 'f' stops. He'll be able to see how the shutter opening is enlarged or reduced with each change of 'f' stop.

Explain that as the shutter opening is reduced, the overall sharpness of the picture, from background to foreground, increases. When the shutter opening is enlarged the foreground remains sharp, but the background becomes increasingly fuzzy. The photographer can control emphasis by using the different 'f' stops. For example, by stopping down the shutter opening as far as it will go, given the proper lighting conditions, the overall effect will be that of a picture postcard in which everything is sharp and there is little distinction between foreground and background. But this is not how the human eye sees; it focuses on what is most important at the moment and blurs the rest. To photograph a closeup, the shutter should be open as wide as possible. The foreground should be in sharp focus if the camera is properly focused. The background will be blurred, as it is in real life when you look close at something.

The 'f' stops must also be related to shutter speed. The speed with which the shutter opens and closes determines how much light strikes the film. This is why fast shutter speed settings are used on sunny days, but slower speeds are required on cloudy days or indoors. The illumination determines which 'f' stop can be used, since it increases or reduces the amount of light that enters the camera.

Suggest to the child that he follows the 'f' stop and shutter speed directions printed on the instruction sheet inside each film package for different lighting conditions, for his first exposures of the film. Then, for the next shot, reduce the shutter speed by one setting and increase the 'f' stop by one setting. Keep changing the exposures for the same photograph for several successive shots, take notes, and compare the results when the roll of film has been developed and printed. This is how a young photographer learns to control his medium.

Film speed (the light sensitivity of the emulsion on the film) is another control factor. Today's fast films make flash and strobe units unnecessary for all except extremely bad lighting conditions and special or professional camera work. Also, by mixing controlled amounts of borax with developer, fast film speeds can be increased even more and film exposed under extremely poor lighting conditions can produce interesting, readable pictures. Finally, by careful printing and paper development, portions of a negative can be 'held back' and others emphasized.

The beginner must learn how to hold a camera. If he wiggles even slightly at the moment of exposure, the picture will be blurred. A tripod is unnecessary for all exposures of a half second or less. Let the child press the camera against his chest while his finger is on the trigger. Then, just before he presses the trigger, let him hold his breath until the picture is taken. This assures relative immobility.

A negative can be cropped (only a portion selected) for printing. But the ability to select, compose and photograph exactly what is wanted with the camera, rather than in the enlarger, is the essence of the photographer's art.

233 Film development

Tools and materials: development tank for the film size used; film developer and hypo; stop bath; red safety light; sink and running water; sponge-tipped squeegee tweezers; thermometer; funnel; clothesline and clothespegs; weighted clips

Follow the directions in the film package about which developer to use. Follow the directions provided with developer and hypo for mixing the chemicals, and for the temperatures at which they should be used. Unroll the film in total darkness or by red safety light and strip away the paper backing. Thread the film on the wire holder of the development tank, then replace and close it again. If the development tank includes a light trap, the rest of the work can be done in daylight.

Pour the developer into the tank through the funnel. Cover the tank opening and let the film develop for the time stated on the chemical package. Shake the tank periodically during the development time. At its end, pour the developer into a brown bottle and store it in the dark for future use. Keep in mind that film developer, like paper developer (see 227), weakens with use and that future development with the same batch of chemicals will require more time. Pour stop bath and hypo into the tank for the required amounts of time. Stop bath halts development; hypo fixes the image on the film. These chemicals can also be re-used two or three times if they are stored where it is cool and dark. After the hypo has been emptied from the tank, let clear water run into it and, after an initial rinse, open the tank and stand it under a running tap for twenty minutes.

When the film is thoroughly rinsed, remove the wire holder from the tank and, grasping the clear leader of the film, unwind it. Run the sponge-tipped squeegee the length of the film from top to bottom to remove excess moisture. Do not repeat this operation or it may streak the film. Hang the film by its clear leader from two clothespegs attached to the line. Attach a weighted clip to the bottom edge of the film and make sure that it does not touch any surface or object while drying. Leave it hanging undisturbed until completely dry. While removing weighted clip and clothespegs, and whenever inspecting film hold the negative by the edges and never touch the surfaces of the negatives. Fingerprints tend to become embedded in the emulsion and they show up in the finished prints.

234 Contact printing

Tools and materials: same as 227;
200mm × 250mm (8″ × 10″) photographic contact printing paper; magnifying glass; scaleograph; red grease pencil

Whether you send exposed film to a commercial processor to be developed, or whether you develop it yourself, it pays to contact-print film before ordering or making enlargements.

Never cut the roll of film into individual negatives. Cut it into strips of a length that enables them to fit, lengthwise, on a sheet of 200mm × 250mm (8″ × 10″) paper.

Contact-print the negative strips as in 227. After the contact sheet is dry, examine each print with a magnifying glass and check off the ones that are worth enlarging. Each picture can be cropped (a selected portion marked) with a scaleograph (see diagram), available from photographic supply shops.

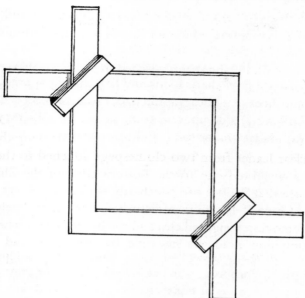

Mark the cropped area with a red grease pencil to decide which portion of each negative should be enlarged.

235 Enlarging

Tools and materials: same as 227;
photographic enlarger with interchangeable film carriage for different film sizes

Photographic enlargers are expensive. Unless one is owned or a dark room equipped with an enlarger is available, the chosen negatives must be sent to a processing laboratory for enlargement. One can be found through the Yellow Pages of the telephone directory. Provide the processor with a marked and cropped contact sheet (see 234) and the desired enlargement size.

If an enlarger is available, place the selected negative in the carrier, leaving the rest of the filmstrip protruding on either side. Switch off the regular white light and switch on the red safety light. Place an ordinary piece of paper, the same size as the photographic paper to be used for the print, on the easel under the enlarger. Move the enlarger head up or down and focus until the portion or the whole of the negative that is to be enlarged is in sharp focus and fills the paper area. Then place one sheet of photographic paper (see 227) on the easel, emulsion (shiny) side up, and print as in 227. Different print densities, gradations of tone, and other effects can be created when printing with an enlarger. Several prints may be required before the best combination of exposure and development time is discovered for a given negative.

236 Colour photography

Tools and materials: any camera; colour film (check size, number of exposures, film speed; whether indoor or outdoor film; and whether colour prints or transparencies are furnished on development)

Colour film cannot be developed by children or in a makeshift or home dark room. Colour film that can be developed and printed by amateurs is now available, but it requires a fully equipped dark room. Most colour film needs to be sent to commercial processors for development. When buying colour film ascertain whether the processed film is returned as transparencies (slides) or as colour negatives and prints. The colour fidelity of transparencies is always better than that of negatives and prints, if the exposure was correct, but they require a projector for viewing. Colour prints can be made from transparencies, but good type C or dye transfer prints are prohibitively expensive. They are used only for commercial reproductions.

Any camera can accommodate colour film, but note that the exposure times required for colour film are very different from those for black and white. Be guided by the exposure directions provided for different lighting conditions in the directions packaged with the film. For best results bracket the exposures by shooting at one more 'f' stop and one shorter exposure, and then at one less 'f' stop and one longer exposure, for each scene, in addition to the combination suggested in the instructions.

The best outdoor results in colour photography are obtained in the early morning or late afternoon, or at any time on slightly overcast, dull or foggy days: in other words, not in brilliant sunshine. Photographs taken under bright, ideal black and white conditions tend to be too highly coloured and to look artificial even when exposures are perfect. For good indoor colour, strobe or flash bulbs 'bounced' off the ceiling or wall are required, unless high-speed film and very long exposures with a camera set on a tripod are used. Once the basic techniques are mastered, suggest to the young photographer that he tries unorthodox effects – shooting into the sun at very fast exposures, or extremely long exposures at night.

237 Animation and movie-making

In a parallel to still photography, a child doesn't need a movie camera to make movies. It is much more interesting for him if he starts making movies without a camera and without film, using only materials to hand. In the following movie-making projects and animations, the use of tape recorders (see 242–7) is implicit to add dimension to the art, wherever possible.

238 Thaumatrope

Tools and materials: 10cm to 15cm (4″ to 6″) white card discs; large sewing needle or hole punch (see 18); thread or twine; wax crayons (see 140); or cut-out photographs, coloured paper and paste (see 24–8)

The thaumatrope was probably the first movie invention. Punch two holes on opposite sides of each disc and thread a loop of thread or twine through each set of holes. Draw or paste two related but different pictures, or paste two such photographs, on each side of the disc. For example, place a bird on one side and a birdcage on the other. Now wind up

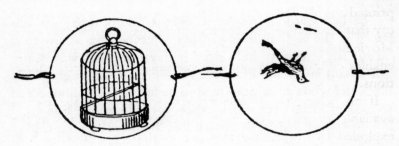

the string by holding each loop in two fingers of each hand and swing the disc in an arc in one direction until it is thoroughly twisted. Then pull at each end in an opposite direction, relaxing the pull as the string unwinds and the disc begins to twirl. The bird will appear to be inside the cage. If the string is pulled and relaxed alternately, the illusion will continue indefinitely. Primitive as this toy may be, it illustrates the stroboscopic effect on which all motion-picture production is based.

239 Zoetrope

Tools and materials: 25cm (10″) diameter × 5cm (2″)-high round cheese box or baking tin; or cardboard constructed turntable (see diagram c); four or more 35cm × 13cm (14″ × 5¼″) strips of white card; or paper pasted together to this length and width; one 35cm × 13cm (14″ × 5¼″) strip of black card; or black paper pasted to this length and width; burnisher; compass; ruler; right-angle triangle; HB pencil; scissors; sharp knife blades and holder (see 69); masking tape; paperclips; crayons; poster paint and brush (see 149); coloured paper and paste (see 24–8); coat-hanger wire and pliers;

two 2·5cm (1″)-diameter washers with a 3mm ($\frac{1}{8}$″) hole in each; blackboard paint and brush; paint solvent; heavy cardboard work surface

The nineteenth century's zoetrope came complete with printed animations. In the nineteen-fifties I designed a similar toy that enabled children to make their own animations – the Movie Maker. The following are plans for a movie maker that enables children to create drawn, painted and pasted animations.

If no baking tin or cheese box of the right diameter is available, construct the zoetrope turntable as shown in the exploded view and diagrams (see diagram c). Punch a hole in the centre of the cheese box, baking tin, or constructed turntable with the hammer and nail. Add the handle as shown and brush two coats of blackboard paint on the outside of the turntable.

Fold one of the 35cm × 13cm (14″ × 5$\frac{1}{4}$″) white paper strips in half; halve twice more. Crease the folds sharply with the burnisher and cut slots on both sides of the folded sheet as shown (see diagram a). When unfolded, use this sheet as the template (see diagram d; and 65) for the other black and white paper strips. Mark the slots on them and cut them out with a sharp knife blade. Place the paper on a thick sheet of cardboard for cutting so that the tabletop is not damaged.

(a)

(b)

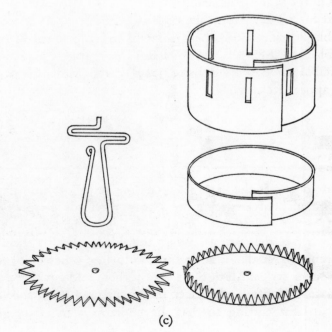

(c)

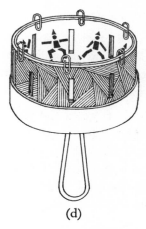

(d)

Paste the black slotted paper strip to the inside rim of the turntable (see diagram c).

After slots have been cut, draw animations between the slots of the white card strips. On completion of each sequence, insert the white strip in the turntable, lining up slots cut into the black and white papers. Attach the white paper strip to the black with paperclips all round (see diagram d). Spin the turntable while looking through one of the slots. The pictures will appear to move.

240 Flip book animation

Tools and materials: several paper signatures, 8–16 pages each,
folded and gathered. Use bond or lightweight drawing paper.
Each page need be no larger than 5cm × 7·5cm (2″ × 3″);
hole punch; paper-fasteners; wax crayons (see 140)

Draw a picture on each page of the gathered signatures in a
sequence, starting with the first page. Use the same animation
techniques described and pictured in 239. When all the
pictures have been drawn and the flip book is filled, run the
edges of the pages through the fingers of the other hand. The
images drawn on the pages will appear to be in motion.

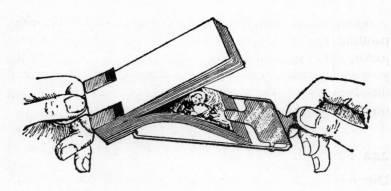

241 Drawing and scratching on film

Tools and materials: 8mm or 16mm movie projector;
720 frames of clear 8mm or 16mm film leader;
acetate inks in different colours; solvent;
student grade watercolour brush; drawing pen nibs and holder;
needle point, or tipped etching tool

Movie film runs through camera and projector at the rate of
twenty-four frames per second; 720 frames of clear leader
will produce a thirty-second film, which is about as much as
a young film-maker can handle without becoming tangled up.

If pre-striped, single-sprocketed clear leader can be obtained, the film-maker, in addition to drawing his animation on film, can scratch sound on to the sound track (see 244).

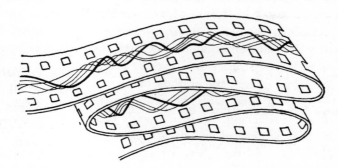

A continuous animation on film can be created by drawing, painting and scratching on film. When run through a projector, the image will appear to be in motion. Suggest to the young film-maker that he lets the design flow together and dissolve over the whole length of the film, rather than drawing on individual frames (see diagram).

242 Recording

Discovering, making and arranging sounds can be highly creative experiences, which call imagination and selective judgement into play, heightening the capacity to listen, to distinguish the meaning of sounds, and to use them inventively. Try turning off the sound on your TV set, letting children guess what sounds go with the pictures unfolding before them, or make up the dialogue.

The skills required for operating a cassette tape recorder are slight. All that needs to be learned is the buttons to push for record, playback, fast forward and reverse winding of the tape, how to insert and remove the cassette and how to clean the sound head. Transferring sound from one recorder to another is only slightly more complicated.

243 Sound instruments

One of the problems that stands in the way of a creative use of sound is that this subject is studied only in elementary science classes. Classroom experiments with sound usually don't concern themselves with meaning and sequence. The human voice is a remarkable solo instrument, able to imitate a wide range of sounds and effects. Encourage the child to mimic animal noises, the sounds of cars, sirens, bells, trains, aeroplanes and boat whistles, water rushing in torrents or rain drops splattering. Scrap materials can aid in such sound production: sticks rubbed or struck on wood; a fingernail scratched over fabric, glass, or eggshell; a dowel or metal spoon struck or rubbed over a cooking pot lid. These are common experiences that enable a child to experiment with sounds.

Homemade musical instruments can be constructed that introduce the child to rhythm and interval. Rubber bands stretched across a box (see diagram a), or a series of water glasses, each filled to a different level (see diagram b) and

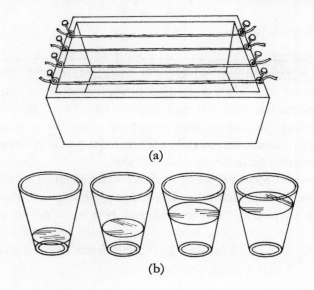

(a)

(b)

struck with a dowel, can produce musical sounds and be recorded on tape. As the child plays back sounds he has created, he'll get ideas for producing others.

244 Scratching sound on film

Tools and materials: 720 frames of pre-striped, single-sprocketed clear leader (8mm or 16mm);
8mm or 16mm sound film projector;
needle point, or tipped etching tool

Given the basic understanding that sound is recorded on magnetic tape in wave form, a child can make a spontaneous sound track on film. Scratch on the opaque coloured band on the unperforated edge of the film with the needle or etching tool. By varying the configuration of the scratches (see diagram), a variety of high, low, screeching and bleeping sounds

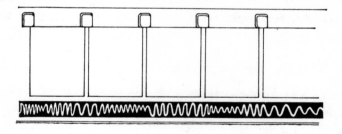

can be created that are made audible when the film is run through the projector. If such a sound track is to accompany a directly drawn animation on film (see 241), it is important to keep in mind that the sound head in the projector 'reads' the sound track twenty-six frames beyond the picture it matches. In other words, the picture projected on frame No 1 is accompanied by the sound on the track next to frame No 26.

245 Finding sounds

Encourage the child to take his tape recorder with him wherever he goes – to the zoo, airport, circus or fun fair, and on any excursion to places where unusual or interesting sounds are likely to be found. At home he or she can record the miaowing of the cat, the barking of the dog, the ring of the telephone, or the kettle boiling on the stove. These sounds, recorded on tape, can be built into a library of natural sound effects (see 246) that the child can use in his or her play and in making animations or movies.

Demonstrate how the meaning of sounds changes when they are rearranged in different sequences:

Cat's miaow	Cat's miaow	Footsteps	Footsteps	Door slam	Door slam
Footsteps	Door slam	Cat's miaow	Door slam	Footsteps	Cat's miaow
Door slam	Footsteps	Door slam	Cat's miaow	Cat's miaow	Footsteps

These, or any other three sounds, can be arranged in six different ways, each sequence conveying a different set of events and meanings.

246 Making sound effects

Professional movie makers and TV producers do not rely exclusively on natural sounds recorded on location; for example, thunder is produced by shaking a large metal sheet; rain, with metal foil or by pouring dried lentils or peas on a wood or metal tray. Inventing sound effects and recording them on a tape recorder is a useful experience. These effects can be edited into story-telling tapes (see 247) or used for animation and film-making.

247 Story-telling on tape

Suggest to children and young people that they tell or read stories into the tape recorder, producing and using sound effects (see 243–6) at appropriate moments to dramatize the story. When the tape is played back, let the child listen and make suggestions for future improvement, slower speech or reading, greater separation of words, better pacing and pronunciation.

10 Fibre craft

If between the ages of five and fifteen, we could give all our
children a training of the senses through the constructive shaping
of materials – if we could accustom their hands and eyes, indeed
all their instruments of sensation, to a creative communion with
sounds and colours, textures and consistencies, a communion
with nature in all its substantial variety, then we need not fear
the fate of those children in a wholly mechanized world.
Bernard Shaw

248 Background

The first likely products of weaving – wind breaks, fences and
palisades – were probably inspired by man's awakening to a
consciousness of animal behaviour – nest building and spider
web and cocoon spinning. This probably led to imitation and
the eventual discovery of original weaves and patterns. These
skills were inevitably applied to various purposes and products – hair ornamentation, baskets, fish traps (still used in
Malta), coracles (wattle-daubed wicker boats), ritual offering

vessels, chests, huts, and even chariot, carriage and wagon bodies. Between the period of the rude beginnings of this craft and its eventual, partial replacement by work in other materials, twisting, spinning, weaving and knotting vegetable fibres became possible as man's ability to make tools – bone awls, threaders and needles – developed.

Many examples of woven baskets, and of course cloth, are pictured in Assyrian and Babylonian murals, sculptures and reliefs, and in later Egyptian and Greek friezes and vase decorations. The common use of wicker baskets is reflected in the story of the infant Moses, left in a basket on the shore of the Nile. Basket-making and its products were frequently considered holy and associated with religious sacrificial rites. During the time of the Roman occupation of Britain, Druids are reported to have woven huge replicas of the human figure, filled with votive offerings, which were burned to the ground during annual religious ceremonies. The bearskin caps of the Guards are lined with wicker even today.

A way had to be found to lengthen and strengthen softer fibres. Flax, jute, sheep's wool, cotton and, in China, the excretion of the silk worm, needed to be twisted into continuous strands to provide fibres for weaves that eventually replaced animal skins as man's clothing. By the time of the flowering of the Incan and Egyptian empires, weaving had become so refined that the closeness and delicacy of the cloth has been seldom matched since.

Primitive weaving was very slow. The warp threads (the vertical strands; see 262) had to be lifted one by one so that the weft (the horizontal strands; see 262) could be passed over and under them alternately to form the weave. The invention of heddles by an unknown genius of the distant past allowed each set of warp strands to be lifted alternately as a group, as shown in the previous illustration; and the shuttle, which holds the weft strand, as shown below, to be thrown rapidly. It is essential to understand these simple principles of weaving,

the proper terms, and the basic mechanism so that they become second nature to the young craftsman. The need to speed up the weaving process made invention and improvement of equipment a matter of concern, second only to agriculture, to those who first experimented with mechanics and water power. This mechanization undermined the consumer's reverence for the product and the labourer's reverence for his work. The latter declined to machine-minding.

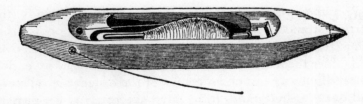

Until some of the basic braids, weaves, and knots are mastered, it is impossible to be inventive. Encourage children to invent their own designs even if they re-invent many that were traditional in the past. Conventional weaves can be readily deduced from the basic ones. Should any child or young person need to know these for practical reasons, he or she can find the particulars in the existing literature.* What is far more important and of primary concern is that the child learns to create and recognize patterns as

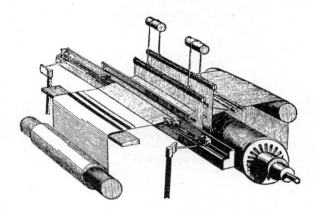

a result of his experience inspired by this and the following chapter. For these reasons some of the less creative aspects of the craft, like caning, have been deliberately excluded. Caning is mostly limited to particular patterns by utility and necessity rather than convention, and the emphasis here as elsewhere in this book is on developmental learning.

Winding and stringing
249 Unravelling

Tools and materials: old wool sweater or other garment; cardboard shuttle (see diagram a)

Unravelling a discarded garment and winding the wool into a ball or on a shuttle can be an interesting activity for nursery and kindergarten age children. The garment should be made of thick, coarse fibre, preferably wool. The turned-over warp

* G. H. Oelsner, *A Handbook of Weaves*: Dover Publications Inc, 1952

strands (see 248), or bound-off knitting (see 270), should be cut through with scissors at the hem so that the child can separate the weft easily (see diagram b). Caution him not to

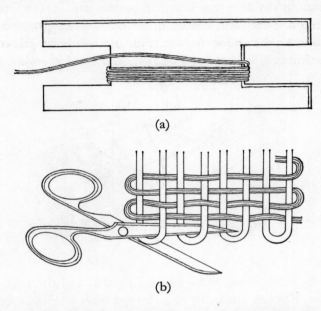

(a)

(b)

unravel more wool than what he can wind on the shuttle at one time. The wool thus unravelled can be used in many of the projects described above and below. (See also 17–20, 29, 30, 89, 127, 158, 183 and 207.)

250 Cord construction

Tools and materials: open cardboard box; cardboard or wooden frame; hole punch (see 126 for round drive punch and mallet), or hand drill and bit (see 93); ball of twine, yarn or wool

Punch holes in the sides and bottom of the cardboard box or construct an open framework of any desired shape and drill holes into all frame members (see diagram a). The constructions shown are representative examples only. The idea is not to thread the twine through every hole but to choose those that, when threaded, make the design interesting.

Start the child by cutting off about 30cm (12″) of twine, knotting one end, and threading the other through any one of the holes in the frame or box. Pull the whole length of the twine through the hole and then choose another hole on any

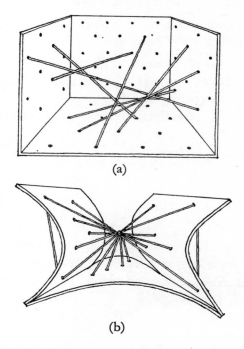

(a)

(b)

opposite side through which to thread it. Pull the twine tight and continue weaving across the box or frame from hole to hole. Whenever the length is used up, knot more twine to its end until the design is finished. Different-coloured yarn can be knotted together for multicoloured effects.

More experienced young people can combine warp (vertical) designs with weft (horizontal) designs, weaving over and/or under to create almost any configuration that grows spontaneously out of the work. Caution the child not to pull too hard on the weft strands, or he may distort the cardboard box sides or frame. If the frame is very solidly constructed, it is possible to distort the warp design deliberately by tightening up on the weft strands (see diagram b).

251 Pasting

Tools and materials: string, twine, wool, thread and fibres; paste (see 21–8); sheet of heavy cardboard or card

String, twine, wool, thread and fibres can be dipped in paste and used as collage materials (see 29); or the cardboard can be given a thick coating of white or acrylic paste and strands laid into it in patterns and combinations of the child's choice. (See also 30, 89, 125 and 183.)

252 Twisting, braiding and knotting

Knots are part of not only the weaver's craft, but the sailor's. There are more than 150 different ways of knotting and splicing twine and rope, but only a small number of them are of practical value to the young craftsman. The first ropes were probably made of twisted vines, thong or animal gut. The knot was an inevitable invention born of the need to keep long hair from interfering with full movement, to secure bundles, and to tie off ends of coarse braids and wicker weaves. The Greek Gordius supposedly tied a knot in 3,000BC, whose ends were so cleverly concealed that no one could discover how to untie it. Legend had it that whoever untied the Gordian knot was to rule the entire Asian continent. According to myth, Alexander the Great severed it with a stroke of his sword and fulfilled the prophecy. Folklore and superstition surround the knot all over the world. The knot has been a part of rituals from tying the umbilicus of the new-born to the marriage ceremony.

A child can be shown how to make his own rope. Take a bundle of single or twisted fibres – twine, string or thread – and gather it evenly at one end. Tape the end securely with masking tape and secure in a vice or G clamp (see 90 and 91). The whole bundle of fibres should be about 6mm ($\frac{1}{4}$″) thick. Cut the other end even and insert it in the chuck of an ordinary hand drill. Turn the drill and a rope will begin to

form (see diagram). It's a good idea to moisten the fibres before twisting and then dry them while still held under tension by vice and drill. Bind the end near the drill chuck with tape before unfastening the rope.

When a child has learned how to tie shoelaces, he is ready for some of the projects described below. Each braid and knot, by itself and in combination with bead work and weaving patterns, can produce individual and inventive results. As with all other craft, don't try to teach too much too soon.

253 Cat's cradle

It is appropriate to mention here this Eskimo and Oriental game, Cat's cradle, played with a loop of string of which the ends are tied together and stretched between the outstretched palms of two hands (see diagram). It develops finger dexterity

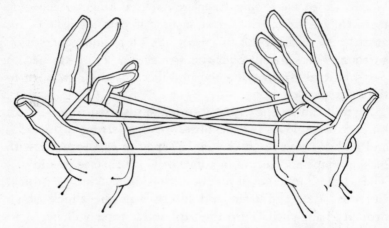

and an understanding of some of the properties of fibres. A child can weave intricate designs of his or her own invention in endless variation, using the basic principle of cat's cradle.

254 Braiding

Tools and materials: cane; rushes; maize husks; grasses; reeds; raffia; hemp; willow twigs; wheat, rye, or oat straw; fern stems; honeysuckle vine; wool yarn; twine or string (see below); scissors

Each fibre used in braiding, as in basketry, caning and weaving, requires special preparation. The following describes the methods appropriate for each material:

Straw: Gather at harvest time. Cut off sheaf with scissors. Select only those straws of which the thin (top) end can be inserted easily into the thicker tubular bottom end to make longer straws if required. Soak straw in water overnight before plaiting or weaving.

Grasses (sedge or slough grass is best): Gather during summer

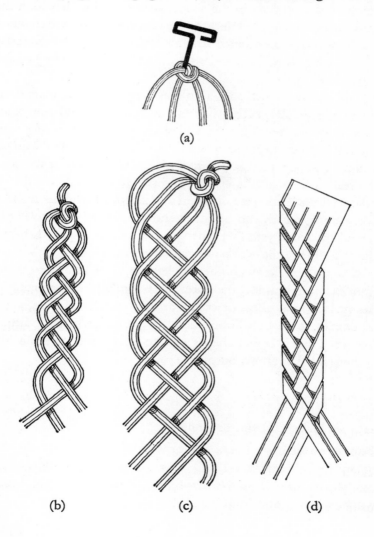

(a)

(b)   (c)   (d)

and autumn. Cut near ground with scissors. Cut off tips and remove outer covering. Dry indoors in the shade. Use dry, but dampen slightly after braiding or weaving and then press between blotting paper and cardboard on which weights are placed evenly.

Willow and rushes: Gather before the end of summer. Clip off tips and dry indoors in the shade. Rushes can be used whole, or split down the middle followed by scraping off the sticky pitch on the inside surface with a knife. Soak in cold water for fifteen minutes before use and keep wrapped in a damp towel until used.

The various braids shown in diagrams b–d are in ascending order of difficulty, each involving more strands. Whenever an even number of strands is braided (four, six, and so on), fold the fibres so that each end is a different length and additional strands can be added at different places. Cross two or more of the folded fibres at the creases and secure the folded end to a board with a T pin (see diagram a). Except for hollow grasses and straws, which can be fitted end to end, overlap the next strand by about 5cm (2″) when an addition is required. Braid the strand into the work rather than knotting it.

When a sufficient number of lengths or a long length of fibre has been braided, the fibres can be coiled and formed into flat or hollow shapes, or coiled around different forms, such as bottles, boxes, balloons and slab-built or other pottery (see 188). Such coiled shapes can be either tied or sewn together (see diagram d on page 259).

255 Knotting

Tools and materials: twine or string

The ten most basic knots and how to splice rope are shown below (see diagrams a–l). One or a combination of several can be used in macramé (see 256), weaving (see 257–65), bead work (see 265) and braiding (see 254).

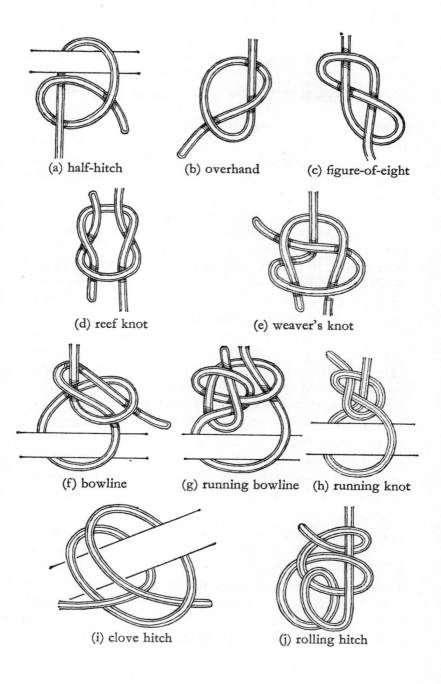

(a) half-hitch   (b) overhand   (c) figure-of-eight

(d) reef knot   (e) weaver's knot

(f) bowline   (g) running bowline   (h) running knot

(i) clove hitch   (j) rolling hitch

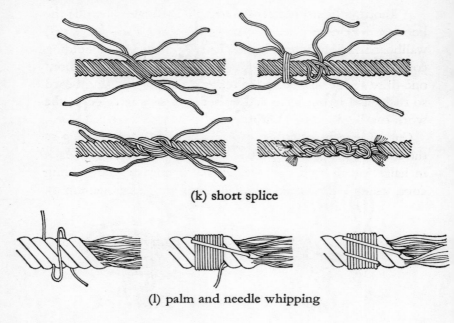

(k) short splice

(l) palm and needle whipping

256 Macramé

Tools and materials: twine or jute; knotting board (see below);
T pins; scissors; embroidery needles (see 268);
crochet hook (see 269); or leather lacing needle (see 127);
beads or metal rings

Macramé consists of tightly knotted patterns made of twine
or thread. The objects made may be utilitarian or purely
decorative – wall hangings, mats, jewellery and belts and other
wearing apparel.

The steps in preparing the material are uniform, no matter
what will be made or which knots or supplementary materials
will be used. Customarily two basic knots are used, the reef
knot and the half-hitch (see 255, and diagram below). However, these, singly or in combination with each other as well
as with those described in 255, can be used to achieve an
infinite variety of designs and effects.

A knotting board is essential to hold the material while the knots are being made. A piece of 20cm × 30cm (8″ × 12″) wallboard or polystyrene is sufficient. Knot and pin a 'holding cord' to the board. The holding cord should be pinned about one-third of the way from the top edge of the knotting board so that, held in one's lap and leaned against a table edge, the work can be done in comfort.

Cut off lengths of twine, each about eight times as long as the estimated length of the finished product, and double each in half. Attach each doubled length of cord to the holding cord, using a double reverse half-hitch knot (see diagram a).

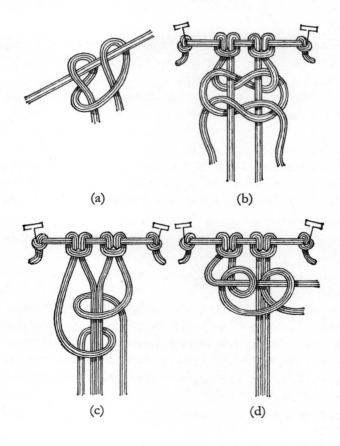

(a)   (b)

(c)   (d)

(The width of the finished work depends on the number of double strands knotted to the holding cord.) Begin knotting, using one or another of the standard macramé knots shown above (see diagrams b–d); but bear in mind that any others can be improvised or combined with those shown (see 255).

It is important to keep the holding cord taut and to add T pins to secure finished portions of the work as close as can be to the cord ends not yet knotted. The finished work should be securely pinned to the holding board. If the work becomes uncomfortable because it is too close to the bottom of the board, unpin the knotted, finished portions and the holding cord, and move both farther towards the top edge of the board.

Beads, rings, and other ornamental findings can be knotted into the work or to its ends or edges as it progresses, depending on the craftsman's purpose.

For children in younger age groups or less experienced young craftsmen, the lengths of twine and the numbers of strands should be kept to a minimum. Two or three doubled lengths of twine, each a foot or so long, tied to the holding cord, suffice for a start. Emphasis should be on spontaneity rather than on formal repeat patterns: no pre-printed pattern should be followed. Examples of more complex forms of macramé can be found in the literature.*

257 Weaving

The weaving process is the same whether spun or natural fibres are used. Weaving as a whole, not by product or material, is discussed below. Once a child has mastered the basic skills, he or she can apply them to any material or purpose. The reader is urged to read 248 and to explain the basic warp and weft principle to the child before introducing him or her to these crafts.

* Mary Walker Phillips. *Macramé*, London: Pan Craft Books, 1972

258 Interweaving

Tools and materials: paper or leather strips (see 20, 42–6, 127 and 128; and diagrams below); or fibres (see 254);
or twine, wool yarn or thread; sheet of heavy cardboard;
heddle sticks (see 262); scissors; masking tape

A sheet of paper or split leather, cut into strips but not all the way through, and taped by the uncut edge to the cardboard (see diagram a), becomes the warp. An identical sheet or strip, cut but not fully separated into strips and laid alongside the warp at right angles, becomes the weft. The weave can be angled (see diagram b).

Fibres and yarn can be used similarly, the top ends of the warp and the ends on one side of the weft being taped together, after the fibres are laid down side by side (see diagram c).

The advantage of this type of interweaving is that it bridges

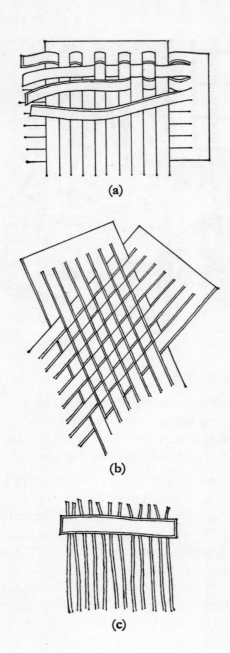

(a)

(b)

(c)

the gap in skills between braiding and weaving. Warp and weft strands are easily arranged and kept in order. If the number of warp and weft strands is kept to seven or nine each, any pre-school nursery or kindergarten child can learn to weave in this manner.

259 Paper weaving
See 42–6.

260 Wicker work and basketry
(See also 254.)

A comparison of the various weaves used in fabrics and in wicker work shows that there is very little difference in the working methods required for weaving natural fibres like rushes, reeds and palm fronds, and spun fibres like wool,

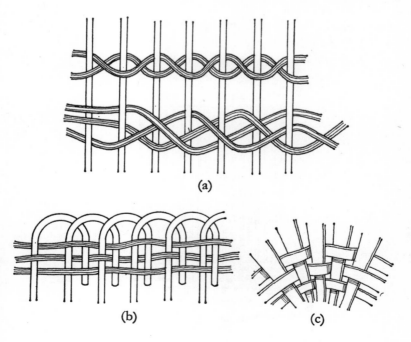

(a)

(b)   (c)

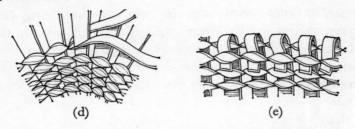

(d)   (e)

cotton and silk. Broad-leaf fibres can be slotted, bent or crossed to form variations in the warp, or the weft can be twisted (see diagrams a–e). Except for these differences, the same basic working methods apply to natural and spun fibres.

261 Stick loom

Tools and materials: wool yarns; thread; or fibres (see 258 and 260); two dowels; heddle sticks (see 262); shuttle; scissors

American and East Indians have used stick looms from time immemorial. Tie an odd number of warp strands, each about 6mm (¼″) equidistant from the next, to one dowel. Tie the other end of each warp strand to the other dowel in the same

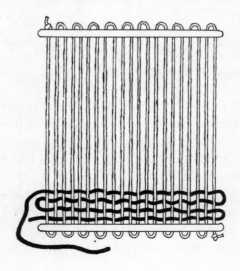

manner, so that the dowels are parallel when hung (see diagram). Suspend one dowel overhead or from a nail in the wall. Insert the heddle sticks as in 262. If yarn or thread is to be used as the weft, wind it on a shuttle and begin the weave from the top, working down. Use the heddle stick to force the last woven weft strand close to the already woven fabric. No shuttle is needed for natural fibres and grasses.

If a shuttle is used, pass it alternately from left to right and from right to left. Do not distort the weave by pulling the warp strands together. When the warp is filled and the weave is completed, withdraw the dowels and heddle stick, tie the end of the weft to the last warp strand, and tie adjacent warp strands to each other, using any knot that serves the purpose (see 255) or seems decorative.

When fibres, grasses, or wicker are woven in this manner, the warp and weft strand ends are either turned over (see diagrams b and e on pp. 241–2) and secured in the weave, or they are sewn together (see 254, 268 and 276).

262 Frame loom

Tools and materials: wood or cardboard frame (see diagram a); wool yarn, string or fibres (see 258 and 260); heddle stick (see diagrams b and c); shuttle; scissors

Though a frame loom is customarily used only for heavy rug weaving, it is especially useful to young people for all kinds of weaving that are adapted especially for the purpose. The wood or cardboard frame can be any size. Drill holes in the top and bottom of the frame, 6mm ($\frac{1}{4}$") or less apart. Leave enough room at the sides (see diagram a) so that the yarn or fibre can be woven. String the warp and tie it top and bottom. Insert the heddle stick (see diagram b). Turn the heddle stick to lift alternate sets of warp threads. Towards the end of the weave it will have to be withdrawn and the remainder woven without it. Weave with a shuttle or threader.

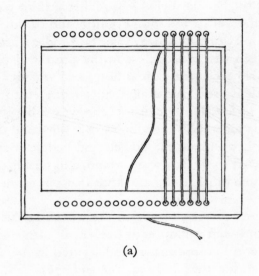

(a)

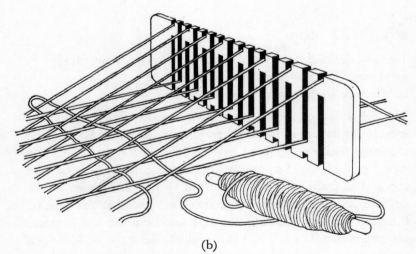

(b)

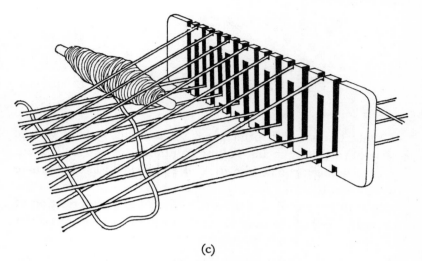

(c)

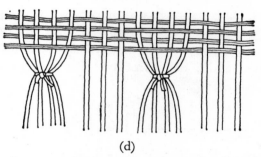

(d)

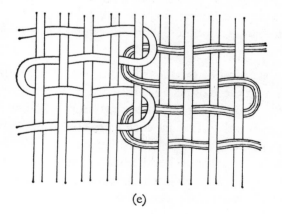

(e)

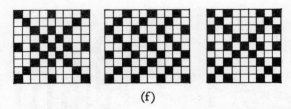

(f)

Once the weaving principle is understood, a great variety of patterns, designs and colour combinations can be woven. Weave without the heddle stick. Bind any section of alternate warp strands with a loosely tied piece of yarn or twine of the colour to be used (see diagram d). Then weave that portion of the warp only to the desired depth before changing the colour or pattern of the weft. Portions of the warp adjacent to what is tied off must be woven so that they overlap as shown (see diagram e). Diagonal or more complex weaves require either careful planning on graph paper in advance or tying off warp strands for the first pass of the shuttle and carefully counting the required additional warp strands for every subsequent pass (see diagram f).

263 Paper, cardboard and wood form looms

Tools and materials: wool yarn, string or fibres (see 258 and 260); heddle sticks; paper or cardboard shapes (see 67–72);
or wooden base (see below); shuttle; scissors; sharp knife blade; ruler

The simplest kind of cardboard loom consists of a flat square or rectangular piece of heavy cardboard in which notches have been cut, top and bottom, at about 6mm ($\frac{1}{4}$″) distances (see diagram a). Wind and secure each warp strand under opposite, matching notches and weave as before (see 260 and 261), either with or without heddle sticks (see 262) or shuttle. When the weave is completed, remove it from the cardboard and tie each warp and weft strand to the next to make a

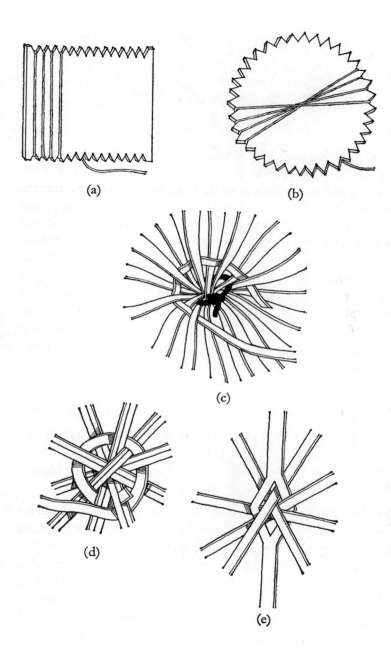

(a)

(b)

(c)

(d)

(e)

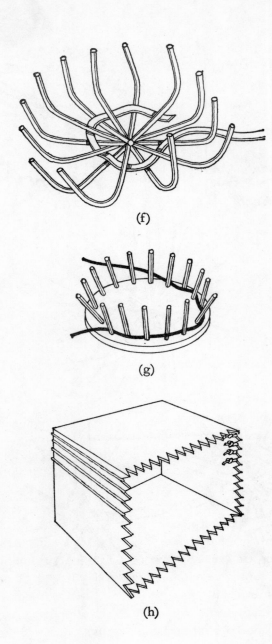

(f)

(g)

(h)

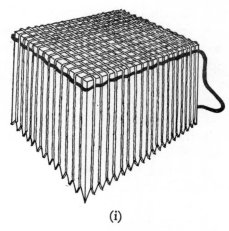

(i)

fringe or, if wicker is used, tuck warp and weft ends under the first and second rows of the weave (see 260). Fibre weaves can also be hemmed or sewn at the edges (see 254, 268 and 276).

A round piece of cardboard can be similarly notched around its edge and the warp threads secured and strung as described above. Start the weft at the centre, weaving around and around, over and under, working towards the outer edge (see diagram b). Flat natural fibres (see 254) do not require such a template for round, flat or hollow woven shapes. They can be notched and crossed (see diagrams c–e) and, if required, the ends can be turned up to form the warp (see diagram f). Permanent wooden bases with holes drilled around their edges are also used for wicker work trays and baskets. Pass the fibres under the wooden base and up through opposite holes to form the warp (see diagram g).

Open dimensional shapes made of paper and cardboard, tubes, boxes, tin cans and bottles can be used as templates for wicker and fabric weaving. Cut notches, drill holes or secure the warp thread with tape on two opposite top edges of the shape (see diagram h). Attach the weft strands to one of the remaining sides. Turn the shape over, its open side facing the table. Now stretch the weft strands across the side to the edge of which they are attached and weave them over and under the previously strung warp strands on the bottom surface only. As each weft strand completes its weave, tie it to the top edge of the opposite side of the shape (see diagram i). Turn the shape right side up when the bottom has been fully woven. Using a new thread or fibre, tie one end to the very edge of the bottom weave at one corner, and start weaving all round the four sides (see diagram i). This method can be adapted to any shape. When the whole weave is completed, the template can be withdrawn if desired, after the ends of the fibres are released from the notches. They can be tied together, hemmed or sewn or tucked into the weave, so that they do not unravel (see 254, 261, 268 and 276).

264 Weaves

Tools and materials: same as 258–63

Whole volumes are dedicated to the wicker and fabric weaves that have been invented through the ages.*† As far as children and young people are concerned, the emphasis should be on experimentation, improvisation and invention, once the basic processes are understood. The warp can consist of multi-coloured strands or strands strung in a sequence of colours or a variety of fibres. The weft need not be woven over and under each warp strand. Two or more warp strands can be woven in regular or irregular patterns. Different-coloured yarns or fibres can be interwoven in regular or irregular sequences (see 261). Or different-coloured weft strands can be joined end to end for random patterns.

The drawings (see diagrams a–d) show some of the conventional weave patterns. These are not to be copied; instead they can suggest how weaves, braids, knots and skills can be

* Navajo School of Indian Basketry, *Indian Basket Weaving*: Dover Publications Inc, 1971

† G. H. Oelsner, *A Handbook of Weaves*: Dover Publications Inc, 1952

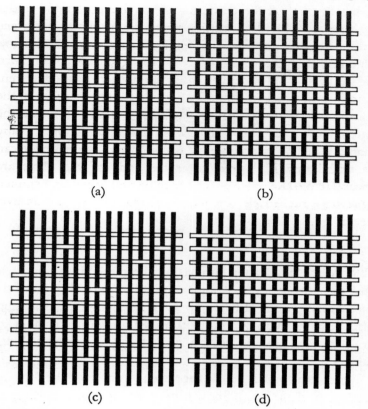

(a)   (b)

(c)   (d)

combined, enabling a child to improvise his or her own fabric
or wicker patterns.

265 Bead weaving and stringing

Tools and materials: beads (see 181);
string and twine; or threader (see 17)

Pre-schoolers enjoy stringing beads, macaroni, and drinking-
straw ends. (See also 17.) This develops finger dexterity and
the discovery of patterns. More advanced bead work is
usually done on a loom,* but for most purposes the bead

* Mary White, *How to Do Bead Work*: Dover Publications Inc, 1972

stringing method shown here suffices (see diagram). In combination with braids, knotting and macramé (see 254, 255 and 256), they permit invention of an infinite variety of bead stringing designs.

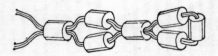

Needlework
266 Canvas work

Tools and materials: plastic mesh; punch needle (see diagram a); coloured wool yarn

Choose the wool after purchasing the mesh. It is important that the yarn is heavy enough so that it cannot slip out of the mesh easily, once stitched to it. This method of stitching, also possible with a simple threader attached to the yarn end, can be used to design and make multicoloured pile fabrics.

Thread the punch needle for the child or attach the threader (see 17, or diagram a). Show him or her how to pass the yarn through the mesh, the slotted side of the punch needle facing as shown, leaving as long a yarn loop on the underside of the mesh as the desired length of pile. Show how to feed yarn through the needle and hold the loop on the underside to assure that successive loops are more or less the same length. Different-coloured yarns, threaded into the punch needle and sewn into the mesh at various intervals, can allow the young craftsman to create colourful designs.

After the mesh is covered with stitching, turn it over and cut through the top of the yarn loops as shown (see diagram b). For permanence, cut a sheet of lightweight cardboard, canvas or linen that matches the size of the stitched mesh

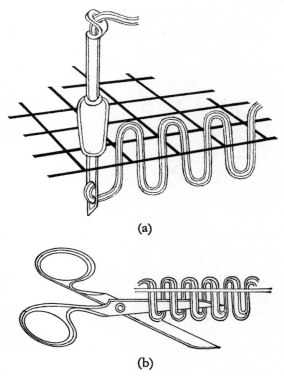

(a)

(b)

exactly, cover it with a coating of fabric glue, and paste it to
the underside of the mesh before cutting the loops.

267 Knotted hook stitching

Tools and materials: latch hook (see diagram a);
coarse plastic mesh; coloured wool yarn

This technique also produces a pile (see 266). Make a loop of
yarn and slide the latch hook over it (see diagram a). Pull the
hook down over the loop but leave it large enough so that
more yarn can be fed through the loop later. Bring the hook
holding the yarn loop down through one of the mesh open-
ings, feeding the loop into the next adjacent mesh opening

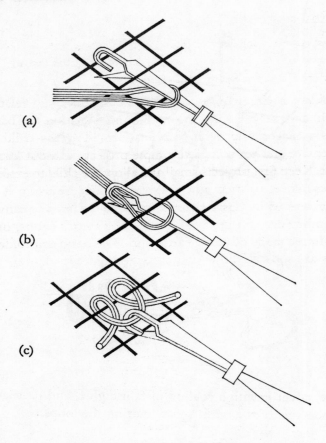

(a)

(b)

(c)

(see diagram b). Pull the free double strand of yarn through the yarn loop to form a double half-hitch (see 255, and diagram c). Cut the doubled yarn ends evenly to form the pile. If a number of different colour yarns are used, designs and pictures can be woven in this manner.

268 Embroidery

Tools and materials: tapestry or lacing needle (see 127);
coarse woven linen or canvas; yarn or heavy coloured thread;
embroidery frame; or heavy cardboard frame

Embroidery is closer to sewing than to weaving. It is related
to both and serves as a good first introduction to basic
stitches which, singly or in combination, allow the child to
be inventive and yet complete simple projects without losing
interest. Keep first projects small and allow the child to explore
the possibilities of each stitch shown to him by using it in
spontaneous sewing. Stretch, tack or staple the linen or canvas
to an embroidery frame, available in needlework shops, or a
simple frame made of heavy cardboard. The basic embroidery
stitches are shown below (diagrams a–k and 276).

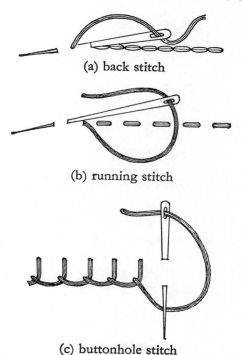

(a) back stitch

(b) running stitch

(c) buttonhole stitch

(d) chain stitch

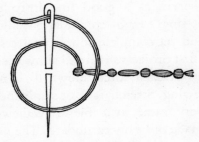

(e) coral knot stitch

(f) stem stitch

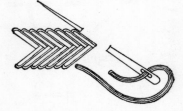

(g) fishbone

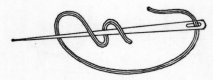

(h) French knot

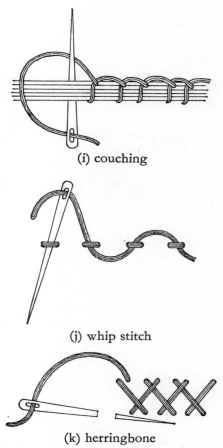

(i) couching

(j) whip stitch

(k) herringbone

Many of these stitches can be 'whipped' and bound with a thread of another colour (see diagram i).

Fine embroidery is usually done on densely woven fabrics; the coarser weaves allow the child to make evenly spaced stitches, using a tapestry or lacing needle without being confused. He can count intervening mesh spaces if he wishes. In couching, two or more threads are laid parallel on the fabric and then sewn on the material, using any of the basic stitches.

269 Crochet

Tools and materials: crochet hook; coloured wool yarn;
wool box (see diagram a)

The ball of wool should be kept in a cardboard wool box in
which a hole has been punched and the end pulled through

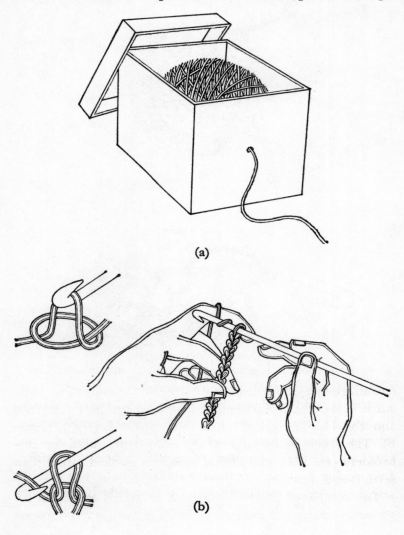

(a)

(b)

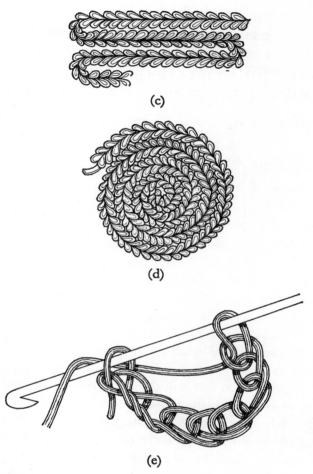

(c)

(d)

(e)

(see diagram a), so it cannot unravel accidentally. The basic stitch is the chain stitch, started with an ordinary slip knot and the loop pulled through and repeated (see diagram b). The stitch is identical to the chain stitch used for embroidery (see 268), except that here it is hooked rather than sewn (see diagram c).

The completed crochet chain can be coiled and sewn together in a variety of designs, round, square or hollow shaped (see diagrams c and d). At more advanced stages it can be crocheted together (see diagram e). Interweave or tie the loose end of a crocheted chain or design to the last loop that has been hooked.

The crochet chain is really the base material. The child can use it to improvise, often in combination with other knots and stitches (see 255, 268 and 276).

270 Knitting

Tools and materials: two knitting needles;
coloured wool yarn (wound in a ball and kept in a wool box; see diagram a on page 258)

Basic knitting includes four operations: casting on; knitting; purling; and casting off. Purling can be left out of the instructions at first, but the other three are essential.

Casting on: It is easiest for a child to learn to cast on using only one knitting needle. Tie the yarn end to the needle with a slip knot. Then twist the yarn into a loop (see diagram a) and slip the loop loosely on the needle. Repeat the slipping on of loops until you attain the width required for the fabric to be knitted (see diagram b). Do not pull the loops tight or they will be difficult to knit, especially by beginners.

Knit stitch: Pass the point of the second knitting needle through the underside of the first loop strung on the first needle (see diagram c) and lift off this loop (see diagram d). The second needle ends up underneath the first. Loop the excess yarn over the point of the second needle, back to front, as shown. Next, push the point of the second needle down close to the first, and lift the inner loop now formed on the first needle on to the second needle (see diagrams d and e). Repeat the series of operations until all loops have been lifted off the first needle and knitted on the second. Reverse the position of the needles in your hand and continue to knit as before.

Purl stitch: Cast the yarn on the first needle. Pick up the first

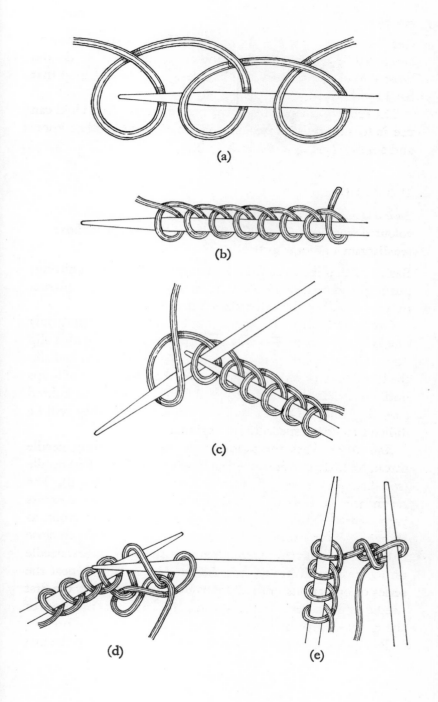

(a)

(b)

(c)

(d)

(e)

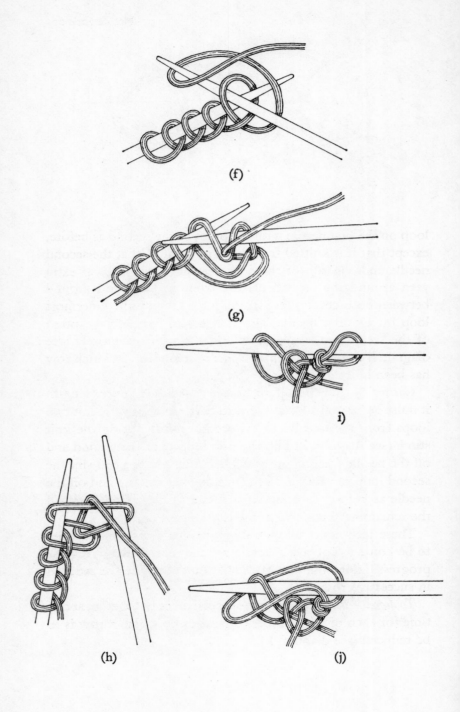

(f)

(g)

i)

(h)

(j)

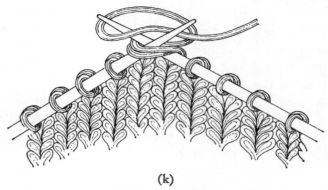

(k)

loop on the first needle with the point of the second as before, except that it is knitted from back to front so that the second needle ends on top of the first (see diagram f). Loop extra yarn around the second needle, front to back and around between both needles (see diagram g). Pick up the innermost loop on the first needle with the second, passing the point of the second up from below and lifting it off entirely (see diagram h). Continue to purl, reversing needles after each row has been knitted.

Casting off: When the fabric has reached the required length, it must be cast off so that the yarn does not unravel. Knit two loops from the first on to the second needle, using the knit stitch (see diagram i). Slip the first loop over the second and off the needle (see diagram j). Then knit another and slip the second loop remaining on the needle over the last and off the needle as before. Continue to the end of the row and tie off the remaining wool end to the last loop.

These techniques allow only square or rectangular shapes to be knitted. To vary shapes from the rectangular, a regular progression of a number of stitches must be added or reduced in successive rows.

To decrease stitches: Knit two successive loops together at one time for each of the number of stitches by which a row is to be reduced (see diagram k).

To increase stitches: Pick up one loop from the row just knitted and knit it into the next row for each of the number of stitches by which that row is to be increased.

Other methods for increasing and decreasing rows exist, but these are the simplest.

Different-coloured yarns used in various portions of a knit design allow the young craftsman to develop multicoloured patterns, cutting off the yarn used up to a point and tying on another of a different colour.

11 Fabric craft

The lif so short, the craft so long to lerne. *Geoffrey Chaucer*

271 Background

This chapter, like most of the others in this book, is not exhaustive. It concentrates on the development of a point of view and the beginning skills that can lead to more mature craftsmanship. The child's development follows that of the historic development of the various crafts themselves. The techniques for joining, fastening and binding cloth were primarily inherited from work with leather. The earliest clothing was mostly bound at the edges, laced and then draped, rather than sewn. Only the need to decorate, to make plain cloth more beautiful, inspired embroidery and stitching that ultimately led to more complex sewing. This in turn made it possible for woven cloth to be cut up in fitted patches which could be reassembled and sewn to follow the contour of the human figure and furniture. Inevitably this led to a need for a large variety of fine needles and other sewing implements and eventually to the sewing machine.

Sewing, other than hemming, was not widely practised in Europe until after the Crusades. But the needleworkers of the Orient and the ladies and their servants in European castles wove, embroidered and stitched decorative cloth for religious and regal ceremonies. Stitching and cloth-working skills served primarily to adorn royalty and nobility, as status symbols of wealth and power, and to enrich ritual. The techniques developed as playful and luxurious art forms before they were applied to everyday life.

Advanced sewing requires patterns. But it is a far cry from making such a pattern to merely following prefabricated patterns. Successful sewing of a garment depends on paper cutting, template making, and designing skills (see Chapter 2), not on just following an existing pattern. Without experience in inventing patterns, following printed patterns can be frustrating – and it results in ill-fitting garments.

To become familiar with the characteristics of cloth the child must first learn to explore and use the different kinds that are commonly available – wool, linen, cotton, velvet, silk and felt – as he would on being introduced to any other craft. He'll discover, for example, that fibres in all fabrics (except felt) unravel at the edges unless they are bound or hemmed. Hole-punching, lacing and binding, in cloth or in paper, give the child experience in joining one piece of material to the next. He needs exercise working in the flat as well as in working dimensionally in the round. He must start with relatively coarse thong or yarn until he can graduate to finer thread.

Cutting and pasting
272 Fabric pasting

Tools and materials: cardboard; fabric and felt scraps; scissors; glue or paste (see 21–8)

When buying glue or paste, check the label to discover whether it is suitable for fabric. Fabric adhesive should retain some elasticity after it has dried completely. Cow gum is not recommended.

Show the young child how to fold, hem and glue fabric edges (other than felt) to avoid unravelling. All the suggestions made for gluing paper apply (see 21–31, 88 and 125). (See also 165.)

273 Hole-punching and lacing

Tools and materials: same as 17–20, 126 and 127; fabric scraps

The same skills, tools and materials apply to cloth as to paper and leather. Lacing through holes punched into the fabric and binding it along the edges give the child a first insight into sewing cloth.

274 Snap fastening

Tools and materials: same as 130; fabric scraps

Snap fasteners are easily attached to fabric by children old enough to punch holes and handle a hammer. They can insert the male and female of parts of each fastener into holes punched into different or the same pieces of fabric and then secure them with the die (see 130). An adult can do this for younger children. Playing with snap fasteners, as with buttons and buttonholes, helps a child learn to dress himself.

Sewing
275 Cutting fabric

Tools and materials: scissors or pinking shears; fabric

Cutting shapes out of fabric with scissors or pinking shears requires prior experience with paper. Start the child with relatively small cloth scraps. Show him that it is best to pin or tape smooth and wrinkle-free fabric to a large sheet of cardboard by one edge before trying to cut it. Hold the bottom edge firmly in hand while cutting. Rather than snipping with the point of the scissors, the child should try to cut fabric from the bottom of the cutting edges, where the scissors blades are joined.

276 Basic stitches

Tools and materials: fabric scraps; large sewing needle;
coarse thread; thimble; pincushion

Show the child how to moisten and twist the end of the thread before trying to thread the sewing needle. Children who suffer vision or coordination defects should have this done for them. See 268 for basic stitches, which apply to sewing as to em-

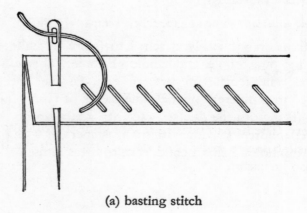

(a) basting stitch

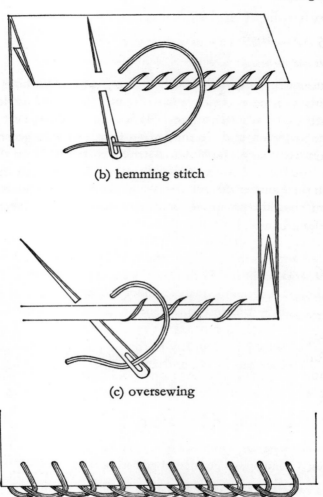

(b) hemming stitch

(c) oversewing

(d) blanket stitch

broidery. The first to be taught should be the running stitch, the easiest one to learn. The stitches shown in the diagram can also be useful.

277 Appliqué and quilting

Tools and materials: same as 268, 275 and 276;
backing fabric (linen, canvas or cotton)

Appliqué is essentially cloth collage, except that cut cloth shapes are sewn, rather than pasted, to a background. A running or back stitch (see 268) is easiest for beginners, but more complex and decorative stitches can be used by experienced young craftsmen. Assure that the child hems each piece of fabric before sewing it on the backing, so that the appliquéd shapes do not unravel at the edges. (See also 272.) Children in the youngest age groups should use felt shapes, or they can hem other fabric with tape.

An appliqué shape can be partially sewn on to the backing, stuffed with cotton wool or kapok, and then fully sewn to form patchwork quilting. Both appliqués and patchwork quilts can be designed spontaneously as the work progresses, or the cut shapes can be laid out in advance and pinned to the backing cloth with straight pins, sewn in position, stuffed if quilted, and then finished, using any of the simple or more decorative stitches described in 268 and 276.

278 Gathering and pleating

Tools and materials: same as 273, 275 and 276;
adhesive binding, or perforated gathering tape

It is easiest for beginners if they apply pre-punched or perforated binding or gathering tape to one edge of the fabric. By lacing through pre-cut holes children can form natural pleats. Or a child can punch holes into one edge of the fabric (see 273) after taping it with adhesive binding, or perforated gathering tape, and then lace and gather it. Pre-punched pleating tapes are available in needlework shops. The pleats can be left loosely gathered or the child can sew them partially or

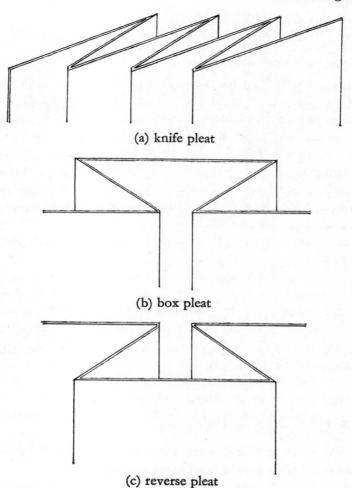

(a) knife pleat

(b) box pleat

(c) reverse pleat

fully, depending on the intended design or purpose (see diagram c). The three basic forms, knife, box and reverse pleats, can be gathered this way (see diagrams a–c, and the diagrams on page 44).

Pattern-making
279 Paper templates

Tools and materials: same as 63–5

Fabric that is to fit a three-dimensional shape requires a pattern. The shape around which the fabric is to be draped – a clothespeg doll, cushion or human figure – must be selected in advance and paper shapes cut to determine size and where the seams will fall. The paper pattern should be cut and assembled like the paper mock-up described in 64, and pieces added, snipped off or folded until they fit the shape to be covered with cloth. When completed, separate the mock-up so that it lies flat on the table. The flattened portions must later be cut out of cloth, hemmed, fitted and then sewn together.

Make sure the young craftsman adds widths of fabric on all edges of any portion that is to be sewn together with other portions, and along hems. Variations in fullness or shape of the finished garment may require tapering of edges, gathering or pleating (see 278). Armholes, for example, need special shaping so that sleeves, when sewn to them, don't bunch under the arms. Give the child opportunities to examine and if possible take apart discarded clothing or furniture covering along the seams, so that he can discover how to design templates for cloth.

The paper mock-up, when cut apart and flattened, becomes the template or pattern for the fabric. Such a pattern can consist of a single, flattened sheet which, when transferred to cloth, requires only folding over at seams and hems and sewing together, or of several individual shapes, each of which is hemmed separately and then sewn to the main body of the work.

280 Transfer from paper to cloth

Tools and materials: paper template or pattern (see 279);
straight pins; pincushion; tailor's chalk; cloth

Flatten the cloth on a tabletop and pin the paper pattern shapes
to it. Make sure that sufficient space is left between the shapes
for seams to be added where needed. Trace the edge of the
paper pattern on the cloth with tailor's chalk, adding a second
parallel line where an additional width for seams and hems is
required (see diagram). Keep the paper pattern pinned to the

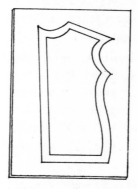

cloth until after it has been cut. Pleats can be indicated on the
paper pattern and then transferred to the cloth. Cover the
back of the paper pattern with a solid layer of chalk, pin it
again to the cloth, and trace the pleat lines marked on the
pattern with a ballpoint pen. They'll transfer to the cloth. Pin
the portions of traced pleats with straight pins wherever they
are to be sewn, after cutting the cloth, so that they can be
found and sewn later even if some of the chalk has rubbed off.

281 Sewing from a pattern

Tools and materials: same as 275 and 276

After the cloth has been cut and the paper pattern unpinned
from it, chalk the lines previously marked again to be sure

they will remain visible. Then sew along all marked seams, hems and pleats. Remind the child that all seams and hems must be sewn on the reverse side of the fabric and the final product turned over or inside out after it has been completed, so that the ragged cloth edges of seams and hems are hidden.

Decorating cloth
282 Painting on fabric

Tools and materials: textile paints and solvent; fabric; bun tin for mixing colours; sable brushes; cardboard mat, embroidery frame or canvas stretcher; newspaper-covered worktable

Textile paints are colourfast, and fabrics painted or stencilled with them can be laundered. Pin or tape the fabric that is to be painted to the mat, frame or stretcher so that all surfaces to be decorated are stretched on top over the opening. Make sure the fabric surface is wrinkle-free and reasonably taut. It must not touch any other surface while being painted or before it has dried completely. Caution the child not to over-load the brush or fabric with paint. A certain amount of crawl or bleeding of colours beyond the width of the brushstroke can be expected at times. Sections 136–9 and 153 apply to fabric painting, as to any other surface.

283 Stencilling and printing on fabric

Tools and materials: textile paints (for stencilling); textile printing inks

See 205–8 for scrap materials printing; 214 and 215 for general printing instructions; 210 for cylinder printing; 211–13 for linoleum-block making and printing; 220 for stencil making and printing. All these processes apply to printing on fabric.

284 Dyeing

Commercial fabric dyes, like those used for leather, are highly toxic. They must be kept out of reach of small children, and even more mature ones should not be allowed to use them. However, young people can learn to make and use relatively non-toxic vegetable dyes. But note that even the most harmless dyes, due to their high concentration, can be irritating to the skin of some young people.

Before fabric can be dyed it must be treated with a mordant so that it is colourfast when dyed. The cautions about dyes apply to mordants too. Young people should wear rubber or plastic gloves, work in well-ventilated areas, and avoid inhaling the fumes from the boiling mordant and dye baths.

To prepare cloth for dyeing, the following are needed:

Tools and materials: copper or enamel pans, large enough so that the fabric to be dyed can be completely immersed and stirred in mordant and dye bath without spilling; mordant (see below); dye (see below); long-handled wooden spoon

Preparing wool for dyeing: Wash the fabric thoroughly in warm water and soap or detergent. Fill a pan with the required amount of water (see caution above) and bring to the boil. Add 25g (1 oz) of alum and 6g ($\frac{1}{4}$oz) of cream of tartar for every 4 litres (gallon) of water. Immerse the fabric in the mordant and boil slowly for one hour. Stir the fabric with a wooden spoon to assure even saturation. Let the mixture and fabric cool until it can be handled safely, and then rinse the fabric thoroughly in cool water. Squeeze out excess moisture without twisting the wool and let dry overnight on a clothesline. Whether or not it is completely dry, the fabric will be ready for its dye bath next day.

Preparing cotton, linen or rayon fabrics for dyeing: Wash the fabric as above and boil the water. Add 25g (1oz) of alum and 6g ($\frac{1}{4}$oz) of ordinary baking soda for every 4 litres (gallon) of water and proceed as with wool fabrics.

Preparing the dye bath: The following dyes can be made by boiling various plants, roots, nuts and berries until the solution reaches the desired colour intensity. Gather plants while they are young – roots in the autumn; leaves as soon as they are full grown; and berries, seeds and nuts when they have ripened.

Vegetable matter	*Colour*
Goldenrod (chop the whole plant into small segments and boil)	Yellow
Pear or peach tree leaves	Pale yellow
Black walnut husks and shells	Yellow-brown
Sunflower seeds and larkspur flowers	Blue
Beets	Violet
Dandelion roots	Dark pink

You can mix and dilute these to obtain other colours and shadings – blue and yellow make green, for example. Add the concentrated dye to a pan of gently boiling water. Be sure not to fill the pan more than enough to soak and cover the fabric (see caution above). Keep the pan boiling gently while the cloth is immersed and keep stirring with a wooden spoon until the fabric is dyed a colour of the desired intensity. Then remove with the spoon, rinse in clear running water, squeeze out the excess moisture gently, and hang with clothes-pegs from a line so that the cloth does not come into contact with itself or any other surface until it is completely dry.

285 Tie-dyeing

Tools and materials: fabric; mordant (see 284); dyes (see 284); thread or twine; steam iron and ironing board

Tie-dyeing is an ancient craft. Cloth is crumpled and tied into a ball, twisted into a spiral and tied, or folded and tied, or sewn temporarily so that, when immersed in a dye bath, the colour penetrates the fabric in certain places only. It is dyed according to the degree of penetration of the colour into the folds and creases of the wadded-together, tied or sewn fabric.

The illustrations show some of the methods of crumpling, twisting, folding, tying and sewing cloth for immersion in a dye bath (see diagram). The fabric must first be thoroughly washed and immersed in mordant and ironed, before it is prepared for the dye bath (see 284).

Index

MARRY IN HASTE

By agreement, theirs is a marriage in name only, but how can Camilla help falling in love with her misogynist husband, Lord Leominster? Marrying in haste, she has much to repent at leisure, particularly her own rash suggestion that her flighty young sister-in-law, Chloe, go with her and her formidable husband to his diplomatic post in Portugal. It is 1807, and things there are in turmoil, with Napoleon's armies poised to crush Great Britain's oldest ally. While Lord Leominster goes about his secret business, Chloe's rashness plunges them all into misunderstanding and disaster. Separated from Leominster by tide of war, Camilla and Chloe spend a hazardous and eventful winter in hiding both from the French and from more intimate enemies. Reunion, next year, is fraught with surprise for them all.

MARRY IN HASTE

by
Jane Aiken Hodge

HODDER AND STOUGHTON

Copyright © 1961, 1969 by Jane Aiken Hodge

First published as *Camilla* in *Ladies' Home Journal*
This edition 1969

SBN 340 10653 0

Printed in Great Britain for Hodder and Stoughton Limited, St. Paul's House, Warwick Lane, London, E.C.4. by Butler & Tanner Ltd, Frome and London

To the Reader

This book was written eight or nine years ago when it appeared, as *Camilla*, in the *Ladies Home Journal* and *Everywoman*, but somehow never achieved book form. I reread it the other day, when I was working on the same period of Portuguese history for *The Winding Stair*, and found myself, shamelessly, enjoying it. If I were writing it today, it would doubtless be different, but not necessarily better. As it stands, it should really be dedicated to Georgette Heyer, to whom we all owe so much pleasure. And, as it stands, I hope you enjoy it too.

Jane Aiken Hodge

Chapter 1

Catkins shivered in the cold spring wind that blew bitter gusts around Camilla's ankles. Shivering too, she pulled her light shawl more closely around her and wished for the warm pelisse that lay in her box. She had packed in such hurry and despair that there had been no time to think of the discomforts of a journey by the mail coach. Mrs. Cummerton, hysterical, reproachful and then hysterical all over again, had insisted that she catch today's coach to London. What with her pupils' lamentations at her going, her employer's reproaches and Gerald's insulting apologies, there had been no time for thought.

And now, at the lonely cross roads, she was beginning to wonder if she could have missed the coach after all. Mrs. Cummerton's coachman, who had deposited her here, had assured her with rough, unspoken sympathy that the mail coach from Bath would stop somewhere between half past four and five. 'Allays does, miss, allays has, allays will, for all I know. Has to pick up Lord Leominster's mail, see, him being a bigwig, as you might say, and own cousin to the Duke of Portland. So rest you here, miss, and wait for it,' he had concluded, 'and you'll be in London by morning, sure as eggs.'

And for a while she had been happy enough, after the day's alarms, to sit quietly on her box in the country road, listening to the evensong of starlings and trying not to think about what was past—and what to come. Memory of Mrs. Cummerton's insults was, she found, rather less unpleasant than expectation of what her father would say. He had told her this project would never do

7

and he had been, odiously, and for once in his life, right. Best not to think about it. She rose to her feet and took a brisk turn down the road to the corner from which the coach should come. The air was colder now, the shadows long, the starlings almost silent. It would be night soon, and where was the coach?

As if in answer to her question, she heard, far off, the rumbling of wheels and soon a carriage clattered into view. At first hearing it, she had hurried back to stand by her box, but as it came nearer, her heart sank. This was not the mail coach, with its sweating job horses, its coachman and uniformed guard, but a gentleman's carriage, drawn by four elegant bays. As it passed her, she heard an order shouted from within, the coachman reined in his horses, and when it stopped a little further down the road the groom jumped down from his perch and came back to speak to her.

'Excusing me, miss,' he said, removing his livery cap, 'but would you be a-waiting for the mail coach?'

'Yes,' she looked at him doubtfully in the gathering twilight.

'Because if you are, master said to tell you it's met with an accident.' Suddenly he became human. 'We passed it not three miles back, as deep as you please in the mud, one wheel gone and splinter bar broke, coachman swearing hisself hoarse, passengers moaning and guard in fits on account of he'd lost the key to the mail box as he fell. Only good thing is, it happened not five minutes' walk from the King's Head . . . Anyway miss, you won't see no coach before morning, if then, and so master said I had best warn you.'

'It was kind of him to think of it. But what am I to do?' The question was addressed more to herself than to him, but he took it seriously enough.

'Why, what but go back where you come from and wait for tomorrow's coach. Master said as how I was to help you with your box, if so be you needed it.'

'It is very good of him,' she said again, almost automatically. Her mind was in a whirl. No coach tonight. What should she do?

To return to Mrs. Cummerton's, after what had passed, was impossible. And yet, what else could she do? She turned again to the man. 'Is there an inn at the village where I could spend the night?'

'Well, miss, I dunno,' he was beginning doubtfully, when an imperious voice summoned him back to the carriage. With an awkward apology he turned and left her at a trot. With him went hope. It had grown darker as they talked and she observed that the coachman had spent his time in lighting the carriage's lanterns. A fine rain was now blowing in the wind and she felt its icy fingers begin to find their way through her shawl. Soon she would be wet through. Should she run after the man and put her plight to his unknown master? Surely no one would be so callous as to leave her benighted here. But it was already too late. The man had jumped back to the box and the carriage had begun to move. She watched with sinking heart, then felt her hopes revive as the coachman took his horses in a wide turn on the grass verge and drove rapidly back towards her. Again the groom leapt from his box, but this time it was to open the carriage door and let down the steps. A tall man in a many caped travelling coat emerged, removed his beaver to reveal close-cropped dark hair and approached her with a bow that would have won the approval of Brummell himself.

'I fear you are like to find yourself benighted here.' His voice was low, pleasant, almost diffident. 'Perhaps I may have the honour of driving you back to your friends' house. My man has informed you, I think, that the mail coach does not run tonight. But allow me to present myself, Leominster, at your service.'

'And I am Camilla Forest, and much beholden to you for your kindness. If you would but be so good as to give me conveyance to the nearest inn . . .' She stammered to a halt, painfully aware of how strange a request this must seem, how odd, indeed, her whole plight. And of all people it must be Lord Leominster who had discovered her—the haughty earl, Mrs. Cummerton called

9

him, too high in the instep to take notice of his untitled neigh-
bours.

'To the inn, Miss Forest?' He could not quite keep the question
out of his voice, but turned nevertheless, to tell his servant to take
up her box and then, taking her arm, helped her up the steps into
the carriage.

'But you are wet through.' He settled her in a corner and
wrapped a fur rug warmly around her. 'This has been an ill-
managed business on someone's part. You will pardon me if I ask
what your parents are thinking of to let you be wandering about
the countryside like this.'

She gave a little laugh, half amusement, half bitterness. 'I fear I
owe you an apology for trespassing on your good nature under
what I fear you may think false pretences. I am not a young lady,
sir, but a governess.'

His reaction to this tragic pronouncement, was, surprisingly, a
laugh. 'You are a very young one then,' he said, 'or your voice
belies you. And you must allow me the privilege of protecting
you just the same. I have yet to learn that it is impossible to be a
governess and a young lady at the same time.'

This came near the bone and she found it, for a moment,
impossible to reply. He was looking at her thoughtfully, and she
was grateful for the near darkness of the carriage that hid her
blush. At last he seemed to come to a conclusion.

'I have no possible right, of course', he said, 'to question you
about the predicament in which you find yourself, but surely
there must be somewhere more suitable than the village inn for
you to spend the night. It is not at all, I feel sure, what you are
used to. And besides, forgive me, even a governess has a reputation
to consider.'

'Particularly a governess,' she said, with some bitterness. 'But
needs must, Lord Leominster, and I shall rely on your goodness
not to mention tonight's happenings.'

'Oh, as to that, it is a matter of course.' He sounded mildly affronted, then returned to the attack. 'And I am to abandon you, then, to the tender mercies of Tom Marston at the Blue Boar and his slattern of a wife? Surely, Miss Forest, it would be better to return to your previous place, however terrible the umbrage in which you left.'

She laughed again with that mixture of bitterness. 'I fear you mistake the matter somewhat, my lord. The boot is on the other foot. I have been turned off, in disgrace. I cannot possibly go back.'

His laugh, in the darkness, echoed hers. 'I see. And what heinous crime, I wonder, have you committed. No, no; a moment; let me guess. I do not for a moment believe that you have been making free with your employer's diamonds — or her port. But, let me see, she has an older son, perhaps, your charges' brother; indeed, I believe I could name him. You are come, I take it, from Mrs. Cummerton's house.'

She gasped. 'How in the world did you guess?'

'Easily enough. You must not think, because I am known as the arrogant earl, that I am not passably well informed as to what goes on in the district. I have a housekeeper who considers it her duty to keep me *au courant* with the local gossip. So naturally I know that Mrs. Cummerton recently engaged a French governess for her children and was thought to be giving herself considerable airs in doing so. And equally I know of Gerald Cummerton — who does not? I can only wonder at his mother's idiotism in engaging you in the first place. But then, I always understood her to be a fool. The only thing, I confess, that does surprise me is that you should be French. You do not sound it.'

'Thank you.' Eagerly. 'I do not wish to.'

'No?' He considered it. 'I remember about you now. Mrs. Lefeu, my housekeeper, said you would never do at Mrs. Cummerton's because — forgive me — you were so much better born than your mistress. You are Mademoiselle de Forêt, are you not, daughter of the Comte de Forêt.'

11

'No!' Almost angrily. 'I am Miss Forest, if you please, English bred, if not English born. I ask you, sir, what is the use of clinging to an empty title? For a year or two, perhaps, it did well enough. One was always going back tomorrow, or at least next week. But it is seventeen years now since we fled from France and I have not found a title much substitute for a competence. Nor does it seem likely that we shall be returning in the near future.'

'No,' he said thoughtfully, 'you are right there. Bonaparte is well in the saddle and I do not suppose you would find it in your heart to compound with him.'

'I should think not indeed.' She flared out at him. 'You do not understand, sir. My only memories of France are of the terror and our escape; of blood and tumult which killed my mother—and my brother too, for all I know to the contrary. Do you think I wish to go back there, on any terms? The only kindness I have known—and I have known much—has been in England. I am as English as you, sir, perhaps more so, because I know how lucky I am.'

He laughed. 'I am glad you think so. I would not, myself, have considered it the height of good fortune to be waiting, in the rain, for a coach that did not come. Nor, indeed, would working, in any capacity, for Mrs. Cummerton be my ideal of worldly bliss.'

It was her turn to laugh. 'Nor mine, I assure you, sir, though in all fairness I should say that it was tolerable enough until Gerald came home from Oxford. One of the advantages of being a governess is that you see so little of your employers.'

'Indeed.' He sounded amused. 'It seems a barren enough recommendation. But, tell me, what possessed your friends to let you go as a governess in the first place?'

'What else could I do?' The bitterness was back in her voice. 'One cannot go on, forever, depending on the bounty of strangers. Oh, they were kindness itself at Devonshire House, but . . .' She paused. The less she said about life at Devonshire House since the Duchess died the better.

12

But he had turned away to look out of the carriage window into the darkness. 'Here we are at the Blue Boar.' The carriage had slowed to a halt and the groom now opened the door and let down the steps. Camilla made as if to rise, but Leominster remained seated between her and the carriage door, looking doubtfully into the darkness.

'I am sure I do not know how to thank you, sir,' she began, but he interrupted her.

'No.' Abruptly. 'It will not do. You cannot possibly spend the night here, Miss Forest. It will be far better to risk your reputation at my house than your health here. And, for the matter of that, though I have no doubt you have heard me described as the proud earl, that, I think, must have been the worst of the slanders against me. Besides, I have an excessively respectable housekeeper in Mrs. Lefeu, who is also, as she frequently reminds me, my seventh cousin six times removed. I think you had much best pass the night at Haverford Hall.' Without allowing her time to answer, he gave the necessary order and then settled back, with a sigh of relief, in his corner of the coach. 'How I dislike making decisions. But you were speaking of Devonshire House. Were you indeed brought up in that *galère*?'

'Yes. My mother made great friends with the Duchess when she visited Paris in 1789.' And then, returning to the matter in hand, 'It is very good of you truly, Lord Leominster, however, I do not know whether I should accept your kind invitation.'

He gave an angry and, to her, unfamiliar exclamation, then continued on a milder though still formidable note. 'You quite mistake the matter,' he said, 'you have not been invited so much as abducted. I am not the arrogant earl for nothing and I intend you shall spent the night at Haverford Hall. If it makes you feel happier about it, I am probably old enough to be your father and have yet to meet the woman for whom I would trouble myself so much as to miss a day's hunting. You will be safe enough with me, a good deal safer than in the hands of the rascally landlord of the Blue Boar, about whom I know nothing good. So, come, let us say no more about it and do you tell me, instead, what you think of Lady Elizabeth Foster.'

'She has always been kindness itself to me.' Her voice was dry.

'And therefore you found it necessary, on the death of your original patroness, to find yourself a situation.' Again there was a note of laughter in his voice. 'But it is not fair to tease you, Miss Forest, and you are right to refuse to gossip about her, and equally right not to remain at Devonshire House under such ambiguous circumstances. It is bad enough for the Duke's own children . . . but I will not gossip either. Tell me, instead, what possessed you to think Mrs. Cummerton a possible employer?'

'Have you ever tried to find a position for a governess?' she asked.

'Why, no, since you ask me, I do not believe I have. But what is that to the purpose?'

'Because if you had, you would not ask such foolish questions.' She was amazed at her own temerity, but, once in, went boldly on. 'There is not such a demand for governesses, specially ones educated at Devonshire House, that I found myself in a position to be particular. I was grateful to Mrs. Cummerton for sinking the gossip in the snob and engaging me.'

'And what will you do now?' he asked.

It was what she had been wondering herself, but she contrived a confident enough answer. 'Oh, visit my father for a little while and redeploy my forces.'

'Your father? Oh, yes, of course, the Comte de Forêt. I have met him, I think, where can it have been?'

'At Watier's, I have no doubt, or one of the other gambling clubs. I hope you did not play with him, sir.'

She was aware of his eyes, in the near darkness of the carriage, fixed on her with an uncomfortably piercing scrutiny. Then, 'I beg your pardon,' he said, 'I would not have spoken of him if I had remembered the whole in time. But consider, Miss Forest,

14

that it is not given to everyone to shine in adversity. His example makes your behaviour the more exemplary.' He broke off. 'I cry your pardon again. It is inexcusable to preach at you so. But here we are at last at Haverford Hall where you are to consider yourself my guest, under whatever protest you wish, until morning. And here, you will doubtless be glad to see, is my cousin Harriet to greet us.'

The carriage door was flung open and Camilla saw a flight of wide stone steps leading up to a lighted doorway in which stood a stolidly middle-aged figure with grey hair under a dowager's turban.

Lord Leominster leapt lightly down, turned to give his hand to Camilla and led her up the gently sloping steps towards the light.

'Cousin Harriet, you should not be out here in the cold.' He shepherded them both indoors as he spoke. 'I have brought you a guest, you see. The mail coach has broken down and Miss Forest was like to be benighted so I have brought her home to you. She is sadly chilled and will be glad, I am sure, to be taken to her room at once.' A footman shut the big door behind them as his master made the two women formally known to each other. Most of the qualms Camilla had been feeling at this unorthodox visit vanished at sight of Cousin Harriet's formidable respectability. What Mrs. Lefeu thought about Camilla was another question, to whose answer she was far too well bred to give the least hint. She was busy, instead, with a speech of warm greeting for Lord Leominster who had, Camilla gathered, been away for some days on a visit to his grandmother, the Dowager Lady Leominster. As he answered his cousin's questions about this lady's health, Camilla was able, for the first time, to take a good look at her rescuer. She liked what she saw, but realised with a little shock of surprise that something positive about his manner, together with his own remarks about being old enough to be her father, had seriously misled her. She had been treating him as she would an uncle, or (if he had had any) a friend of her father's.

Now, looking at him by the warm candlelight of his hall, she decided he could not possibly be more than thirty, which, though a great age when viewed from the standpoint of twenty, is still hardly decrepitude.

More alarming still, he was formidably handsome. His dark hair curled shortly round a high forehead and his large and piercing eyes gave a romantic impression to his face which was somewhat contradicted by a straight nose and a small, firm mouth. Looking at him, Camilla was perfectly certain that she should never have agreed, however tacitly, to spend a night in his house.

He too, while apparently absorbed in talk with his housekeeper, was getting his first real look at his guest. He saw a slight, graceful girl, not beautiful, although there was something appealing about the large brown eyes in the thin face, and something else about her that he had recognised even in the dark carriage. An aristocrat through and through, he had been aware of breeding in her despite the governess's drab costume and awkward plight. He had known her for a lady; now looking at her, with her soft brown curls escaping from under the unbecoming bonnet, he thought her almost a child and it was with an adult's impatience that he broke off what he was saying to Mrs. Lefeu to exclaim: 'But Miss Forest is soaked to the skin and we keep her standing here. Had you not best take her to your apartments while a fire is lighting in the Blue Room?' Having thus indicated to his housekeeper that this unexpected guest was to be treated as an honoured one and given the best guest chamber, he took a quick leave of Camilla, hoping formally that she would do him the honour of dining with him when she felt more herself.

Camilla, appalled now at what seemed in retrospect her incredible boldness, merely curtseyed, too shy to speak and thus, though she did not know it, did much to win over Mrs. Lefeu, who had so far been regarding her with well concealed distrust. She had seen too many lures thrown out for her handsome cousin not to be suspicious of this child's story. Now, however, she reserved judgment, confining herself to polite nothings as she led the way up a handsome flight of stairs and down a long corridor to her own apartments, where Camilla, shivering as she removed her sodden shawl in front of the fire, turned to her with an impulsive gesture.

'Dear madam, what *am* I to do? I beg you will advise me. He said he was old enough to be my father and I believed him. He sounded so . . . so composed that I thought there could be no harm in spending the night here with him and his—excuse me—his housekeeper. But now I see it will not do at all. What shall I do?'

Thus approached, Mrs. Lefeu, who heartily agreed with her as to the impropriety of her visit, found herself in something of a quandary.

'Well, my dear,' she temporised, 'it is not perhaps an arrangement that would quite satisfy your friends. Can you not send to have them fetch you away? I am only surprised that Lord Leominster did not propose it.'

'But that is just the difficulty.' Camilla plunged headlong into the story of her troubles. Mrs. Lefeu, who had begun to purse up her lips when she heard that her cousin's protégée had been brought up at Devonshire House, relaxed a little when Camilla turned to her after describing the death of her patroness the Duchess: 'I loved her so. And then, when she was gone, Lady Elizabeth just stayed and stayed, "To look after the poor dear Duke," she said. And how could I stay then? It was bad enough for the others; but he was their father, they had to. But I—I could not bear it.'

'And quite right too,' said Mrs. Lefeu. The gossip about Lady Elizabeth Foster and the Duke of Devonshire had been widespread enough so that there was no need to pretend ignorance. 'So what did you do?'

'I went to stay with my father, but I found that would not do. either.' Camilla coloured. She did not wish to tell anyone how appalled she had been by her father's way of life. It was all very well to meet him, the man about town, sauntering elegantly in the park, but something else again to be let into the sordid secrets of his ménage. 'So . . . I could not think what to do for the best. We have no money, you know, Bonaparte has taken our estates. Father says we shall get them back one day, but what is the use of "one day"? Besides, I do not believe it . . . Anyway, one day is too late. I have to live now. So, altogether there seemed nothing for it but to go for a governess, and Miss Trimmer—she was the governess at Devonshire House you know—was so good as to find me a place with Mrs. Cummerton.'

'Oh!' Mrs. Lefeu was beginning to see.

'Yes. Mrs. Cummerton was only too happy to have someone recommended from Devonshire House. I do not believe she would have minded if I had been as ignorant as herself; all she cared about was to be able to tell her friends that she had me "from the dear Duchess" which was not true, since the Duchess died a year ago. But it went well enough, just the same, and I was fond of little Harry and Lucy. They were just beginning to mind me when Gerald came home from Oxford.' She stopped, colouring.

'I have heard about Gerald,' said Mrs. Lefeu helpfully.

'So I can imagine. Even the housemaid warned me about him. But what could I do? He was forever making excuses to come to the schoolroom, and how could I give him the setdown he deserved in front of his brother and sister? But to have his mother say that I encouraged him—' She stopped, scarlet with mortification at the memory of that scene in the shrubbery, where Gerald had come upon her unexpectedly; of the stale smell of wine on his breath as he forced his kisses on her, and the hot moisture of his hands on their rough way down the front of her dress. At first, when his mother had irrupted upon them, she had felt nothing but relief, but when she found that it was upon her and not Gerald that Mrs. Cummerton's reproaches fell she had flared up in self-defence. The result had been instantaneous dismissal and that weary vigil at the cross roads where Lord Leominster had found her. And so she was back at her immediate problem. 'Dear madam,' she said again. 'Advise me. What must I do?'

'Why, make the best of things, I think, my dear,' said Mrs. Lefeu kindly. 'And be grateful you have fallen into such good hands. At least you have nothing to fear from my cousin, who is indeed . . .' She stopped, then made a new start.

'For a moment, when he handed you out of the carriage, I hoped . . .' Again she paused. 'But what am I thinking of to keep you gossiping here? The fire will be lit in your room by now and you must be changing for dinner. Leominster always dresses, even when he is alone.'

'Alone? But dear madam, you will dine with us surely?'

'No, no. Our arrangement was, when I came to live here, that I would dine with him only by invitation. And tonight,' once again she paused, 'tonight I have not been invited.'

Chapter 2

Camilla found the Blue Room full already of firelight and dancing shadows. Her box had been unpacked and her best muslin laid out for her, but she gratefully declined Mrs. Lefeu's offer of her own woman, Hannah, to help her dress. 'I am used to manage for myself,' she said with truth, forbearing to add that her shattered nerves cried out for a few minutes alone before the ordeal of dining with Lord Leominster. And yet, when she was at last alone, she could not help a thrill of enjoyment at the unwonted luxury of the room. Life had been like this before, at Devonshire House, and now, as she brushed out her curls in front of the fire, the whole misery of the cold and dreary attic at Mrs. Cummerton's seemed like a dream. This was her world, and she was back in it at last.

But only for one night, she reminded herself, as she turned to the glass to adjust the soft folds of her dress and then, with hands that would not stop shaking, tied her one jewel, the miniature of her mother, on its ribbon round her neck. Ready all too soon, she turned from a last reassuring glance in the glass, then stood for a moment, hesitating, in front of the fire. The sound of a gong, growling somewhere below-stairs, alerted her. She must go down and face her host. And after all, she told herself, what was there to be afraid of? How often as she ate her meagre supper in the schoolroom at Mrs. Cummerton's had she longed for one more civilised evening. Now, she was to have one. Why not make the most of it?

Just the same, it was with some trepidation, and a becomingly

20

heightened colour, that she joined her host in the small salon Mrs. Lefeu had pointed out to her, and allowed him to conduct her, as formally as if they had just met for a great dinner, across the hall into the dining room. To her relief, this was not so formidable an apartment as she had feared. The mahogany table had been contracted to its smallest extent and as the room's whole light came from the heavy silver candelabrum that stood in its centre, it was possible almost to forget the outer reaches, where only firelight flickered. Settled on Lord Leominster's right, Camilla was able, for a moment, to consider him unobserved as he turned to give an order to a footman, and congratulated herself, as she took in his impeccable evening attire, on the trouble she had taken with her own.

The meal was a simple one, but was accompanied, to her slightly shocked surprise, by champagne. Catching her eye as her glass was filled, Leominster smiled at her for the first time. It changed his face entirely, transforming the rather formidable handsomeness into something infinitely more engaging. 'My butler thinks I am run quite mad,' he said, lifting his glass to hers, 'to be drinking champagne with my soup, but I hoped it would be what you would like. Besides,' his smile included her in a small conspiracy, 'I like it myself. I trust I do not need to reassure you that this is not the prelude to a scene of seduction. Nothing, I promise you, is farther from my thoughts.'

Camilla who had been wondering that very thing, smiled, blushed, disclaimed and drank to him. It was not exactly a complimentary speech, but it was certainly a reassuring one. 'Though indeed,' he went on, 'I have what you may think a slightly unusual proposition to make to you—later, when we are somewhat better acquainted. In the meantime, pray let me help you to some of this pâté which my chef, being a compatriot of yours, makes to perfection. But I beg your pardon, I remember that you did not wish to be considered as French. You have no hankering then, to return and throw in your lot with Bonaparte?'

'Good God, no. You must understand, sir, that I do not *feel* French. After all, I have lived in England ever since I was three years old. Patriotism, I think, is a plant of later growth.'

He seemed pleased with her answer. 'Yes, I suppose so. Though I cannot think that your treatment at the hands of the English has been such as to fill you with any great gratitude.'

'You are mistaken, sir.' She flared up at once in defence of her friends. 'Everything I am and have I owe to the Duchess of Devonshire. You do not understand – how can you? – what it is to be a refugee, to have nothing. If it had not been for her . . . I . . . I do not like to think what might have happened to me.'

He smiled at her very kindly. 'It becomes you to defend her, but surely to end up as a governess – and in such a house as Mrs. Cummerton's, is hardly the pinnacle of worldly bliss?'

'But that was no one's fault but my own,' she said. 'I could have stayed at Devonshire House forever, I am sure, if I could have borne it, and I have no doubt, if the Duchess had lived, I should have done so. Everything was different when she was alive. It did not seem to matter then that I was the object of charity, penniless, without a dowry, but when she died, everything changed. You have no idea, sir, how difficult it is to be the victim of benevolence.'

He smiled, signalled to the footman to refill their glasses and changed the conversation to politics. 'I collect, since you were brought up at Devonshire House, that you are the fiercest of Whigs,' he said, 'and think nothing Government does is right.'

'Why, not exactly.' She considered it for a minute. 'Because, you see, we *must* beat Bonaparte, or he will tyrannise over the whole world, and the Whigs do not seem even to be sure about that. But what are your politics, sir?'

He smiled at the direct question. 'Why, Tory of the deepest dye. In fact, I rather expect to be employed in the new government that is now forming – the Duke of Portland, you must

22

know, is my cousin, and you will, I am sure, have heard that we Tories carry nepotism to the point of scandal.'

'Nepotism, sir?' she raised delicate eyebrows at him.

'I cry your pardon. I am lecturing you as if you were a political meeting. Nepotism, Miss Forest, is the gentle art of giving jobs to your relations. You must have heard that we Tories are perfect in it.'

'Well,' she considered it, 'the Whigs seem to do pretty well at it too.'

'Ah, yes, but in their case, of course, it is pure coincidence. Or so they say. But tell me, now we have reached our second glass of champagne, is it possible that you have come out of Devonshire House heart whole? Are you not secretly wearing the willow for young Hartington? Or one of those noisy Lamb boys who hang about there?'

She coloured – what an extraordinary conversation this was – but answered composedly enough. 'Why, as to Hartington,' she said, 'no one who knows him could help loving him – as a brother – but I am not quite mad, sir. To be Duchess of Devonshire is something above my touch. Besides,' she added with transparent candour, 'I think I lived too closely with them all to fall in love with any of them.'

'So here you are, a full fledged governess, and, if I am not very far out in my calculations, twenty years old, and without a romantic attachment to bless yourself with?'

She laughed. 'You make my condition seem deplorable indeed, but I refuse to despair. We French, you know, are a practical race. I gave up dreaming of a grand romance when I was seventeen and began to understand that all the men I met were quite beyond my mark. Since then, I have had various plans. I should make an admirable wife for a country clergyman, I think; and a governess, you know, has frequent chances of meeting *them*. And, if all else fails, I can always set up as a *modiste*.'

'What a talented young lady you are, to be sure. You will be

23

telling me next that you are skilled in cookery and made that charming dress you are wearing. I cannot, however, think that you know Portuguese.'

'Portuguese?' She looked at him in amazement. 'What is that to the purpose?'

'Why, perhaps, a great deal, if you are indeed as practical as you suggest. Do you drink port, Miss Forest? No? I thought very likely not; it is hardly a young lady's drink. Marston,' he turned to the butler who had been, for some minutes past, hovering nearby in a faintly threatening manner, 'fill up our glasses, set the dessert on the table, and leave us. Miss Forest will take pity on my solitude and drink another glass with me. You see,' he turned back to Camilla, 'that I am something of a tyrant in my home.'

She had been thinking that on the contrary he seemed oddly ill at ease. Throughout the meal she had been aware of a curious tension behind the miscellaneous questions he had fired at her, and this awareness of strain in him had done much to ease her own nervousness. Just the same, now, with the room empty, the candles flickering and the fire burning low, she found her hands uncontrolledly shaking as she helped herself to the cheese Leominster recommended. What could the proposition be that he had spoken of at the beginning of dinner? Why had he asked her so many questions, almost, she thought, as if she were applying for a position? What was the cause of the strange excitement she felt burning beneath his outward calm?

'A glass of wine with you, Miss Forest.' His voice interrupted her thoughts. Solemnly they drank, then, his glass empty, he pushed his plate aside and leaned over the table towards her. 'Will you bear with me, Miss Forest, while I tell you something about myself?'

'Of course.'

'Good. Then to begin with, as I think I told you before, I do not like women. Anyone will tell you that. I do not understand them, I do not appreciate them, I do not want them. Please remember that. I never had a mother; my sister might just as well be my daughter. My cousin Harriet is well enough; she teases me, but not beyond bearing; but as for young ladies—heaven defend me. I know nothing about them, and I do not wish to learn. You will forgive me, I know, for making this plain from the start. You are, you have told me, a practical Frenchwoman; very well then, I have a practical proposition to put to you. Will you marry me, Miss Forest?'

'Marry you?' She could not believe her ears.

'Yes, marry me. On the strict understanding that it is a marriage of—shall we say—appearance only. You look confounded, Miss Forest, and I do not blame you. I fear I have set about this quite the wrong way. Let me explain. I have a grandmother, the Dowager Lady Leominster, to whom I have just been paying my yearly visit of duty. She is a fierce old lady with a great sense of family pride—and a close hand on the family purse. I have the title, this house, and a pittance with which to support them. My grandmother has millions, which I had always assumed would come to me, in the fulness of time. Yesterday, she told me that unless I marry, she will leave the whole to my cousin. So you see you are not the only one to know what it is to be the victim of benevolence.' His voice was bitter. 'You, with your spirit, which drove you out into the world as a governess, will perhaps ask why I do not snap my fingers at my grandmother and her money. But I have family pride too. I love this house and cannot bear to see it falling to pieces about my ears. Besides, a title has its responsibilities; there is my cousin Harriet; there are others, whom I feel bound to support. I had hoped, perhaps vainly, that I might find a solution to my difficulties in Government office. Now, I have been offered a place by my cousin—he wishes me to go as special assistant to Lord Strangford, our Minister Plenipotentiary at the Court of Portugal. It is a position of the greatest dignity and difficulty—and one that will cost me infinitely more than it brings in. And as if that was not enough, my grandmother has to tell

25

me that she wishes to see me married before I go. I tell you, Miss Forest, I was in despair when I met you, but since then, I have been beginning to hope. You are everything of which my grandmother would approve, and—forgive me—you are in a position where even the half marriage I offer might be—well, preferable at least to turning *modiste*. If you were head over ears in love, I would not have ventured this proposition, but you tell me you are heart whole. Would it amuse you to come to Portugal with me, Miss Forest?'

She had heard him out in amazed silence, now she thought for a moment before speaking. 'It is indeed a remarkable proposition, my lord. But have you thought closely enough, I wonder, about what you are doing? Your grandmother, you say, wishes you to marry out of family pride. Surely, if I may speak plainly with you, this means she wants you to marry and get an heir. May you not find, if you venture into the kind of arrangement you have done me the honour of suggesting, that you are saddled with the wife, and still deprived of the fortune for lack of the heir?'

He looked at her with a new respect. 'I confess that is an idea that has occurred to me. But my grandmother is a woman of her word; she has not stipulated the heir; she will hold to her side of the bargain. Besides, she is hardly to know on what terms we live —and—she is a very old lady. That is the ground on which she insists on my marrying forthwith. She wishes, she says, to see me established in life before I go to Portugal because she does not expect to live until my return. As a matter of fact, I have no doubt she will live to be a hundred, but there it is: she has delivered her ultimatum and will abide by it. And anyway, if I must marry, there could be worse times. It is bound to be something of a nine days' wonder, and we would be safe away from it, in Portugal. Besides, a wife is always a useful adjunct to a diplomat.'

Camilla could not help laughing. 'I must say, sir, that your proposal is scarcely a flattering one. "If you must marry" indeed. What do you expect me to say to that?'

'Why, anything to the purpose.' There was a note of impatience in his voice. 'I have been at some pains, already, to explain to you that this is anything but a romantic proposal. Flattering, on the other hand, in some ways, I think it is. You are the first young lady I have met with who has enough sense to entertain it for a moment.'

'Or enough foolishness.' Thoughtfully. 'But then, you must remember, sir, that I am only by courtesy a young lady. Do you really think your grandmother will be delighted at the news that you are to marry a governess? Not,' she hurried on, 'that I have at all decided to agree to your remarkable proposition, but I think we would do well to have all clear between us. And she does not sound to me like the kind of person who will take kindly to a déclassée grand-daughter in law.'

'What a sensible girl you are,' he said with approval. 'All your objections are admirable ones. Of course we would have to handle it with care, but I think if we make you known to her first, and tell your story afterwards, we will do well enough. Besides, she will be too delighted at having me marry at all to throw many rubs in our way.'

Again she laughed. 'More and more flattering. Well, sir, it is an odd enough proposition, but I tell you frankly I find myself so circumstanced that I must at least consider it. Since you have dealt plainly with me (and I am grateful to you for it) I will do as much by you. A year ago, I would not have entertained such a proposal for a moment. I was still full, then, of dreams of romance. Now, I am not so sure. Romance, I begin to see, is something of an expensive commodity and I am not sure that I can afford it. But tell me, when do you need your answer? I would like, if I may, to see my father before I decide. Not, of course, that I would tell him anything about your proposition. I can see that one of the terms of our agreement would have to be most absolute secrecy on both sides. It is not the kind of arrangement one would wish to discuss even with one's dearest friends.

Not,' she added reflectively, 'that I have any very dear friends. Which would make it all the easier. But, frankly, I would like to see if my father has any more eligible suggestion for me. Perhaps —who knows?—he has won a fortune at cards since I saw him last, and I may set up heiress on the proceeds. It is not, I can tell you, likely, but I would like to make sure before I commit myself to—forgive me—so desperate a hazard.'

It was his turn to laugh, somewhat wryly, and she found herself thinking with amusement that he liked her plain speaking no better than she had his. But he spoke with his usual grave courtesy. 'Of course, Miss Forest, you must have time to decide. That you will even consider my proposal is, to my mind, a great point gained. I must, in any case, go to town tomorrow to discuss the terms of my appointment and begin my preparations. It will hardly be possible for me to set out for Portugal until, at the earliest, the middle of May, and, in my opinion, our marriage, if you agree to it, should take place at the last possible moment.'

'Naturally,' again she could not help a little laugh.

'Before then,' he went on, 'we should, of course, have to pay a visit to my grandmother, and you, too, would have your preparations to make. You will want, I suppose, a trousseau, for which, in the circumstances, I shall consider it my privilege to pay. Altogether, the sooner you make up your mind, the better. Besides, I should be glad to have my anxiety at an end.'

'To be put out of your misery,' she said kindly. 'Yes, and, of course, if I should refuse, you will have to start looking about for another candidate.'

'Quite so.' He refused to be roused. 'So, all things considered, I would suggest that you do me the honour of accompanying me to London. We will take Cousin Harriet too, in deference to the proprieties. If you are to be Lady Leominster, you cannot be jauntering about the countryside alone with me.'

'Caesar's betrothed?' she said, teasingly.

'Exactly so. Indeed, I must ask Mrs. Lefeu to look out for a maid for you. And,' a new thought struck him, 'where are you to stay? I do not imagine that your father's lodgings will be quite the thing for my future wife.'

This was suddenly too much. 'Not your future wife yet, sir,' she said. 'You are going a little too fast for me. And naturally I had not the slightest intention of staying with my father. I am quite as well aware of what is suitable as you are, and plan to return to Devonshire House, where I have *carte blanche*. You would not, I collect, consider it beneath your dignity to take a wife from there.'

'I beg your pardon,' she was aware of his increasing respect. 'No, even my grandmother can hardly quibble at Devonshire House, though your coming from there may give her ground for some anxiety about your politics.'

She laughed, in charity with him once more. 'So that is why you asked me whether I was a fierce Whig. I can see that would hardly do for the wife of a Tory diplomat, any more than a secret passion for Lord Hartington, or one of those tiresome Lambs. But it is getting late, and you do not, I am sure, wish your servants to be gossiping about this any more than is inevitable.' She rose. 'I shall be most grateful for your escort – and Mrs. Lefeu's – to London. When do you intend to start in the morning?'

'Why, as soon as Mrs. Lefeu can be ready, which will be early enough, if I know her.' He too had risen and now escorted her ceremoniously upstairs to Mrs. Lefeu's apartments, where the arrangements for next day's journey were quickly completed, Camilla noticing, not for the first time, how absolutely he was obeyed and how entirely he took such obedience for granted. What kind of a husband, she wondered as she undressed in the luxurious warmth of her bedroom, would he make? Was she not mad even to consider his strange proposal? But on the other hand, what else did the future hold for her? She had spoken truly when she said that she had outgrown her romantic dreams. For some time now she had considered her future with a cold and gloomy realism. In this spring of 1807, Bonaparte remained all-powerful in France and even if she could bring herself to submit to him, the chances of his restoring the family estates were so slight as to be pitiful. She was condemned, as far as she could see, to be a displaced person for life, dependent on her father's slight support and her own resources for a livelihood. Her first experience as a governess had hardly been an encouraging one and what chance of marriage had she, dowerless as she was? Her hopes along that line had been dashed once and for all when the elder of Lady Elizabeth Foster's sons, after showing all the signs of a *tendre* for her, had made it clear that it was very far from being marriage that he intended. If she was not good enough for Augustus Foster, what hope of a respectable establishment had she? No, she told herself, as she began to drift off to sleep, she must think very seriously of Lord Leominster's proposal. After all, to be Lady Leominster . . . and besides however odd his proposal, there was no denying his attractiveness. And already, she thought, she had learned something of how to deal with him. He might dislike women (why? she wondered sleepily) but he could be brought to respect one who would not let herself be browbeaten. It might do . . . it might very well do. And she drifted into a sleep incorrigibly troubled by romantic dreams.

Waking, she told herself briskly that that would not do at all. If she did decide to marry Lord Leominster, it would be strictly upon his own terms. If it was to work there must be no romantic nonsense about it, on her part any more than on his. Just the same, she was human enough to take particular pains about her appearance, exchanging the governess's drab in which she had been expelled from Mrs. Cummerton's house for a most becoming travelling dress of dark red sarsnet which had been a present from Harriet Cavendish.

Hurrying downstairs, she saw, in daylight, much that last night's candles had failed to reveal, and began to realise the truth of Lord Leominster's remarks about his straitened circumstances.

The red Turkish carpet that covered the main stairway was frayed in several places, and the shadows of many years' candle smoke darkened walls and ceilings. In the breakfast room, where she found herself the first, it was the same story; the brocade curtains were faded and the chair seats that matched them had been exquisitely mended in several places. The house might be luxury itself compared to the governess's quarters at Mrs. Cummerton's, but compared instead with the extravagant elegance she had been used to at Devonshire House it was scarcely fit to live in.

The rooms, however, were beautifully proportioned and the window, to which spring sunshine drew her, showed a handsome prospect of beautifully kept lawn and parkland. It was like a man, she thought, to have spent all he could on the grounds and let the furnishings go. She was mentally repapering the breakfast room and hanging it with rose coloured curtains when she was interrupted by the fluttered appearance of Mrs. Lefeu, who apologised breathlessly for being late, explained that she had been at her packing since six o'clock, offered Camilla a choice of green tea or bohea, exclaimed about Leominster's absence and then, all in the same breath, greeted him warmly as he appeared from a door at the further end of the room. He in his turn greeted Camilla with the automatic courtesy of a host, announced that they had fifteen minutes before the carriage would come round, and applied himself to the consumption of devilled kidneys with a concentration fatal to the romantic visions that had wreathed themselves among Camilla's dreams. Very well (she helped herself largely to scrambled eggs) if he could play at detachment, so could she.

It was only later in the carriage that she began to be aware of the difference between them. However collected an appearance she contrived to present, behind it her emotions were in a constant whirl of indecision. Whereas he, having made his proposition and left her to decide, really seemed to have forgotten all about it, and was soon deep in a serious discussion with Mrs. Lefeu as to the comparative urgency of various repairs and refurbishments of the house, which she had apparently been pressing upon him. After listening for half an hour to their earnest discussion of the woodworm in the attic and the dry rot in the cellar, Camilla was in a fair way to flying into a miff, and had to remind herself that so far as Mrs. Lefeu was concerned she was merely an object of casual charity; a poor little governess who had been given a night's lodging out of kindness. Braced by this thought, she endured another hour or so of dilapidations and retrenchments, merely making a mental note, from time to time, that if *she* should chance to find herself in charge of the house, she would go quite otherwise about things. But then, of course, if she did marry Lord Leominster, his grandmother would be bound to increase the allowance she made him. Everything would be different.

Different indeed. But that was not the way to achieve detachment. She had told herself she would attempt no decision until she had found out how her father was circumstanced, and now firmly put the problem out of her mind, and turned instead to listen to her companions' talk. Mrs. Lefeu and Lord Leominster had reached the subject of the stables by now, and here it was evident that he would allow of no economy. His guests might suffer some diminution of luxury, his horses never would. Camilla, who had noticed with approval the handsome team of matched bays that drew his carriage, saw nothing out of the way about this. It would have been equally ridiculous to suggest that some local tailor might dress him as satisfactorily as the master hand that had cut the capes of his travelling coat.

Thanks to their heroically early start, they reached London betimes in the afternoon and Camilla was quite human enough to enjoy being driven up to Devonshire House in an elegant travelling carriage instead of dwindling to the door in a hackney as she had expected. She parted from Mrs. Lefeu and Lord Leominster with many expressions of sincere gratitude, and a little niggling worry at the back of her mind was set at rest when he promised himself the pleasure of calling upon her next day to make sure that she was none the worse for her journey. So he had meant it, last night. He would no doubt expect her answer tomorrow. She must lose no time in getting in touch with her father. To her relief, she found no one at Devonshire House but Miss Trimmer, who welcomed her with her usual reserved affection and told her that the family were in the country and likely to remain there for some time longer. This suited Camilla admirably and she sat down at once to write a note to her father, urging him to call upon her that very evening. He arrived with suspicious promptness and greeted her with an enthusiasm that boded no good, as his guardian angel, his '*Camille bien aimée.*'

Detaching herself as best she might from his port wine flavoured embrace, she observed with the still patience of constant repetition that she preferred to be called Camilla and asked him how he did.

'Villainously,' he replied, with that faint but unmistakable French accent that had won him so many female hearts, years ago, when French refugees were still a novelty. 'I am *au déséspoir*, Camille — Camilla, I should say, since you insist. You arrive most happily to be my saviour, *mon ange guardien* — and to make your own fortune, my love, which, no doubt you will think more to the purpose. I was on the point of writing to you, when I received your note.'

'Really, father?' She looked at him with a suspicion based on long experience. 'And how pray am I to set about being your saviour — and making this fortune?'

'Why, so easily, my love, that you will hardly believe it possible. But 'tis something of an *histoire*. Shall we not be seated and will you not, perhaps, offer your *vieux père* some refreshment?'

'Of course, father.' She rang and gave the necessary orders, while he prowled about the room with a restless air that made her wonder more and more just how he proposed to make their fortunes. Established with his necessary glass of wine, he raised it at once to drink her health, emptied it, refilled it from the decanter, drank again, and said, 'Well, *mon amour* what do you think of an advantageous marriage?'

'Marriage? For me? Father, you cannot be serious. How can I expect to marry well with no dowry?'

'But that is exactly the point of the whole *affaire*,' he said. 'The dowry will be provided, the groom is willing, it is but for you to say yes and our troubles are over.'

'And who is to be the lucky man?'

'Oh, *ma Camille*, always the cynic, always the sceptic.' He burst into one of his fits of exaggerated and unconvincing laughter, while she wondered more and more what was coming. 'But I have much to tell you, and first for a piece of news that will make you *folle de joie*. What think you of your brother's being alive all this time?'

'My brother? Charles?' She could not believe her ears.

'Yes, Charles. My son, your brother. Not dead in the Terror as we thought, but alive and well, the adopted son of some good people in Clichy who told him, only the other day, who he really was. Only fancy my heir, the future Comte de Forêt, masquerading all this time as M. Boutet, a butcher's son. And only see how blood will tell, for even as a butcher's son he has achieved distinction.'

There was a cold dread now around her heart. 'How, father?' she asked.

'Why, as one might expect, serving his country. It is a trifle embarrassing, I confess, but understandable enough that he should have thrown in his lot with Bonaparte. After all, he was not to know that he was an aristocrat—and besides, let us be a little realistic, *ma petite*. Nothing will shake Bonaparte now; he is master of Europe and will remain so. These bungling fools of Englishmen will be lucky if they can keep their own freedom. Any idea of their invading and freeing the continent is merely laughable—*à faire rire*. All they think of here is their party

34

squabbles; there is not a man among them fit to set up against Bonaparte. And then, only consider that poor exiled king, fit for nothing but the gout stool and water gruel. Who is he to rally the French to his cause? And what has he ever done for us, despite the years of faithful service we have offered him? Now, through your brother, only see what prospects open up before us!'

'You have heard from him then?'

'But *naturellement*, how else do you think that I know all this? There is a friend of his, even now, in London, who sought me out with the most proper messages of filial regard from Charles.'

'A friend of Charles's in London? But you said he was a follower of Bonaparte!'

'And so he is.' Not for the first time she recognised embarrassment under her father's joviality. 'And so, of course, is his friend, who passes, for the nonce, as M. Mireille, an emigré. In reality, he is here on a secret mission of the greatest consequence.'

'You mean, I collect, that he is a spy.'

'Oh, *ma Camille*, why must you always take things so awkwardly? I tell you of your brother's friend, and you must talk to me of spies. Do you not think the English have their agents, too, in Paris? But when you meet M. Mireille, as you will shortly, you will realise how wide you are of the mark and how greatly things must be changed in France. He is an aristocrat to his fingertips. I will not tell you his title—the less you know, perhaps, the better—but to find such as he serving Bonaparte—*ma foi*, it makes me sure it is time we went home, you and I. This England is well enough for a while, but to tell truth, I am passing weary of their roast mutton and that dishwater they call coffee, and as for their manners! I have stood their condescension long enough. To be treated as an inferior by such *canaille*; it is a wonder I have endured it so long. Why, only the other day, when I was walking down St. James's—'

'But, father,' she cut him short, recognising the beginning of

35

one of his long stories of offended dignity, 'what is this to the purpose?'

'Ah ha, *ma petite*, always so practical. You wish to hear about the handsome husband and the dowry *n'est-ce pas*? Well, so you shall. As for the husband, Mireille is the man and head over ears in love merely from hearing your praises, and, for the fortune, what say you to your share of our own estates, which I am promised on my return to France.'

'And what must we do in exchange, father?'

'Why, nothing of the slightest importance. Nor indeed would you have to return to France for the moment. Mireille is fixed in London for some time, so you would not be leaving your friends. I know how much the connexion with Devonshire House has meant to you; I am too good a father to snatch you away from all that.'

She saw it all now. 'And how much does the connexion with Devonshire House mean to M. Mireille?' she asked. 'Does he expect me to assist him in his spying?'

'Oh, Camille,' he shrugged despairingly. 'We are given a chance to recoup our fortunes, to go home to France, to see once more the brother you adored, and all you do is to make difficulties. Well, let me tell you then what I had hoped to spare you, that if you do not marry Mireille, I am a ruined man.'

'Ruined? What do you mean?'

'Why, merely that I owe him more than I can possibly pay. He has it in his power to disgrace me, Camilla, and all you can think of is your British niceties.'

Now she was beginning, indeed, to see. 'And because he has done this to you,' she said, 'you wish me to marry him.' She rose and took an angry turn about the room, then came back to face him. 'Father, you have surpassed yourself. But, tell me, how much, in fact, do you owe this M. Mireille?'

He was extremely reluctant to tell her, but she got it out of him at last. The figure, it seemed, was upwards of five hundred pounds and she knew only too well how impossible he would find the payment of such a sum. She was pacing the room again, in distracted consideration of his plight, when a disapproving footman appeared to announce that, 'A M. Mireille' was below asking for her.

'Tell him I am not at home,' she said at once, and then, when the man had withdrawn, turned on her father, who had made as if to protest. 'Really, father,' she said, 'this is the outside of enough. I collect you told him to give you the meeting here. Have you so little thought for my position that you would have me entertaining every Tom, Dick and Harry of your acquaintance, and with the family away, too.'

'But, *mon amour*,' he protested, 'your intended husband? Surely that alters the case? I wish you may not have affronted him by having him sent away. I had best hurry after him, I think, and explain.'

'Yes,' she said, 'perhaps you had. Say to him what you please, but do not tell him I have accepted him. He is no intended husband of mine.' And she cut short his further protests and exclamations by ringing for a footman to show him out.

Alone at last, she paced the room in an agony of indecision. So this was the help she had hoped for from her father. Well, she told herself, she should have known him better than to allow herself even to imagine the chance of assistance from him. But what should she do? He was all too evidently on the high road to ruin. Could she save him? Almost, for a moment, she was tempted to sit down and write to Lord Leominster, accepting his offer on the spot and asking his help. Then she thought better of it. That his offer must be accepted, and his help asked, seemed certain, but, from what she had already seen of him, she thought she would do better to leave him tonight in doubt, rather than to seem to fall too easily into his hands.

This decided, she went up to her room and unpacked her box, then joined Miss Trimmer for an evening of handwork and polite conversation. It was, she found, strangely soothing to be exchanging, once more, dry comment on the new ministers, the course of the war, and the new style in sleeves with this calm and reliable friend. Only, at last, alone in her room, did she let herself think of the future. 'Well, my Lady Leominster,' she told the pale, large-eyed reflection in her glass, 'and how, pray, do you do?' There was, of course, no answer.

Chapter 3

The morning had its own terrors. Suppose Lord Leominster should have changed his mind? But she would not even consider that possibility, setting herself instead to decide how to receive him. Theoretically, she certainly should not do so alone, and yet this was obviously essential. After some thought, she decided, inevitably, that the time had come to take Miss Trimmer into her confidence, and did so, telling her, of course, as little as possible of the story, and nothing about the strange nature of Lord Leominster's proposal. Always reliable, Miss Trimmer congratulated her warmly on forming so eligible a connexion and came, with her usual good sense, straight to the point. 'And he is calling on you today for your answer, you say? Well, I think I had best play mamma to you, my dear, since the family are all away. We will receive him together, if you will be ruled by me, and then I will act the part of a wise parent by leaving you alone with him.'

Since this was exactly the reaction Camilla had hoped for, she received it warmly and settled down to learn from Miss Trimmer whatever she knew of her future husband. This was not much, since Lord Leominster, as a Tory, moved in a very different circle from the Devonshire set. But Miss Trimmer had heard enough about his charm and promise to make the time pass very pleasantly for Camilla, who allowed herself, for a little while, to be soothed into the illusion that this was an ordinary marriage she was contemplating. At least, there was something very encouraging about the warmth of Miss Trimmer's congratulations, confirming, as they did, her own belief that a respectable marriage was worth achieving at almost any cost.

But the time passed slowly and when Lord Leominster was announced at last, it was with a sensation of astonishment that Camilla realised that he had come almost as early as politeness warranted. Nothing else about him betokened the eager lover, and Camilla, watching him exchange polite nothings with Miss Trimmer, could hardly believe that his proposal had ever been made. Only, when he turned to her with a gleam of—what was it? Irony? Solicitude? Or something between the two?—and asked her how she had found her father, did she know that it was all real enough. Suddenly overwhelmed with nerves, she stammered out an incoherent reply and was still further shaken when Miss Trimmer took this as her cue to rise and take her leave.

Alone with her, Leominster wasted no time. 'Well,' he said, 'you do not look, Miss Forest, like a young lady whose father has just won a fortune in the lottery. Nor,' he twinkled at her suddenly, 'like one who awaits a proposal of marriage. Is it so very bad? Do you wish you had never encountered me?'

Again she found herself at a loss for words. This would never do. With a fierce effort she pulled herself together and contrived to match his lightness of tone. 'On the contrary, my lord, I think I may have much cause to bless the day we met. But whether you will do so, I cannot but doubt.' And then, with a sudden rush: 'Tell me, my lord, have you any money at all? Without recourse to your grandmother, I mean.'

He laughed. 'Well, that's a frank enough question,' he said, 'and one, I hope that you find yourself entitled to ask, for the best of reasons. Yes, I have a few pounds to command at a pinch. Why? Am I to take it that you have found your father not so much fortunate as embarrassed.'

Not for the first time, she blessed him for his quick comprehension. 'Precisely so,' she said, 'and there is worse than that. I think, before there is any more talk of marriage between us, I must tell you the whole. You may well feel, when you have heard it, that as a wife I should prove more of a liability than an asset.'

40

And without stopping for any further doubts, she poured out the whole story, only minimising, as best she might, the sordid part played by her father and, by implication, her brother. At last she paused, looking at him expectantly, rather, he found himself thinking, like a young bird hoping for crumbs. A sudden, unfamiliar wave of feeling swept over him, part anger at her father, part pity for her desolate position in which, instead of being protected, she had herself to play the protector's role. But his voice lost none of its lightness as he replied. 'So, I take it, as a bride's present, you would wish your father cleared of debt? Well, with a little contriving, I believe it can be done, and you are right when you think I do not much want a father-in-law in Bonaparte's camp. You say he admits to five hundred pounds debt? Then, I suppose we had best assume that the total amounts to half as much again. Well, I am afraid Cousin Harriet must say goodbye to her improvements at Haverford Hall.' He rose to his feet. 'You had best give me your father's direction, Miss Forest, and let me handle this. But, first, have I your permission to announce our engagement in the *Gazette*? It will infinitely strengthen my hand in dealing both with your father and with this M. Mireille, whose pretensions I propose to myself the pleasure of depressing.'

'Yes, of course,' she said, then hurried on to a point that had been troubling her. 'You will not have M. Mireille arrested, will you?'

He laughed. 'As an acceptance, it lacks something of enthusiasm, but I thank you, just the same.' With a sudden, courtly gesture he bent to kiss her hand, then continued, 'And I promise I will do my best to make the married state tolerable to you. As for M. Mireille, do not trouble yourself over him. For one thing, he is not worth it; for another, I do not propose to do anything so drastic as having him arrested, which might, just remotely, involve you; but shall merely drop a word in the proper quarters. Once he is known for a spy, he can do little harm and may indeed do us good. But now, for our plans. My grandmother is most happily come to town—she wishes she says, to see the last of me—and I am sure you will agree with me that we should lose no time in making you known to her. With your permission, I will call on her even before I see your father and ask her leave to bring you to visit her this evening.' Again came that irrepressible twinkle. 'I think I can promise you that she will be the most surprised dowager in London. It is but three days since she made me her ultimatum, and here I present myself to her as a happily affianced man.'

'Yes,' Camilla considered it somewhat doubtfully. 'Do you think she will really *believe* it?'

'You are not exactly flattering, Miss Forest. Do you find it so impossible that I should be able to woo and win a young lady in three days?'

It was her turn to laugh. 'I cry your pardon. I am convinced you could do it in one. And besides your grandmother will doubtless be too charmed at your obedience to look too closely into my motives. But, my lord, I do not know how to thank you—'

He interrupted her. 'Then do not try. Or rather tell yourself that I rescue your father merely out of motives of self-interest, which, you must long since have realised, is paramount in my nature. And, Miss Forest, I must beg you to give over calling me "my lord" which might, indeed, rouse some justifiable doubts in my grandmother's breast. If you boggle at Maurice—and I should not blame you—my family name, Lavenham, will do well enough until we are better acquainted. And what, pray, am I to call you in return?'

'Camilla, my lord—I beg your pardon, Camilla,' she said, colouring deeply as once again the extraordinary nature of this engagement was brought home to her.

'Camilla,' he said with approval, 'a pretty name, and suits its owner.' And with this, the first compliment he had paid her, he took his leave, promising to call for her, that evening, and conduct her to his grandmother's house in St. James's Square.

He arrived punctually upon his hour and greeted her with a reassuring, 'All's well so far,' as he handed her into his carriage. 'I have seldom had the pleasure of seeing my grandmother so surprised.'

'And pleased?' she asked, somewhat wryly. 'Is she prepared to sink my past in my future?'

He laughed. 'You make marriage with me sound like some kind of barbaric sacrifice.' I promise you I will do my best to make it something less unpleasant. As for my grandmother, to tell truth, she reserves judgment until she has seen you, which in my opinion is more than half the battle. My only fear was lest she condemn you unseen, but she is all eagerness for the meeting. It has given her, she says, a new lease of life. And, of course, to see you will be to approve.'

She inclined her head gravely. 'That is the second compliment you have paid me,' she said, 'this is better and better. . .'

'It is more, I think, than you deserve, with your hints that I am some kind of modern minotaur merely because I am no lady's man. But I have more news for you, and what, I know, will please you. I have seen your father.'

'Already? Oh that was *kind* of you.'

He laughed. 'Think rather that I wished to have your mind clear for this important interview with my grandmother. Yes, I am happy to say that I now appear as your suitor approved by your father. No, that is putting it mildly; welcomed, I should say, and indeed kissed, most enthusiastically, on both cheeks.'

'Oh dear,' she sighed, 'I can imagine how you must have enjoyed that. I only hope it is the worst you will have to suffer for my sake. But what of M. Mireille, sir? What has my father's approval cost you?'

'Why, to tell truth, less than I had feared. I have met your other suitor, too, and put him roundly to flight. When I suggested to M. Mireille that a word from me in the proper quarter might put an end to his capacities for wooing for some time to come, he was only too happy to waive his claim to your hand and is now, if I mistake not, busy packing his traps ready for a precipitate return to France.'

'And the five hundred pounds?'

'I suggested to him that it would be well worth his while to waive his claim to that too. Blackmail, Miss Forest, is a game two can play at, and I was in very much the stronger position. No, you will have no more trouble from M. Mireille and your father is my very dear friend already.'

'Dear me', she said, 'how—' she hesitated for a word—'how competent of you, my lord.'

'Lavenham,' he corrected. 'I beg you will remember not to go "my lording" me at my grandmother's. I can see that you are disappointed in me, Camilla—I must get into practice too,' he explained in parenthesis. 'Does my method of ridding you of your difficulties seem odiously unromantic to you? I suppose it must, but you will, I hope admit that it has many practical advantages. Mireille dead at my hand—or even in prison—would prove a continuing embarrassment to us, Mireille in France is none. Besides, I have warned you already to expect no romance from me. But here we are. Remember, I beg, that my grandmother is a very old lady indeed and used to say what she pleases.'

Camilla laughed. 'I am glad to think somebody bullies you.'

Lady Leominster's house differed most remarkably from Haverford Hall. Here were no peeling paint and shabby curtains. The very smell of the house suggested beeswax, and everything shone, from the silver candelabra to the footmen's wigs. They were conducted, at once, to Lady Leominster's own apartments where they found her enthroned in an enormous velvet-hung fourposter bed. She was a little monkey of an old lady, so small, so shrunk, so shrivelled up with age that it was hard, until one saw her eyes, to imagine her as a rational being, still less as the powerful tyrant of a whole family. But her eyes told another story. Large, dark and brilliant as Leominster's own, they seemed, to Camilla,

44

to have an added something that his lacked—was it, perhaps, wisdom?

She held out a fragile claw to Camilla. 'I shall not kiss you— yet.' And then with a laugh, 'Very likely you will not want to kiss me at all.' Both voice and laugh were an astonishment, deep, resonant, and beautiful. 'But I am old enough to be tyrannical, as Lavenham will doubtless have told you, and you are young enough, I hope, to learn something from me. As for you, Lavenham, you will be so good as to leave us. We will get on very much better without you. Tell Chatteris to give you a glass of whatever you wish. I will send for you when I am ready.' And she held out her tiny begemmed hand to him in greeting and dismissal.

Alone with Camilla, whom she had imperiously motioned to a seat by the bed, she looked her up and down for a moment, then said, with a sigh of satisfaction: 'Well, at all events, you look ladylike enough.'

Camilla could not help a little laugh. 'Thank you, ma'am.'

'Hmmm—and got some spirit, too, have you? Why, this may do well enough yet. Tell me then, what makes you wish to marry my grandson?'

Camilla looked at her thoughtfully for a moment, then, 'Why, his money, ma'am,' she said simply.

Once again that amazing laugh rang out. 'And a very good reason, too,' said the old lady. 'If you had told me some stuff about love at first sight I would never have trusted you more. But as it is, we may deal admirably yet, you and I. So you have been out as a governess, hey?'

'Yes. I told Lord Leominster I thought you would not like it.'

'Not Leominster,' snapped the old lady. 'Lavenham to you and me—his first name is too ridiculous for use—Maurice—pah! But there were Lavenhams at Haverford Hall long before the house of Hanover was thought of—or the Stuarts either, for that matter. You are yourself of good family, I understand, despite the

45

governessing. The Comte de Forêt, is it not? Surely I know something of him?'

'Nothing good, I fear, ma'am,' said Camilla calmly. 'I come to you with many liabilities.' She made it a statement rather than an apology and it was taken as such.

'Oh, as to that,' said the old lady, 'you will find that we have enough of our own. To begin with, I must tell you that I hold the purse strings and shall continue to do so. Since you tell me that you are marrying Lavenham for money you had best understand at once that it is mine.'

'So it is easy to see, ma'am, by the state of this house compared with Haverford Hall,' said Camilla dryly.

'*Touché,*' again came that swashbuckling laugh. 'You have me there, Miss Forest. Is it so very shabby? I have not been there this age.'

'Deplorable,' said Camilla simply. 'It is worse than shabby, ma'am, it is falling to pieces. It will cost a pretty penny to set in order again.'

'Well, there is time enough to be thinking of that,' said the dowager. 'But let us return to you. This Mrs. Cummerton was your first employer was she not? And until you went to her you had lived at Devonshire House – as one of the family,' she added sharply.

'Yes, ma'am.'

'And are now back there?'

'Yes, ma'am.'

'And will remain there until your marriage, of course. Will the Duke give you away?'

'I have no doubt he would if I were to ask him. But you forget, ma'am, that I have a father. Whatever may be said against him, I will be given away by no one else. Besides, I do not wish it suggested that I am another of the Devonshire House miscellany.'

'That's good,' the dark eyes flashed approval. 'That's excellent good; the Devonshire House miscellany! No, we'll not have you

46

confused with that. But the Cavendishes will be there to dance at your wedding, I take it? Oh, it might be worse – it might very well be worse.'

'Leominster – I mean Lavenham – said you would be too happy he was marrying at all to make many objections to me,' said Camilla, greatly daring.

'Why, to tell truth, child, he was right there. I do not know when I have been more astonished – or more delighted. I only hope you know what you are doing. We want no more scandals in our family: if you marry Lavenham, you are to stick to him, understand?'

'Of course, ma'am, That is my idea of matrimony. But,' Camilla hesitated, 'you say, "no *more* scandals"?'

'Ha' It was a grunt almost of satisfaction. 'I thought he'd not have told you. Well, you'd best know, since it explains much about Lavenham that might puzzle you else. Besides, if I do not tell you, there will be enough kind friends to do so. Best hear it from me. What has Lavenham told you about his parents?'

'Why, nothing, ma'am. We have not, to tell truth, had much time for conversation.'

'No, I suppose not, since you only met – am I right? – the day before yesterday. But it would be years before Lavenham told you, and you had much best know now. Lavenham's father – my son – was killed in a duel defending his wife's honour (as he thought). She watched from her lover's carriage and left England with him afterwards. They are living still, in Italy. Lavenham was a child of ten at the time, his sister a mere baby. He has not, I think, forgotten.'

'Oh.' There seemed nothing to say, but then, 'He . . . he told me he did not like women. I could not understand it, but now I begin to see.'

The dark eyes snapped. 'Told you that, did he? A good sign, a very good sign. This may do yet. But you will have to be patient, child, patient as Job. Do not delude yourself this is a romantic

47

history you are embarked on . . . it is something quite other . . . Hmmm,' she paused for a moment, 'told you he did not like women, hey? Did he tell you he's had all the eligible girls in town dangling after him and paid them as much attention as he would a flock of sheep when he's hunting? I tell you, my threat to disinherit him if he did not marry was the throw of despair: I never thought it would work. But now, we must talk business, you and I.'

'Business? You mean I have passed?'

'Passed? Why, child, I am thanking heaven for you, on bended knees, or would be if it were not such a confoundedly awkward position. You'll do far better for Lavenham than one of those milk and water society misses who think marriage is just another kind of nursery game. You seem to have some idea of practical living, and I tell you, you'll need it with Lavenham. But now, to business. I shall buy your trousseau and put Haverford Hall in order for you. I shall also deal with Mrs. Cummerton—which should not, I think, be difficult—and launch you in society. If you are to be a diplomat's wife, no one must be able to cast the least slur on your antecedents. You have not, I take it, been presented, or made your appearance at Almack's, or done any of the things a young lady should? Well, it will be difficult, and that will make it interesting. I have not the least doubt in the world but that we shall succeed, if you will keep your head and do as I tell you. I shall also provide your dowry and give you an allowance independent of what I give Lavenham—which I shall, of course, increase. But I think it will be better for you—and for him—if you are in some sense independent of him. I would rather I was your tryant than he. And, one more thing, when you bear us an heir, your allowance will be doubled. Now, I am tired. Ring, and have Lavenham sent for.'

So there was to be no more discussion, and Camilla was relieved. The question of the heir was something she did not feel she could discuss even with her remarkable old grandmother-to-be. Nor, needless to say, did she mention it to Leominster who was, however, heartily satisfied with what she did tell him of the interview. She had wondered how he would take her separate allowance, but he welcomed it with evident relief. 'So you are to be independent of me. Admirable; we shall agree much better so.' It was one of those remarks of his that gave her each time a strange little pang about the heart and each time she told herself, angrily, not to be a fool. If he did not for a minute forget that this was a business arrangement they were embarked on, nor at all costs must she.

Lady Leominster had announced, in parting, that she was tired of being, as she put it, 'a bedridden old crone' and would be up betimes in the morning to take Camilla shopping for her trousseau. 'Clothes come first, always: society must wait.' Arriving, Camilla found her dressed in the very height of fashion of ten years ago and looking more like a performing monkey than ever. This morning, she offered a brown, rouged and wrinkled cheek for Camilla's kiss saying as she did so, 'I am glad to find you so punctual, child: we have much to do today. Lavenham has been here already this morning. His orders are changed: he must leave for Portugal before the month is out.'

'So soon?'

'Yes; they are having some crisis or other over there and apparently his presence is urgently required. He seemed doubtful whether you could be ready in time, but I told him not to trouble himself: we shall do it if it means hiring every mantua maker and milliner in town. He has gone off to arrange for a special licence, and you have but to decide, since it must be done at hugger mugger like this, whether you would liefer be married quietly in town or at Haverford on your way to Falmouth.'

Something in the course of this speech had alerted Camilla. 'Dear madam,' she said, 'forgive me, but I must ask. Does Lord Leominster *wish* me to go with him now?'

'Lavenham, child, Lavenham, if you love me,' barked the old

lady, and then, with her cavalier's laugh. 'What a sharp little thing you are, to be sure. I confess it had crossed my mind too that Lavenham was, shall we say, prepared to bear a delay. But I am not, and we'll not discuss it further. In many ways, too, 'tis an admirable arrangement. There will be no question, now, of presentation, or appearing in society. You marry Lavenham, leave for Portugal and return, at leisure, Lady Leominster full blown. I must look out some Dowager's purple: I have ladied it in the title alone for so long I shall hardly know how to conduct myself. But, come up to my room: I have commanded the attendance of all the best *modistes* in town and we must apply ourselves to tricking you out as every inch the diplomat's wife.'

That was the most exhausting week of Camilla's life. She did, between fittings, manage to make an opportunity to speak to Lavenham alone and ask him with a straightforward anxiousness that he found oddly touching, 'Do you very much mind having to marry me so soon?'

He laughed. 'Surely an odd question from bride to groom? No, of course I do not mind. The sooner, in many ways, the better.'

And with this Camilla had to be satisfied, though she could not help feeling that he sounded uncomfortably like someone swallowing a disagreeable dose of physic, to get it over with. Perhaps it was as well for her that she was too busy for much thought: it was not only her personal trousseau that had to be assembled, but almost the entire furnishings for a house. Her betrothed, who knew Portugal well, assured her that although the houses were handsome enough, she would not find a towel or a pair of sheets fit for an English beggar. They must take with them everything necessary for comfort, let alone luxury. 'You see how selfishly wise I have been in getting myself a wife to do all this for me.'

After he had left to make one of his long visits to Mr. Canning at the Foreign Office, Camilla nibbled slowly and luxuriously on the crumb of comfort he had offered her. She might, after all, be able to earn her keep as a wife, and perhaps his gratitude, by looking after his comfort in Portugal. She threw herself with a new enthusiasm into the choosing of the household linen for which old Lady Leominster was so lavishly prepared to pay.

After some discussion, it had been decided that the wedding had best take place in the village church at Haverford. Lady Leominster, who normally proclaimed herself far too aged and infirm to travel, was so miraculously rejuvenated by a week of hard labour and constant bullying of tradesmen that she pronounced herself easily fit for the journey. 'And besides,' she twinkled at Camilla, 'it will give me an opportunity to see just what kind of a fortune I have committed myself to spending in setting the house to rights for you.'

She and Camilla's father were to be the only witnesses at the wedding. Camilla, on learning this, had raised a problem that had been troubling her. Lavenham had come in, briefly, on his way to the Foreign Office to discuss the arrangements for shipping their household stuff and he and his grandmother had then turned to the order of the journey down. Learning from this that only her father was expected to go with them, Camilla had ventured to interrupt. 'But surely,' she said, 'will not your sister be accompanying us?' She had wondered several times why no move had been made to make her known to Lavenham's sister, who was, she knew, at a school on the outskirts of town, and now it seemed that Lady Chloe Lavenham was not even to be present at her wedding.

'Chloe?' Lavenham raised an eyebrow. 'I confess I had not thought it necessary. What think you, ma'am?' As usual, he referred the point to his grandmother.

'I think she had much best stay at school and try to learn some conduct,' said the old lady roundly. And then, seeing Camilla's amazed expression, she laughed. 'I collect Lavenham has told you nothing about his sister. Oh well, unpleasant duties always fall to my share. Go to your appointment, Lavenham, for which I suspect you are already late, and I will explain to Camilla why Chloe had best not grace your wedding.' And then, after Lavenham had taken his leave: 'You will think our family cursed with scandal, child, when I tell you that, young though she is, Chloe has already come near to disgracing us all. What think you of her trying to elope, at sixteen, and with the music master? Did you ever hear of anything so gothic?'

'Well,' said Camilla thoughtfully, 'I suppose it is not really so much worse than marrying a governess. But, tell me, how far did they get?'

'Not too far, by God's mercy, though far enough in all conscience. Lavenham was in Portugal at the time, so it fell to my lot to rise from a sickbed and pursue them on their very inefficient way to Gretna. Luckily, the young man was a fool of the first water, and all their arrangements went awry. By the time I caught up with them I think poor Chloe was positively glad to see me. She has never spoken of him since. That was six months ago, and we told her that a further year at school must be her penance. I think when you return from Portugal will be time enough for you to meet her.'

Camilla could not help but be sorry for the motherless girl, who had had, she suspected, all too little of thought or affection from either her brother or her grandmother, but she had learned that when Lady Leominster spoke with that touch of finality, it was best to let a subject drop, and therefore did so, only resolving that if she could not contrive to meet Chloe before she left, she would at least enter into a correspondence with her. She had learned the direction of her school and kept hoping for an opportunity to go there, greatly daring, and visit her without consulting either Lavenham or his grandmother, but the press of work was too great, the day came for their move to Haverford and the opportunity had still not arisen.

It was an oddly assorted quartet that set forward in two travelling carriages for Haverford Hall. Camilla's father was resplendent in gleaming new buckskins and topcoat that she shrewdly suspected her betrothed had paid for, and was more Gallic than ever in his flowery attentions to her and to Lady Leominster. In some ways, it was a relief to find she was to drive down with him, while Lavenham escorted his grandmother. At least he would not be troubling them with his airs and graces, but nevertheless she could not repress an illogical pang of disappointment. It had been absurd to hope that Lavenham would accompany her, but she had done so just the same, and had counted more than she had quite realised on this time alone with him to allay some of the doubts and fears that tormented her. Instead, she had to listen for the intolerable length of the journey to her father's enthusiastic congratulations on her good fortune—and his. In the course of his long and exclamatory monologue it came out that Lavenham had undertaken to make him a small allowance—on condition that he kept away from the gaming tables. Camilla did not know whether to be more touched at this instance of Lavenham's thoughtfulness, or amused at the ungrounded optimism that made him believe her father's asseverations that he would never touch another pair of dice. She would as easily believe him if he told her he would never draw another breath. Still, it was clear from a slight bitterness in his tone that the allowance was so tied up that it would be impossible for him to anticipate it. At least it should help to safeguard him from blackguards like M. Mireille, who, she was relieved to learn, had indeed packed up and left at once for France. But here, too, was matter for a slight pang. To have been so nearly in touch with her long lost, dimly remembered older brother and then to have had nothing come of it, was a sad blow. But the fact remained that he was only dimly remembered—and he had thrown in his lot with Bonaparte. Perhaps, after all, it was best this way. If peace ever came, which seemed unlikely, it would be time enough to resume relations with him.

At Haverford Hall, as in London, she was too busy for thought. Lady Leominster, after a volley of horrified exclamations at the state of the house, turned to with a will to plan its renovation.

And Camilla must be consulted about everything. If she suspected that this was a device of the old lady's to keep her, as she had done in London, too busy for thought, she was, in the main, grateful. The die was cast. What was the use of thinking? Instead, she must decide which paper should be hung in the dining room, and whether the curtains there should be of green or of rose coloured brocade. She must decide the colour scheme of her own suite of apartments, which Lady Leominster intended entirely to remodel: 'We'll have no memories of his mother lingering here to haunt Lavenham,' she explained, when Camilla protested at the expense. This was a silencer. Impossible to suggest to the old lady that the chances of Lavenham's ever visiting these apartments were remote indeed.

As their wedding day drew relentlessly near, he seemed more and more a courteous stranger. Considering her in everything, he nevertheless contrived really to talk to her about nothing. They might, she thought in despairing tears one night, be the merest of chance acquaintances, not a couple who were to marry in two days. And, as so often before, she pulled herself up, dried her tears angrily, turned over the pillow and composed herself for sleep with the thought that they were indeed mere acquaintances, and likely to remain so. Since this did not, somehow, prove conducive to slumber, she made herself, instead, catalogue the items of her trousseau, which despite the speed at which it had been assembled, overwhelmed her by its richness and variety. But not even the enumeration of silks and gauzes proved soporific and it was with a tear still trembling on one eyelid that she fell asleep at last – to dream, maddeningly, of Lavenham.

She woke to something like panic. Tomorrow was her wedding day. They were to be married early in the morning, then leave at once for the long journey to Falmouth. By spending one night in Exeter, they would break the journey and reach Falmouth in time to go aboard their ship the evening before she sailed. It all seemed too near, too soon, in short, impossible. And yet to retreat was equally impossible; she was caught a helpless prisoner in the web of Lady Leominster's kindness. The certainty that this was exactly what Lady Leominster had intended made no difference. She had gone too far, now, to turn back she; must go through with her mad bargain.

But it was with an aching head and a pale face that she joined the others at breakfast. Lady Leominster looked at her sharply, said nothing, and presently engaged her grandson to drive her out to pay a morning call on Mrs. Cummerton. 'I will not go so far as to invite her to your wedding, my love,' she told Camilla, 'but I warrant you I'll silence her effectively enough without.'

At last, it seemed, Camilla was to be allowed thinking time, though whether, at this late date, she really wanted it was another question. Anyway, the formidable dowager soon took care of her. 'Camilla, my love, you look pale this morning. Perhaps you would do me a kindness and yourself a benefit by taking a message to Forbes for me? Your father, I know, will accompany you.'

Since Forbes, the bailiff, had a cottage at the farthest end of the estate, this would have entailed a ride of several miles there and back, but soon after Lady Leominster and her grandson had left, Forbes appeared in person and Camilla was able to give him the message. This done, and her father having vanished with scarce concealed relief to the billiard room where he would, she knew, spend the rest of the morning pushing the balls about and betting left hand against right, Camilla found herself alone indeed. At once she knew it was the last thing she wanted. She prowled about the house, trying to think of anything but tomorrow, and it was with a sensation of pure relief that she saw a dusty hired carriage turn into the drive and come to an awkward stop at the front door. She had been half-heartedly considering colours for the drawing room curtains, now she stood and unashamedly watched as an untidy postilion let down the steps. A golden haired girl in a maroon travelling dress bounced out of the carriage, said something to the man, hurried towards the house, and vanished into the front entrance.

Camilla had hardly time to wonder who she could be, arriving thus unheralded and, it seemed, unaccompanied, when Marston, the butler, appeared, looking even more melancholy than usual. After apologising for disturbing her, he came quickly to the point. 'Here is Lady Chloe arrived, Miss Forest, in a hired chaise, and wants the man paid off, and my lord out and my lady too. I am sure I don't know what to do for the best.'

'Why, pay the man of course, as Lady Chloe tells you,' said Camilla with an assumption of authority that surprised herself. 'And bring her in here to me.'

This further instruction, however, proved unnecessary, for Lady Chloe had followed the butler and now stood hesitating in the doorway, a look of mixed fright and amusement on her exquisite face. Why, Camilla found herself wondering as she went forward to greet her, had no one thought to tell her that her future sister-in-law was a beauty? The explanation flashed into her mind almost as soon as the question. For Chloe Lavenham's golden ringlets, exquisite pink and white complexion and huge blue eyes must proclaim her, for all the world to see, her errant mother's child. The less said about it, perhaps, the better. She was tiny, too, and had to reach up to plant an impulsive kiss on Camilla's cheek.

'I *knew* I should like you,' she said. 'You are not going to give me a scold, are you?'

Camilla laughed as she returned the kiss, and temporised. 'That must depend,' she said, 'on what you have been doing.'

'Why, nothing so very dreadful,' said Chloe, taking off her bonnet and gloves and throwing them on a chair. 'And, besides, it serves Lavenham right for trying to keep me away from his wedding. It was perfectly boneheaded of him to think I would stay virtuously minding my books at such a time. You do not mind my coming, do you?'

'Of course not. I have been longing to meet you.' And then,

aware that Lavenham and his grandmother might think her sadly lacking in firmness, she changed her tone. 'But I trust you have at least your school mistress's permission to come, if not your brother's?'

Chloe threw back her head in a fit of delighted — and delightful — laughter. 'Permission,' she crowed. 'I should just about think I had. I am not only permitted to leave, but most earnestly entreated not to return. I told Lavenham I'd make him regret it if he left me mewed up with those old women much longer. I am seventeen, you know,' she confided. 'All my friends are being presented, and I must stay muddling over French verbs and the pianoforte. Well, I have taken care of that now: the old cats will not have me back even if Lavenham goes on bended knees to them — which, mark you, he is quite incapable of doing.'

'Oh dear,' Camilla could see trouble ahead. 'Have you done something so very dreadful?'

'Of course not. Do not look so grave: I have been in enough trouble already as I have no doubt they have told you: I do not wish for more. No, no, I took the most particular pains to make it something the old pussies could not forgive — and Lavenham could not mind too much: it was only what he had taught me anyway.'

'What was?'

'Why, the composition they gave me to write. It was a punishment, of course, for whispering in church: I was to write about what religion means to me. Well, I told them right enough, just what Lavenham has said to me, all about enlightened self-interest and the church being a bogey to frighten children. No, no, they will not have me back, and I do not see how Lavenham can be so *very* angry.' But her voice shook a little, and Camilla, recognising fright, put out an impulsive hand to her. 'Never mind,' she said, 'I will stand your friend, and truly I am glad to have you here for my wedding.'

Just the same, it was two visibly frightened girls who greeted

Lavenham and Lady Leominster on their return. And the scene that followed amply justified their fears. But it was over at last, and, as Lavenham said, if Chloe had indeed been turned out bag and baggage, there was not much to be done about it. 'But, in your mighty contriving,' he turned on her with a renewal of anger, 'what do you propose to do with yourself after you have graced my wedding? Perhaps you are not aware that I leave for Portugal tomorrow.'

'Oh; I did not know.' Chloe's face fell.

'Exactly! You did not know. Now, you had best go on bended knees to your grandmother to ask for house room in St. James's Square, for I am most certainly not going to leave you here alone with Cousin Harriet to get into what scrapes you please.'

It was clear to Camilla that this proposal was equally unwelcome to both the parties concerned, nor did she wonder at it. Lady Leominster was too old to go much into society and too selfish to change her habits for the sake of a young visitor. And Chloe visibly thought that this would be but to exchange one form of servitude for another. Camilla let the unenthusiastic discussion dwindle towards deadlock before she intervened.

'May I propose another plan?' she said. 'Could not Chloe come with us? I am sure I should be glad of her company, Lavenham, when you are away, as you tell me you will often have to be.' She felt herself colouring at her own temerity, but was rewarded by a quick kiss from Chloe: 'I *knew* you would stand my friend. Oh, Lavenham, do, do let me come. I will behave like an angel and not give you or Camilla a moment's anxiety, I promise it, cross my heart.'

Lavenham laughed. 'For you to talk about keeping out of trouble, puss, is like a fish planning to live on dry land, but to have your promise that you will try is something, I suppose.'

Since Lady Leominster warmly seconded this plan, all obstacles to it were quickly dealt with, and indeed Camilla soon began to suspect that after his first doubts Lavenham himself had come to greet this breaking up of their tête à tête existence with considerable relief. For herself, she was not sure what to think, only that there was nothing else she could have done.

Certainly Chloe's presence added a gaiety that had hitherto been lacking in the wedding preparations and her warm sympathy carried Camilla through the trying hours, while the extra preparations entailed by her joining the travelling party kept everyone too busy for thought. It was Chloe, of course, who helped Camilla dress for her wedding, exclaiming in dismay at the simple dove coloured travelling dress she had chosen and then keeping up such a stream of chatter about what *she* would wear when her turn came that Camilla had hardly time to be frightened. Chloe talked all the way to the village church and only paused, at last, to give Camilla a little reassuring pat on the shoulder and say, 'You look like an angel.' She reached up to pinch Camilla's cheeks in an attempt to bring some colour into them and added, 'A rather frightened angel, but there's no need for it. Lavenham's bark is much worse than his bite, I tell you, and I should know.'

And with these encouraging words ringing in her ears, Camilla took her father's arm and started up the aisle to meet her husband.

Chapter 4

It was over, it seemed, in a flash. Lavenham's cold hand slipped the ring on her finger, the clergyman finished the short service and she clung grateful and uncontrollably trembling to her husband's arm as they walked down the church through the sparse and curious congregation to the vestry where, for the last time, she signed as Camilla Forest. Then her father was kissing her enthusiastically, shaking Lavenham warmly by the hand and seizing the chance to press a more than paternal kiss on Chloe's flushed cheek. Glancing up, Camilla saw Lavenham's dark eye taking this in.

'I should kiss you?' he said.

'It is, I believe, customary.' She held up her cold cheek to his still colder kiss. Then they were all outside, grateful for April sun after the winter cold of the church. There was laughter, a scattering of flower petals from the village children, a volley of farewells. The day's journey to Exeter was so long that Lavenham and his grandmother had decided that any delay for a wedding breakfast was impossible. So bride, bridesmaid and groom were loaded forthwith into Lavenham's travelling carriage, while Camilla's new maid Frances took her place with the valet Jenks in the second carriage with the luggage.

'Well,' said Chloe into the stretching silence as the carriage swung out on to the main road, 'that was quick. I shall expect something quite other when my turn comes, and so I warn you, Lavenham.'

He laughed shortly. 'I doubt if there are bride's cake and champagne at Gretna Green.'

'Oh, that,' she dismissed her elopement as a youthful folly, long forgotten, then turned with a pretty gesture to Camilla: 'You cannot conceive what an encumbrance I feel. To be acting third on a honeymoon party is a most monstrous piece of ill manners. Should I, do you think, ride with Jenks and the maid?'

Camilla, whose gratitude to Chloe for breaking the silence had indeed been mixed with a shade of regret at her presence, began a polite protest, but Lavenham interrupted her, telling his sister not to be more absurd than she could help. 'You wished to be of the party, now you will put up with the consequences.'

Even Chloe found this something of a silencer and after exchanging a glance of quick sympathy with her new sister-in-law, settled down to gaze out of the carriage window. Camilla, too, was silent, sorry that Lavenham had given his sister such a set down, and yet sympathising with the almost intolerable strain under which she recognised him to be labouring. She longed to make some gesture of sympathy — after all, she was his wife — but restrained the hand that would have gone out towards him. The first advance, if there was to be any, must come from his side, not hers. She remembered Lady Leominster's warning, 'You will have to be patient . . . patient as Job,' and sat back quiet, in her corner. So they travelled across the heart of England all day, almost as silent as if they had been three strangers in the public coach. By the time they reached Exeter, late in the evening, the silence of constraint had given place to that of fatigue and Camilla observed a crease across Lavenham's brow that she had never seen before. Was he, she wondered, regretting their marriage already?

Chloe brightened up at the sight of the outskirts of Exeter, with its promise of food and rest. For all her seventeen years and attempted elopement, she was enough of a child still so that the mere passage of time could put her at her ease in any situation. By now, her sense of the awkwardness of intruding on her brother's honeymoon was lost in the excitement of the journey. She began to chatter excitedly to Camilla and was soon running from side to side of the carriage in her attempts to see Exeter Cathedral. A lurch of the carriage as it hit the paved road overset her and she cannoned heavily into her brother, who let out an exclamation of such black rage that Camilla shrank back in her corner.

Chloe did not seem particularly surprised, however, but settled back in her own corner with an apology and added, 'Have you one of your migraine headaches, poor Lee?' Her sympathetic tone and the use of the pet name, which Camilla had not heard before, showed that his start of bad temper neither surprised nor alarmed her.

He admitted to the headache. 'I am afraid I have been vilely bad company all day,' he said to Camilla, 'you must forgive me, M—' He had almost said 'Miss Forest', but remembered himself in time, coloured deeply and contrived to turn it into 'my dear'.

The mild endearment moved Camilla almost to the point of tears, which she however took care to conceal, remarking instead, in her gentlest voice, on the length of the day's journey and enquiring what treatment he found best for the headache.

'Oh, nothing but to endure it,' he answered a shade impatiently as the carriage turned into the inn yard, and she could only admire the fortitude with which he endured the bustle of their late arrival. Fortunately, rooms and a meal had been bespoken for them, and a question which had been troubling Camilla, of whether she and her husband were to share a room, had apparently been settled in advance. They found two large bedrooms with a sitting room between them ready for their occupation. Chloe's presence, of course, had not been provided for, and the obsequious host was soon deep in apologies because he had no other room available that was fit for her occupation. But this was easily settled, 'Of course, she must sleep with me,' said Camilla and felt herself amply rewarded for the sacrifice of comfort and privacy by her husband's grateful look.

Dinner, the host told them, would be served immediately, and they retired to their rooms at once to repair the ravages of the long day's journey. To Camilla's relief, Chloe did not comment on the odd allocation of bedrooms, being far too busy hanging out of the window and counting the number of gentlemen's carriages in the inn yard below. 'If only Lavenham would eat at the ordinary like anybody else,' she wailed, 'we might see their owners, but he is so mortally high in the instep he would never even think of it. And how am I to find myself a husband if I meet no one?'

Camilla paused with the comb in her hair and looked across the room at Chloe. The time, she felt, had come to be firm. 'You must not speak like that of your brother,' she said, 'and most particularly not to me. As for a husband, there is time enough to be thinking of that when the world has forgotten about your excursion to Gretna,' and then, seeing the ready tears in the child's eyes, 'come, that is enough for a first scold, and I promise you we will never speak of Gretna again.'

When they joined Lavenham in their sitting room they found him staring pale and gloomily at the table which a man and a boy were engaged in loading with food. Chloe exclaimed with delight at the plenty before her, but it was soon obvious to Camilla that Lavenham ate only by a heroic effort of will. At last, she could bear the sight of his struggles no longer, and as Chloe embarked on her third helping of devilled chicken, asked, 'Would you not be very much happier in the quiet of your own room, my dear?' She ventured the endearment he had used. 'Chloe and I will do very well without you and, with your permission, I will come presently and see if I cannot massage the pain away. I used to do it for the poor Duchess of Devonshire when she had one of her headaches and she said it was wonderful how it eased it.'

He protested, but was obviously glad to leave them. Later, when she knocked timidly on his door and found him stretched fully clothed on his bed in the darkened room, he was obviously in too much pain not to be grateful for any chance of alleviation. He turned over obediently and lay flat on his face while her gentle hands worked their way over the tense muscles at the back of his neck where the dark hair grew close and curling. Gradually, as she sat there in the half dark, she could hear his breathing ease off into sleep and at last, very quietly, she rose to leave him. At the door, his voice stopped her: 'Camilla,' he said, and then, as she paused, 'thank you.'

'Goodnight,' she whispered, closing the door softly behind her.

They had another long day's journey before them, and were up early again, but Camilla had already lain for a long time, listening to the noises of the inn yard, and Chloe's quiet breathing, and thinking about her husband and the strange life before her. Later, the first sight of Lavenham was encouraging: he was visibly better, his colour nearly normal and the furrow gone from above his eyebrows. But if she had hoped for any increase in warmth on his part this morning, she was to be disappointed. He was brisk almost to the point of rudeness, both to her and to Chloe, and it was a subdued little party that climbed punctually into the carriage as the cathedral clock struck the hour. Chloe, however, had had enough of silence and having ascertained that his headache was indeed gone began to tease him with questions about Portugal. What was he to do there? Where were they to live? Did he like the Portuguese, and was their Queen really mad? And a thousand other questions, which he began by answering monosyllabically enough, but gradually as the carriage rolled on through sunshine and the sounds of spring he began to thaw a little and answer her questions and those that Camilla now dared to raise, more fully.

Yes, he told them, Lord Strangford, the Minister Plenipotentiary, had already secured a house for them on the eastern outskirts of Lisbon; they would be able to go there directly from the boat. 'I found the dirt and discomfort of my lodgings intolerable when I was last there and insisted that this time I would have a house—fortunately, as it has proved. You will find the Portuguese a good enough kind of people, I think,' he was addressing Camilla now, rather than Chloe, 'if curiously unaware of dirt and discomfort. But the climate, I am sure, will make up for much, though I hope you neither of you find hot weather oppressive.'

They both assured him that it was of all things what they liked best and took advantage of his mellower mood to ply him with more questions, which he was glad enough to answer. 'You are to form part, remember, of the diplomatic colony and much may depend on your behaviour.' This time, the speech was made very directly to Chloe, who laughed, blushed, stammered a promise of good behaviour and changed the subject by reiterating an earlier question about the Queen.

'Oh, yes,' he assured her, 'she is as mad as you please, and shut up in her palace of Queluz while her son Dom John governs as Regent—and but a poor business he makes of it, I am afraid, though he is a good enough sort of man.'

'Is it true that he and his wife never speak to each other except on state occasions?' put in Chloe.

'True enough, but not the kind of thing upon which you will remark in Portuguese society,' was his repressive answer.

She was not to be cowed. 'That is all very well, Lavenham, but how are Camilla and I to avoid making gaffes if we do not know these things?'

There was such obvious sense in this that he unbent still more and proceeded to give them a lively account of Portuguese society, its delights, such as they were, its tedium, and its pitfalls. 'And above all,' he ended warningly, 'you will avoid comment of any kind on their religion which is, to the Regent certainly, and to many of his people, the most important thing in life. And, equally, you will avoid association of any kind with the French—oh,' he remembered, 'forgive me, Camilla, but at least you are English now.'

She laughed. 'And a good thing too, I can see. But do the French maintain an Embassy in Lisbon then? I had not thought of it.'

'Of course they do, since Portugal is, officially at least, neutral.'

'How do you mean, officially?' asked Chloe.

'Why, merely that, in past years, Portugal has always been our very good friend both at land and sea. Now, Bonaparte is trying to change all that and is exerting the utmost pressure on Dom John to persuade him to close his ports against us.'

'And would that be bad?' said Camilla.

'Disastrous.'

'And you are going to Lisbon to persuade the Prince Regent that he must not give way!' exclaimed Chloe. 'What a great man you are, to be sure, Lee!'

He laughed. 'Well, call it rather, to assist Lord Strangford in his persuasions. My cousin thought my knowledge of the country might prove of some service. I spent several years there when I was a very young man indeed,' he explained to Camilla, 'since the rest of Europe was closed to me by this unending war. I hope you will find the countryside and the people to your taste. I have grown to find them good friends, for all their faults.'

She could not help laughing at this characteristically reserved commendation. 'Do not praise them too high,' she begged, teasingly, 'or you will raise expectations quite impossible of fulfilment. But I can see that we will have plenty to do, Chloe and I, in insuring that we do not handicap you in your negotiations. Tell me, though, in what language we will converse with these paragons of yours, for I must confess that I know no more Portuguese than I do Greek.'

'I am afraid that with the ladies you may find yourselves largely reduced to sign language,' he said, 'for you will find their ideas of female education amazingly behind ours.'

Camilla laughed again. 'So Chloe and I will find ourselves miracles of learning,' she said. 'Well, at all events, it will make the chances of our offending considerably less if no one can understand what we say. Do you know any Portuguese, Chloe?'

'Why, yes,' she said surprisingly, 'I do a little. I tried to learn it when Lavenham was there last, but I am afraid I did not make a great deal of progress: to tell truth, I could not believe that any human being could make such strange noises; but perhaps I will recall it when I hear it spoken.'

'You never told me that,' said Lavenham, with a mixture of surprise and pleasure that Camilla found most promising for his relations with his sister.

'You never asked me,' said Chloe simply.

The day wore on endlessly. They had left the red Devon fields behind now and were rattling over the dreary uplands of Cornwall. The fatigue and tedium of travelling had them all in its grip and conversation dwindled and died. Chloe curled up in her corner and fell asleep with the easy abandon of a child, Lavenham, in his, leaned back with eyes half closed, brooding—about what, Camilla wondered, and then warned herself against the vanity of imagining his thoughts were of her. It was far more likely that he was considering the difficulties of the mission ahead of him.

She had difficulties enough of her own to face. Impossible not to like Chloe, but equally impossible not to wonder just how their curious *ménage à trois* would develop. The prospect of working out some kind of possible life with Lavenham had been frightening enough without the addition of his lively sister to the party. And yet, she could not regret her suggestion that Chloe accompany them. It was obvious that much of her thoughtless behaviour was the direct result of her forlorn childhood. She had been a baby when her father was killed and her mother ran away, and no one had really thought about her since. Her grandmother cared nothing for her; her brother hated women; she had been brought up by servants, bandied about from this casual relative to that, and finally deposited at a school in Wimbledon from which she had been lucky if she escaped once a year. It was really no wonder, Camilla thought, that she had leapt at the proffered affection of a music master. After all, no one else had cared for her. Nor was it surprising that her one idea now was, apparently, to get herself married as quickly as possible. She was pining, Camilla thought, for family life and this was the only way she could secure it. Well, she and Lavenham would have to form themselves into a family, however odd a one, for her sake. At least after his first outburst Lavenham seemed to have resigned himself easily enough to her accompanying them and indeed, considering how little they had seen of each other, brother and sister seemed to be on remarkably easy terms, and Lavenham had been visibly touched by her attempt at learning Portuguese for his sake. Perhaps it would do well enough yet. Perhaps, even, she and Chloe between them might contrive to teach him that women were not so very dreadful after all. And, smiling at this idea, she fell asleep.

In his corner, Lavenham was asking himself if he had, perhaps, gone raving mad. Here he was, at the outset of what he intended to be a successful career in the diplomatic service, burdened with not one, but two of the females he detested. Now that there was time to think—for his wily old grandmother had allowed him quite as little as she had Camilla—he could only decide he was recovering, too late, from a fit of insanity. It would take more than his grandmother's fortune to compensate him for its results. With an impatient sigh, he looked from the corner where Chloe slept, her face flushed, her mouth half open, her curls dishevelled under a lopsided bonnet, to Camilla in her dove-coloured dress, as neat asleep as awake, her face a little pale, as it had been all day, her eyes dark-shadowed, her hands loosely clasped in her lap. His wife. If he was mad, he thought, suddenly sorry for her, so was she to have accepted his terms. There was nothing ahead for either of them but trouble and sorrow. The migraine headache began to flicker once again behind his eyes. Best try not to think about it. He reached into a pocket of the coach, drew out the instructions Mr. Canning had had drawn up for him, and tried to make himself concentrate on them.

The inn at Falmouth was far from luxurious and it was a weary little party that boarded the packet next morning. Once out at sea, the fresh land breeze seemed to become a hurricane, the little ship tossed and shuddered, and Camilla found it increasingly difficult to endure Chloe's tearing spirits. To Chloe, everything was exciting; even the idea of possible pursuit and capture by a French man-of-war seemed to delight her. She was free at last, the world before her, and nothing could subdue her.

Camilla, on the other hand, was worn out with the events of the past week and it was with a sensation almost of relief that she finally found herself so overcome by nausea that she had to admit her sickness and hurry below to her cabin. Chloe was all sympathy at once and during the wretched week that followed, Camilla thanked heaven, over and over again, for the lucky chance that had brought her with them. The maid, Frances, who had never even seen the sea before, had retired to her cabin before the boat left harbour; if it had not been for Chloe, Camilla would have been entirely dependent on her husband's ministrations. It was an appalling thought, for it was all too obvious that he found a sick woman even less attractive than a well one. After the first visit of duty he paid her, she begged Chloe to keep him away and Chloe laughed and promised to do her best. 'Not that it will be difficult,' she added. 'Poor Lee never could abide the sight of sickness. I think perhaps it was from seeing our father die,' she added as she prepared to bathe Camilla's forehead with lavender water.

'Seeing what?'

'Did you not know? I thought my grandmother would have told you. You know about the duel, I collect?'

'Oh, yes, Lady Leominster told me.' This was dangerous ground. If only her head did not ache so.

'Oh well, then,' Chloe went on cheerfully, 'she cannot have

told you that when they fought not only was my mother in the other carriage, she had Lee with her. If it came to flight she was going to take him too.'

'Good God! But what happened?'

'Why, when my father fell, Lee saw, jumped out of the carriage and ran to him. They could not drag him away and the Runners found him there when they came up. Of course, my mother was gone by then; they could not afford to stay.'

'She left him there alone?'

'Yes, it is no wonder that he cannot abide the sight of blood, or, indeed, of illness of any kind. You can see,' she went on, 'that in a way I was lucky. My mother never thought of taking me. I would have been far too much trouble. Indeed, I have been nothing but a trouble to everyone ever since,' she added with sudden passion.

Camilla reached out to catch her hand. 'Not to me, Chloe,' she said. 'I cannot think how I would have managed without you.'

Chloe pressed her hand fiercely. 'I will never be a trouble to you, Camilla, I promise you.'

Chapter 5

Life in Portugal proved everything that Lavenham had said. Chloe seemed neither to notice nor to mind the dirt, but Camilla was Frenchwoman enough to be appalled by the condition in which she found their house, and spent the first few weeks of her stay battling—in sign language—with her Portuguese servants in an effort to have it made habitable. They thought her quite mad, but, luckily, liked her, and liked blonde Chloe, with her smattering of Portuguese, still more. If the crazy *Inglesas* wanted their floors scrubbed to a fantastic standard of cleanliness, they should have them. Only in the servants' quarters did Camilla have to give up the struggle. There, by an honourable compromise, chaos still reigned, with pigs and poultry happily sharing the apartments with the staff.

When they arrived, the Court was at the *Caldas da Rainha* taking the waters, and, since Lord Strangford was there too, Lavenham felt obliged to join him, leaving his wife and sister to their domestic devices. It would be time enough, he said, for them to make their appearance in society when he—and the court—returned. They had found British society there sadly shrunk since he had been there last. Bonaparte's demands on Dom John, the Prince Regent, had not been limited to the closing of his ports against English ships; he also wanted the thriving British colony banished from Portugal and their possessions expropriated. And the Regent, while trying desperately to please both sides, had strongly advised the English residents to sell up and go while the going was good. The English factory was closed, its staff gone, and until they had made their debut in Portuguese society, Camilla and Chloe were almost entirely dependent on each other for companionship.

But then, there was so much to do and see and talk about. The climate was everything that Lavenham had promised, but so far they had not found it too hot, revelling in a warmth and richness of sunshine that made their light muslins practical almost for the first time in their lives. Their house, which stood on a hill to the eastern end of Lisbon, had a broad marble terrace overlooking the harbour, and here, every evening, they sat, alternating between sun and shade as the spirit moved them, Chloe growing browner every day, while even Camilla was gradually losing the sallow tinge that had previously marred her pale complexion. Soon, she too was faintly brown, with a glow of health that made Chloe exclaim one evening as they settled themselves with books and work, 'Why, you are growing quite a beauty, Camilla, Lavenham will be amazed when he returns.'

Camilla laughed. 'If he notices,' she said. She found Chloe wonderfully easy company these days and was increasingly grateful for the chance that had brought her with them. Though in many ways an adult, Chloe still had a child's easy acceptance of a situation. She did not seem to find it strange that Lavenham should have abandoned his bride to go and dance attendance on the Court, nor that he and Camilla had their own independent apartments in the house. If no one else appeared to find this odd, then neither would she. Perhaps, Camilla thought, she was too happy to notice much. Freed at last from the tyranny of the schoolroom, she blossomed each day into new life and gaiety. Hers was not, Camilla thought, a deep or serious nature and it was indeed remarkable how happily ignorant she had contrived to remain after all those years of forced study. Her genius was for happiness, not learning, and she contrived to find and convey to Camilla a fresh delight in every detail of their new life. Presently, Camilla feared, she might, since she had so few resources within herself, begin to find their simple daily round monotonous, but by then, no doubt, Lavenham would have returned and Portuguese society would provide a new scene of pleasure and interest.

As for Camilla, she, too, was very happy in her own, quieter way. This breathing-space of Lavenham's necessary absence could be given up to the pleasure of being a married woman, someone with a place in the world at last. And it was all Lavenham's doing. There was a deep, quiet pleasure in setting his house in order against his return, which, she hoped, would not be much longer deferred. A feeling of tension hung about Lisbon these hot days of early summer: rumours ran the streets in the daytime, as packs of scavenging dogs did by night, and Camilla did not know which she found more disturbing, the whispers that ran, incomprehensibly, through the Great Square by day, or the desolate howling of the dogs by night. She would be glad when Lavenham returned, with his understanding of the language and the situation.

The Prince Regent came back at last, rowing down the Tagus in the royal barge on the eve of the festival of Corpus Christi. Chloe was delighted, and spent the morning watching the animated scene on the river from the terrace of the house, running in, from time to time, to urge Camilla to come out and join her, or to ask if there had been any news of Lavenham. Her anxiety for his return was considerably heightened by the fact that Camilla had positively refused to take her to see the procession next day unless he should be there to escort them.

When he arrived at last, tired and travel-stained, from a morning's jolting over the rough Portuguese roads, Chloe rushed to throw her arms around him and put her request. 'Lee, you are here at last! Oh, Lee, you will take us tomorrow, will you not? Camilla will not go without you; she is grown positively matronly while you have been gone. Oh, Lee, we can go, can we not?'

With something half way between a laugh and a groan, he disengaged himself from her embrace, and held her at arm's length, looking over her head to Camilla, who had followed her, more calmly, into the carriageway behind the house. 'Quiet, child, a moment.' To Camilla's relief, the rebuke was a gentle one. 'You are both well, I can see,' he went on. 'I must ask your pardon for leaving you so long alone,' he was addressing Camilla now, 'we have been expecting, daily, the order to return, but Dom John, excellent man, has a perfect genius for vacillation. I am only relieved that his beloved church has brought him at last. It is, I collect, unthinkable, that one of the great festivals should take place in his absence.' And then, to Chloe. 'So you wish to see the procession tomorrow? I promise you, it will prove disappointing and tawdry enough, but if you have been behaving yourself, why, we shall see.'

'Oh, Lee, I have been a perfect angel, a model of all the virtues, have I not, Camilla? We have hardly stirred from the house, and I have sewed, and studied and slept like an absolute paragon. Truly, I deserve a treat, and so does Camilla, who has been so busy and domestic that I doubt you will not recognise the house. Why, it smells almost like Haverford Hall, instead of the stables it seemed when we arrived.'

Laughing, he took an arm of each and led them indoors, through the enthusiastic crowd of servants who had hurried out to welcome him. In the main salon, Chloe seized his hand and hurried him enthusiastically here and there to see the improvements Camilla had made, but Camilla, who had noticed the telltale furrow between his eyes, soon intervened, partly, she realised, to protect Chloe herself from the explosion she could see was imminent.

'Your brother is tired, my love,' she said, and then, to Lavenham, 'would you not be glad to retire for a while and recover from the fatigue of the journey? We do not dine till six; it will be time enough then to hear your news, and talk of tomorrow.'

Chloe laughed. 'I told you she was the complete matron, Lavenham. You had best do as she bids you.'

It was spoken thoughtlessly enough, but Camilla coloured up to the eyes at the suggestion that she was acting the part of a managing wife, and began a stammered apology.

Lavenham cut her short, addressing Chloe in repressive tones. 'I shall indeed do as Camilla bids me,' he said, 'since she has suggested the very thing I most desire, rest. As for tomorrow, we will talk of that later. In the meantime,' he had reached the door, but now turned to speak once more to Camilla, 'are you very busy, or could you, perhaps, spare the time to give me some more of that massage that proved so miraculous for my head at Exeter? I have been plagued with the headache since I saw you last, and if we are to take this bad child to see the procession tomorrow, I had as lief be rid of it.'

Camilla, who had been longing to volunteer her services, was equally delighted at his request, and at the kinder tone he used towards Chloe. Besides, she was glad of the chance to accompany him to his rooms and talk to him alone. She had done her best to keep her anxiety about the state of things in Lisbon to herself, considering Chloe too young to be burdened with such worries, but it was an immense relief to be able to ask Lavenham whether he thought an invasion by France, or Spain, or even both, to be imminent. It was an even greater relief to have him pooh-pooh her fears. 'Do you think I would have left you and Chloe alone if there had been any chance of it? No, no, there will be much more of the kind of political blackmail of which Bonaparte is such a master before he moves to the attack. I do not expect any trouble before autumn. Ah, that is better,' and he gave himself up, with a sigh of relief, to the soothing pressure of her hands.

Camilla was waked at first light next morning by a hideous din, which, as she came gradually to complete consciousness, resolved itself into the jangling of all the church bells in the city, mingled with the rolling of drums and the harsh braying of

75

trumpets. The festival of Corpus Christi had begun. They met early for their breakfast of excellent coffee and coarse indifferent bread, and Camilla was glad to see that Lavenham's brow was clear and to have him assure her that he had quite slept his headache away. She had given up the effort to persuade the servants to produce an English breakfast for herself and Chloe, but was amused to see ham and eggs appear, as if by magic, for Lavenham. Clearly, she teased him, men were still the lords of creation, at least in Portugal.

Chloe's thoughts, of course, were all on the procession this morning, but, warned by Camilla, she managed to refrain from mentioning it until her brother had finished his breakfast. She was rewarded for her patience when he rose from the table Camilla had had set up in the sunshine of the terrace, smiled from one to the other of them, and asked, 'And now, how do you ladies wish to celebrate my first day at home?'

Chloe, who had been wandering restlessly to and fro between the garden and the terrace, ran to him at once. 'Oh, Lee, by going to see the procession, please . . . It is quite near, I have found out all about it, and it starts from the Church of Saint Vincent at our end of the town. We could almost walk there, and everybody says it is something quite out of the ordinary.'

He turned to Camilla. 'What say you, my dear? Shall we gratify this child's passion for spectacles?'

Camilla, who would gladly have done anything for him when he called her his dear, agreed at once.

'Very well then, we had best start as soon as you ladies can make yourselves ready. Is it not fortunate that my friend Dom Fernando has arranged to make a balcony available to us in the square opposite the church? I fear you would be sadly crushed if we had to watch from the street itself.'

Chloe reached up to give him a resounding kiss on the cheek. 'You monster, Lee, you had planned to go all the time. What a tease you are to be sure; I do not know how Camilla abides you!'

And she danced away to fetch her shadiest hat and most becoming scarf.

Alone with Camilla, Lavenham seized the opportunity to explain to her that Dom Fernando de Casa Molinha, who had arranged for them to have the use of the balcony, was one of the leaders of the British party in Lisbon and to ask her to try and make sure that Chloe did not, as he put it, 'fly off in one of her mad starts' and offend him. Camilla promised to do her best, though she felt slightly daunted when he reminded her that an unmarried Portuguese girl of Chloe's age and position would be immured almost as completely as a Turk or Moor. She hurried away to fetch her own hat and sunshade and pass on the warning to Chloe, who promised that butter would not melt in her mouth all day.

Their mule-drawn carriage made its way with difficulty through the crowded streets towards the square in which the church of Saint Vincent stood, and they had to leave it some distance off and walk through back streets to the building from which they were to view the procession. There, they were greeted with the greatest courtesy, and in fluent French, by Dom Fernando, and Camilla, answering him as fluently, breathed an inward sigh of relief that the conversation was to be conducted in this language of which, she had discovered with surprise, Chloe was almost entirely ignorant. It would be difficult for her to shock Dom Fernando with the few words she knew of Portuguese.

When they reached the balcony, she forgot her anxiety in amazement at the sight that met her eyes. Every house in the square was hung with damask, tapestry, or cloth of gold, and the rich fabrics, gleaming in the sun, made it seem rather an Eastern encampment than a European city. Below them, the square was thronged with people, and on the far side rose the vast flight of steps that led to the church. Here were massed the Yeomen of the Queen's Guard in their parti-coloured velvet uniforms, and, among them, priests and friars bearing crosses and banners. Even Chloe, after her first exclamations, was awed almost to silence by the splendour of the scene and when, after a short interval, the doors of the church were flung open and the Patriarch of Lisbon appeared under a regal canopy, accompanied by the dignitaries of the church in their scarlet vestments, and the Prince Regent and his court in all the splendour of full dress, she was equally silenced by the excitement of the scene, the roar of artillery and the clangour of all the church bells in Lisbon.

The procession wound slowly away down the flights of steps and lost itself at last in a winding street decorated with splendid hangings. Chloe caught Camilla's hand. 'May we not follow it?' she asked.

Camilla shook her head, but was distracted by Dom Fernando asking how she had liked the procession. By the time she had thrown together enough French adjectives to convey her delight and gratitude, and turned again to speak to Chloe, she found, to her horror, that she had disappeared. A winding stairway led down from the balcony to the square, which was rapidly emptying as the crowd hurried after the procession. She thought she saw Chloe's Italian straw bonnet whisk around the corner among the crowds. Her heart plummeted. What should she do? What would Lavenham say? With a half intelligible apology, she left Dom Fernando and crossed the balcony to where Lavenham stood in an animated group of Portuguese to whom he was talking in their own language. Even in her distracted state, she noticed that the foreign language seemed, in some curious way, to liberate him. She had never seen him talk so freely or so vigorously in English. But she must spoil it.

'My dear,' she said, as he turned to greet her, 'Chloe—'

He looked around. 'Where is she?' They were speaking in English, of course, and the group around him had withdrawn a little with a natural courtesy she had already noticed in the Portuguese.

No use beating about the bush. 'I am very much afraid she is run off to follow the procession. I was talking to Dom Fernando,' she blanched at his frown. 'I beg you will forgive me.'

'Forgive *you*? What's that to the purpose? I should have known better than to bring her. Well, we must just hope she comes to no harm, that's all.'

'Will you not go after her?'

'Of course not,' he kept his tone casual, but she could feel the anger seething below the surface. 'She has played us this trick. She must take the consequences. Because she is a reckless hoyden, am I to leave you alone here? Besides, I have invited Dom Fernando and his friends to come home with us.'

'But what will you tell them?'

'About Chloe? Why, that she was overcome by the heat, and is gone home already.' And before she could answer, he had turned away from her to speak to Dom Fernando in his rapid Portuguese.

The rest of the afternoon was an agony to Camilla. The whole party came back with them to the house and she found herself acting hostess for the first time, offering the wine and sweetmeats Lavenham had recommended as the correct thing, and automatically exchanging polite French nothings with her visitors, while all the time her mind was in a turmoil of apprehension about Chloe. She had hoped against hope to find her indeed at home when they returned, but there was no sign of her, and increasing anxiety on her behalf was mixed with a more mundane fear that she would appear unexpectedly and thus give the lie to her brother's apologies on her behalf. Fortunately, the slight absence of mind that she showed was attributed, by her courteous guests, merely to anxiety for Chloe's health. To her intense, if well concealed, relief, Dom Fernando took the lead in rising to make his adieus at almost the first moment politeness allowed. The farewells themselves, however, were prolonged and enthusiastic, and when, alone at last with her husband, she turned to him impulsively to ask, 'Did I do, Lavenham?' he smiled at her very kindly.

'You were perfect. My grandmother would have been proud of you.'

She would much rather he had been proud of her himself, but there was something more important to think about. 'And now,' she asked, 'will you not go and look for Chloe?'

His face hardened. 'And where, pray, should I begin? In all the public haunts of Lisbon? Should I, do you suggest, blazon her disgrace by enquiring her out from street to street? No, no she must pay the penalty of her folly and find her way home as best she may.'

When Chloe finally appeared, some half an hour later, Camilla's heartfelt relief at sight of her, dusty but apparently unharmed, was considerably qualified by fear of what Lavenham would say. He looked his sister up and down from under furrowed brows, then turned to Camilla: 'You would oblige me by leaving us,' he said. 'I have something to say to this termagant that will go better, I think, without even your audience.'

Camilla made as if to protest, but there was something in his face and voice that warned her to comply, and, with one last anxious glance from one to the other, she withdrew.

Chloe, whom she found, much later, in tears in her bedroom, never told her what her brother had said to her, but appeared, from then on, considerably chastened and quieter in her behaviour. She also, to Camilla's grief, seemed to avoid her brother, spending much time wandering by herself in the alleys of their garden, and even, as Camilla discovered one day when she went out to look for her, among the tangled shrubberies of the deserted garden next door.

When Camilla mildly queried the wisdom of this, Chloe was up in arms at once. 'Oh, Camilla,' she exclaimed impatiently, 'must you play the prude so unmercifully! Were you never young yourself? What kind of a life do you think I lead, cooped up here to watch you and Lavenham billing and cooing. Oh, I know I asked to come,' she anticipated Camilla's remonstrance, 'but I did not know it would be like this.'

'Nor would it have been,' Camilla felt bound to say, 'if you had not made Lavenham so angry at Corpus Christi.'

Chloe took another tack. 'Besides, if I wish to be alone some-times, so surely must you and Lee. I am not quite blind, Camilla, though I collect you think me so.'

Camilla was silenced. It was true that she found their trio an awkward one enough these days, on many counts. To begin with, Lavenham was still displeased with his sister, and took any excuse to leave her at home when he took his wife out visiting among his Portuguese friends, and it was a sore point between him and Chloe whether she should be included in Camilla's forthcoming presentation to the Prince Regent. But there was more than this. Camilla could not help feeling that, but for the presence of this third party, whom she had herself invited, it should have been possible, by now, to come to what she thought of as more human terms with her formidable husband. Lavenham had been home for some weeks, but though he frequently complimented her on the difference her presence made to his domestic comforts, he behaved to her still with a stranger's calm courtesy. Walking back now, alone, through the orange and lemon groves of their garden —for Chloe had made a point of being left behind to pick the armful of jasmine she wanted for the house—Camilla took herself to task for the thousandth time, for the irrational hopes she had allowed herself to entertain. Lavenham had promised her a mar-riage in name only and had been true to the letter of his bond. She had no cause for complaint, except against herself. Hating her own folly, she knew now that she had never taken Lavenham quite seriously. She had fallen into the age-old female fallacy of think-ing that marriage would change everything—particularly her husband. Lavenham thought he hated women: she would convert him. Well, she had failed, as his cold demeanour to Chloe, his distant civility to herself made daily more plain. And, she plucked a rotten lemon from the tree and threw it, furiously, down the hillside towards the river, there was worse than that. Lavenham still hated women — herself included — and she, idiot that she was, had fallen in love with him.

She had never admitted it to herself before, and rather wished she had not now. Ignoring the strong sun, she turned and hurried up the last terraces to the house, then stopped short at sight of Lavenham himself awaiting her on the verandah.

'You look flushed.' He greeted her with his usual cool civility. 'Surely you have not been hurrying in this heat? It is high time we moved to Sintra. The Prince Regent leaves for his palace in Mafra next week and Lord Strangford is finding country villas both for us and for himself. You will be glad, I am sure, of the cool and quiet of the hills. But where is Chloe? I thought her with you.'

'In the garden.' For the first time Camilla found herself prevaricating with her husband, but it would only make trouble to tell him that she was in the garden next door. 'I have just left her; she is picking a bunch of jasmine for the house.'

'Touching and domestic,' said Lavenham. 'I wish I might consider her a reformed character, but, if I know her, it is only skin deep. I wish she may not lead you a dance when I am away.'

'Away?' She seized, at once, on the important point.

'Yes, I must leave you tonight, and do not exactly know when I shall return. I have asked Lord Strangford to make our apologies to Dom John. Your presentation will have to be postponed till I return, and we make the move to Sintra. Perhaps, by then, Chloe's conduct will have justified her inclusion in the party. I can only hope so.' He did not sound optimistic.

To Camilla's surprise, Chloe took the news of her brother's departure, and their consequent return to a life of cloistered seclusion, with equanimity. It was a sad comment, Camilla thought, on the way relations between brother and sister had deteriorated since Corpus Christi. As for her, she was glad enough of an excuse to avoid the heavy round of Portuguese hospitality, but found herself missing Lavenham with infuriating sharpness. Besides, this time, she found herself anxious about him. He had refused to tell her where he was going and she had forborne to press him, but something about his manner told her that it was into danger. When Chloe, on the first afternoon of his absence, stretched herself like a luxurious little cat in the sunshine of the terrace, and said, 'Now I call this peace and quietness,' she was surprised at the sharp answer she received from her usually gentle sister-in-law. Camilla was restless and unhappy all day, and grateful for the distraction provided when Chloe, surprisingly, asked to be taught French, promising, in return, to help Camilla in her stumbling attempts at Portuguese.

So they settled down to domesticity, spending long hours on the verandah, sewing, and exchanging French and Portuguese verbs. Only, towards evening, Chloe seemed to grow restless, would jump up, drop her book and proclaim her intention of taking a stroll in the garden. Once or twice, Camilla volunteered to accompany her, but, though Chloe always welcomed her with apparent pleasure, the time passed so dully, with Chloe obviously thinking of something else, that Camilla gave up the attempt at sociability. She remembered well enough what it had been like to be seventeen in Devonshire House, where somehow, for all the vast number of rooms, there was never any privacy, and sympathised with Chloe in this need of hers to be alone. And when she saw her return from these solitary rambles with flushed cheeks and happy step she congratulated herself on her decision. The child was growing up, finding herself; she must be left to do it in her own way.

As the hot days and moonlight nights passed, Camilla was amazed at Chloe's visible, bubbling happiness. She did not walk, she danced; she sang instead of talking. What a monstrous thing it was that this child (for Camilla, from the height of twenty-one, still thought of her as little more) with her extraordinary gift for enjoying life, should have been cooped up for so long, learning little or nothing from a parcel of old women. In her sympathy with Chloe's past, she was prepared to bear with her present heedlessness. Sometimes she found herself wishing that Chloe was not quite so set on these evening walks of hers. For with the approach of night, the air, intolerably hot all day, began to cool, and a fresh little breeze sprang up off the harbour. Now would have been the time to order out the carriage for a drive along the sea shore. But Lavenham had explained, before he left them alone for the first time, that if they wished to drive out, it must be together, chaperoning each other. He had been equally firm about any chance of their being benighted in the sudden dark. And by the time Chloe came wandering back from the garden, her golden curls in disorder, her arms full of jasmine or myrtle blossom, the first shadows of night would have begun to creep along the terrace and it was too late to think of anything but candles and bed.

Camilla was brooding about this, one golden afternoon, and wondering whether she was allowing Chloe to over-indulge her passion for solitude, when she was disturbed by a servant announcing Dom Fernando and his sister. Surprised and alarmed, for she had thought them already at Mafra with the court, she hurried to greet them and offer refreshment, waiting impatiently, as they completed the solemn ritual of meeting, for the moment when she could ask the question that had flashed at once to her mind.

'You have news, perhaps, of my husband?' she said in French.

'Why, no.' Dom Fernando seemed ill at ease. 'That was what I had come to ask you. Can you tell me, perhaps, where I could get in touch with him? The Prince Regent is anxious to speak with him.'

Camilla, explaining that Lavenham had not told her where he was going, found much to disquiet her about this speech. Dom

Fernando was supposed to be a friend of the English, but she knew enough already about the Portuguese court to be aware that his message from the Prince Regent must be a mere pretext. Why, then, was he so anxious to know where Lavenham was? A creeping feeling along her bones confirmed her earlier certainty that he had gone on a mission of danger, and one, it now seemed, unknown even to his Portuguese friends. But there was no time for anxiety; she was too busy concealing it, laughing with Dom Fernando and showing herself the kind of giddy wife to whom no man in his senses would think of giving precise information.

'He said he would be back—presently.' She fluttered her eyelashes at Dom Fernando in the best imitation she could manage of Chloe. 'Perhaps Lord Strangford would know where he is. I have not seen him this age.'

'No,' said Dom Fernando. 'He is away too.' The words fell coldly on Camilla's ear and she was relieved when he put down his wine glass and said something in Portuguese to his plump and docile sister. They rose together and took their leave; only, as Dom Fernando kissed Camilla's hand in parting he paused for a moment. 'Ask him to come to me as soon as he returns. I am,' he paused for a moment, 'I am anxious about him.'

Chloe, returning late and glowing from the garden, found her sister-in-law so short-tempered that she retired at once to the dreamy seclusion of her room.

Chapter 6

The anxious days that followed were made no easier for Camilla by the constant visits she received from Dom Fernando and his family. He brought his sister again, he brought his grandmother, he brought his plump and widowed aunt and his three giggling sisters-in-law. If a day passed without his visiting her, urgent messages would summon her to his house where, among an indescribable medley of sounds and odours, she was expected to join them in their oily and indigestible meals of fiercely flavoured rice. Dom Fernando's pretext was the enormous fancy his sisters had taken to Camilla, though since, as Lavenham had warned, none of the females of the family spoke either English or French, it was difficult to see what satisfaction they could get out of her company. An aged, wrinkled priest, part father confessor, part hanger-on, acted, when Dom Fernando was absent at court, as interpreter on these occasions, translating Camilla's French formalities into Portuguese and then, laboriously, conveying his mistresses' trite answers. It would all have been comic enough if Camilla had not been wracked with anxiety for her husband, and convinced that all this solicitude on her behalf merely masked Dom Fernando's curiosity as to Lavenham's whereabouts. Every day, regularly as clockwork, if with careful casualness, came the question from one or the other of the family: Had she heard from milord yet? And every day, equally casual, she replied, with perfect truth, that she had not. It was galling enough thus to have to expose Lavenham's neglect, and yet she had to admit to herself that if he had expected this kind of inquisition on her, he had been well advised to tell her nothing of where he was going. It would have been hard work, if she had known where he was, not to give something away under this courteous barrage of apparently trivial questions. On the other hand, her anxiety for him was exacerbated by the thought that he did not trust her to keep his secret. He might at least have warned her what to expect.

Chloe was no help these long anxious days. Her one idea was to escape visiting the Molinhas with whose cloistered daughters Dom Fernando had done his best to force her into reluctant friendship. After one session with them in their private apartments, Chloe told Camilla frankly that if she was compelled to go again she would not be answerable for the consequences. 'I do not know which is worse, the girls' giggling or their brother's laboured attentions.'

Camilla found herself reluctantly sympathising with Chloe. So far as she could see the Molinha girls' entire occupation was to sit on the floor of their apartment searching each other's jewelled hair for lice and gossiping about possible husbands, while their brother had so obviously been instructed by their uncle to lose no opportunity of paying court to Chloe that Camilla felt faintly anxious lest, in Lavenham's absence, Chloe, whose position as a comparatively emancipated young English girl obviously left her open to misapprehension, might not be in some way compromised. So when Chloe pled unconvincing headache or unlikely fatigue, or just vanished into the garden when it was time to go to the Molinhas', Camilla usually took the line of least resistance and went alone. She did, however, insist on Chloe's accompanying her when Dom Fernando arranged a party to cross the river and go to a bullfight on the other side. Camilla had done her best to be excused, saying with truth that she thought it of all things what she would like least, but Dom Fernando overruled her, insisting that she must take the opportunity which might easily not recur before the impending move to Mafra and Sintra. When she hoped to nonplus him by querying the propriety of her attending it in her husband's absence, he silenced her by telling her that the Prince Regent's wife was a constant spectator. Of course, he admitted, if Chloe had been a Portuguese young lady, it would have been unthinkable that she should have accompanied them, 'but your English young ladies have such liberty, have they not?' And, since Chloe had gone with them to see the Corpus Christi procession, Camilla could only agree with him, while feeling privately that if she must go she would be glad of Chloe's support.

The day of the bullfight dawned fine and clear, with a welcome little sea breeze to temper the heat, and Camilla and Chloe, festive in their freshest muslins and shadiest hats, found themselves immensely enjoying the crossing of the Tagus, which they made in the Molinhas' sumptuous, if shabby, private galley, rowed by twenty oarsmen.

They landed in a pleasant hilly country shaded by pines and overgrown with a wild shrubbery of low aromatic bushes, and Camilla would gladly have remained there to explore the little paths that wandered beside rivulets among a tangle of wild orange and bay trees. But mule-drawn carriages awaited them and they had to climb in for a stuffy jolting over hill roads to the amphitheatre, where they were hurried straight into a box, and had hardly time to agree that the place was about the size of Ranelagh but very much less splendid, when a dozen hideous negroes dressed in a sort of Indian Chinese style tumbled into the ring driving a placid herd of bulls. A tawdry procession introduced the matador, who proceeded to slaughter one passive bull after another until Camilla and Chloe, sickened by the bloody spectacle and the remorseless heat, had to beg Dom Fernando to let them retire. He, it seemed, was a devotee of the ring — or had to pass as one in deference to his royal mistress — but he deputed his eldest nephew, Dom Pedro, to accompany them, and they retired, grateful, for once, for the escort of this very young man, to the shady garden of a nearby monastery. To Camilla's relief, it was quite impossible for females to enter the monastery, so they were able to sit in the shade of a gigantic cork tree and recover something of their spirits before they were rejoined by Dom Fernando and his sister. As Dom Pedro's attentions to Chloe were very much less pressing when his uncle was not present, the interval was refreshing enough and they were able to enjoy the homeward journey across the Tagus in the cooling evening among a throng of other boats from some of which rose the strains of song, the catchy Brazilian *modinhas* for which Chloe had developed a passion.

Reaching home late in the afternoon, Camilla was able to put more conviction than she had expected into her thanks to Dom Fernando. The bullfight itself might have horrified her, but the rest of the day had been pleasant enough. To her relief, he merely left them at their door, but then spoiled it by promising himself the pleasure of calling on them later to make sure they had not suffered from the fatigues of the day. She would gladly have dispensed with this courtesy, but forced herself to welcome it, putting an extra touch of enthusiasm into her voice to make up for the defection of Chloe, who, after the briefest of thanks, had already vanished into the garden.

Glad to be alone, Camilla settled herself with a book on the terrace but was soon aroused by the sound of a horse's hooves on the carriage drive behind the house. Her first thought was of Lavenham, but he had left by carriage. Still, she jumped to her feet; this might, at last, be a messenger from him. She hurried through the main salon and reached the front door in time to see Lavenham himself being helped to dismount by one of the servants. The fact that he needed help was alarming enough, but his pale face and torn and dusty clothes told their own story.

Camilla hurried forward: 'My dear, you are hurt?'

He managed an apology for a smile. 'A trifle. Nothing to signify.' But he let the man help him towards the house, while another servant led away the exhausted horse.

Once in the salon, Lavenham dropped with a sigh into a chair and dismissed the man with a few rapid sentences. Then, once again, he did his best to smile at Camilla. 'Lord, it's good to be home. But I must ask your pardon for so melodramatic an entrance. Where is Chloe?'

If Camilla suffered a little at this evidence that his first thought was for his sister, she did not show it, merely replying, 'In the garden as usual, and you, my lord, should be in bed.'

'All in good time. First I must eat. I rather think I have not done so since yesterday. No, no,' as she jumped to her feet, 'never trouble yourself, I told the man to bring it presently. In the meantime, I am glad Chloe is out of the way. I need your help.'

'It is yours.'

'I knew I could count on you. You are not, I am sure, one of the young ladies who faint at the sight of blood.'

She was on her feet at once. 'You are wounded! I knew it. Of course I do not mind the sight of blood. I used, often, to assist the surgeon who attended the poor Duchess of Devonshire. Only come to your room and I will fetch ointment and bandages. But should we not send for a doctor?'

He had risen somewhat shakily to his feet and now gratefully accepted the support of her arm. 'No, no. We cannot have a doctor, and indeed it is not necessary. You will see it is but a scratch, but has bled most confoundedly. I am in a sad state I fear, and no object for a lady, but the deuce of it is I cannot afford a doctor and his gossiping.'

More and more alarmed, she was relieved to get him to the privacy of his room where a servant had already brought warm water. Bidding him sit quiet until she returned, she hurried off to her own apartments to fetch salve and bandages. Returning, she found him shrugging himself awkwardly out of his dusty blue jacket and hurried to help him, letting out a gasp of horror when she saw the clotted blood through an awkward looking bandage around his left arm. But it was no time for talk, she set at once to work and was relieved, when she removed the bandage, to find that the bleeding was from a clean sabre cut.

'You see,' he said, clenching his teeth as she gently sponged the wound, 'I told you it was nothing. Ah, that feels better. What an admirable woman you are, to be sure. Not a question yet?'

She laughed with relief at his stronger tone. 'I have no doubt you will tell me what you wish me to know in your own good time. For now, I would rather see you in bed than talking. You must be fatigued to death.'

'I am a little weary,' he admitted, 'since I have been riding all night, but, tell me, you do not expect company tonight?'

'Oh, I forgot. Dom Fernando is coming. He has positively haunted us since you have been gone, Lavenham, and is coming to see we are not unduly fatigued by the bullfight we went to this afternoon.'

'A bullfight! But you shall tell me about that later. In the meantime, you must help me to my clothes. If he is coming, I must see him. No one, I tell you no one, not even Chloe, chatterbox that she is, must know I am wounded.'

Now she could not forebear a question. 'But, Lavenham, why?'

'Because I have been where I should not have. Tell me, does the wound on my head show?'

'On your head?' She had finished binding up his arm now and noticed for the first time the place where his dark curls were matted together. Gently probing, she found an enormous lump which, luckily, had bled only a little so that she was able by gentle bathing with spirits of lavender to remove all traces of it. By the time she had finished, a servant appeared with a tray of food and Camilla was able to appreciate her husband's forethought in making her hide away the bloodstained bandages as she worked. Lavenham, in a clean shirt over his dusty buckskins, merely looked as if he was tired out with travelling, Camilla was the devoted wife bathing his temples with lavender water. When the man had gone and she had seen Lavenham take his first few

91

hungry bites, and a good draught of wine, Camilla ventured another question.

'But where is Jenks?' she asked. For Lavenham's valet had accompanied him on the journey as well as several Portuguese servants.

He put down his fork. 'Dead, I am afraid. We were taken by surprise. I thought no one knew where we were. No one should have. Jenks was on the box; an easy mark. I was able to use the coach as a defence—I do not think they had looked for so stout a resistance. At all events, when I killed their leader, they soon took to their heels, and I was able to avail myself of his horse, since the carriage was useless.'

'And the other servants?' She kept her voice calm, aware that any exclamation from her would be intolerable to him in his exhausted state.

'One dead, the others fled. We shall not see them again. Nor, I hope, will they come back to Lisbon to tell tales of the encounter.'

'But, Lavenham,' now that he had eaten she must ask it. 'Who? Why?'

'Who but the French? It would suit their book very well to have me out of the way. They know, I am afraid, more than I could wish about the real purpose of my coming to Portugal.'

'The real purpose? Is it not, then, to help Lord Strangford in his negotiations?'

'Not entirely. I suppose I should have told you sooner, but it is a secret to be shared by as few as possible. No, my main purpose in coming is to get in touch with the various military agents in this country and in Spain, to get what information and make what preparations are possible against the outbreak of war with France. I am not, you must know, quite the do-nothing I must have seemed, but have had to play the court butterfly to conceal the real purpose of my coming.'

'I see. And these journeys of yours—'

'To meet the various agents. This time I have been to Spain.

92

I only wish I knew who blew the affair to the French, but I have been beginning to wonder, for some time past, whether Dom Fernando was quite the friend of Britain he would have one think.'

'He has certainly been most anxious for news of your whereabouts, and has positively haunted the house for tidings of you. To tell truth, I was quite glad Chloe and I did not know where you were, or it would have been hard, without rudeness, to have concealed it.'

To her moved surprise he took her hand and kissed it. 'I owe you many apologies, Camilla, for having done you less than justice, and you are generosity itself not to chide me for leaving you so in the dark. But you, with your good sense, will realise, I am sure, that it was not a secret to be entrusted lightly to a stranger.'

She managed a laugh. 'What a mortal inconvenience it must have been to you to find yourself saddled with a parcel of females.'

'Not altogether.' He considered it. 'You and Chloe have provided me with a most admirable cover, and will, I hope, continue to do so. Though I am afraid you will find it harder now that you know what you are doing.'

'Yes, I shall be anxious about you. As for Chloe, of course she must know nothing of this. And now, if you are convinced you must give Dom Fernando the meeting, I had best act valet (poor Jenks, he was a good man) and find you your evening dress. Is there none of the servants you could trust to help you?'

'I think not. But if you will find me what I need and leave me to my struggles, I can, I think, make shift to dress myself. And indeed, I shall have to, for there, if I mistake not, is Dom Fernando now. Go to him, please, and tell him I am a trifle fatigued from travelling but will join him forthwith.'

'Very well, and for good measure, I will tell him I am quite exhausted with the bullfight and have the headache, and if that does not shift him soon, do not be surprised if I suffer a public attack of the vapours. After all, a bullfight is a tiring experience for an English young lady.'

'Admirable girl.' He pressed her hand gratefully. 'But have you a headache?'

'Not the least in the world. I have never felt better—since you are safe home.' And then, colouring fiercely at her own unexpected vehemence, she left him hurriedly, and ran down the shallow marble stair to the great salon, where she found Dom Fernando awaiting her.

After assuring himself, and her, that she was in most remarkable looks and clearly none the worse for her exhausting day, he came quickly to the point. Complimenting her on her colour, he continued archly, 'But I am not coxcomb enough to think you fly these flags on my account. I understand that milord is most happily returned. I hope you have chided him for his long absence from so charming a bride.'

'Oh yes.' She gave her best imitation of Chloe's laugh. 'I have read him a fine lecture and he is a chastened man. He is making himself presentable, for indeed he was sadly travel stained, and bids me tell you he will be with you directly. What a fortunate thing that so good a friend should be here to welcome him home.'

He made her a gallant rejoinder, and she continued to keep the stream of small talk alive, while all her thoughts were with Lavenham. Would he really be able to shrug his wounded arm into his dress jacket? Not for the first time, she congratulated herself that he was not one of the town dandies who insisted on a fit so rigorous that it was impossible to put on their own clothes. But time was passing.

'I trust,' Dom Fernando said, 'that milord is none the worse for his journey. You are wishing me no doubt at the devil for troubling your reunion, but I must just wait long enough to welcome him home. That is, if you think him well enough to see me?'

'Well enough? But why should he not be? I hope he is not such a weakling as to be knocked up by a long day's journeying, though he is, in truth, more than a little fatigued and I shall certainly do my possible to ensure that he retires early.'

'I am sure you will.' And then, seeing her colour, he changed the subject. 'But, tell me, where is the charming Mademoiselle Chloe? I trust that she is not worn out with the exertions of her day, or disgusted with me for taking her to the bullfight.'

'Oh, no.' For some time past anxiety for Chloe had been mingled with that for Lavenham. What could be keeping her out so long? 'She is out, I think, walking in the garden.'

'In the garden? So late?' And indeed a servant had just brought in candles, which made the terrace and garden below suddenly a place of twilight shadows. Camilla moved restlessly over to the window, while throwing back over her shoulder to Dom Fernando, 'I know you must think our English girls sadly unprotected, but Chloe will come to no harm in our own garden.' She only wished she was sure of it. 'Ah, here she comes.' And she opened the folding door that led on to the terrace to call, 'Chloe, what are you doing out in the dew so late? Here is your brother home, and Dom Fernando come to enquire after our health.'

'Oh!' Chloe's moue was for the second half of the sentence. She had clearly been intending to skirt round the house and go in by the other door, but now came reluctantly up the terrace steps, where candlelight from indoors caught golden lights in her tousled curls and showed up the brilliance of her complexion and the rich red of the roses she carried. Pausing in the doorway, she greeted Dom Fernando with what Camilla could only think deplorable casualness and then looked about her. 'But where is Lee?'

'Here.' He appeared in the doorway, dead pale but erect and with a courteous speech of welcome for Dom Fernando and a quick smile for Chloe, who, Camilla saw, was about to rush towards him for one of the quick fierce embraces he tolerated from her. But not tonight. Camilla caught the hand that was not full of roses. 'Your brother is tired, Chloe. He has been riding all day. And you, my love, are in no state to see company. I beg you will tidy your hair and your dress before you rejoin us.' Thus positively commanded, Chloe made a little rebellious face for Camilla alone, smiled brilliantly at Lavenham and withdrew, with the merest sketch of a curtsey for Dom Fernando.

He was already pressing Lavenham with courteous questions about his long absence. His friends had missed him . . . Had he found the roads passable? . . . Had his business not taken him longer than he had expected? One must hope that at least it had proved prosperous . . . And so on, with each half question circling closer to the crux of the matter — the purpose of Lavenham's journey.

To Camilla's relief, a servant interrupted one of Lavenham's courteous, vague replies by appearing with the wine and cakes she had ordered, and she made a little business of being sure that the men were served with what they liked best, then took advantage of the interruption to change the subject, bursting into an exclamatory description of Dom Fernando's kindness during Lavenham's absence and then proceeding to a detailed and falsely enthusiastic description of the bullfight. Dom Fernando listened with his usual grave politeness, then returned to the attack. If they had only known milord was to return today, they might have extended their journey to ride out and meet him. Or was he wrong in assuming that milord had come from south of the river?

Lavenham laughed and parried the question by replying that he had been in no mood to be met by a party of pleasure. 'Your roads and your inns do not leave one in festive spirit.'

The men's glasses were empty. Camilla rose to her feet to replenish them, hoping that this would give Dom Fernando his cue to leave, but he let her fill his glass and sipped at it absent-mindedly as he returned to his questioning. Lavenham, too, was drinking quickly, and a little flush of colour had mounted in his cheeks. Camilla, who knew him to be moderate to the point of abstemiousness, watched anxiously and was relieved when Chloe danced back into the room, her crumpled muslin changed for a fresh one, her golden curls agleam with brushing. But the distraction she provided was only half successful for she, too, wanted to know where her brother had been and what had kept him so long away. Since her questions were put in English, Dom Fernando could not, presumably, understand them, though Camilla, watching his absorbed expression, found herself wondering whether his ignorance of English was as complete as he had led her to suppose.

Lavenham was taking no chances, but rebuked his sister roundly in French for talking a language their guest could not understand, and then, breaking into English with an apologetic glance at Dom Fernando, continued, 'And if you do not understand that, I will tell you in plain English that I am tired out and have no wish to discuss my travels tonight.'

Chloe, always unpredictable, amazed Camilla by bursting into a golden peal of laughter. 'Why, Lee, you are disguised! I have not seen you so since your coming of age. Did you know you had a toper for a husband, Camilla?'

Camilla had been watching Dom Fernando throughout this interchange and was now convinced from his expression that he understood every word they were saying. She noticed something else, too. A dark patch was forming on the sleeve of Lavenham's evening jacket. His wound was bleeding again and had already soaked through the bandage. It was only a matter of time until either Dom Fernando or Chloe noticed; and Dom Fernando had just poured himself another glass of wine and seemed to have settled down for the night. She rose to her feet, exclaiming: 'My head aches so,' and moved towards the window, then, as she passed the chair where Dom Fernando was sitting, swayed on her feet and fell towards him. To her intense relief, he caught her, and laid her on a nearby sofa with exclamations of solicitude and alarm, in which the others joined. For a few minutes, she let herself lie there with closed eyes, listening to the little tumult her collapse had caused. Then, as Chloe held a vinaigrette under her nose, she let her eyes flutter open, looked vaguely around and tried to sit up, with a murmured apology: 'The heat . . . the blood . . . Dom Fernando, what will you think of me?'

Lavenham had taken his cue. 'I was afraid the bullfight might prove strong meat for English stomachs,' he said. 'Chloe, ring for your sister's maid. She will be best in bed.'

Camilla allowed herself a sigh of pure exhaustion. 'Oh, yes,' she said, 'I fear the excitement of the day has given me the vapours. All that blood . . . Lavenham, you'll not leave me?'

He took her hand in his, which burned ice cold. 'Of course not. You must forgive us, Dom Fernando. Perhaps we may continue this most interesting conversation tomorrow?'

Thus directly applied to, Dom Fernando took his leave at last, and Camilla, who had been thinking rapidly, allowed herself to be supported to her room by Lavenham and her maid. Better that Chloe should think her a weak and neglectful wife than that she should guess at her brother's condition. Chloe showed signs of lingering with further offers of smelling salts and spirits of lemon, but Lavenham disposed of her with a brother's firmness before turning to Camilla, whose maid was busy on the other side of the room.

'Admirably acted,' he pressed her hand. 'At least,' anxiously, 'I trust it was acted? You are not really unwell?'

'Not the least in the world. I will come to you as soon as I can rid myself of Frances. Your wound needs dressing again. Best get to your apartments before it is noticed.'

He looked quickly down at the dark patch that was spreading over the cloth of his sleeve, pressed her hand once more and then, as Frances approached with her negligée, made her a speech of husbandly solicitude and took his leave.

By the time Frances left her the house was quiet. Camilla jumped out of bed and put on the swansdown-trimmed blue satin negligée Lady Leominster had chosen for her. What a mockery, she remembered, it had seemed at the time. Now, impatiently sliding her feet into the matching slippers, she was glad of it with its look almost of a morning gown. In the main hall, a night light burned dimly; no lights showed under Chloe's door; the house seemed asleep. She tapped gently on the door to Lavenham's apartments at the end of the hall and opened it quietly. The light of his guttering candle showed that he had managed to struggle out of his blood-stained jacket before collapsing, exhausted on the bed. Now he slept heavily, his flushed face and loud breathing bearing witness to the unusual quantity of wine he had drunk under the strain of Dom Fernando's visit. For a moment, beside his bed, Camilla hesitated. It seemed wicked to rouse him. But the blood was still seeping through the bandage on his arm, and besides it would be dangerous to let him lie all night like this. Very gently, she shook his good shoulder: 'Lavenham, it is I, Camilla.'

He stirred in his sleep, then woke all at once, gazing at her with wild and startled eyes, then, obviously remembering: 'Oh, it is you—I was dreaming.'

'Yes, I am come to change your bandages. I will not disturb you for long.' And she began deftly unwinding the bloody bandage. Involuntarily, he winced at her touch. 'This is no work for a young lady,' he said. 'You will be wishing that you had seen me at Jericho before you married me.' And then, wincing again as she reached the wound itself, 'Pour me a glass of wine, will you? And one for yourself. It will make the work go better.'

Reluctantly, for she was convinced that he had already had rather more than was good for him, she poured two glasses from the decanter that stood on a side table and brought him one, leaving hers, for the time being, where it stood. But he insisted, with an invalid's fierceness, on her drinking with him before she finished bathing and binding up his wound, and toasted her solemnly: 'My invaluable wife.'

Colouring with pleasure, she raised her glass to his and drank, recognising, as she felt the strong wine bloom within her, that she needed it. It seemed to have revived him too, for as she began once more to work on his wound, he began to talk, quick and freely, as she had heard him do in Portuguese but never, before, in English.

'Do you know,' he was saying. 'Out there, when they attacked the carriage, I was afraid? Afraid of death. I have never feared it before. Do you think I can be beginning to wish to live?'

'I hope so. There.' She had finished and laid his arm gently on the pillow. 'Now I wish you will let me help you to bed. You will catch cold, lying thus.'

He caught her hand with his good one. 'No, do not dismiss me so: I will be your obedient patient presently, but tell me one thing first; when you so admirably pretended to swoon, you called for me: "Lavenham, do not leave me," you said. Of course, that was feigning too?'

She sat there for a moment by his bedside, looking at his flushed face, wondering what to say. Pride, which had stood by her so well, told her to lie, to tell him it had all been pretence, but something else in her, was it the wine, or something stronger, would not be denied. 'No,' she said, 'that was not feigning, Lavenham.'

'Then drink up your wine.' He drained his glass as she obeyed him. 'Perhaps there is no need to be afraid any more.' And with a sudden, fierce movement of his good arm he pulled her down on the bed beside him while his lips closed hungrily over hers. For a moment, some sober instinct made her resist, then, as his kisses became fiercer and more demanding, she felt her need of him rise up to meet his. On the table beside the bed the two glasses stood empty, the candle guttered out, the cool moonlight shone into the room as there, among his bloodstained sheets, she found herself, at last, his wife indeed.

Chapter 7

Waking, much later, to quick happiness and the first morning sound of birds, Camilla was alarmed at once by Lavenham's restless tossing and muttering at her side. He was all too evidently in a high fever, his broken murmurings part dream, part delirium. She slipped quickly out of bed, pulled the bedclothes closer around him and shut the large casement through which cool morning air was pouring into the room. Returning to the bed, she found Lavenham's pulse was rapid and disordered. His hot forehead and flushed cheeks added to her anxiety. But what should she do? Her first instinct was to summon a doctor, but it would be impossible for him to tend the invalid without discovering his wound. For a moment she thought of explaining this away as a domestic accident of some kind, but who would believe her? And besides, there was Dom Fernando to be considered. It would be well nigh impossible to invent an accident that could convincingly have happened after he had left. No, she would have to pray to God and nurse Lavenham herself. She was slightly encouraged in this determination by memory of his strictures on Portuguese medicine. Perhaps after all she would be saving his life by keeping the doctor from him.

Only the deep unspoken happiness of her new relation with Lavenham carried her through the anxieties of the next few days. He continued half conscious or, worse still, delirious, while his fever resisted all the medicaments she had brought with her from England. The only point of consolation was that, miraculously, his wound continued to heal and she thought that the fever must be due mainly to exhaustion and, perhaps, to the blow he had received on his head. As he continued deliriously calling out for his mother and, it seemed, acting over again the duel of long ago when his father was killed, she became increasingly anxious lest his brain should have been affected. If only she could get expert advice. But Lord Strangford was still away and there was no one else to whom she felt she could turn.

Chloe's anxiety and Dom Fernando's daily visits of polite inquisition exacerbated her misery. For them, as for the servants, she had to pretend that Lavenham's illness was merely trifling, a matter of over-fatigue and inevitable recovery. But as the anxious days passed, it became increasingly difficult to keep up the pretence, and on the third day, as she sat by his bed bathing his hot forehead with spirits of lavender, she had almost made up her mind to give way to Dom Fernando's pressure and let him summon a doctor. Surely she was a murderess to keep expert attention from him. And yet, she was sure, a Portuguese physician would bleed him at once, and he had lost enough blood already. She was sitting there, a prey to the most agonising kind of uncertainty, when he suddenly reached out and grasped her hand, 'Mother,' he said, 'mother, you will not leave me?'

'No, never.' How truly she meant it. 'Lie still, my love, lie still and rest.'

'You never called me that before.' To her delighted surprise he seemed to have taken in what she said, though attributing it, no doubt, to the mother he had lost so long ago. 'Stay with me,' he went on, 'stay with me always.'

'Of course.' Very gently, still holding his hand in hers, she used the other to stroke the disordered curls away from his brow. Was she imagining it, or did this feel cooler to her touch? Scarcely daring to hope, she sat there and watched as he fell, still holding her hand, into a deep and refreshing sleep. Time passed. The shadows lengthened in the room and Chloe came scratching at the door to whisper that Dom Fernando was below, asking for her. Camilla did not stir from where she sat, merely turning to whisper over her shoulder that Lavenham was better, but she could not leave him.

Towards night, he woke at last, a characteristic apology on his lips. 'I have been ill, and a monstrous trouble to you, I fear.'

'No trouble, my love.' The endearment slipped out without thought, and she saw a look of faint puzzlement cloud his face. Was she going too fast for him? Hastily recovering herself, she went on, 'Do not trouble yourself about anything; I have not had the doctor to you. Nobody knows what has been the matter with you.'

'No one knows? No doctor?' He looked more puzzled than ever. 'But why not?'

A cold finger of fear touched her heart. 'But do you not remember?'

'Remember? Let me see.' His head moved restlessly on the pillows. 'I was dreaming of my mother . . . but that's not it. Ah, now I have it. I went to Spain, did I not? And was attacked, returning . . . Poor Jenks, was he killed, or did I dream it?'

'You told me so.' She watched his restless movements anxiously.

'And then—what? I remember nothing more. I must have come home somehow, for here I am. And you have not had the doctor to me—Of course, it was all to be secret. I remember planning it with Strangford. He thinks Dom Fernando less than a friend. Has Fernando been here?'

'Yes, soon after you arrived, but do not trouble yourself, he knows nothing, although, I think, he suspects much.'

He managed a flicker of a smile. 'So you have nursed me single-handed and kept the world at bay. I see I am more indebted to you than ever. It was a lucky day for me when my grandmother made us marry. But you must be worn out. Tell me, how long have I been ill?'

'Only three days.' Her thoughts were in a turmoil. His tone, as much as his words, told her that he remembered nothing of the night that had changed her world. What could she do?

He was looking at her anxiously. 'Have I been so great a trouble? I wish I could remember . . .' Again his head moved restlessly among his pillows. His colour was rising.

She reached out to feel his pulse: 'Do not trouble yourself about anything. You must rest. You will remember soon enough.' Deeply and desperately she hoped it was true, as she sat and watched him drift off again to sleep. If he did not? What could she do? The answer was obvious: nothing. That moonlight night must be forgotten. She must return to the old formality, the old pretence. She had never known such chill despair before, but sat there, quietly, by his bed, watching him as he slept, while, silently, following each other, the tears ran down her cheeks.

There was at least some consolation in his rapid and continued recovery, but with it came no blessed return of memory. In answer to his questions, she had told him of his exhausted return and how, between them, they had kept Dom Fernando's curiosity at bay, but this did not, as she had hoped, rouse any answering gleam of remembrance. 'So you got me to bed and I turned lunatic on your hands,' he concluded. 'What a plague I must have been to you. It is no wonder you look exhausted. We must lose no time in moving to Sintra, where I hope the cooler air will refresh you.'

She laughed. What an effort it was to get back the old lightness of touch. 'You are scarce flattering. Am I indeed looking so hagged?'

He reached out to press her hand. 'You look like someone who has just saved her husband's life,' he said.

She slept better that night. Surely, it was only a matter of time, and all would be well. Dreaming she was in his arms again, she woke to fresh hope and resolutions of patience. Lady Leominster had said she must be patient as Job, and had come nearer the mark than she knew, for by now Camilla had learned only too well how an unguarded tender word or look could startle her husband back into his lonely shell. At all costs, she must keep up the light and teasing relationship she had managed to evolve between them, and leave the rest to time.

Luckily for her, as soon as Lavenham was well enough to go out, he plunged into the arrangements for their move to Sintra, and indeed the idea of a mountain change after the dusty July heat of the city was most welcome to Camilla. But to her surprise, Chloe proved almost mutinous. They were well enough where they were, she said. What was the use of going off to ruralise in the mountains and exposing themselves at the same time to all the tedium of attendance on the Court. For the villa Lavenham had taken would be all too convenient both for attendance at the Prince Regent's Court at Mafra and for visits to his estranged wife who was living on her estate of Ramalhao in Sintra itself. It was in vain that Camilla pointed out how necessary such attendance was for the success of Lavenham's mission. Chloe refused to be comforted and sulked ostentatiously until Camilla could have shaken her. Not for the first time, she found herself grateful for Lavenham's detachment, which kept him from noticing his sister's bad behaviour.

He came home early one evening to announce, rather sooner than Camilla had expected, that all was ready: they could make the move to Sintra next morning. Camilla's own preparations were well in hand, but she suspected that Chloe had done little or nothing about getting ready, and hurried out into the garden to break the news to her. Not finding her in the shady walks of their own garden, she crossed the little stream that separated their estate from the deserted gardens of the Marvila palace next door and wandered through the overgrown thickets of myrtle and jasmine calling softly for Chloe. But the evening wind, fiercer than usual tonight, was tearing early fruit from the plum trees and her voice was lost in its wailing among the branches.

So it happened that she turned the corner of one of the orange groves and came, unawares, on Chloe, sitting on a rustic bench, her arm entwined with that of a man Camilla had never seen before.

'Chloe!' At the sound of her voice, the absorbed couple sprang to their feet, and apart. Chloe coloured crimson, the man, who was thin, brown, wiry and considerably older than her, made a low bow and stood his ground, still holding Chloe's hand in his, somewhat, Camilla suspected, against her will. For a moment, the silence stretched out. Chloe was tongue-tied, Camilla could think of nothing to say that would not seem unduly melodramatic, the stranger looked, she thought angrily, faintly amused. It was he who broke the silence at last.

'Well, *mon ange*,' he said to Chloe, 'will you not make me known to your sister—and mine?' He spoke in English, but with a marked French accent.

Camilla would not believe her ears. 'What do you mean?'

He made her another bow, elegant, courtly—infuriating. 'I would have known you anywhere,' he said, 'Your likeness to our lamented mother is startling. But it seems I have the advantage of you, and since this dear child will not do it, allow me to present myself: M. Boutet, the butcher's son, or, being translated, your long lost brother. Is this not a touching reunion?'

'I do not understand. Chloe, what does this mean? When did you meet this gentleman?'

Chloe spoke at last. 'At Corpus Christi,' she said. 'He brought me home, when Lavenham would not even trouble himself to look for me. I was like to sink when he told me he was your brother, Camilla. Is it not the most romantic circumstance? Of course, it is tedious that he is one of the enemy Lee fusses about, else I would have made him known to you long ago. Indeed, I am glad you have discovered us now; you can give us your counsel as to how best to make Lee see reason. How can I be expected to come to Sintra, when my heart,' she made a wide dramatic gesture, 'my heart is here.'

106

Camilla had never been so angry. She looked at her brother and wished that his strong and discouraging likeness to their father did not convince her of the truth of his claim. 'I do not know what to say to you.'

'Why, what but "Welcome, long lost brother"? It is, as Chloe says, a somewhat inconvenient circumstance that we should find ourselves, for the moment, in opposite camps. But time will put that to rights—and soon enough, I can tell you. It is but a matter of months until England is a province of the French empire, and then, little sister, you will be glad enough to have a friend in Bonaparte's army. In the meantime, I agree with you that we had best say nothing to your husband who seems, from all I hear, to be a marvellously stiff-necked English prig and would doubtless make an international incident of me forthwith, which, I know, is what you would not at all wish for any of our sakes.'

Though it was infuriating thus to have him take her course of action for granted, she had to admit the sense in what he said. To present Lavenham with a brother-in-law in the enemy's camp would be enormously to complicate his position, and at the same time, inevitably, the discovery of Chloe's clandestine romance would put him fatally out of patience with her. Thus provoked, he might do anything—would almost certainly send Chloe back to England, and Camilla, who flattered herself that by now she had at least some influence over her volatile sister-in-law, dreaded the consequences of any such drastic action. This affair with her brother was bad enough, but who could tell what mischief Chloe might get up to alone in England? As these thoughts flashed through her mind, she also remembered, with relief, the reason for her coming to look for Chloe. After all, they were leaving for Sintra tomorrow: this would put an end to the lovers' meetings that had been carrying on, she realised with a shock of dismay, since Corpus Christi.

She had been looking at her brother gravely as these thoughts hurried through her mind and finding little in his appearance to

107

reassure her. No use to appeal to his better nature; everything about him proclaimed him a gambler like their father, but, she feared, a gambler not so much with money as with life. He was becoming, she noticed with satisfaction, somewhat restive under her prolonged scrutiny, while Chloe, incredibly, had drifted away to pick and nibble at a ripe apricot. Nothing could have brought home so forcibly to Camilla her sister-in-law's basic childishness. She simply had no idea of the gravity of the situation in which she had plunged them.

It was time to speak: 'Come, Chloe,' said Camilla, 'your brother is looking for you.'

This recalled Chloe's wandering attention at once. 'Lee? You will not tell him, Camilla? Promise! I dare not face him, else.'

'It is a pity,' said Camilla, 'that you had not thought of that sooner. But do not cry, child,' as the easy tears began to roll down Chloe's cheeks, 'I shall not tell Lavenham — yet. M. Boutet is right. Silence, for the moment, will be best. But I must have both your promises that you will not meet again.' No need to tell them this would be impossible anyway because of the impending move to Sintra.

After a quick exchange of glances, both of them promised so readily that Camilla was convinced they had not the slightest intention of keeping their word. It was lucky that circumstances were likely to make them more scrupulous than they intended. She hurried their farewells, ignoring a protest from her brother that she was heartless in calling him M. Boutet like a stranger. 'Am I not to be Charles after all these years?'

'I will call you Charles when you behave to me like a brother,' she said austerely. 'So far, I see no reason to consider you anything but a stranger. I only wish you were one. Come, Chloe,' she said again. 'Your brother will come looking for us if you do not hurry.'

This threat was effective on both Chloe and Charles, whom Camilla began to suspect of being as much of a cowardly braggart as his father. For all his slighting words, he clearly had no wish to encounter Chloe's formidable brother. One swift look passed between him and Chloe, promising, Camilla was sure, a meeting on the morrow, whatever obstacles might be placed in the way. She merely smiled and took Chloe's hand. 'Goodbye, M. Boutet,' she said, 'give my regards to your friend M. Mireille when you next see him.'

The shot went home. He coloured angrily and withdrew down a shady walk of lemon and orange trees. Alone with Chloe, Camilla did not hurry her away at once. Her threats of Lavenham's impatience had served their turn, but she did not, in fact, think he would come looking for them. When she had left him, he had been busy sorting papers ready for tomorrow's move. So occupied, he would not notice the passage of time. And before they went in, she must find out how deeply Chloe had committed herself. Anxiously, she began her questioning, and to her relief Chloe, who obviously felt that she was being let off lightly, answered readily enough. Yes, they had met almost daily since Corpus Christi, but in answer to Camilla's delicate but persistent questioning, she maintained that her beloved Charles had behaved to her with the most perfect propriety, had hardly, in fact, done more than kiss her hand. The naïve irritation that she showed in revealing this went far to convince Camilla that she was speaking the truth, and she decided, with a deep inward sigh of relief, that whatever unprincipled game her brother had been playing it had not involved actually disgracing Chloe, or at least, not yet. It was with an anxious heart and an almost absent-minded air that she administered the scold Chloe expected, trying to convey, as she did so, that this was a business too serious for mere scolding. In vain she tried to show Chloe how her behaviour might endanger her brother's position as a diplomat. Chloe merely sighed, shrugged, and asked what importance the behaviour of a mere girl like herself could have. At last, Camilla lost her temper. 'Well,' she said, 'fortunately, it is not of the greatest importance that you insist on playing the fool. We leave for Sintra tomorrow. I hope you will have time there to come to your senses.'

Now the tears came in good earnest, convincing Camilla once more that Chloe had not for a moment meant to keep her promise not to see Charles again. For once, she could not find a scrap of sympathy for Chloe's presentation of beauty in distress, but merely shrugged and turned to lead the way back to the house. 'You had best dry your tears if you do not want Lavenham asking questions.'

Tossing on her sleepless bed that night, Camilla wondered over and over again whether she had been right in what she had done. Should she not have taken this deplorable piece of news at once to Lavenham, whose chief concern, after all, it was. She could not make up her mind. If things had been right between them, she would not have hesitated for a moment, but as it was, she could be sure of nothing—except that he was still over-tired from his illness and that she could not bear to put another strain upon him. No, she decided at last, this burden must be borne alone, at least for the time being.

To her relief, Chloe seemed to have decided she had best conceal her reluctance to go to Sintra, fearing, no doubt, that any recalcitrance on her part might end in Camilla's telling Lavenham the whole story. As a result the drive to Sintra was less of an ordeal than Camilla had feared and she was even able to enjoy the wild and romantic views of valley and mountain, parched and dry from the summer drought, the occasional aloes, splendid in yellow bloom, and the strange aromatic perfumes that were wafted into the carriage by a fitful breeze. Lavenham, too, bore the rough journey better than she had feared, though he was pale and tired by the time they crossed the desolate heath at the foot of the Sintra mountains and reached the house that was to be theirs.

But there, to her dismay, an urgent messenger was awaiting Lavenham to summon him, at once, to a conference with Strangford and the Prince Regent who were visiting the mad old Queen at Queluz. At her insistence, Lavenham delayed long enough to drink a glass of wine and eat a handful of dried fruits, but rest longer he would not, starting at once for the ride back to Queluz. Left alone, she and Chloe plunged once more into the business of house cleaning, for here, as at Lisbon, they found the apartments intended for them scarce fit for habitation by a well bred English pig.

Lavenham did not return until late at night, and then his face was grave as he told them the news. France and Spain together had presented an ultimatum to the Prince Regent, demanding once again that Portuguese ports be closed to British shipping and that British residents be arrested and their property confiscated. This had plunged the Prince Regent into an agony of indecision and all the English Minister's representations of the folly of acceding to so unreasonable a request had merely prevailed upon him to delay his answer. The Spanish and French representatives in Portugal were threatening to ask for their passports if Dom John did not agree to their demands, and this, Lavenham explained, would mean war. Undecided himself, he paced about the room, pale with exhaustion and anxiety, as he debated part with himself, part with Camilla, what was best for her and Chloe to do. Ideally, they should leave for England at once, but how? The regular sailings of the packet had been discontinued, and he knew of no other ship on which he would trust them unescorted. Camilla seized on this at once. If he did not propose to accompany them, how would he return if war did break out? When he explained that a battleship would certainly be sent to pick up the British Ministers she urged that it would be best for her and Chloe to wait with him, pretending a greater reluctance than she actually felt at the idea of travelling unescorted. For she could not bear the idea of leaving him to the casual mercy of Portuguese servants in his still uncertain state of health. Besides, she did not want to leave him. But this must not be said. Instead, she talked of the hazards of a journey alone, and was enthusiastically seconded by Chloe, who had, of course, her own reasons for not wishing to leave Portugal.

In the end, he gave in, reluctantly, and insisting that if a suitable ship should, by any miracle, arrive in Lisbon before the port was closed to the British, as he feared it soon would be, they must agree to sail with her. To this, Camilla yielded readily enough. It would be time for argument when the ship appeared. Besides, Lavenham looked more and more exhausted, and had told her that he must be at Queluz again early the next morning. This was no time for unnecessary talk.

From then on, she and Chloe lived a strange life, marooned, as it were, in their country villa. Although the Prince Regent had still not answered the French and Spanish ultimatum, Lavenham was increasingly afraid that he would, in the end, yield to the demands upon him. In these circumstances, he thought it best that Camilla and Chloe should not appear at court, but remain as quietly as possible in the country. As for him, he spent every day adding his arguments to Strangford's in the vain attempt to persuade Dom John that an attack by Bonaparte was inevitable and that his best and indeed only course was to move his entire court to his American province of Brazil and wait out the coming storm in safety there. When Camilla protested at this defeatist advice, Lavenham explained that the Portuguese army was negligible while both it and the country in general were riddled with secret supporters of France, who still believed in Bonaparte as a liberator. Only bitter experience, he thought, would convince them of their mistake and this they were all too likely to have. Strangford, too, who rode back once or twice with Lavenham to dine and sleep at the villa, was gloomy about the prospects and made no secret of his doubts as to the wisdom of Camilla's and Chloe's remaining. But as the hot August days followed each other, and the surrounding hills grew more and more parched and brown, no English ship was reported at Lisbon, and Camilla and

Chloe remained where they were, force perforce, much to Camilla's relief. For she was increasingly anxious about Lavenham who continued pale and withdrawn beyond what the situation seemed to her to merit. He was brief with her, almost abrupt with Chloe, their earlier teasing relationship a thing of regretful memory only. It was almost a relief when the Prince Regent moved his court back to Mafra and the distance was too great for Lavenham to return home every night. Alone together, Camilla and Chloe resumed a seemingly peaceful life of reading and work. The French lessons, whose purpose had been only too obvious to Camilla since she had discovered Chloe's affair with her brother, had been tacitly discontinued, but both were making rapid strides with their Portuguese. As for Charles, or, as Camilla insisted even of thinking of him, M. Boutet, they never mentioned him. Camilla felt she had nothing to add to the scolding she had administered on the day of discovery, and was indeed only too grateful that Chloe seemed to be bearing the enforced separation so placidly. She wondered, occasionally, whether the lovers still contrived to correspond, but thought it best not to provoke an explosion by enquiring too closely. After all, they would undoubtedly be leaving for England soon enough and this would put an end to everything. For Lavenham, on the rare occasions when he contrived to visit them, was more and more gloomy. Arriving, one night, drenched with the first September rain, he announced that the French and Spanish envoys had, as they had threatened, packed up and left Lisbon. And instead of taking this as the signal for positive action, the Regent continued to hesitate and temporise, now asking the English for assurances of his safety and convoy to the Brazils, now hovering near to granting the French requests, refusing to admit that the time for this – if there ever had been one – was past.

It was later that rainy night, after Chloe had gone off, as usual, early to bed, that Lavenham, who had been pacing restlessly about the chilly room, came suddenly to stand beside Camilla as she sewed. She put down her work and looked up at him in suddenly anxious enquiry.

'I have been meaning to ask you,' he paused for a minute, took another rapid turn about the room and returned to stand over her again. 'The day before we left Lisbon,' he said. 'You remember it?'

'Of course.' She was cold with more than the chill of the fireless room. What could be coming?

'You were out in the garden—not ours, the one next door. I came to look for you.' He spoke in short, disjointed sentences. 'It was growing late. The dew was falling. I thought it time you and Chloe were indoors.' Again he stopped, listening to the desolate patter of rain on the marble terrace. Then, in a rush, 'Who was the man you were talking to?'

'The man?' At all costs she must have time to think.

'Yes. Do not, I beg, think that I was in any sense spying on you. I heard your voices: that was all, thought I saw someone with you. I did not wish to seem to intrude. I should have asked you sooner.' He passed a hand over his forehead. 'You do not, I think, quite understand, you and Chloe, what a nest of spies we live among.' He was looking at her now, almost, it seemed appealingly. What a blessed relief it would be to tell him. But how could she now, so long after the event, expose poor Chloe, who thought herself safe, to the explosion of his wrath? It was all over: let it be forgotten. And yet, how she hated to lie, and to him of all people. She looked up from her sewing, where it lay, neglected in her lap. 'What man?' she said. 'I remember no one.' She regretted the lie as soon as it was spoken, but, to her relief, he seemed to accept it.

'Strange,' he said. 'Can my memory have been playing me tricks again? I was positive . . . You are sure you were not talking to one of the gardeners?'

'So late at night? You know they would not think of working after evening. But ask Chloe, if you are still in doubt.'

'What?' He took her up on it at once. 'As if I would not trust

114

your word. No, no . . . I must have imagined it. I shall be glad when we are back in England. My mind has not recovered its tone since my accident . . . it is the pressure of events, I suppose, I am wretched company for you and Chloe, I'm afraid. I only wish I could send you home.'

She rose and put away her sewing. 'You are worn out,' she said. 'That is all the trouble. Let me give you some laudanam to make you sleep.'

'No, no, I thank you just the same. My mind is troubled enough. I will not tamper with it further. But neither will I keep you talking here. It is too cold to be sitting so late without a fire. I only wish we could move back to Lisbon, where the house is more fit for cold weather, but the Prince Regent seems fixed at Mafra and so long as he stays, I must. Nor do I think it safe for you and Chloe to return without me.'

'No, anything rather than that.' His sudden questions had re-awakened all her anxiety on Chloe's behalf. She hoped, of course, that M. Boutet would have left with the rest of the French mission, but nothing was certain. Much best not risk exposing Chloe once more to his dangerous proximity.

Lavenham was looking at her strangely. 'You really prefer it here, with all the discomfort of draughts and cold?'

'Of course. So long as you are here.' So much, surely, she could say.

He smiled at her more kindly than he had done for some time. 'Very well, that is settled, then. So long as I remain, you and Chloe shall do so too. We will all freeze together.'

Alone in her own apartments, Camilla allowed herself the relief of a passion of tears. If only she had had the courage to tell Lavenham the truth . . . Now, looking back on it, she was sure she had been wrong to shield Chloe at the expense of a direct lie. It was frightful to have convinced Lavenham that his memory was playing him false, while his kindness, his confidence in her and refusal to apply to Chloe for confirmation of what she had said, was more than her guilty conscience could bear. If he should ever learn that she had lied to him, he would never trust her again.

She woke next morning feeling ill and wretched, her first thoughts of the unlucky interview of the night before. But it was too late now for regret, she had committed herself to the lie, and must stick to it. Resolutely putting the thought of it out of her head, she dressed and went down to the breakfast room, where she found Lavenham already eating a hurried meal preparatory to leaving for Mafra. She crumbled at a roll, pretended to drink her coffee and made an early excuse to leave the room. To her relief, Lavenham appeared to notice nothing. He was busy giving last minute orders to the steward, for this was to be an absence of some duration. He had had news that Antonio de Araujo, the Minister for Foreign Affairs, had been urgently summoned to Mafra, and as he strongly suspected Araujo of belonging secretly to the French party, neither he nor Strangford would think it safe to leave the palace so long as he remained there. But he urged Camilla to have everything ready for a sudden move to Lisbon in case this should become necessary. She promised to do so, said the formal goodbye that was all she allowed herself, watched him anxiously as he rode away along the hillside, and then retired to her room to be sick.

Chapter 8

September passed, the sun came out to shine on hills that were green from recent rain. The heather on the plain below them was in splendid blossom, and Camilla and Chloe, in their afternoon rambles, were delighted to find enormous pink and white lilies, blooming among the wild moss under the cork trees of a nearby village. But all the sunshine could not warm Camilla, who continued chilly and wretched, shaken by alarming fits of nausea and faintness. It was Chloe, one golden afternoon, when Camilla had been compelled to sit for a time on a mossy bank to recover from a giddy spell, who suggested an alarming explanation of her state.

'Can it be that you are breeding, Camilla?' she asked, with her devastating schoolroom frankness. 'How delighted Grandmamma would be.'

Camilla, with a sinking heart, pooh-poohed the idea. She was merely suffering, she said, from nerves and the intolerably greasy Portuguese food. She convinced Chloe easily enough, but convincing herself was another matter. More and more, as September darkened towards October, she began to fear that Chloe was right. If so, what should she do, how break it to Lavenham that she was to bear his child? How bitterly, now, she regretted that she had not told him the whole story of their night together when he first recovered his senses. And yet, in the face of his total oblivion, his almost unbearable return to the old formal relationship, how could she have? Would he, even, have believed her? Wary as she knew him to be of female guile, might he not have thought she was taking advantage of his admitted forgetfulness? No – it would have been impossible to tell him – and yet, now, how she wished that she had. If it had seemed impossible, before, to tell him that he had broken through a lifetime's suspicions and slept with her, how much more so now, when she must tell him, as well, that in that one ecstatic, forgotten night, he had got her with child.

How could she hope that he would believe her? Distrustful, always, of women, he must inevitably think this a ruse on her part to conceal her own unfaithfulness. As she grew, morning by morning, increasingly, despairingly certain of her condition, her one, pitiful consolation was that there was no one else, after all, whom Lavenham could possibly suspect of being the father.

But even this forlorn consolation was snatched from her, one mild October morning, by an unexpected visit from Dom Fernando. Chloe, to whom Camilla had allowed increasing liberty since the departure of the French mission, was out gathering arbutus berries on the nearby hillside, and Camilla, welcoming Dom Fernando with apologies for her husband's absence, found herself, alone with him, unaccountably ill at ease.

As always, they spoke French, and it was in that language that he assured her that he had known Lavenham was still at Mafra, had, in fact, left him there that morning to return to his own house in Lisbon. He had not been able, he told her, to pass so close to her villa without calling to find out how she did. And then, to her appalled surprise, he seized her hand and burst into a speech of passionate love. He could no longer bear, he told her, to stand by and see how Lavenham neglected her, how carelessly he exposed her to danger. Why, at any moment, the French might be over the border, and here she remained, on their very line of march to Lisbon. It was enough to make a man mad, he said, to see so much beauty and goodness so treated. How pale she was, how thin, her appearance distracted him! He had not meant to speak, had meant to love on in silence, but, seeing her thus, how could he help himself? He must tell her how completely he was her slave, how entirely hers to command.

She had contrived, at some point in this long and vehement

speech, to withdraw her hand from his, but there was no stopping him. When he was silent at last, looking at her with a mixture of hope and despair, she found herself strangely moved. He asked nothing, seemed, indeed, to hope nothing. For the first time in her life she found herself the object of disinterested affection — but with what disastrous possibilities. Here, ready made, if he should not believe her story, was a suspect for Lavenham. Every moment that she continued talking with Dom Fernando was fraught with danger, and yet, she could not bring herself to be less than gentle in dismissing him. She did her best to convince him of the injustice of his criticism of Lavenham, assuring him of her devotion to her husband and explaining that it was at her own insistence that she remained at Sintra. He listened to her patiently enough, but refused to be convinced, and continued to beg her to call upon him if she should find herself in any difficulty. 'For, say what you will, I will not believe that husband of yours as devoted to his wife as he is to his politics.'

This came uncomfortably near the bone, and it was a profound relief to Camilla when she heard Chloe singing 'Lady Fair' in the garden. When she appeared with her basket of arbutus berries, Dom Fernando stayed only long enough for the necessary polite speeches, then took his leave, begging Camilla, once again, to let him know if he could be of the slightest service to her.

'Do you know,' said devastating Chloe after he was gone, 'I really believe the old goat is sweet on you, Camilla. And if he did not stink somewhat of garlic and salt fish, he would be a proper enough conquest.' She was quite surprised and hurt when Camilla rounded on her, telling her to mind her manners and try to speak like a lady, if she could not think like one. And Camilla herself was so taken aback by her own vehemence that she ended by bursting into tears, apologising to her sister-in-law and retiring to bed.

Morning brought no comfort. Ill and wretched as usual, she wandered from room to room under the pretence of making arrangements for the sudden move Lavenham had warned them might be imminent, but in reality driven by the restlessness of despair. Until yesterday, she had continued to hope that it might yet be possible to tell her story to Lavenham and be believed. Dom Fernando's outburst had changed all that. When she remembered how he had haunted the house while Lavenham was away, she could not bring herself to hope that Lavenham would not suspect him. In fact, now that her eyes had been opened, she felt that she had been mad not to have thought of him as a possible suspect sooner. Perhaps it was as well she had not tried to tell Lavenham . . . and yet, how she wished she had. Her thoughts went round and round like this, till, finding them and the house alike intolerable, she made her way out on to the terrace and down into the sloping walks of the garden. The day was fine, with a new crispness in the air that helped to revive her spirits and she drifted up and down the alleys, trying not to think, and noticing instead the mosaic patterns of the fallen leaves, red, black and yellow, that strewed the walks. They were another reminder that winter was coming, and she found herself passionately hoping that before it began in good earnest the crisis that had been looming over them for so long would break, Anything would be better than this desperate inaction. If only the French would attack, they might at last go home. At the thought, a pang of fierce homesickness overwhelmed her and with it the glimmering of an idea. It was cowardly, perhaps, but might she not persuade Lavenham that she was not well enough to stay? At home, she might be able to convince his grandmother of the truth of her story. Old Lady Leominster would be a powerful ally, and surely her desire for an heir would help to persuade her. And yet . . . it would mean leaving Lavenham, for however eagerly she had defended him against Dom Fernando's criticisms, she was sure he would put his work first and stay to see it through. And quite right too, she told herself angrily, particularly as her illness must seem to him nothing but an affliction of the nerves.

Returning at last, reluctantly, to the house, with nothing decided, she found Chloe looking for her. Her first words chimed oddly with Camilla's thoughts. 'I have been looking everywhere for you,' she said reproachfully. 'Do you think you are well enough to be wandering off alone? The girl tells me you have eaten no breakfast. I wish you will sit down and take something now. And will you not let me send a messenger for Lavenham? You do not sleep, you do not eat . . . Camilla, do you not think we should go home?'

'But how?' Camilla had sat obediently down, enlivened by a faint amusement at this odd reversal of their roles, and begun to pick idly at a bowl of fruit.

'Someone told me there was an American boat at Lisbon. We could take passage on her. I know you do not wish to leave Lavenham, but truly Camilla, he is much better; it is about your health that we must be thinking now. Do, pray, send for him at once. The *Jane* has already unloaded her cargo, I believe. There is no time to be lost. Oh, Camilla, think of London, the blessed English food and clean sheets at night. Or we could go to Brighton; I know you would recover your spirits there: it is the enervating Portuguese air, I am sure, that has made you ill. Please, let us go home, Camilla; I am tired of it here: I do not wish ever to smell garlic again, and as for their sunshine, they are welcome to it: I would give anything for a comfortable London fog.'

Camilla could not help laughing. 'Ungrateful girl, I am sure you will sing another song when we do get home and encounter one. But, tell me, how do you know about this American boat —the *Jane*?'

Chloe was elaborately casual, 'Oh somebody told me—one of the men, whose family is in Lisbon. Was it Pedro? Or Jaime? I vow I do not recall, but it is certain enough, I tell you, and no time to be lost. Only let me send for Lavenham and he will arrange everything.'

Camilla knew Chloe well enough by now to be sure that she

was lying. Who, then, had told her about the *Jane*? Could it be that she was still seeing—or at least corresponding with M. Boutet? Had he not gone with the French mission after all? With a chill memory that his friend M. Mireille was a self-acknowledged spy in England, she wondered what sinister role her brother filled in Portugal. 'Chloe,' she had just begun the essential question when they were interrupted by an excited servant who announced that milord was riding up the hill.

Inwardly noting Chloe's look of relief, Camilla ran with her to welcome Lavenham who had just dismounted from his exhausted horse. He, too, looked infinitely weary, and Camilla hurried him indoors to comfort and a glass of wine, before she would do more than exchange the most routine greetings. Sitting, he sighed with relief. 'Ah, I was ready for this. I have been to Lisbon and back since yesterday,' he explained. 'And on a fool's errand, too, I fear. There is an American ship in harbour.' Camilla and Chloe exchanged glances as he took another long draft of wine. 'The *Jane*. I hoped to get you passage on her, but my information came too late. She was loaded to the gunwale when I arrived; her captain said he could not take aboard as much as another child. They are paying £1,200 for one family's passage to England. I wish I had heard of her sooner. I am afraid I have done wrong, gravely wrong, in letting you stay so long.'

He looked so tired and depressed that Camilla forgot her own anxieties and hurried to comfort him, reminding him that it was she who had insisted on staying. 'And, besides,' she went on, 'surely there will be other ships? It is true that Chloe and I have been saying, only this morning, that we should be glad to get home. Should we, perhaps, move to Lisbon and await the next one?'

He made an impatient gesture. 'But that is the whole point,' he said. 'Dom John has signed the edict. Tomorrow all Portuguese ports will be closed to British shipping, and who knows how long it will be before another American boat touches here? No, I have done wrong,' he said again, 'and regret it too late. For I fear that now he has yielded this point, the Regent will soon give way to the other French demands. It is only a matter of time until he orders the arrest of any British subjects that remain and the confiscation of their property.'

'But surely,' protested Camilla, with sinking heart, 'that will not apply to us? You have diplomatic immunity: he cannot touch us.'

'I wish I could believe it. I fear I have let Araujo lull me into a false sense of security. I am increasingly convinced that it is he, not Dom Fernando, who is playing the French game. I only wish I had realised it, and listened to Dom Fernando's warnings sooner. He has been urging me, this month or more, to send you both home without delay. And now it is too late. I shall never forgive myself,' he stopped in the middle of this gloomy sentence and changed his tone. 'But there is one crumb of comfort. Strangford has received information that a British Squadron, under Sir Sidney Smith, is on its way to Lisbon. We must hope that they arrive before conditions here become impossible, or before the French invade, which I am sure they intend to, whatever last moment concessions Dom John may make. In the meantime, I think you had best move back to Lisbon: this house is too lonely, and too close to what must inevitably be the French line of attack for it to be a suitable home for you now. Can you be ready to leave this afternoon, for if so I shall be able to give myself the pleasure of escorting you.'

Camilla assured him that they had everything in readiness, and could easily make their final preparations in time for an afternoon journey, but could not help asking, 'And you? Will you be able to remain with us in Lisbon?'

'Not beyond tonight, but at least the Prince Regent plans to move his court tomorrow to Queluz, to join his mother. So at least I shall be only an hour's journey away from you.'

Comforted by this news, Camilla set about her preparations with a will, and felt better, so occupied, than she had done for some time, so that when, over a light luncheon preparatory to departure, Chloe raised the question of her health with Lavenham she was easily able to scout their anxieties. It had been, she assured them, nothing but an affliction of the nerves: the move back to Lisbon would doubtless be a cure in itself. And indeed the drive back, in mellow afternoon sunshine, was a pleasant one. The heath below their house was still brilliant with a profusion of wild flowers and when they reached the valley of Alcantara, which had been so parched and dry when they last traversed it, they found it resplendent with an almost springtime green. The orange and lemon trees under the pillars of the gigantic aqueduct that crossed the valley were vividly green again and brilliant with ripening fruit. When, at Chloe's insistence, they stopped the carriage for a few moments so that she could pick some of the flowers that enamelled the close and fragrant turf, they could hear larks singing, far above them. Camilla, who had found the carriage's jolting over the rough roads far from pleasant, was delighted at the excuse Chloe had given her to sit for a while in the benevolent sunshine with Lavenham beside her. He seized this opportunity, when Chloe had wandered away a little in search of some particularly luxurious myrtle blossom, to question Camilla more closely about her indisposition, and did it so kindly that she was on the point of risking all and telling him the truth when Chloe came running back with her armful of blossom, and the opportunity was gone.

Still, it was a happy day, with Lavenham kinder than he had been for some time, teasing Chloe and taking care of Camilla so that she began to feel that if this had been achieved by her lie to him on his last visit, it was almost worth it. She was relieved, too, to find that he no longer seemed to suspect Dom Fernando of spying on him and began to hope that before he left she might have the chance, and the courage, to tell him her secret. But the chance never came. They found the servants they had left to look after the Lisbon house in a state of panic, the house itself in rack and ruin with a family of toads six inches across in the cellar. Lavenham was busy all evening putting some heart into the servants, who had been convinced they would never see master or mistress again, while Camilla and Chloe had their work cut out for them in making the home habitable once more.

And first thing next morning Lavenham rode off to visit Dom Fernando, explaining to Camilla that since he had no reliable English manservant to leave as their protector, he intended to intrust their safety to Dom Fernando. 'He will be, I am sure, a reliable protector, for really, Camilla, I believe him to be more than a little in love with you,' he finished teasingly. And Camilla, laughing and blushing, longed to seize the chance to tell him of Dom Fernando's amazing declaration. But Chloe was there, and Lavenham's horse awaiting him: once more she let the opportunity slip.

Lavenham returned to assure them that Dom Fernando promised to watch over them like a brother and that he himself would come at once if any new crisis arose, and then took his leave urging Chloe to look after Camilla, and Camilla to take care of herself. 'I hope to see your health quite re-established when I next visit you.'

Camilla, who was now thoroughly convinced that it would be nine months before her health was re-established, found cold comfort in this speech, with its suggestion that her husband was only on visiting terms with her. Left alone once more, she resumed the old round of 'if only's'. If only she had told Lavenham in the first place . . . If only she had seized that chance in the Valley of Alcantara . . . If only . . . if only. . .

A visit from Dom Fernando was almost a relief, because a distraction, and she was grateful for his assurances that she and Chloe should come to no harm that it lay in his power to prevent. To her relief, too, he made no reference to the scene he had made two days before, behaving once more merely like her husband's friend. As such, she found him easy and entertaining company

125

and was surprised when he rose to take his leave and commented on Chloe's prolonged absence. Apologising for her, and bidding Dom Fernando a grateful farewell, Camilla found herself a prey to renewed apprehension. Surely, it was impossible that M. Boutet was still in the country? Or, if he was, secretly, he would never risk visiting Chloe here? And yet—Chloe had been out in the garden for over an hour. She wandered out on to the terrace and stood there irresolute, unable to decide whether to go and look for Chloe. After all, she told herself, Chloe had never made any secret of the boredom Dom Fernando's visits caused her. She might well have seen him arrive and contrived to avoid him. So hesitating, Camilla accused herself of cowardice. Her real reason, she knew well enough, was that she could not face the possibility of another scene with her brother, for whom, on the strength of one brief meeting, she felt an aversion so strong as to amount almost to terror. Even thinking of him brought on one of her faint spells; she was compelled to hurry indoors and lie down on an uncomfortable *chaise longue* in the salon. And it was thus that Chloe found her when she came running up the steps from the garden, her cheeks flushed, her arms full of late gleanings from the rose bushes.

She was all contrition at sight of Camilla. She had left her too long alone: she would fetch smelling salts and the cordial Camilla found reviving. Dropping her roses on a small table she hurried upstairs, to return almost at once with the medicaments and a light mohair shawl which she folded lovingly round Camilla. 'There,' she said, 'now you will be better, will you not, Camilla? But I wish you would let me fetch a doctor to you: I am sure Lavenham would wish it if he knew how often you were having these giddy spells.'

'What?' Camilla's spirits were reviving. 'And be dosed, as like as not, with crushed snails and viper's broth? No, thank you, Chloe, I will wait to call a doctor till we are safe home, which I hope will be soon now.'

The light went out of Chloe's face. 'Very soon?'

'I hope so. But are you not glad? Chloe,' the question came out almost despite her, 'have you been seeing him again?'

'Him?' All too obviously Chloe was playing for time.

'The Frenchman . . . M. Boutet . . .' and with a final effort. 'My brother. Is he not gone with the others? Chloe, tell true! I must know.' And she sat up on her couch with a look of such feverish anxiety that Chloe, alarmed in her turn, hurried to take her hand and offer the smelling salts once more. But Camilla waved them away. 'No, no: I am well enough; if only you will tell me the truth. I must know, Chloe,' she said again, 'or else I will send a messenger to Lavenham telling him the whole.'

Thus threatened, Chloe dissolved into one of her fits of easy tears. 'Why are you so hard to me, Camilla? One would think you had never been in love in your life.' And then, drawing herself up proudly, 'Yes; I am this minute come from Charles. He has stayed in Lisbon, at great risk to himself, merely in the hope of seeing me again. Camilla, I beg you will try to understand: we have so little time. Who knows when we shall meet again? I know Lee would not understand, but that you—Charles's own sister—that you should be so hard, so unsympathetic: it is beyond bearing! Sometimes I think I shall go mad. And I thought you would be so pleased: I shall never understand you: to treat your own brother as if he was an enemy.'

'But he is one, Chloe. I fear I have done wrong in not telling Lavenham of this affair long since. But I tell you now that unless I have your solemn word that you will not see M. Boutet again, I shall send to Lavenham tonight.' And yet, she told herself, this too was cowardice. What was the use of extorting promises from Chloe, who would break them as lightly as the leaves she was stripping, as they talked, from one of her roses.

'Oh,' she had pricked herself and put her finger into her mouth to suck away the blood, then smiled reassuringly at Camilla. 'No need to promise,' she said, 'Charles leaves tonight: I do not know when I shall see him again.'

127

'For good?' Camilla did not conceal her relief.

'Oh no, but for more than a week.' Chloe made it sound an age. 'You do not think we shall be gone by then, Camilla? If I did not see him once more, to say goodbye, I think my heart would break.' And Camilla, wryly amused, found herself, of all things, consoling her incorrigible sister-in-law for the absence of her untrustworthy love. And so the scene between them ended with nothing settled, though Camilla, thinking it over afterwards, told herself that next time Lavenham came, he must be told, at whatever cost either to herself or to Chloe.

But when Lavenham did ride up to the house, a few days later, he looked so distracted that Chloe and Camilla, after a quick exchange of glances, devoted themselves entirely to his comfort, without daring even to ask the questions that trembled on their lips. At last, setting down the glass of wine he had hardly tasted, he spoke. 'You do not ask my news?'

'I fear it is bad,' Camilla said.

'Yes, the worst. It is but a matter of days before Dom John signs the decree confiscating British property. And the squadron we were promised, under Sir Sidney Smith, has not arrived. But there is worse than that.'

'Worse?'

'Yes. At least for me . . . for us, I should say. Chloe, I beg you will leave us.'

Chloe protested, but her brother was firm. 'No, this is no concern of yours, thank God. I must speak to my wife alone.' With an anxious glance at Camilla, Chloe rose and left them.

Closing the door behind her, Lavenham took another distracted turn about the room before he came back to stand over Camilla. 'Do you remember my asking you, some time since, at Sintra, about a man I thought I saw you talking with in the garden there?'

'Yes?' Camilla's voice shook on the word.

'And you denied having done so?'

'Yes,' she said again.

'God, I should have known.' He stood beside a tall vase of myrtle, systematically stripping the white blossoms from their stalks. '"Trust the devil before you trust a woman," my father told me as he died. *Why* did I not listen? Now I am disgraced — a laughing stock. I hope my grandmother will be pleased with what she has done to me. "No, no," you said, you had talked with no one. My poor mind, you hinted, must have been deceiving me again . . . And so it was . . . When I took your word. I must have been mad. The Court has its spies, you must know, on all of us foreigners. I collect you did not think of that. And most particularly have there been agents about you, being the Frenchwoman, God forgive me, that you are. This morning, when I was urging Araujo to persuade Dom John to throw in his lot with ours and sail at once for the Brazils, he turned on me. "Is that the advice your wife wishes me to give?" I did not understand what he meant. "My wife?" I said. "Yes," he said, "that French wife of yours. Or did you not know that she has been constantly in touch with a notorious French spy? I have no doubt it would suit the French admirably to have me run away, bag and baggage, leaving our country for who will to snap up, but we'll not do it, I tell you, and so you can tell that wife of yours you have kept so close — and no wonder, a spy and the accomplice of spies".' Lavenham broke off and took another furious turn about the room, while she watched him, speechless. At last he returned to loom over her more threateningly than ever. 'And I — poor fool,' he went on, 'I spoke up for you, refusing to believe what Araujo said — only to be faced with proofs, the reports of his men who have watched you.'

'Araujo's men?' she asked, grasping at a straw. 'But did you not say he was for the French.'

'What's that to the purpose? No, no, do not shilly shally with me like that. You have ruined me, and there's an end of it. I trust you are satisfied with your work.'

Camilla had been thinking the rapid thoughts of despair. If they had indeed been spied on, surely the informer must know perfectly well that it was Chloe, not she, who had been receiving the Frenchman's visits. His reports must have been deliberately falsified in order to give Araujo the strongest possible hold over Lavenham. Or could it be that Charles Boutet himself was the source of the information and had deliberately misinformed Araujo for some sinister purpose of his own? Groping among these possibilities, each one more desperate than the last, she sat tongue-tied under Lavenham's furious stare. What could she say, what do? Useless to tell him that Boutet's visits had been to Chloe: they remained just as damaging, and anyway she felt herself responsible in that she had let them continue. But there was one question she must ask. 'And Strangford,' she said, 'does he know?' Before the words were out of her mouth, she realised how he would take them.

'Ah,' it was something between a sigh and a groan. 'So you admit it. As calmly as that. Is it nothing to you that you have destroyed everything I had hoped for in life? Do you know—it will make you laugh, I have no doubt—do you know that I had begun to think we might find happiness together, you and I. I had begun to believe a woman could be trusted—might even be safely loved. Yes, have your laugh, for you have earned it: I had begun to love you, poor fool that I was. And all the time, you were laughing at me with that French accomplice of yours. Tell me, accomplished wife, is he your lover too? But I've not answered your question. No, Strangford does not know, nor will he, Araujo tells me, if I will but contradict everything I have ever said, change my advice to the Regent. Urge him to stay in Portugal, and my secret is safe. If I betray my country I may continue respected there; if not, I must be ruined. And this you have done for me. You, the girl I picked up in the gutter and gave my name—and almost gave my heart, too. But I have learned my lesson. Only tell me, mistress spy, what shall we do now? Do you propose to continue gracing my board—never my bed—or do you intend to join your Frenchman when he welcomes Bonaparte's armies into Portugal—all too soon? I had best know, had I not, that I may guide my conduct accordingly.' His eyes glittered dangerously as he bent still more closely over her, but she was too angry now for fright.

'I thank you, my lord,' she said, 'for your confidence in me. So I am to be tried, judged and condemned, am I, on the word of Araujo, whom you have always proclaimed a French agent! You do not come to ask me if there is any truth in his accusations. Oh, no, merely to tell me that I am false, and pour out your accumulated spleen against womankind on my innocent head. Yes, I said innocent and it is true, though I can see you will never believe it. I have been foolish, I admit, and would ask your pardon, if you were in any state to listen to me. As for Araujo, go to him, tell him he has been misled by his agents, if that is the story they have told him, and see how he takes that. As for me: I have no French accomplice and never have had. Your board I have shared—and your bed too, though you have paid me the compliment of forgetting the occasion—and carry the consequences with me now. It is a little late in the day, my lord, to banish me from your bed when I am carrying your child. Oh, I grant, you were drunk— not yourself at the time—you would doubtless never have touched anything so loathesome as a woman else. Well, I too have learned my lesson. I have had my delusions, too; my hopes of a happy marriage, but, believe me, my lord, they are at an end. Let us but get back to England and I promise you my child and I will never trouble you more.'

'Your child? What madness is this?'

'Yes, my child—and yours, though I can see you will never believe it. Well, so much the better for it, poor baby. Better no father than one as incapable of human feeling as you . . . a man who will believe anyone rather than his own wife.'

He was silent for a moment, white faced and shaking, then,

as she succumbed to a passion of tears, he broke out again: 'A likely story, madam, and told in a most happy hour. So I am to acknowledge some French spy's bastard as my heir . . . You say I believe Araujo before you: well, why should I not, when I have, to confirm his story, the evidence of my own eyes? Did I not—though, in my folly, I let you persuade me I was mistaken—did I not, myself, see you with your French paramour in the gardens?'

He was interrupted by a voice from the doorway, where Chloe stood, whitefaced and trembling. 'Oh, Lavenham,' she said, 'it was I.'

He looked at her, for a moment, in appalled silence, then, at a cry from her, turned back to catch Camilla as she fell.

Chapter 9

For Camilla there followed an interval of blessed unconsciousness. The doctors came, sighed and shook their heads. It was brain fever, said one, and recommended shaving off her hair. It was merely the culmination of a nervous affliction, said another, and urged frequent bleeding. It was homesickness, said a third: Lavenham had best send her back to England without delay. In the same breath he warned that it would mean certain death to move her. None of them discovered her condition, and Lavenham, wracked with an intolerable uncertainty, at once cursed and congratulated himself for his silence on this point. If she was false — as he mostly believed — what better than that she should die, undisgraced, here in Portugal? But — suppose her story was true? Pacing the house, sleepless, night after night, he tortured himself with the doubt, and the vain attempt to remember. It was true enough that when he had waked, the morning after he came home wounded, he had remembered nothing of what had happened the day before. Camilla had had to tell him. And how could she have told him this? And yet — how easy for her to use his brief forgetfulness to mask her own guilty secret. True, Chloe had confessed the whole of her affair with Charles Boutet, though suppressing, from a delicacy of her own, the fact that he was Camilla's brother. But there were other men . . . Suspicious of women since childhood, Lavenham found it impossible to believe one now.

And yet, as Camilla lay there, day after day, so white, so silent, so nearly dead, it was impossible not to be moved by that strange feeling—could it be love?—that had crept upon him, almost unawares, since the first day when he had seen her in his carriage, drooping, exquisitely asleep—his wife. Sometimes, as he paced his room, those still, intolerable nights, he found himself praying for proof of her innocence, for another chance, for life . . . But still she lay there silent, the doctors came, their advice conflicted on every point, and Lavenham and Chloe, united in an uneasy truce over the sickbed, agreed tacitly to ignore it. As for the maid, Frances, she had fallen into such a state of panic since the first decree against the British that she was worse than useless and the main burden of the nursing fell inevitably on Chloe and Rosa, the plump kind-hearted Portuguese girl who acted as her maid.

Despite his racking anxiety and tormenting doubt over Camilla, Lavenham still had to spend much of his time with the Prince Regent at Queluz. Things were moving rapidly to a crisis. It was only a matter of days, perhaps of hours, he told Chloe, before the Prince Regent signed the decree confiscating British property. And still the promised British squadron had not arrived —not that its coming would do them much good, as Chloe gloomily pointed out, since the one point on which all the doctors were agreed was that Camilla could not be moved without grave risk to both life and reason. Fortunately, when the decree was signed, it excluded the property of diplomats, and Dom Fernando, whose solicitude for Camilla's health had been unfailing, and had added considerable fuel to Lavenham's suspicions, arranged for a police agent to be stationed at their house to ensure that they were not molested. But it was uncomfortable enough, just the same, to hear of the forced sale of such British possessions as had not been already disposed of, and Chloe was not surprised when Frances's nerve gave way entirely and she accepted an offer of a passage home with an Englishwoman who had contrived to bribe her way on board an American ship.

Chloe was glad enough to see her go. She had been more of a liability than an asset for some time, and, besides, it was a relief

134

to have no English ears to hear the bitter scenes between her and her brother. For the discovery that it was Chloe who had been associating, all the time, with a known French spy, had combined with Lavenham's suspicions of Camilla to reawaken all the old bitterness against his mother, and through her, against women in general. Only the fact that most of their meetings took place over Camilla's sickbed saved Chloe from the full tide of his wrath. Inevitably he blamed her more than himself for Camilla's illness and found her devoted nursing the smallest of amends. Conscience-stricken herself, she bore his reproaches for some time with the patience of guilt, but gradually her spirit reasserted herself and she turned on him roundly. Whose fault, after all, was it that she and Camilla were still here? 'I do not blame you on my own account,' she went on, 'since I begged to come, and must take the consequences, but as Camilla's husband I should have thought you would have taken more thought for her safety. The truth of the matter is you want a wife for convenience but do not propose to yourself to take any responsibility for her. And besides,' she was well and truly roused now, 'if you ask me, the main cause of Camilla's illness has been your continued neglect of her. She has borne it like the angel she is, and therefore, I have no doubt, you have not even perceived that she felt it, but I have. It has never, I collect, since you are incapable of such a feeling yourself, occurred to you that she loved you and suffered from your treatment of her. If you could not *feel* towards her as a husband, you might at least have compelled yourself to *behave* like one. I only wish I knew what madness made you propose for her in the first place—or her accept you, for the matter of that.'

Thus roundly attacked, Lavenham was silenced for once, and he left soon afterwards for Queluz with much to think about. It was a relief, both to him and to Chloe, when circumstances kept him there for several days. When he next came to Lisbon, it was to announce the imminent arrival of the British squadron and to bring bad news arising from it. Lord Strangford had felt compelled to ask for his passports and intended to go aboard Sir Sidney's flagship as soon as he arrived to begin his blockade of Lisbon harbour. To make the gesture complete, it was essential that Lavenham should accompany the Minister Plenipotentiary. He came to ask Chloe whether she thought it safe to take Camilla. Once more the doctors came and once more they shook their heads. There had been no change in Camilla's condition; she still lay in the stupor into which she had fallen, accepting Chloe's ministrations passively, like a child, or, more frightening, an imbecile, but otherwise entirely withdrawn into some shadow world of her own. The doctors looked grave, each one blaming her failure to recover on Lavenham's refusal to take his original advice. As for moving her — and on board ship at that — they were unanimous in agreeing that it was out of the question. Death or madness were the alternative consequences. Then, gravely accepting their fees, they shook their heads a last time and took their leave.

Alone with Chloe, Lavenham turned to her in despair. She had had the main charge of Camilla, what did she think? Reluctantly, she found herself compelled to agree with the doctors. 'But do not trouble yourself, Lee. I shall stay with her. We will do well enough. Dom Fernando will protect us, and you will be within easy call, will you not? If the worst comes to the worst, and, for any reason, Sir Sidney proposes to leave Lisbon, we will have to risk moving her, but until then, I think she and I had best remain here.'

However reluctantly, Lavenham found himself compelled to admit the sense of what she said. Since the terrace of their house commanded a clear view of the harbour, he arranged a code of signals by which Chloe would be able to communicate with him on Sir Sidney's flagship, and promised to seize every opportunity of visiting her. At last, reluctantly, he took his leave, all his earlier fury forgotten in the unwilling respect he found himself feeling for her. But when he tried to say something of this, she just laughed at him: 'Never mind, Lee, you will have plenty of chances to be in a passion with me again before we are old and grey and gouty.'

He returned to Queluz, to join Strangford in making arrangements for their move aboard ship with an uncomfortable feeling that he was not, somehow, showing up very well in contrast to his flibbertigibbet younger sister. It was a new experience for him, and one, like his torturing doubts of Camilla, and Chloe's own disconcerting attack on him as a husband, that kept him awake for many an uncomfortable night's tossing on the uncertain water of Lisbon harbour.

His only comfort, those wretched days, was that he had at last told the whole story of Chloe's indiscretion to Lord Strangford. The confession, though painful enough, had at least been an easier one than if it had concerned his wife instead of his sister. Luckily for his peace of mind, Chloe had not thought it wise to tell him that her French lover was Camilla's brother, and Camilla had been in no state to do so. He had been soundly rebuked by Strangford for not keeping his household in better order, had felt, with dislike, that he deserved the rebuke but had at least had the consolation that Araujo's blackmailing overtures had not been repeated. His career was safe, but as the gloomy November days passed, it seemed more and more likely that it had been saved at the expense of his wife's reason. Night after night, the signal Chloe flashed from the shore indicated no change in the invalid's condition, and night after night Lavenham paced the decks for hours, in turns blaming and excusing himself. If only he could *remember*. If Camilla was indeed carrying his child, how different the world would be to him . . . And yet, how could he believe it? Never trust a woman, his father had said. What cause had he to do so now? And yet . . . and yet . . . Camilla had *seemed* so different, so calm, so good . . . so lovable. Still, despite himself, he loved her, and his love, stronger than any reason, argued the truth of her story. If it was indeed his child . . . and he had destroyed mother and child together . . . So he went on, suffering, doubting and arguing with himself, hour after hour, in a squirrel's cage of wretchedness until Strangford, increasingly anxious about him, was almost relieved when an urgent messenger summoned them to the Prince Regent at Queluz.

The news was as bad as possible. A French army, under Junot, who had once been French Minister in Lisbon, had entered Portugal. And now, at last, the Prince Regent had been forced to open his eyes. By some freak of luck an old copy of the Paris *Moniteur* had reached him, and in it he had read Bonaparte's announcement that the house of Braganza had ceased to reign in Europe. Even he realised that the time for compromise was past. He summoned his Council of State and announced his immediate departure for Brazil; a Provisional Government, of which Dom Fernando was a member, was named to rule Portugal in his absence.

The news brought chaos to the city, and despair to Lavenham. It was to be his honourable task to accompany the Portuguese royal family on their arduous voyage to the new world. Out of the question that Camilla should accompany him, but equally imperative that, at whatever risk, she be placed on board one of the British ships that were to return to England. With Strangford's permission, he made a detour on his way back from Queluz to visit Chloe and tell her the news. She received it with unconcealed anxiety. There had been no change in Camilla's condition; the risk of moving her was as great as ever. She led her brother upstairs to Camilla's bedroom, where she lay, white and still, her only movement a restless convulsive clutching and unclutching of her fingers.

'What is she holding?' Lavenham asked.

'Her wedding ring. She has been doing it for some days. It is the only change.'

They stood together, silently, for a few minutes, then Lavenham spoke with a brisk cheerfulness he was far from feeling.

'Perhaps it is a good sign. Should we have the doctor again? No?' As Chloe shook her head vigorously. 'I am inclined to agree with you. Very well then. We must simply arrange to move her, as gently as possible, and at the very last moment. It will take some days for the Court to embark . . . many of their ships are still fitting for the voyage; the provisions of others need replenishing. We can count, I think, on four or five days' grace . . . and, besides' — he looked gloomily out of the window and across the harbour — 'if the wind does not change, it will be impossible to sail anyway.'

'You mean Junot may catch us here?'

'It is possible. By all reports, he is only a few days' march from the city and no attempt has been made at stopping him. General Freire and his troops are still on the coast. So far as I know they have not even heard of Junot's advance. They have certainly made no move to check it. Not,' he added with his usual fairness, 'that they would have the slightest hope of doing so. Junot's troops, I understand, are something of the rawest, but the Portuguese army can hardly be said to exist at all. The fact remains that Araujo has made no move to alert it. I am more and more convinced that it has been he, all the time, who has played the traitor. I owe Dom Fernando a hearty apology for my suspicions of him . . . and hearty thanks too, for his care of you and Camilla.'

Chloe smiled wickedly at him. 'I am not sure that it is not Camilla who should be thanked for that. If he is not head over heels in love with her, I miss my guess very sadly. But what are we going to do, Lee?'

'Why, leave her here until the last possible moment. This movement of her hands [he did not like it] is new. Who can tell what other change it may presage. Do you come out on the terrace every night at first dusk. If the fleet is ready to sail, and the wind favourable — if, in short, I feel that the time has come when, at whatever risk to her, you and Camilla must come aboard, I will burn a green and a red light, together, on the stern of the *Hibernia*.

139

That is your signal to get the men to carry Camilla, as gently as possible, down to the cove below the house. I will meet you there, with one of the *Hibernia*'s boats. We must pray God that the movement does not hurt her.'

'Yes,' Chloe said, 'I do not see what else we can do.'

. . .

Camilla's dreams had been troubled and restless. Now, waking suddenly, she was relieved to see Chloe bending anxiously over her. Chloe had been in the dreams, surely? And Lavenham, too? She was sure of it, yet could remember no detail. She was tired, too tired for remembering, or even for thought. But she must think. She must consider Chloe who looked thin and pale, and who was, unaccountably, crying. To confirm this, a large tear splashed on to Camilla's right hand which was clasped, she noticed, over her left, the fingers rubbing feebly over—oh, her wedding ring of course. Lavenham . . . Chloe . . . bad dreams. It was no use, she could not remember.

Chloe's voice distracted her. 'Camilla! Can you hear me?'

What an effort it was to speak. 'Of course. Why not?' The question left her exhausted and she lay with closed eyes, trying to take in Chloe's answer. She had been very ill: that was why she was so tired. Of course, that was all . . . She was beginning to remember now; a little, slowly. And at once there was another question. 'Lavenham?' she asked.

'Coming for us tonight,' Chloe said, and then, in a rush that sounded more like her usual self, 'Oh, Camilla, I am *glad* that you are better. But no more questions now. Rest . . . try to sleep. It will be tiring enough tonight.'

It was good advice. Camilla was glad to close her eyes. Only, as she did so, another memory came to her and she opened them again. 'And the baby,' she asked, 'what does Lavenham say now?'

Chloe's look of puzzlement was answer enough. 'The baby? Camilla, what do you mean? . . . are you . . .' and then, in a rush: 'Oh, those doctors . . . Oh, Camilla!' Again her tears began to fall and then, unaccountably, she was laughing. 'Oh, Camilla, I am so *pleased* . . . and Lavenham kept it to himself! Just wait till I see him.'

'No, no . . .' It was all too much. She was relieved when her protest was interrupted by the girl, Rosa, who brought Chloe a note. Chloe read it, coloured, and rose to leave the room, telling Rosa to watch by Camilla and urging Camilla, once more, to rest. Drifting off to sleep, Camilla found herself a prey to a vague anxiety. Chloe had had a note . . . Why not? . . . What was there frightening about that? . . . It was no use, she gave up trying to think and drifted off again into a place of troubled dreams.

When she next woke, Chloe was back by her bed watching her anxiously. The room was full of evening shadows and Camilla could hear, outside, the steady rush of rain. She shivered. 'It is cold,' she said, and then, 'How long have I been ill?'

'Not long; though it seems an age. A little more than two weeks. Camilla, are you really strong enough to talk?'

'Of course. But, tell me, where is Lavenham? You said he was coming for us tonight. Why? Where are we going?'

'Home, I hope. As for Lavenham, he is aboard the *Hibernia* with Strangford and Sir Sidney Smith, and mad, I can tell you, with anxiety for you. The doctors said you could not be moved, you see.'

'So you stayed here with me? Thank you, Chloe. But I still do not understand . . .' Once more, her hands began their restless movement, and Chloe, noticing it, hurried to give her a brief explanation of the events that had taken place during her illness, of Junot's approach and the Prince Regent's belated recognition of danger.

'You should just have seen the harbour two days ago, when the court were going on board: I spent all day at the window here, watching; you never saw anything like it. The whole court, the archives, the treasury — everything, out there in the pouring rain.

The mad old Queen, they tell me, crying "Ai Jesus", harder than ever, the Prince Regent with tears running down his cheeks, the proudest ladies of the court wading into the water to beg for passage . . . And many of them without a scrap of baggage to their name. It will be an unhappy enough voyage even for those who have managed to beg or bribe their way on board.'

'But when do they sail?' asked Camilla.

'Why, that's the rub. They have been ready for two days now, but the wind is against them. They cannot stir. And all the time, Junot is getting nearer. That is why Lavenham is coming for us tonight. He thinks it possible Junot may be here tomorrow and dares not risk a further delay. We are to meet him down at the little harbour. What a happy man he will be when he sees you recovered. Tell me, are you strong enough to dress? The men will carry you down, but you would be better dressed.'

Camilla laughed. 'I should rather think I would. Well, let us make the effort.'

She found it an exhausting enough business, but with Chloe's loving assistance managed, at last, to put on a warm travelling dress of dark green sarsnet and its matching pelisse. After the effort, she was glad enough to lie back on her bed while Chloe hurried away to make her own preparations. Lavenham had told her that they must bring as little as possible, but her jewels and Camilla's must be packed into the smallest compass, together with a minimum wardrobe for the voyage back to England. 'We shall be nothing but a pair of waifs and strays when we get home,' she told Camilla, 'but luckily grandmamma will be so delighted with your news I am sure nothing will be too good for you.'

'My news?'

'Why, the baby. Or were you funning? Oh, Camilla, surely not?'

It seemed an odd enough kind of a joke to Camilla, although she was tempted, for a moment, to pretend that it had been a mis-understanding. But what was the use? The truth would have to come out sooner or later. If only she knew whether she had succeeded in convincing Lavenham in that last dreadful scene, of which she had only fragmentary memories. But the fact that he had not spoken of her condition, even to Chloe, was anything but hopeful. Her hands resumed their nervous movement as she begged Chloe to say nothing about the baby to anyone: 'Do not, I beg of you, tease Lavenham about it . . . there will be time enough on the voyage home.'

Chloe looked appalled: 'Oh, Camilla, how could I be such a muttonhead. Did I not explain? Lavenham does not come with us. He has been appointed to escort the Prince Regent to the Brazils. It is a great honour, of course . . .' Chloe was dwindling to an unhappy silence when she was interrupted by an agitated servant who announced that there were men below who insisted on speaking with the ladies.

'Men? What men?' Chloe was beginning, when she saw another figure enter the darkening room behind the servant. 'You?' she said.

'Myself. And entirely at both your service.' Monsieur Boutet removed his hat with a flourish, dismissed the man in fluent Portuguese and advanced towards the window where Camilla sat transfixed. 'My dear sister, I am delighted to see you better. When our beloved Chloe told me the good news I was transported with joy . . . for many reasons.'

'What do you mean?' It was no comfort, in her cold terror, to see that Chloe shared it.

'Just what I say. That I am glad to see you better. Whatever risks milord your husband might have been prepared to take with you, I should have been most reluctant to move you against the advice of the doctors. But now, everything is altered, and just in time. I am come to offer you asylum, my dearest sister, and to you, my ever beloved Chloe, my heart and hand.'

'What can you mean?' For all her illness, it was Camilla who spoke.

'Why, that I am come to take you home. You did not, surely, think that I would stand by and let you return to England with that tyrannical husband of yours? No, no, I am a better brother than that, and a better lover too, as my dearest Chloe will admit, I am sure, before many days are past. For the moment, there is no time to be lost in talk. You, I am sure, have no more desire than I have for an encounter with your braggadocio husband, in which he must inevitably be defeated. So come, you are packed and ready, I see. We have not far to go: I am much too considerate a brother and [once again there was a proprietorial smile for Chloe] lover for that. We will just take you to a safe shelter far enough away so that milord the husband cannot find you, and, there, for tonight, you may rest. Tomorrow, Junot will be here, and all Lisbon yours. You will find it somewhat different from playing the beggarly British suppliants, I can tell you.'

Chloe spoke at last. 'Traitor,' she said. 'I should have known. And all your talk of love was time-serving and treachery. Camilla, will you ever forgive me? It was I—I am the traitor. I told him all our plans. I wanted—God help me—I wanted to say goodbye to him. Because you see, I loved him. Or,' she was standing beside Camilla now, one hand protectively—or for protection—in Camilla's, 'I thought I did.'

Charles Boutet smiled mockingly. 'A pity to change your mind now, when everything is in train to make me the happiest of men. But, come, we are wasting time. Tell me, ladies, do you propose to accompany me willingly? It will be very much your wiser plan. I should be sorry to have to mar our relationship with any show of force, but, believe me, I shall not hesitate to do so, if you make it necessary. Dom Fernando's officer has been dealt with; your servants have taken our hint and fled; there is no other house within earshot; my carriage is outside. And I am sure you, my love,' he turned to Chloe, 'will agree with me that any scene of violence will be the worst possible thing for our dear sister's precarious health.'

Chloe and Camilla exchanged despairing glances. It was all too evidently true. The house was silent, and Chloe, white with rage, could see that Camilla was near fainting. Charles Boutet settled it. 'Of course,' he went on, 'if your pride compels you to make some show of resistance, I shall feel myself constrained, however regretfully, to separate you from our sister who would I am sure, sadly miss your nursing.'

Once more the two girls exchanged glances. Then Camilla spoke, 'Very well,' she said. 'We will go with you, but do not imagine that we will ever forget or forgive this outrage.'

'No?' He raised mocking eyebrows. 'Speak for yourself, my dearest sister. Perhaps you may be so foolish as to continue resenting my freeing you from an unloving husband, but I am sure my beloved Chloe will forgive me soon enough when once we are man and wife.'

'Never,' Chloe began, but he had turned to summon his men. Speechless with indignation, she nevertheless found herself helping in the business of carrying Camilla down through the deserted house to the closed carriage that waited outside. To the last moment, both girls had refused to believe that this could really be happening to them, but no miracle took place. With a careful solicitude that was, somehow, the last straw, Charles Boutet's followers laid Camilla down on the back seat of the carriage, where Chloe supported her as best she might. Charles Boutet stepped in beside them, gave an order to his men, pulled down the shades and settled himself on the front seat with a little sigh of satisfaction. '*Bon*,' he lapsed comfortably into French. 'Now no one will disturb us. Besides, the world has other things to think of, today. Come, my dearest sister, do not fret,' — for tears were slowly following each other down Camilla's cheeks. 'I have left a note for that bullying husband of yours telling him not to derange himself on your account since you have followed your heart, to France.'

It was too much. Camilla, who had been fighting for consciousness with every breath she took, slid once more into a faint. When she came to herself again, she was lying on a hard bed, with Chloe once more anxiously beside her. 'Was it a nightmare?' she asked.

'No,' Chloe said. 'It is all true, and all my fault. But if it has not killed you, Camilla, perhaps there is some hope for us yet.'

'Hope?' Camilla asked sardonically. Then, looking around the darkening room. 'But at least we are alone.'

'Yes. That is why I dare speak of hope. When we reached this house—and God knows where it is, for I certainly do not—there was a messenger waiting for Charles, an urgent summons to join Junot on the march. I am glad you taught me some French, Camilla, for Charles thinks I do not understand it. He has left us here, with only two of his men on guard. We are locked in, of course, and they think us safe till morning. I heard them say so. They are downstairs, in the servants' quarters, with a cask of wine. We are at the very top of the house: they think we cannot possibly escape!'

'Well,' Camilla said reasonably, 'how can we?'

'By climbing down the vine that grows up the side of the house. You should just see it, Camilla, it has branches as big as your arm. It will be a ladder for us—a ladder to freedom. Camilla, say you can do it.'

But Camilla, all too evidently, could not. When she tried to rise to her feet, it was only to fall back, half fainting, on the hard bed. 'It's no use,' she said. 'I cannot do it. Chloe, you must go alone. If you cannot get to Lavenham, go to Dom Fernando. He will help us, I am sure.'

'But Camilla, how can I leave you?'

'You must. It's our only chance. And besides, consider; Charles can only hold me to ransom, but he means to marry you.'

It was a clincher. Chloe kissed Camilla, asked her once more for her forgiveness, pinned her skirts up carefully around her knees and disappeared, with one last near-smile, out of the window. Camilla, listening desperately, heard a continued rustling, then silence. No sound of a fall; no sound of pursuit. Perhaps there really was hope. Amazingly, she slept.

She woke to morning light and the sounds of altercation down-stairs. And also to an almost forgotten feeling. She was actually hungry. I must be better, she thought, and then suspended even thinking in her effort to make out what was going on below. A few more anxious moments and she heard voices on the stairs. Chloe burst into the room, followed by Dom Fernando. 'Thank God,' she said, 'you are still here. We are safe, Camilla.'

'But Lavenham?'

Chloe's face fell. 'You must be brave, Camilla. He was gone when I reached the house. And — the wind has changed; the fleet is putting out of the harbour. Listen?' A volley of gunfire sent her running to the window. 'It is the British and Portuguese fleets saluting each other,' she said, 'and, oh, Camilla, I fear Lavenham must be aboard. He must have believed that lying note Charles left. Though how he could leave us so passes my imagining.'

'I collect he could not help himself.' As always, Camilla rallied to her husband's defence. 'He has his duty, after all.'

'Duty! And leave us to the mercy of the French! Were it not for Dom Fernando we would be in their hands tonight.'

'And may be yet,' interposed Dom Fernando himself, 'if we lose more time talking here. I am told that Junot's advance guard are already on the hills above the town.'

'Oh,' Camilla sank back despairingly on the bed. 'Then how can we be safe? Lavenham gone . . . Junot coming . . . what hope have we?'

Chloe took her hand. 'Do not despair, Camilla. It is bad, I know, but not so bad as it might be. Dom Fernando has an admirable plan for us: we are to pose as his two mad nieces who used to live on his estate south of the Tagus. It is but to row across the river — and vanish. Charles will think we succeeded in rejoin-ing Lavenham and have sailed with the fleet. Besides, the French will be occupied enough for some time in taking over Lisbon. By the time they get south to Almada we will be perfect in our disguise; I promise you, they will never find us.'

'And then what?' Camilla asked.

'Why, then,' Dom Fernando said, 'as always, we must trust in God.'

Chapter 10

While Camilla and Chloe were being hurriedly rowed across the Tagus by Dom Fernando's servants, Lavenham was pacing up and down the deck of the *Marlborough* in an agony of indecision. The combined British and Portuguese fleets were clear of the harbour now, all except one frigate that had had difficulty in crossing the bar, and as Lavenham stood, looking longingly back towards Lisbon, he saw a puff of smoke from the cannon in the fort of Saint Julian. The French advance guard must have taken the fort already and had lost no time in turning the guns on the last straggler from the fleet. But their shot fell short, and the frigate crossed the bar at last and joined the rest of the fleet.

Realisation that the French were already on the outskirts of Lisbon gave the final twist to Lavenham's anguish. He had not been quite a reasonable man since he had found Charles Boutet's note pinned to the door of his house the night before. His sense of duty had made him return to the *Hibernia* after his fruitless search of the house and garden and even of the deserted Marvila palace next door. Of the servants there was no sign, and everything he found in Camilla's and Chloe's rooms seemed to indicate that they had indeed left of their own free will. Searching almost frantically among their possessions, he had found that each had taken her jewels and, he thought, a few personal necessities. Camilla's enamelled hairbrushes, a wedding present from Lady Leominster which she had particularly treasured, were missing, and various other things that he remembered. And yet—how could Charles Boutet's message be true? How could Camilla have left him voluntarily, when she was not even conscious? It was at this point that he had heard movement in Chloe's room, and, throwing open the door, discovered the maid, Rosa, who had come back to collect her possessions. What she told him merely confirmed his despair, although he found himself oddly comforted by the news that Camilla had recovered her senses. But what was that to the purpose, when the first use she had made of them was to leave him? For Rosa insisted that she had hidden in the bushes and watched Camilla and Chloe go. They had not been forced, she said. Milady was carried, it was true, but Doña Chloe had walked beside her freely enough and had seen to it that she was comfortably settled in the carriage. Throughout, the Frenchmen had behaved with the greatest possible courtesy, brutes though, of course, they were. At this point, something in Lavenham's face had frightened her, and she had taken flight, not even pausing long enough to remove a few coveted trifles of Chloe's that had been the real reason for her return.

And Lavenham had gone, almost mechanically, back to the *Hibernia*, to be greeted with the news that the wind had changed and they were to sail at dawn. Hardly knowing what he was doing, he had accompanied Lord Strangford and Sir Sidney Smith when they went to pay their respects to the Prince Regent on the *Principe Real* and only returned to full consciousness when he heard the Prince request once more that he be detailed to accompany the Court to the Brazils. He had had no chance to tell Strangford of the disaster that had befallen him, and his training forbade him to breach Court etiquette with an instant protest. There would be time enough later, he told himself, to explain his predicament to Strangford and ask for an exchange from the *Marlborough*, which was to accompany the court to the Brazils, to one of the ships that were to continue the blockade of Lisbon. It had been a blow when Lord Strangford had accompanied Sir Sidney Smith back to the *Hibernia* without giving him a chance for a private word, but he had reassured himself that the fleets would be sailing together for some time yet. Now, with the wind rising, and Lisbon dwindling in the distance, he cursed himself for a vacillating fool. He should have spoken up roundly at once, royal presence or no royal presence. But it was still not too late. Determined to lose no more time, he hurried to the captain of the ship to ask for a boat to take him over to the *Hibernia*. The captain's answer was short and brutally to the point. They were in for a storm—a hurricane perhaps. The very idea of launching a boat was madness. He had no time for landsmen's idiocy. When they had survived the storm would be time enough to talk of boats. He turned from Lavenham to shout an order against the roar of the wind, then turned back, for he was a kind man at heart, to answer Lavenham's last question. 'When will it blow out? God knows. Best ask Him.'

The storm raged for four days. The fleet was scattered and the *Marlborough* alone in a hell of wind and green water. For Lavenham, the private hell was worse. The captain, pitying his evident distraction, had told him their only hope was to run before the wind. With luck, they would be reunited with the rest of the Brazil-bound fleet when the storm was over. But for better or worse, they were committed to the long journey to the New World. How much of the fleet ever reached it was, he said, another question. The Portuguese ships had been unready and ill-equipped; they were grievously overloaded; only the hand of God could bring them safe to shore. 'And trust you in Him, too,' said the captain, who had heard something of Lavenham's story.

But Lavenham was beyond trust, beyond hope. Alternately, he blamed, with desperate rage, himself, Chloe, Camilla. He could not sleep; he could not eat; he was not even granted the distraction of sea-sickness, but prowled about the boat, a Jonah, the sailors whispered to each other, if ever there was one. And yet, though he sometimes half hoped it would, the ship did not sink. On the fourth evening the wind began to fall, and on the fifth morning they woke, those of them who had contrived to sleep at last, to a brilliant sunrise, and sight of the *Principe Real* on the horizon. Gradually, in the course of the next calm days, the little fleet reassembled and exchanged bad news. Surprisingly, no ship had sunk, but the sufferings of the refugees, crammed into the ill-equipped Portuguese fleet, had been frightful and there had been many deaths, including that of the aged Duke of Cadaval. Lavenham, harvesting what news he could, learned that his old enemy, Araujo, was on board the *Medusa* and, with relief, that Dom Fernando had remained behind in Lisbon. If Camilla and Chloe should need a friend, he told himself, they would find one in him. And then, in one of his fits of bitter rage, he told himself to quit his folly: Camilla and Chloe were probably in Paris now, fêted by the Emperor. Chloe was doubtless married to her lover; Camilla—but he could not imagine Camilla curtseying to Bonaparte, could not help remembering her voice the first night they met: 'I am as English as you, sir, perhaps more so, because I know how lucky I am.' Had he not been mad to believe Boutet's note? And yet, what else had there been to think? Camilla and Chloe had gone willingly enough, the girl, Rosa, had said. He was back, once more, on the round of doubt and self blame, half realising that his very rage at Camilla and Chloe as renegades was an attempt to ease his own conscience. Had he failed them, or they him? Would he ever know? The voyage, in calmer waters now, was an eternity of wretchedness, his only comfort the knowledge that his application for recall was ready written and sealed, waiting only the chance of despatch.

This came at last at the end of January when they sighted land and the tattered little fleet sailed into Bahia where the once-proud Portuguese court tottered to shore, thin, emaciated and dirty. Dom John's estranged wife, the Spanish Princess Carlota Joaquina, who had travelled with her children on the *Affonso D'Albuquerque*, came ashore, like them, in a white muslin cap to hide her head, shaven in the endless unavailing battle against lice and infestation on board. The exhausted court decided to rest for a while at Bahia before sailing on to a formal welcome at Rio de Janeiro, and Captain Moore seized the opportunity to send a ship home with the news of their safe arrival. By this ship, too, went Lavenham's impassioned plea for recall, and then there was nothing for it but to settle down to count the days and, as the kind captain had suggested, to pray.

.　　.　　.

Meanwhile, in Portugal, Camilla and Chloe had had their share of terror and of prayer. They had hardly landed on the south bank of the Tagus when the storm broke, and their first few days in the little house Dom Fernando had given them were made horrible by the lashing of wind and rain against the shutters and by their fears for Lavenham at sea. In Lisbon, they were told, the storm had been so fierce that even in the sheltered harbour boats were thrown up on the steps of Corpo Santo. Was it possible that Lavenham could have survived? And, if he had, what must he be thinking of them? Could he really have believed Charles Boutet's note? But if not, how could he possibly have sailed without them? These speculations were as painful as they were useless, and they soon abandoned them by tacit consent. Chloe could see that the mere mention of Lavenham's name was calculated to renew the hectic flush in Camilla's cheek and start once more that restless, anxious movement of her hands. And Camilla, for her part, felt too truly sorry for Chloe to wish to remind her of the part she had played in their disaster. Besides, maternal instinct was at work in her now, warning her that agitation was bad for the child she carried. The only way not to be agitated was not to think, and she was amazed how successfully she managed.

Of course, they had enough of a practical kind to do and think of. Dom Fernando had not dared accompany them himself to their new home, but had sent his steward along to introduce them to his cousin, the Mother Superior of the Convent in whose grounds their house was situated. Its two previous tenants, his

mentally defective illegitimate nieces had lived there, incon-
spicuously, most of their lives and had recently died there just as
quietly, of typhoid. The old nun, who received Camilla and
Chloe with the greatest kindness, told them she thought they
would be perfectly safe. Dom Fernando's nieces had hardly stirred
from their house except to visit the Convent, whence they had
obtained all their supplies. The nearest village was some miles
away and its inhabitants had thought the two women witches
and had given their cottage a wide berth when they visited the
Convent. Their superstitious terrors could be relied on to keep
them away from it now. Like them, Camilla and Chloe would
receive all their supplies from the Convent, and should be safe
enough so long as they did not stray beyond its grounds. Only
— here the old lady looked doubtfully at Chloe — perhaps they had
best assume the habit of lay sisters. It was most unusual for a Portuguese young lady to be conspicuously blonde and at all costs
they must avoid drawing attention to themselves. In gowns and
hoods, they might walk safely where they pleased. Chloe pulled
a face, but had to admit that the nun's argument made sense, and in
fact she and Camilla found the voluminous robes surprisingly
comfortable and a great blessing in their cold little house.

As the slow months passed Camilla was increasingly grateful
for the robes' lavish, concealing folds. She had told the Superior
of her condition and had been amused, despite herself, at the
worldly calm with which the reverend lady took it. 'Admirable,'
was all she had said. 'If questions should be asked, I shall put it
about that you are a young lady of family saving her good name
by a timely retirement — it happens often enough, I can tell you.'
She urged Camilla robustly not to worry about anything: when
her time came, the sister who cared for sick nuns would come to
her. 'And she is not without experience, I promise you.'

Amazingly enough, Camilla found that she was not worrying.
As the days passed, and she and Chloe settled into their almost
primitive daily round, her strength and spirits improved. 'Take

no thought to the morrow' might have been her motto, so successfully did she live from day to day, while her colour crept back, her quivering fingers relaxed and her child stirred to life within her.

'Chloe, he kicked me,' she exclaimed, one mild morning in earliest spring when she and Chloe were out together working in their little garden.

Chloe straightened up and laughed. 'He?' she asked.

'Of course. How shall I face Lady Leominster, if it is not an heir.'

'Well,' Chloe said reflectively, 'it is true that in our family the first child always *is* a boy. First Maurice, then Edward, then Maurice, then Edward and so on, back to William the Conqueror and forward—who knows, till kingdom comes, I suppose. Oh, Camilla, I wish I might see Lavenham's face when he hears the news.' For they had heard, at last, that none of the fleet had been lost, and felt themselves safe in assuming that Lavenham was alive and, probably, at the Brazils. If they both, in their different ways, found this knowledge of his distance rather restful, they did not discuss the matter.

But there was something else Camilla had been waiting a chance to ask. 'Chloe,' she said now, after a moment's consideration of her sister-in-law's brown and cheerful face.

'Yes?' Chloe dropped her primitive spade and ran earth-stained hands through her tangled hair. How would they ever be young ladies again?

'Chloe, tell me, do you still think of Charles?'

'Think of him!' Chloe exclaimed. 'I should rather think I do. I have guillotined him, and boiled him in oil, and—oh a thousand torments, but it is all no use: it still exasperates me, just to think of him. Camilla, how could I have been such a fool? To imagine I loved him! It makes me mad, merely to think of it.'

'You do not mind any more?'

'Mind? You mean, do I still love him? Camilla, I don't think

I ever did. Is it not shameful? To have made all this trouble for you, just out of a whim, out of liking flattery, wanting to be important . . . when I think of it, I am so ashamed . . .'

'Then do not think of it,' Camilla said. 'What is the use? And, besides, it is foolish to talk of making trouble for *me*—the misfortune is just as much yours as mine, and you have made up for it a thousand times in all you have done for me since . . . After all, he is my brother. I am only grateful to learn that you are not suffering too much.'

'Suffering? Do you know, Camilla, I do not think I have ever been so happy before in my life. Does that surprise you very much.'

'Why no,' said Camilla, 'for I believe I have not either.' And they returned contentedly to their digging.

News came to them rarely, by way of the Convent, for Dom Fernando, much concerned with the problems of the French occupation of his country, did not dare visit them in person, nor write often. They knew, however, that the French were behaving more like the masters they were than the liberators they pretended to be. 'We are unable to entertain you as friends, or to resist you as enemies,' Dom Fernando had told them, but, as time went by, their behaviour proclaimed them all too clearly as enemies. It was a long, hungry winter for the Portuguese, who found themselves penalised by severe laws and heavy, enforced contributions to the war chest of France. Writing of this, Dom Fernando told Camilla that, for them, and for all true friends of Portugal, it was good news. 'The spirit of revolt is growing,' he said. 'It will not be long now.' He had other good news for her, too. Her brother had been recalled to France on the very day Junot had taken over Lisbon, and had not returned. 'So long as he is away, I think you safe enough.'

Reading this, Camilla found herself blushing: how extraordinarily good Dom Fernando had been to her; it was reassuring just to think of it. The very fact of his keeping away from her now was proof of his thought for her. He had never referred again to that scene at Sintra. No doubt the Mother Superior had told him of her condition and his only thought was to make things as easy as possible for her. How different from Lavenham's behaviour. And then, angrily, she repudiated the thought. After all, Lavenham had never asked her to love him. She had taken him on his own terms, and must abide by them. Or must she? Alone in the garden, she thought that their child must change all that. If she ever lived with its father again, it must be on her terms, not his. But then, the chances of their ever doing so were slight enough. But Dom Fernando wrote encouragement. It was only a matter of time before he would contrive to smuggle them out of the country and home to England. He was still secretly in touch with the English fleet that continued to blockade Lisbon and hoped that, sooner or later, the French vigilance would relax and he could find a way to get them home. Later was soon enough for Camilla. She was very big now, very placid, and more than ready to wait out her time in this quiet corner of Portugal, where no one expected anything of her except Chloe, who merely wanted her to drink goat's milk, and rest in the afternoons.

They were excellent friends now, each of them glad of the sister she had never had. Chloe had grown up a great deal since the shock of discovering what a fool she had made of herself over Charles Boutet, or rather, as Camilla insisted, how he had contrived to fool her. Camilla blamed herself as much as Chloe for their plight. She should have suspected that Chloe and Charles were still meeting and done something about it, but, absorbed by her own relations with Lavenham, she had been almost wilfully blind. Chloe would not allow this, insisting that the fault had been entirely hers, and they soon abandoned the fruitless subject. Nor did they talk often about Lavenham, since each, in her heart of hearts, could not help but feel that he had let them down, and either would have died rather than admit it. So they lived contentedly enough from day to day, baking their bread and working in their garden, and turning, as Chloe often exclaimed, into a quite capital pair of housewives. No one had ever taught her anything more useful than beadwork and embroidery, and as Camilla's domestic education at Devonshire House had been almost as frivolous, they found themselves shamefacedly compelled to go to the fat and jovial Convent cook for lessons in cookery, which involved their learning a good deal of Portuguese, since she spoke nothing else.

Dom Fernando, paying them one of his rare visits early in April, congratulated them heartily on the progress they had made in the language. It would be invaluable when the time came for them to make their escape. For he had almost abandoned hope of being able to get them out to the blockading fleet, and thought they would have to make their way northwards across country to make contact with one of the British ships that called, from time to time, to drop spies—or as they were more politely called, military agents—in the little harbours around Corunna. Their chances of getting successfully across so much occupied territory would be much increased if they could learn enough Portuguese to pass as visitors from the Brazils, who might be expected to speak with an outlandish accent.

The news Dom Fernando brought them was mixed bad and good, with the bad preponderating. No word had been received from the Brazils, but no news, he said, was good news. In Europe, Bonaparte seemed all powerful. Russia and Austria had given up the struggle, and England faced him alone. But in Spain and Portugal, he told them, the scene was changing. Spain, too, had been occupied, treacherously, by Bonaparte's armies and there, as in Portugal, the people at large were awakening slowly to a realisation of disaster. Passive at first, the people of both countries were rousing to fierce resistance under the goad of French tyranny. 'They have learned at last,' Dom Fernando said, 'that France is not the saviour they hoped. Now when it is too late, they begin to sigh for their lost rulers. I think we shall have a hot summer of it in Iberia; I only wish I could see you safe home before the fighting really begins. How long do you think . . .' he stammered to a halt.

Camilla laughed. 'Not long now,' she said, 'Sister Maria says it is a matter of days.'

'Good.' He rose to take his leave. 'I confess I shall breathe more freely when you are safe away from here. I find that your identity is an open secret in the village by now: they are all your devoted friends and I hope you have nothing to fear . . . But,' he shook his head and repeated, 'I shall feel safer when you are gone.'

Camilla laughed. 'And so shall we. It seems little less than a miracle that we have been unmolested so far.'

He smiled at her very kindly. 'Perhaps it is one. Who knows?' And took his leave.

Two days later, Camilla roused Chloe in the small hours of the morning. 'Chloe, I think it is time to go for Sister Maria.'

Chloe was out of bed in a flash. 'Are you sure? Will you be all right while I am gone? Oh, Camilla, I wish we were at home.'

'So do I, but never mind, it has happened before, and will again. I have no doubt I shall do well enough . . . Only, hurry, Chloe.'

Chloe ran all the way to the Convent, but Sister Maria, who was as lazy as she was good-tempered, refused to be hurried. 'Time enough, time enough,' she said, in her broad, country Portuguese. 'These first mothers always think the end of the world is at hand, but, I promise you, we will have time for breakfast— yes, and lunch too, before we see his young lordship.' Wheezing with the exertion, she packed up her sinister looking tools, and Chloe, equally alarmed by her grimy equipment and the delay, could finally bear it no longer and ran on, alone, to their cottage. As she crossed the garden, a sudden almost unrecognisable scream from Camilla gave wings to her feet. She entered the tiny bed-room, gasping for breath, just in time to receive her squalling nephew. Sister Maria, arriving placidly ten minutes later, found herself with nothing but the tidying up to do and could hardly forebear scolding Camilla for her unladylike speed. But Camilla, white and exhausted, was too happy to care. 'Edward,' she whispered, and fell asleep.

It was Sister Maria who first noticed the thin webbing between the baby's smallest toes and pointed it out, with eldritch shrieks, to Chloe. Chloe, an aunt and entirely grown up now, merely dismissed her from the house with unearned thanks and a string of beads the sister had admired and now accepted with enthusiasm: 'For the blessed Virgin, of course.' Then she returned to the little room where Camilla and the child slept peacefully. If she could help it, Camilla should not be troubled with news of her child's deformity before she was strong enough to bear it.

To her delighted surprise, Camilla's return to strength was very much more rapid than she had expected. It almost seemed that there was something to be said for bearing a child in an atmosphere of domesticity and gardening and without society's benefits of laudanum plasters, devoted relatives and straw in the streets. At any rate by the fourth day, Camilla insisted that she was tired of lying in bed and wanted to bath her son herself: 'You are not to have all the care of him, Chloe, Aunts have their rights, I know, and you have most certainly earned yours, but his mother must come first.'

Chloe protested, but in vain, and watched in anguished expectation while Camilla removed little Edward's clothes with loving, unskilled hands and held him gently in the large cooking pot they used for a bath. In a moment, Camilla looked up at her. 'I see,' she said. 'That is why he was always dressed. Did you think I should mind it, Chloe? I shall only love him all the more. Do you know, I was beginning to be afraid there was something really *wrong* with him; but this—who cares about this?'

'Not I, for one,' said Chloe robustly, but could not help adding. 'I only wondered—Lavenham and Lady Leominster . . .'

'Who cares what they think, or the world for that matter?

And besides, why should anybody know? It is not yet the fashion that I know of for gentlemen to dance barefoot, is it, my precious?' And she bent to concentrate on the intricate and unfamiliar task of washing her son who was beginning to wriggle in her hands like the fish he resembled.

He was a wonderfully well conducted baby, but then, as Camilla said, so he should be, with the entire attention of a devoted mother and aunt. When Sister Maria called to see how he and Camilla were going on, she was amazed to find them both out under a huge cork tree in the garden and raised her hands in horror, prognosticating all kinds of disasters from such an early risking of fresh air. As for the baths, when she learned of them she was convinced the baby would not survive its second week. 'And perhaps as well,' she said to Chloe, who was shepherding her out of the garden, 'poor little monster. What good can come of it? Let me but baptise him and he will be better off with the angels.'

Grateful that Camilla had not heard, Chloe paid a visit to the Convent that night and begged the Mother Superior, who had always been their understanding friend, to prevent Sister Maria from visiting them again.

The old nun nodded her comprehension. 'Yes,' she said, 'perhaps it would be best. Sister Maria is well enough for the peasant women, and even for our own girls when they go astray, but perhaps I will take her place from now on. She has told me, of course, about the poor little boy. We can only pray that it will prove, by God's grace, a blessing to him in disguise.'

Chloe could hardly see how it could do so, but was too relieved at the success of her mission to care. From then on, the Mother Superior visited them daily, cheering them with her robust common sense and her hearty and convinced praise of the baby who grew and throve in daily contradiction of Sister Maria's prophesies.

He was a month old, and a picture of placid health, when Dom

Fernando paid them an unexpected visit. He arrived late in the evening, when the shadow of the cork tree had lengthened across the sunny garden and they were beginning to think about bed. One look at him told Camilla that something was wrong, and she helped him to hurry through the formal greetings and congratulations as fast as possible. He came quickly to the point: 'I am more relieved than I can say to find you so well, for I fear I bring bad news.'

Camilla turned white. 'Not Lavenham?'

'No, no. How could I be so stupid? I have good news of him. We have heard at last that the court are arrived safe at Bahia, though after a sufficiently grievous voyage, poor things. Your husband is alive and, so far as I know, well. No, my news is not of him but of Charles Boutet, who is returned to Lisbon and who, I fear, must have learned that you did not escape with the fleet as he first thought. I discovered only this afternoon that he has been tampering with my servants, asking them all kinds of questions about my movements. That is why I am come so late; I did not dare let anyone know where I was going. But now he has started making enquiries it is only a matter of time — and not very much at that — until he discovers your whereabouts and then, I gravely fear, I would be powerless to protect you.'

Camilla had taken Chloe's hand. 'But what shall we do? Where can we hide?'

He answered her with another question. 'Are you truly better? Strong enough to face a journey, and, I fear, an exhausting one?'

'To go home?' Camilla asked. 'I could face anything for that. And indeed I am entirely recovered. Chloe will tell you that I have been working in the garden all afternoon, and none the worse for it.'

'I cannot tell you how relieved I am to hear it. No hope of getting you out to the blockading fleet. Since Boutet arrived, the French vigilance in the harbour has been redoubled. It was with the greatest difficulty that I made the crossing to visit you tonight.

162

To attempt to get out to the British ships would be to court disaster. But I have another plan which I begin, now I see you so well, to think may be possible. There is a British agent, a Mr. Smith, who is returning from a visit to Spain. He is to be picked up by a British frigate north of Lisbon, where the French watch is less close, and I have suggested to him that you might accompany him.'

'You have seen him then? Where is he? Can we really go with him? What did he say?'

He smiled a shade reprovingly. 'One question at a time, I beg. Or rather, the fewer questions, the better. The less you know, the safer for you. But, yes, he has agreed to take you with him, always provided that you are strong enough to stand the journey. He has vital information to take home to England and asks me to warn you that he must travel fast and can stop for nothing. Luckily his rendezvous is not for another three days, or he could not stay for you. But as it is he will be delighted to escort you and, indeed, thinks that your company will much improve his chances. The French are, we believe, on the lookout for him, but are not likely to suspect a family travelling together. Only,' he paused to look anxiously at Camilla, 'are you strong enough? And what of the baby?'

'To get home,' Camilla said again, 'I can face anything.'

Chapter 11

Neither Camilla nor Chloe slept that night. Excitement would have prevented it, even if there had not been so much to do. Before he left them, Dom Fernando had explained that Mr. Smith could not risk the detour to join them; instead they must make their way alone up the south side of the Tagus and would find him waiting for them where the road turned off for Badajoz. He would, of course, recognise their little party easily enough and would identify himself by asking them, in Portuguese, 'What news, today, in Lisbon?' To make assurance doubly sure, Camilla must then answer, 'None worth the hearing.'

After they had met Mr. Smith, Dom Fernando warned them that they would have two days' hard riding over rough country, if they were to keep their rendezvous with the frigate. His cousin, the Mother Superior, would provide them with mules, peasant costume, and a man to escort them to the meeting place with Mr. Smith: after that, they would be in his hands. He left at last with many good wishes for what seemed a mad enough venture, and promises of a happier meeting when Bonaparte was defeated and peace restored. At the last minute, he came back with a final injunction: 'I had almost forgot. Mr. Smith urges that you make yourselves look as much like peasant women as possible. The clothes my cousin will provide will help, but can you, perhaps, bring yourselves to dirty your faces and untidy your hair?' And on this semi-comic note he left them.

The Mother Superior came bustling over soon afterwards and added her advice to his. Better than advice, she brought a jar of black and viscous fluid with which she urged Chloe to dye her hair: 'Those golden locks of yours are as good as an advertisement that you are a foreigner.' Chloe made a face, but agreed and by morning her hair had been turned a muddy black and her face liberally streaked with the glutinous dye. She insisted, somewhere between laughter and tears, that Camilla, too, daub herself with this strong-smelling substitute for dirt, and by the time they had put on the bedraggled clothes the Mother Superior had brought them, and tied dirty black shawls over their heads, they made, in their own opinion, as convincing a pair of filthy peasant women as anyone could wish to see. The Mother Superior, however, was not so sure, and insisted, at the last moment, that the baby, too, must be wrapped in one of the grimy shawls she had brought, Camilla nearly rebelled at this, but her good sense made her yield soon enough, and she even rubbed a very little of the black dye on Edward's pink and somnolent cheek, where it stood out like a clown's paint.

By now it was morning, and the man was waiting outside with the mules of which, they realised at the last moment, the Mother Superior was making them a present. Protests were vain. There was no possible way to arrange for the animals' return, and they left with a warm feeling of gratitude and the kind old nun's blessing in their ears. They rode for the most part in silence, since Dom Fernando had urged them to speak as little as possible, and never in English: 'Imagine that the very aloes have French ears.'

They had to admit the justice of his advice, although the enforced silence added very considerably to the misery and fatigue of the day's journey. In order to be sure of their rendezvous, they must ride steadily through the noontide heat, pausing only for brief rests, to feed the baby and to encourage themselves with the lavish refreshments the Mother Superior had provided. Their guide was silent to the point of taciturnity, the sun blazed down, their only consolation was that little Edward, carried first by his mother and then by his aunt, slept like an angel, soothed, no doubt, by the rocking gait of the mule.

Towards evening, however, he woke and began to whimper in his mother's arms; the fatigue of the journey had made him hungry earlier than usual. But their guide rejected Camilla's suggestion that they stop to feed him with a surliness that was all too evidently the mask for anxiety. They were late already, he said. There was an hour's hard riding still to the cross roads and Dom Smith would be already awaiting them there—if he waited, added the man gloomily, troubled by visions of having to escort his awkward companions back to the Convent.

The last hour's ride was a silent misery. Both Camilla and Chloe were proficient riders, and had had plenty of practice on mule-back over the rough Portuguese roads, but neither of them had realised what an awkward addition little Edward would be to the party. Even asleep, he was a problem to carry; now that he was awake, crying and wriggling, it was all that they could do to hold him and still keep their beasts on the road. 'Truly, my angel,' Chloe exclaimed as she handed him back to his mother, 'if I did not adore you, I should be in a fair way to thinking you a little pest.'

She had spoken in English, and Camilla was beginning to reply in the same language when a warning exclamation from their guide silenced her. Absorbed in the handover of the baby, they had neither of them noticed that they had come to the outskirts of a village. It was an encouraging sight, for the cross roads at which they were to meet Mr. Smith was only a mile or so further. But just as Camilla and Chloe were exchanging glances of mutual congratulation, their guide's hand on the knotted rope that served as bridle halted Camilla's mule. Without a word he turned its head towards a filthy alleyway leading past a group of hovels and away from the Tagus. A fierce glance silenced the question that rose to Camilla's lips, and she and Chloe followed him without a word down the stinking lane and into the untidy orange grove to which it led. There, at last, he let them come up with him. 'You did not see them?' he asked.

'Who?'

'The French soldiers.' He spat expressively. 'The village was full of them. I hope it does not mean they have caught Dom Smith. But it means we must avoid the village. How long it will take to go round it, God knows. I only hope Dom Smith will wait—if he is not already in French hands.'

The next hour or so was pure nightmare. Camilla and Chloe had thought the riding over country roads bad enough, but now they were following mere goat tracks. Brambles slashed their faces; even the sure-footed mules slipped and slid on the rocky ground; carrying the baby was so difficult that when their guide, with an impatient exclamation, snatched him from Camilla, she was simply grateful. When they finally returned, down a precipitous slope, to the little road on the far side of the village, they were already two hours late for their rendezvous. Their guide's face was a picture of gloom; Camilla and Chloe were both near tears and the baby, in Chloe's arms now, wailed on the despondent note of exhaustion.

A sudden turning of the road showed them the cross roads— and a small group of French soldiers camped at it . . . They had been seen already; there was nothing for it but to go on, with sinking hearts and as bold an appearance as possible. The soldiers, they now saw, were grouped around a tattered figure and his dejected mule. Camilla and Chloe exchanged quick glances. Impossible that this vagabond, who was holding forth to a French officer in rapid Portuguese, could be Mr. Smith, the British agent. But he had seen them, and broke, all of a sudden, into a loud wail of thanksgiving to all his patron saints, who he named in exhaustive catalogue, while the French officer listened impassively. 'Mary, Mother of God, and all the saints be praised,' he concluded, when he was sure that Camilla and Chloe were within earshot, 'here, at long last, are my beloved wife, my sister, my child.' He ran towards them, mule and Frenchmen alike following him closely, embraced Camilla in a cloud of garlic and salt cod and then, to her utter amazement, gave her a resounding slap across the face. 'And that,' he said, 'is for keeping me waiting. As for you, neighbour Tomas, I'll not ask you to escort my wife again! Two hours I have waited for you, here in the sun.' And he turned on their guide in such a threatening manner that the man kicked his mule into a gallop and disappeared around the corner in a cloud of dust.

The French soldiers found all this highly entertaining, and laughed still harder when their prisoner, for such he obviously was, fetched Chloe a box on the ears, and then snatched the baby from her and covered it with dirty kisses, calling it his lamb, his only son, his treasure, his hope in heaven. Handing little Edward back to Camilla he turned to the French officer and broke into what seemed an endless tirade against the whole of womankind, describing their shortcomings in such a wealth of unprintable detail that Camilla and Chloe were grateful for the dirt that hid their blushes, and for their limited Portuguese, which spared them full comprehension of what he was saying.

At last, the officer grew impatient, 'Enough,' he said, 'I am sure your wife and sister are everything you say, and more so,' he spared them a quick, contemptuous glance, 'but we have work to do. Away with you, and do not let me find you loitering about the highways again.' He gave him a push that sent him staggering into the filthy ditch, shouted an order to his men, and wheeled his horse back in the direction of the village.

The man lay in three inches of stinking water and watched them go, muttering a mixture of prayers and curses, while Camilla and Chloe sat speechless on their mules. Of their guide there was no sign; he had taken his cue and vanished. At last, when all the Frenchmen were out of earshot, the man crawled out of the ditch, shook himself and approached Camilla and Chloe with a smile that gave a sparkle to his grey eyes and revealed startling white teeth in his filthy face. 'Well,' he said, 'what news, today, in Lisbon?'

'None worth the hearing,' Camilla, who had noticed with fury that he had contrived to filthy the baby's face all over, controlled her voice as best she might. 'Is it really you?' she went on, still in Portuguese.

'Yes, and never more glad to see anyone. If you had not kept your tryst, I should have been a dead man. I apologise to you both,' he made an awkward peasant's bob, 'for the blows I gave you, but you must admit that they saved you questions I was afraid you might not be able to answer. There is nothing more husbandly than a few matrimonial slaps. And now, we must lose no more time.' And without more ado, he mounted his bedraggled mule and led them at a brisk pace away from the village. They exchanged despondent glances and followed. He might, despite appearances, be an Englishman but he seemed no more considerate a guide than their Portuguese one. Too exhausted to make the effort of speech in Portuguese, they followed him as best they might, drooping in the saddle. But their mules, too, were tired. They found themselves dropping further and further behind their guide. At last he disappeared into a little wood and they exchanged a glance of mute despair. Could he have decided, already, that they were too much of a liability, and abandoned them? They did the best they could to kick their unresponsive mules into a trot and reached the wood with sinking hearts, only to find Mr. Smith lying full length at the side of the road, waiting for them.

'Good,' he said, 'we are out of sight at last. But we will still speak Portuguese, I think. Now, tell me, have you the strength to ride another two miles – to safety? I have good friends in the next village, where you may rest in peace.'

After a glance at Chloe, Camilla assured him that they would manage. 'Then let me take the baby,' he said. 'I can see that he is an awkward burden,' and then, seeing Camilla hesitate, 'I know

169

you think me a brute for blacking his face, but it was touch and go with us, then, and when did you see a clean Portuguese baby? I am sure, when he grows up, he will thank me.'

There was such obvious good sense in this that Camilla handed him the child gratefully enough and settled down to concentrate all her energies on the exhausting problem of keeping her weary mule on the road. Chloe, too, was swaying with fatigue and she and Camilla rode silently, side by side, some way behind Mr. Smith, who rode steadily on ahead, hardly sparing them a glance. Added to their fatigue, there was something infuriating about this neglect and by the time he finally dismounted outside a lonely hovel by the road and stood awaiting their approach they were both seething with silent rage.

When they drew level with him, he merely said, 'Good, we are arrived at last,' and handed the baby to Camilla who had lost no time in sliding to the ground. Chloe, who had fallen a little behind, now drew up, swaying with fatigue and sat, for a moment, too tired even to make the effort of dismounting. When Mr. Smith made no effort to help her, rage overcame her. 'Pray,' she said in English, 'do not trouble yourself to help me dismount.'

For a moment he looked as if he would strike her again, then answered in Portuguese. 'I most certainly shall not. When did you see a Portuguese peasant help his women? It is far enough out of character that I should have been carrying the baby. I could not risk even that where there were people about. Most fortunately, here, we are among friends, but I warn you, if you speak English again, I shall leave you behind. The news I carry is too important to be jeopardised by a girl's foolish tongue.' And he turned on his heel and began to lead his mule around to the back of the hut.

Following him in chastened, if irritable silence they were greeted by the hut's ragged owner, who kissed Mr. Smith enthusiastically on both cheeks, greeting him in a flood of Portuguese so rapid and so strangely accented that neither Camilla nor Chloe could understand him. They followed the two men mutely into the hovel and then stopped to gaze in horror at its single, filthy, earth-floored room. But their host was bustling hospitably about, drawing stools up to a rickety table and fetching dirty bread and sinister dark sausage from an odoriferous cupboard in a corner.

Mr. Smith eyed the two of them coolly: 'I hope,' he still spoke Portuguese, 'that Dom Fernando passed on my warning about the roughness of our trip.'

Camilla was too busy trying to soothe the now frantic Edward to answer, so it was Chloe who answered. 'Naturally we are prepared for some discomfort, but the baby needs to be fed. Surely my sister should have some privacy.'

'Privacy? In a peasant's hut? Are you mad? You should be grateful that my friend here has sent away his wife and children, for fear that contact with you should endanger their lives. Be thankful for the shelter he risks his life to give us, and spare me your complaints. As for the baby, why should he not be fed? I promise you, we have other things to think about.' And he drew up a stool beside their shabby host, who had just produced a bottle of local wine, and filled two glasses. In a moment, the two men were deep in conversation and Camilla, who had, of course, heard everything, gave one defiant look round, opened her dress and put little Edward to suck. A contented silence replaced his previous wailings and was broken only by the murmur of the two men's voices as they disposed of their wine which they accompanied with great slices of greyish bread spread liberally with sausage. Mr. Smith turned once to invite Chloe to join them, but she indicated haughtily that she would wait for Camilla and busied herself with unpacking the bundle of provisions the Mother Superior had given them, of which a lavish quantity still remained for their supper. When the baby finally fell into a contented sleep, she handed Camilla her share and they fell to with a will. Mr. Smith, after a quick and, Camilla thought, hostile

171

glance in their direction, turned back to his incomprehensible talk with their host, who was busy opening a second bottle.

The talk went on and on. Camilla and Chloe swayed on their stools and still the two men talked and drank, drank and talked. At last, Chloe could bear it no more, but jumped to her feet. 'We wish to sleep, my sister and I.'

Their host looked at her in puzzlement, and Mr. Smith merely answered, 'Well, why not?'

The two girls exchanged glances, then, without a word, began to make their travelling shawls into the best approximation of a bed that they could manage in a dark corner of the little room. Seeing what they were about, their host leaped to his feet and produced two filthy blankets, which he pressed upon them. Chloe was about to refuse hers, when a warning glance from Camilla stopped her, and later, when the chill of midnight crept into the hut, she was glad that manners had forced its acceptance, and pulled it around her, dirt and all.

They were roused, far too early, by Mr. Smith. Even little Edward was still asleep and Chloe, stiff and sore from exercise and the hard bed, awoke with a rebellious murmur. Mr. Smith was looking down at her with his calm grey eyes. 'Very well,' he said. 'I will leave you behind to have out your sleep, if you prefer.'

She was up in a flash and began to make her morning toilet as best she might when a word from him stopped her, 'No, no,' he said 'leave it, you are much better as you are. I tell you, I trembled at every step we took yesterday. This morning, you are almost convincing if you will only remember to speak in Portuguese.'

Chloe turned from him with an angry moue, but nevertheless abandoned her efforts to tidy herself, and set to work, instead, to prepare breakfast for herself and Camilla out of the remnants of the Mother Superior's supplies. Mr. Smith had already sat down with their host to more of the inevitable bread and sausage and as soon as Camilla had finished feeding the baby, the two girls made their own breakfast in peace. When they had done, Chloe began to pack the last fragments back into the bundle, but Mr. Smith intervened. 'No, no,' he said, 'you have insulted our host enough. If he had not been my very good friend, I do not like to think what would have happened when you refused his bread last night, but this morning, you shall make amends.' At that moment, their host, who had been out of the hut on some errand, returned and Mr. Smith at once offered him the remains of the girls' food 'as some small token of their gratitude'. The man accepted with a sudden grace that pricked Chloe's conscience far more than Mr. Smith's rebuke had done and they set out on their day's journey with many protestations of affection on their host's part and gratitude on theirs—and some more of the stinking bread and sausage for their wayside luncheon.

Once more they rode through the long, hot day in silence, the two girls always some little distance behind Mr. Smith who showed no sign of caring whether they followed him or not. When Chloe, who was very far from being in charity with him today, murmured about this to Camilla, the latter looked up from little Edward to say reasonably, 'But, Chloe, look at the people we meet. The men always ride ahead. Mr. Smith is right and I beg you will do your best not to annoy him further. I only hope we are not being too great a burden for him as it is.' And she kicked her mule to make it keep up with Mr. Smith's beast, which despite its shabby appearance, seemed to be able to go steadily on for ever.

When they stopped for lunch, Camilla asked Mr. Smith anxiously whether they were going fast enough, and to her relief, his answer was reassuring. If they kept up the pace he had been setting, they would reach his friend's hut at a reasonable hour in the evening. And tomorrow they would have an easy day's ride. Their rendezvous with the frigate was not until after dark; they would have ample time to reach it. 'You may catch up on your beauty sleep in the morning, if you wish,' he told Chloe, but she was too irritated with him to answer.

Their afternoon's ride was uneventful and as Mr. Smith had promised they reached his friend's house early in the evening. The two girls saw with pleasure that this house, which stood alone in its orange grove, was very much larger than the hovel in which they had spent the previous night. They dismounted and received the obsequious greetings of their new host with visions of some possible modicum of comfort dancing in their heads. He shouted to one of his sons, who were playing in the dust outside the house, to take their mules to the stable, and led them indoors with an extravagant speech of welcome which Chloe, at least, found almost comprehensible. She and Camilla were delighted to find that the house consisted of three rooms, one of which was to be put at the disposal of their little party. Of course, it would have been better still if Mr. Smith could have slept elsewhere, but this was too much to be hoped. Besides—alone, for a moment in the room that was to be theirs, Chloe whispered to Camilla, in English, 'Camilla, I do not like this place.'

'Not like it?' Camilla was feeding the baby. 'Why not, Chloe?'

'There is something wrong here. I can feel it. Did you not hear how the man received us—as if we were honoured guests. It is absurd: we are fugitives; he endangers his life harbouring us. Remember that man last night, how frightened he was . . . And he had sent his family away, lest they be implicated. What makes everything so different here? Listen to them.'

She was silent for a moment, listening to the chatter of female voices in the next room, then went on: 'I tell you, I do not like it. There was something wrong in his tone as he greeted us. Do you know, I am glad Mr. Smith is to share our room. I shall feel safer so.'

She was interrupted by Mr. Smith himself, who entered at this moment with a look of controlled rage. 'I believe I asked you not to speak in English,' he said, in furiously whispered Portuguese.

'I am sorry; I forgot.' Chloe refused to be cowed. 'But, Mr. Smith,' she too was whispering, 'I was telling my sister. Do you not feel something wrong here?'

'Wrong? What do you mean?'

'About our host. I do not like him. Do you think it is safe to stay here?'

He made an impatient gesture. 'What nonsense is this? I thought you would be glad to spend a night of comparative comfort and instead you start refining at God knows what imaginary terrors. I see nothing wrong with the man. It is true, he is a stranger to me, not a close friend like last night's host. Doubtless that accounts for any difference you may have noticed in his behaviour. But, come, leave these megrims and join the family at their supper. And, remember, you are to eat whatever is given you, and show your gratitude. If you do not value your life, I do mine, and both lie in our hosts' hands.'

'Yes,' said Chloe mutinously, 'that is exactly what troubles me.' But he had already turned to leave the room.

The evening dragged on interminably. There was the usual fierce sausage to be washed down with coarse red wine, and, tonight, doubtless as a hospitable gesture, there was salt cod too, cooked with a lavish flavouring of garlic. But appetite was on the two girls' side, and they ate their way staunchly through everything they were offered, making what conversation they could with their hosts as they did so. But it was an enormous relief when a cry from Edward in the next room, and a confirmatory nod from Mr. Smith, gave them the signal to say goodnight.

'Do you still say you feel nothing?' whispered Chloe, in Portuguese this time, when they were safe in their own room.

Camilla temporised. 'Well, naturally, it was not the easiest evening in the world, but I am sure that is all, Chloe. You are tired, and refining too much, as Mr. Smith said. Try and sleep, now, and forget it.'

Much later, however, when Camilla heard the party next door

175

breaking up, and Mr. Smith tiptoed in, Chloe stirred and sat up to whisper to him. 'Lock the door, for the sake of my megrims, will you?'

He gave an impatient exclamation, but went back to the door, which turned out to have no lock. He shrugged his shoulders, made his brief preparations, and settled down among his blankets in the farthest corner of the room from Chloe. Much later, just as she was drifting off to sleep at last, Camilla heard Chloe get up and go over to the door; she remained there for a minute and then, just as Camilla was about to rouse herself and ask what she was doing, returned to her makeshift bed. It was nothing . . . megrims . . . Camilla slept.

She woke with a start to darkness and terror. Chloe was shaking her shoulder. 'Camilla, someone just tried the door. I wedged the latch with a bit of wood; otherwise they would have been here. Do you still think nothing is wrong? Get Edward, while I wake Mr. Smith.'

Half asleep, Camilla's first thought had been to pick up little Edward, who stirred as he slept, then settled once more against her breast. Meanwhile, Chloe had crossed the room, silent in the darkness, to rouse Mr. Smith. He was on his feet in a moment and listened to her whispered explanation. 'Tried the door, did they? You wedged it you say? You may have been wise. At all events, we will take no chances. It is probably nothing, but better safe than sorry. Get together your things, and come.' He moved to the one window of the little room, which was closed by a wooden shutter, and began to remove its bolts. 'I loosened these earlier,' he explained in a whisper as the girls followed him. 'When you spoke of danger. Better, always, safe than sorry. There,' he had the window open, 'out you go: quietly.'

Obediently, Chloe slipped out into the darkness and turned to receive the baby from Camilla, who followed her. Last came Mr. Smith with their bundles. 'This way,' he whispered. 'For the moment, we will not risk staying for the mules.' And he led them along a little path, fitfully moonlit, that ran down through the orange groves towards the main road. Suddenly he stopped. 'Hush!' Mercifully, the baby still slept, and they followed him in absolute silence as he slipped down off the road and into the shadows of an enormous cork tree. Safe behind it, he stopped, and touched a finger to each of their cheeks in warning. As their quick breathing steadied, they heard what he had, the sound of men and horses approaching from the main road.

They stood there, as still as statues in the warm darkness, as a detachment of French soldiers marched past. They, too, were silent, moving almost stealthily through the fitful moonlight. And as the last of them went by, the moon came out more clearly, to reveal their host marching amicably beside the officer. Mr. Smith's hand on each girl's arm, constrained them to stillness for what seemed an incredibly long time after the men had passed. Then, 'Hurry,' he whispered and led the way back on to the track. 'When they reached the main road he turned back the way they had come. 'Safer so,' he whispered. 'And I remember a side road soon.'

The side road, when they found it, climbed precipitously among the foothills of the Sintra mountains, and presently, when at long last Mr. Smith allowed them to stop for breath, they looked down and saw how wise he had been in bringing them this way. For below them lay the village from which the soldiers had come and they could see lights moving everywhere about its streets. The hunt was up for them.

'Time to move on,' said Mr. Smith and then, matter-of-factly, to Chloe, 'We all owe you our lives, Lady Chloe. And I, an apology.'

She inclined her head, all at once the society beauty. 'I thank you.'

After that, no one had the breath for speech. If the rough roads had been hard work on mule-back, on foot, and in the dark, they were torture. But at least the little road continued to rise and to lead away from the village where they had so nearly been captured and towards the bay where they must keep their tryst with the British frigate. Light was beginning to show in the East, and early birds to twitter here and there around them when Chloe voiced the question that had been in all their minds. 'Have we any chance of getting there on foot?'

Mr. Smith signalled a halt and looked thoughtfully from her to Camilla before he spoke. 'Yes,' he said at last, 'we have a chance. If you can walk all day.'

Chloe and Camilla exchanged glances and this time Chloe spoke for both. 'If we must,' she said, 'we can.'

'Good. Then let me take the baby.' He settled the sleeping Edward gently in the crook of his arm. 'The longer he sleeps, the better. We can neither afford to draw attention to ourselves by his crying, nor to stop often for him to feed.'

'If the worst comes to the worst,' said Camilla, 'I shall just have to feed him as we go.' It was a far cry from the time when she had been embarrassed to feed him in public.

Mr. Smith rewarded her with an approving glance. 'If you continue in that spirit,' he said, 'I have no fear of our failing to keep our rendezvous.'

The sun rose higher, dust everywhere made breathing difficult and speech too much trouble, and still they walked on, one foot placed relentlessly in front of the other, Mr. Smith, with the baby, a few yards in front, Camilla and Chloe stumbling speechless behind. Only, once, when they had climbed breathlessly for what seemed an eternity, Mr. Smith stopped at a turn of the road commanding a wide view of the sea. 'There,' he pointed ahead, 'there is our goal.'

Camilla and Chloe looked at the distant promontory and their hearts sank. Could they possibly get there by night? But they had got their second wind by now and plodded on valiantly for another hour or so as the sun rose towards noon and the heat grew more intense. At last, little Edward began to cry in Mr.

Smith's arms. He looked up at the sun, then paused. They were passing a thicket of myrtle and wild orange through which ran a little laughing stream. 'We will stop here for a while,' he said, 'and rest.'

Safely out of sight of the road, Chloe and Camilla sank down with sighs of relief and Camilla began at once to feed little Edward while Chloe unpacked the bundle in which she had wrapped the scanty remains of their yesterday's luncheon. She was sharing the dry bread and now stinking sausage into three meticulously equal, pitifully small portions when Mr. Smith stopped her, 'No, no,' he said, 'share it between you. I have gone without food often enough; it is no hardship.'

All too soon, he gave the signal to resume the march. The two girls found that their muscles had stiffened as they sat and stumbled along slowly enough at first, Mr. Smith slackening his pace to theirs. But as Camilla got back into her stride she found that Chloe lagged behind, walking as if each step was an agony. Mr. Smith had gradually increased his pace. Now, as Chloe fell further and further behind, Camilla called to him softly.

He stopped and turned back. 'What is the matter?' He spoke with the brusqueness of anxiety.

'I don't know.' They waited in silence as Chloe came up.

As she approached, Mr. Smith spoke bracingly. 'We must go faster than this. If your sister can keep up, surely you can?'

Chloe coloured, bit her lip, and was silent. Camilla took her hand. 'It is just the stiffness from sitting,' she said encouragingly. 'It will pass off soon. Mine has already. Come, Chloe.'

Still silent, Chloe stepped out faster and they resumed their dogged march. But Chloe was limping more and more. At last she sat down by the roadside. 'You go on, Camilla,' she said. 'Leave me here. I can go no further.'

'Leave you? What madness is this?' Looking down almost impatiently at Chloe, Camilla suddenly noticed blood oozing over her left shoe. 'Chloe, what's the matter?'

179

'My shoe.' Wearily Chloe lifted her foot and showed that the rope sole of her shoe had worn clean through. For some miles she had been walking almost barefoot on the rocky road. Her foot was bleeding from a dozen wounds and lacerations. 'You see,' she said. 'It is no use. I cannot go on.'

Mr. Smith, who had been some distance ahead, came back to join them. 'What new absurdity is this? We cannot afford these delays.' He saw Chloe's foot: 'Good God!' He said no more, but hurried to a nearby stream, brought water and bathed the foot before bandaging it gently with strips of his shirt. 'No, no,' he ignored her protest, 'I shall do well enough without. But—you cannot go on thus.'

'No,' Chloe said. 'You must leave me. Take my sister, and the baby. Remember, the news you carry is too important to be jeopardised by a foolish girl.'

He stood for a moment, looking down at her silently, then 'Wait here,' he said, 'rest, and, if you know how, pray. If I do not return, you must try to get back to Lisbon. Dom Fernando will look after you, if you can reach him.'

'But what are you going to do?' Camilla asked.

'Beg, buy or steal a mule—or two, or best of all three. If I am not back before the shadow of that tree falls across you, you will know that I have failed, and you must find your way back to Lisbon as best you may.'

'But,' Camilla protested, 'you could go on alone without taking the risk. Leave us here. As you say, Dom Fernando will protect us.'

'If you reach him. No,' he anticipated her further protest. 'It is no use. I cannot reconcile it with my conscience to abandon you here. The message I carry is important, it is true, but there are other things more important still. Besides, we must hope that we will all carry it together.' And then: 'Goodbye. Rest well. You will need all your strength when I return.'

He was gone. For a few moments, as they settled themselves

in the little glade by the stream, neither girl spoke. At last, 'Do you think he will return?' Camilla asked.

'Of course,' said Chloe. 'He said he would.'

'I am glad you are so sure. We know so little about him. I did wonder whether this was not a gentler mode of leaving us.'

'What? After what he said? Camilla, how can you!'

Surprised at her vehemence, Camilla said mildly: 'Well, why not? We are nothing to him, the message he carries doubtless everything, his career, his future . . . Tell me, Chloe, what do you think he is? Do you realise, we have never heard him speak in English, nor seen what he is really like: that filthy face — those ragged clothes — how can one possibly tell what is underneath. Do you think he is a gentleman?'

'I have no idea,' said Chloe. 'I only know he is a man, and will return. And now, he told us to rest. It is a pity we cannot eat first, but for myself I am tired enough to sleep through worse hunger than this. I do not believe I slept at all last night.'

'And lucky for us you did not,' said Camilla as she obediently composed herself and little Edward for sleep. 'I suppose Mr. Smith feels he owes it to you to return. After all, as he said, you did save his life last night.'

'Oh — obligations!' exclaimed Chloe with a burst of temper that surprised Camilla. 'Stop talking, Camilla, and go to sleep.'

Drifting off into a doze of nervous exhaustion, Camilla thought with amusement that her position and Chloe's seemed to have reversed themselves of late. Now, it was Chloe who gave the orders, she who meekly obeyed. Well, it was restful . . . she slept.

She woke at last, to see Chloe bending anxiously over her. 'Camilla? what time do you think it is?'

Camilla stretched, shivered, and tucked the shawl more closely round little Edward who still, blessedly, slept. 'I have no idea. Oh! the sun has gone in.'

'Yes. I think there must be a storm coming.'

Camilla looked up at the tall tree whose shadow was to have

181

been their clock. 'For once,' she said, 'Mr. Smith has not thought of everything. Now what do we do? I have a feeling it is late, Chloe. Surely, if he was coming, he would have returned long since. And it is certainly going to storm. Should we not try and find shelter? These trees will be useless if it really rains — and dangerous if it thunders.' She picked up little Edward as if ready to start at once.

'Are you mad, Camilla?' asked Chloe. 'What is a wetting, compared to our chances of safety? Find shelter for yourself and Edward, if you must, but I shall stay here and wait for Mr. Smith.'

'Oh very well.' Camilla sat down again faintly relieved at having her mind so definitely made up for her. 'We will wait here a while longer.'

'We will wait till Mr. Smith comes,' said Chloe.

'But, Chloe, have you considered . . . it is not only that he may have decided to go on alone . . . he may have been discovered . . . he may be dead by this.'

'I do not believe it,' said Chloe.

The minutes dragged, the clouds darkened, the air grew colder, and the two girls sat close together for warmth. They were silent now. There seemed nothing to say. A few large drops of rain fell in the clearing and the wind began to grumble among the trees.

'Chloe,' Camilla said, 'it is getting dark.'

'It is the storm,' Chloe answered, and she jumped up and arranged her shawl over the branches of a tree so that it formed a kind of makeshift tent over their heads.

'But, Chloe, you cannot intend to stay through this.' For now the rain was falling fast, and the thunder rumbling nearer.

'I most certainly do.' Chloe's look of white determination carried even more conviction than her words.

Camilla shrugged. 'Very well then. But I tell you it is madness. Mr. Smith is doubtless at the rendezvous now.'

'I do not believe it.' Once again they fell silent. Huddled together, they felt strange little currents of hostility playing between them as the rain began to penetrate their shelter. A large drop fell on Edward's nose and he woke with a cry as forked lightning slashed to the ground dangerously near them.

'Now I am going, Chloe.' Camilla was on her feet.

Chloe was up too. 'Listen,' she said. They stood, for a moment, silent in the teeming rain and then Camilla, too, heard the terrified braying of a mule nearby. Her hand found Chloe's. 'It cannot be,' she said.

'It is,' said Chloe.

A few moments later, Mr. Smith entered the clearing, riding a drenched mule and leading two others. 'Thank God,' was his greeting. 'I hoped the storm would prevent you from knowing how late I was. Now, we must lose no time. You have slept, I hope.'

'Yes.' Like him, Chloe was oddly matter of fact.

'Good. Then up you go.' He helped them to mount and led the way, without further words, out of the little clearing.

The rain teemed down, the thunder roared, the lightning flashed, and Mr. Smith rode on ahead as unconcernedly as if he had been in the Mall. Only, once, he turned to shout back, as always, in Portuguese, and with the flashing white grin they had come to know so well: 'This is luck for us. No one but lunatics will be abroad tonight. We will risk taking the shortest way.'

So once more it was nightmare on mule-back. The girls were drenched to the skin and so, despite Camilla's best efforts, was little Edward, and howling resentfully as a result. But his cries were lost in the roaring of the wind and the fitful crash of thunder. There was no question of stopping; they rode on doggedly through the storm while its darkness was swallowed in that of night. At last, when they could hardly see Mr. Smith riding ahead of them, he paused to let them catch up.

183

'It is the next valley,' he said. 'One more hill, and we are there. Keep close behind me, and let the mules find their own way.'

In single file, drenched and numbed beyond thought, they made the last climb and the even more precipitous descent into the valley of their rendezvous. There they found Mr. Smith, who had drawn slightly ahead during the descent, busy looking for dry bits of undergrowth. 'It will be a pity,' he remarked calmly as they drew up, 'if I cannot light the signal fire.' But even as he spoke he had it going, the flames crackling up in defiance of the slackening rain. 'Watch,' he said to the girls, 'Watch the sea as if your lives depended on it.'

'I collect they do,' said Chloe, then, 'Look, there!'

And indeed far out to sea an answering flash had shown for an instant, then vanished. Once more it showed, and then again, before Mr. Smith extinguished his own fire. 'Now it is but to wait.'

'How long will it take?' Camilla asked.

'For them to get here? Some time, I fear, in this storm.'

And indeed it was a long, cold, desperate wait before they heard the sound of muffled oars and a boat pulled into the tiny harbour. Mr. Smith had warned the two girls to lie low until he had explained their presence to its occupants and now he went down alone to meet it. There was a brief colloquy and then he returned to fetch them. 'All's well,' he said, with his usual calm. And then, 'Come.'

Chapter 12

Cold, drenched and exhausted, the two girls were hauled aboard His Majesty's Frigate *Indomitable* more dead than alive, far beyond caring about their bedraggled appearance. Conducted at once to a cabin that showed signs of having been hurriedly vacated, they collapsed on its narrow beds pausing only to strip off their soaked outer garments and settle the baby in an open sea chest. For the time being, exhaustion was more powerful than hunger. All three of them slept heavily for the rest of the night while outside the storm raged with increased vehemence. They woke to find the little cabin a swaying inferno and the next three days were a mere struggle to keep themselves and little Edward alive and unhurt. From above, they heard, from time to time, the sound of orders, and hurrying feet as the ship battled her unsteady way through the gale. Their only communication with the outside world was through the tongue-tied sailor who appeared, at irregular intervals, with meals they did not want. Questioned, he bobbed shyly, said they were weathering the storm—he did not know where they were, or when they would reach England—and left them once more to their struggle for survival.

On the fourth day, the storm subsided, little Edward turned pink again and Chloe began to fret about her clothes. 'To think that we shall have to land in England like this.' She shook out the skirts of her black, peasant's dress which had been shabby when she first put it on and was now merely deplorable.

'Yes,' Camilla agreed, 'like two bumboat women—or worse. Still, better to land in rags than not at all, and I fear it is rags or nothing. It seems hardly likely that there will be anything on board that we can borrow.'

Chloe laughed with something of her old light-heartedness. 'I certainly do not intend going ashore in the full rig of a First Lieutenant. Mr. Smith is luckier than we are. He is doubtless on deck this very moment, enjoying the sunshine in the guise of a Rear-Admiral.'

'Or a ship's cook,' said practical Camilla. 'Remember, Chloe, that we know nothing in the world about him.'

'Except that he saved our lives,' said Chloe.

They were interrupted by a tap at the door and their sailor attendant appeared with a beaming face, and breakfast, to announce that it was a fine morning, a calm sea and they were three days out from Falmouth. 'And,' he concluded, 'Capn's compliments, and will you ladies dine with him and the dook tonight?'

'Him and what?' asked Camilla.

'The dook, ma'am—his grace, cap'n says we're to call 'un. Can't think why, though a prettier sailor I never wish to see . . . been on his legs right through the storm he has and never so much as turned green—and eat! I wish you could see 'im. Would a' et an 'orse, he said, when he come aboard, and blimey but I believe him, only we didn't have one 'andy.' He made his customary awkward bob and left them.

Alone, the two girls exchanged glances. 'A Duke?' said Chloe.

'Mr. Smith?' said Camilla.

'It cannot be,' said Chloe.

'Then who else?' asked Camilla.

'But what shall we wear?' wailed Chloe.

She spent the rest of the day trying to persuade Camilla that they should make an excuse to refuse the captain's invitation: they were tired, they could not leave the baby, anything . . . But Camilla was firm. A captain's invitation, on his own ship, she said, was the equivalent of a royal command. There could be no question of refusing. As for their clothes—he must have known how they were circumstanced when he invited them. 'It is but to carry the thing off with an air — and at least we have our jewels.'

But Chloe remained rebellious and it was with the greatest difficulty that Camilla prevailed upon her to do what she could for her appearance. This was, admittedly, not a great deal, for the dye provided by the Mother Superior had proved all too fast a one. Repeated washings had merely reduced Chloe's golden hair from greasy black to dirty brown. Camilla sympathised, but pointed out that at least Chloe's face was now clean, as were her own and the baby's. 'And, besides, Mr. Smith — I mean the Duke — I wonder, by the by, what he is Duke of — has seen us looking much worse than this. And who cares about the captain?'

'I do,' said Chloe crossly. 'As for Mr. Smith, he has already made it clear that we are nothing but an encumbrance to him: I do not care if he is a Royal Duke — as indeed he might well be, from his manners, or lack of them.'

'But hardly from his appearance,' said Camilla. 'Has it occurred to you that without his disguise he might be positively good looking?'

'No,' said Chloe and began furiously to curl her sticky hair.

Even Camilla felt a slight sinking of the heart when they were ceremoniously ushered into the captain's cabin. If anything, she thought, her diamonds and Chloe's pearls merely added a final touch of absurdity to their appearance. But she held her head high, and greeted the captain with all the ease of a great lady, while noting with sinking heart that he was in full dress uniform and Mr. Smith, behind him, in impeccable evening attire and looking, as she had forecast, deplorably handsome without his mask of dirt. His bows to her and Chloe, as the captain presented him as the Duke of Weston, carried the faintest hint of laughter, and Camilla, recollecting the awkward peasant's bobs he had made them in Portugal could not help laughing herself in sympathetic pleasure at the transformation. But she could feel Chloe bristling beside her, and hurried to mask an ominous silence on her sister's part by what she herself felt to be a slightly over-eloquent flow of gratitude. Mr. Smith — or rather the Duke — would have none of it.

'If I have helped to save your lives,' he said, 'you — or rather your charming sister — have most certainly reciprocated by saving mine.' And he told the captain the story of their adventures on that desperate last night of their journey. Camilla, taking wine, first with the captain and then with the Duke and listening to the Duke's praises of their fortitude on the long march was soon in charity with both men, forgiving them what had seemed, at first, their quite odious elegance of appearance. But she looked in vain for a similar softening in Chloe, who continued to act what was almost a parody of a great lady. When the Duke drank her health and called her his preserver she merely tossed her head and re-marked that he had surely changed his tone: 'I seem to remember that I was "a foolish girl" back in Portugal.'

Camilla was appalled, but the Duke merely laughed and turned back to entertain the captain with a description of their first meeting, and his manhandling by the French: 'I can tell you,' he concluded, 'if these two young ladies had not arrived when they did — and looking as they did — there would have been one Duke-dom the less in England.'

Chloe raised elegant eyebrows. 'Truly?' she said. 'Have you then no heir ready to step into your ducal shoes?'

'Why no,' he turned back to her at once, 'oddly enough, I have not; we Smiths have dwindled most deplorably off into the female line.'

If Camilla had not been so fond of Chloe, she would have thought she snorted. 'Deplorable indeed,' she said, turned her shoulder to him and began ostentatiously to ply the captain with questions about the state of things in England.

It was not a comfortable evening, and Camilla, for one, was heartily glad when it was over and she felt that it was politely possible to plead anxiety for little Edward (who was being minded by the tongue-tied sailor) and take their leave. Back in their cabin, she turned on Chloe to administer a well-earned reproof—but found herself forestalled. Chloe had subsided on her bed in a passion of tears.

They did not see either the captain or the Duke again before they reached Falmouth. Camilla, who was beginning to fret at the narrow confinement of their cabin, urged Chloe more than once to join her in a turn about the decks, but Chloe was adamant. Nothing, she said, would induce her to expose herself once more to the Duke's censorious eye. 'Did you not see, Camilla, how he took in every detail of my—I mean our appearance? No doubt it will make an admirable tale for his friends at White's, just as our meeting provided food for the captain's mirth all evening. No thank you, I shall stay below decks and deprive him of more grist for his humorous mill.' And so, since Camilla did not feel she could properly venture up by herself, they all three stayed in their cramped cabin, Edward increasingly fretful for lack of fresh air, Camilla suffering for his discomfort and Chloe in what seemed a permanent fit of the sullens.

It was, therefore, with the most profound relief that Camilla welcomed their arrival at Falmouth, although she also found herself suffering, more even than she had expected, from the inevitable memories that the green harbour roused of the last time they had been there—with Lavenham. Her eyes filled with tears as she looked across the harbour at the little hotel on the hill where she had stayed, with Lavenham, so newly her husband, the day before they had sailed for Portugal. What mad hopes she had fostered then: Lavenham would learn to love her; in the end they would be man and wife indeed. Well, she shook herself and picked up little Edward, they were, and he did not believe it—perhaps never would. And she had before her the painful task of convincing old Lady Leominster, perhaps in the teeth of her husband's denial, that her child was indeed the heir Lady Leominster wanted. It was not a happy prospect, and when Chloe,

189

who had been miserably silent all morning, opened her mouth to complain at the prospect of going ashore looking like a couple of women of the town—or worse—Camilla turned on her so roundly that Chloe, shaken at last out of her private wretchedness, suddenly put her arms round her and kissed her. 'Oh, Camilla, I am a brute; it is worse for you than it is for me, and I have been behaving like a bear. Forgive me.'

In a flood of mutual, soothing tears, they forgave each other, and then dried them because little Edward had caught the infection and was screaming heartily in Camilla's arms. Chloe took up the little bundle that contained their jewels and they went up on deck to find the captain awaiting them. The Duke, he told them, had gone ashore at first light and was now on his way to London with his despatches. But he had left his carriage behind for the use of Lady Leominster and Lady Chloe. He begged that they would allow his servants to take them wherever they pleased.

'But how, then, is he gone to London?' asked Chloe.

'On horseback,' said the captain, 'he said it would be quicker so.'

'Then he lied,' said Chloe, with a return of her previous bad temper.

But she had to admit that the lie was a very handy one for them. They had no English money, and the prospect of pawning their pearls, one by one, in order to pay for their journey across England was not pleasant. Now they were to travel in luxury, for the Duke's elderly and formidably respectable coachman made it clear that he was to be responsible for all expenses on the way. 'It is as much as my place is worth, my lady,' he explained, when Camilla began a protest. She yielded gratefully enough—it would be time to think of repaying the Duke when they were safe at home—and even went so far as to suggest to Chloe that they might borrow enough from Mr. Banks, the coachman, to equip themselves in somewhat more suitable clothes for the journey. Oddly enough, it was Chloe, who had previously complained so bitterly about their tatterdemalion appearance, who now exclaimed, just as vehemently, against the very idea of borrowing any more from the Duke than strictest necessity demanded: 'Do you, if you feel you must, Camilla, but I am too intolerably obligated to him already.'

Camilla gave up the idea readily enough. She was too bone weary to care for the idea of shopping; little Edward was fretful from the long journey; the sooner they got home the better. And she soon discovered that Mr. Banks had had the fullest possible orders from his master. Not only did he manage not to show the least sign that there was anything odd about their appearance, he also always contrived an excuse to go ahead and announce their arrival at the wayside inns where they stopped. When they arrived they found themselves greeted as heroines. England, it seemed, was war mad all of a sudden, and Spain's unexpected resistance to Bonaparte's tyranny the subject of universal enthusiasm. Heralded as the heroines of a romantic escape from the French, their odd appearance was forgotten in the glamour Mr. Banks contrived to cast around them.

'You must confess,' Camilla remarked as they remounted the coach after a positively festive meal of the best of everything a little country inn had to offer, 'that the Duke is well served.'

'Of course he is,' Chloe replied, 'tyrants always are.'

Camilla sighed, and shrugged and dropped the subject. If Chloe must persist in this unreasonable aversion to the Duke, she, for her part, had worries enough of her own to occupy her. They had decided to go straight to Haverford Hall. It would be time enough, after they had somewhat recovered their strength and, incidentally, refurbished their wardrobes, to face old Lady Leominster, to whom, inevitably, they would have to apply for funds. 'Unless,' remarked Chloe, momentarily forgetting her own preoccupations in concern for Camilla's, 'we find Lavenham home before us. I cannot believe that he will stay long in the Brazils, ignorant, as he must be, whether we are alive or dead.'

Now it was Camilla's turn to be unreasonable. 'I do not see why not,' she said. 'After all, you know as well as I do that he has always put his duty before our welfare. And quite right, too,' she added belatedly, and without entire conviction.

'Camilla, I do not think that quite fair of you,' Chloe protested. 'If you had but seen his anxiety when you were ill, you would think otherwise.'

'It did not stop him going on board ship with Lord Strangford and leaving you to nurse me,' said Camilla. 'If he had stayed with us, we would never have got into this scrape.'

'But no more should we, if I had not been such a fool as to trust your brother,' pointed out Chloe.

It was a silencer for Camilla. The part played by Charles Boutet was not one she much liked to remember. Monstrous to have reminded Chloe. She put out a hand. 'Forgive me.'

'Of course. Camilla, do you realise we are almost there?' The milestones were beginning to carry familiar names, and to revive, for Camilla, painful memories of that hopeful journey on which she had set out, a lifetime ago, with her new husband at her side. Where was he now, and what did he think of her? Could he possibly believe that she had gone willingly with Charles? She was actually grateful to little Edward when he burst into the tears of total exhaustion and effectively distracted her from thoughts that were equally painful and useless.

When they drew up at last on the wide carriage sweep in front of Haverford Hall, the first shadows of night had fallen, and they were surprised to see that the entire front of the house was illuminated. Camilla clutched Chloe's hand: '*Someone* is there.'

For a moment, her courage failed her. Suppose it was Lavenham, how would they meet? She had not spoken to him since that desperate day when he had hurled such furious accusations at her that she had fainted. And now, she was returning with his child in her arms, a child he had called a French spy's bastard. But Mr. Banks had beaten a resounding tattoo on the big front door and it now swung open, revealing the brilliantly lighted hall. Even in this moment of tension, Camilla found time to notice, as she carefully alighted from the carriage with Edward whimpering in her arms, that old Lady Leominster had been as good as her word: the house shone with new paint, and the servants, who were hurriedly assembling in the hall, were resplendent in new liveries. What an odd contrast, she thought as she slowly mounted the steps, she and Chloe must present in their bedraggled black.

She forgot everything as an inner door opened and old Lady Leominster appeared. More bent, more wizened and more brilliantly garbed than ever, she hurried forward, arms outstretched. 'My dears,' she gathered first Camilla, then Chloe into a highly perfumed embrace, paused for a quick, satisfied glance at little Edward who had fallen silent in the dazzle of the lights, then urged them forward into the little drawing room from which she had come. 'I know it all,' she said, 'I had a message from the Duke of Weston this morning and hurried here to have all ready for you. You are heroines, I collect, both of you, and the Duke your servant for life.' Here a sharp glance, bristling with question, flashed from Camilla to Chloe and back, before she resumed: 'And my grandson, I understand, a perfect paragon among babies. Tell me,' to Camilla, 'has he the Lavenham foot?'

'The what?' A long, involuntary tremor ran through her, and she was glad to have Lady Leominster take Edward in fragile but surprisingly competent hands. Speechless, Camilla looked on while the old lady deftly unwound his shawls, lifted the long dress to reveal his poor little webbed feet and let out a sigh of satisfaction. 'Ahh,' she said, 'most satisfactory.' And then, to Camilla. 'But did no one tell you? Of course, Chloe was a child—she would not know—but Lavenham? Every boy in the family—since anyone can remember. It would have been—awkward, if you had come back with an heir born God knows how in Portugal and he had not had it . . . as it is; come here, my dear, and let me kiss you.' But Camilla had burst into helpless tears.

Later, she told Lady Leominster the whole story, or as much as she could bear to, and received, in return, her promise of every possible assistance when Lavenham returned. 'He will not be reasonable,' said his grandmother, 'he never was. But we must contrive to make him so.' She had told Camilla already that Lavenham had asked for, and received, permission to return to England. She looked for his arrival daily. 'But I am inclined to hope, my child, that it may be somewhat delayed. I would rather you had a little colour in your cheeks, and flesh on your bones, before we have to deal with him. And now, tell me,' once again the large eyes flashed questions, 'what is this about the Duke of Weston?'

'The Duke?' Camilla asked, puzzled. 'Why, nothing, except that he has been most kind to us.'

'Kind!' The old lady snorted. 'I should just about think he has! Can you really be as ignorant—or as innocent, as you seem? Do you not know that the Duke who has been so "kind" to you and Chloe has about as sharp a reputation as any young rakehell in town? Why, I have it on the best authority that when he took it into his head to go on this dangerous mission to Portugal his family let out a sigh of relief and secretly prayed that he would never come back. And you wish me to believe that he nurse-tended you and Chloe across the country—yes, and the baby too —out of pure philanthropy? And sent you home in his own coach —though I grant you that is more in character, since he has always been known for his wild rides across country and was doubtless glad to get rid of coach and servants as a pack of encumbrances. But to take the trouble to send and tell me of your arrival—no, no, it must be for one of your sakes, and I only hope it is Chloe. Though come to that,' her bright eyes snapped, 'it might not be such a bad thing after all if Lavenham were to come home and find you pursued by the most notorious Duke in town. But mind you do not let him catch you; I'll not have any of your Devonshire House goings-on in my family.'

Half angry, half amused, Camilla did her best to convince the old lady that she was far wide of the mark in her suspicions. The Duke had never showed the slightest partiality for either of them, she said, and had indeed tended all too obviously to treat them as the encumbrances they must have been to him. 'Though,' her natural fairness forced her to add, 'he could not, in truth, have been kinder. He even carried little Edward much of the way.'

'What!' exclaimed Lady Leominster. 'Best not noise that around, if you wish him to remain your friend. But I begin to think I see—treated you as encumbrances did he? No wonder Chloe is so out of charity with him. Well, I think we had best go to London at once.'

Camilla, who pined for nothing more than a long rest in the peaceful unfamiliar greenness of the English countryside, protested in vain. Lady Leominster had made her decision and nothing would shake her. There were, she pointed out, a few weeks left of the London season: it was of the most vital importance that Camilla should make her appearance in society at once. 'I wish Lavenham to find you thoroughly established when he returns.'

Camilla, who could not help seeing the good sense of this, merely asked, 'And Chloe?'

'Chloe comes too,' said the old lady. 'She has been kept in the schoolroom long enough. And, besides, who knows what may come of it?'

Chloe, of course, was delighted with the idea of London and even Camilla became gradually reconciled to it after she had won a short sharp battle with Lady Leominster about Edward. His devoted great grandmother had found a wet nurse for him and arranged for him to stay at Haverford Hall and was quite amazed when Camilla, fierce for once in her gentle life, sent the wet nurse packing and announced, once and for all, that where she went, Edward went too. 'If he inconveniences you, ma'am, it is but to open our own town house instead of staying with you.'

That silenced Lady Leominster, who made no secret of the fact that she wanted both girls under her immediate eye during their first tricky weeks in society.

As it turned out, she need not have worried about their reception. London was Spain mad. Bonnets, dances, military jackets . . . everything had a Spanish name, and the two heroines from Portugal found themselves taken to society's heart. No breakfast was complete, no ball a total success, unless they were present. The fact that Camilla either insisted on taking Edward with her, or left early in order to feed him, merely added to the glamour that surrounded her. Not only was she a heroine: she was the best kind of modern mother. It was all very exciting, and, after a while, rather boring, since Lady Leominster insisted on their accepting every suitable invitation, and as Chloe said, yawning, one hot July morning, one breakfast was really very like another, and each conversation the same as the last. 'And if anyone else asks me if I do not adore the dear Duke of Weston, I vow I shall throw something.'

'Yes,' said Camilla, 'I do not altogether blame him for beating a retreat from London and going to join Sir Arthur Wellesley in Ireland, though I own I could wish to have seen him and thanked him before he went.'

Chloe tossed her head. 'If he had wanted to be thanked,' she said, 'he could have stayed in London till we got here.'

'Perhaps he will come back when Sir Arthur sails for Portugal,' said Camilla, for Wellesley had been given command of the expeditionary force that was to sail from Cork any day now, to the relief of the Portuguese and ultimately the Spaniards.

'Much more likely he will go too,' said Chloe crossly, and as it turned out she was right. When the news came that the British expeditionary force had sailed at last, they learned that Weston had gone too as an additional aide de camp. 'I should think he would be of the greatest assistance to Sir Arthur,' said Camilla. 'Think how well he knows the country and the people.'

'Yes,' said Chloe. 'I expect he has gone back to some black haired girl in Lisbon.'

'Very likely,' said Camilla.

'Or several,' said Chloe.

'Why not?' said Camilla, whose heart was increasingly heavy these days. It was all very well to be the toast of the town, but where was Lavenham? He had applied for leave to return, and received it weeks ago. And still time dragged on and there was no word from him. The season had drooped to an end by now and Lady Leominster had agreed at last to the longed-for move back to Haverford Hall, since neither Camilla nor Chloe had showed the slightest enthusiasm for her suggestion that they should follow the *beau monde* to Brighton.

Their determination was amply justified when they reached Haverford Hall and found a letter from Lavenham awaiting his grandmother there. She read it quickly, with pursed lips and furrowed brow, then handed it, silently, to Camilla.

Chloe watched impatiently as Camilla in turn struggled to decipher the fine small handwriting of the letter, which had been many times redirected and, it seemed, at some time thoroughly soaked in water. 'Well,' she asked at last, 'what does he say, Camilla? Where is he?'

Camilla handed her the letter with a hand that shook. 'In Portugal,' she said. 'Looking for us.'

Chapter 13

Lavenham had reached Portugal only a week after his wife and sister left. Landed secretly, at night, some distance north of Lisbon, he had made, in reverse, almost the same journey that they had, and had contrived, after lying low for a few days, to get in touch at last with Dom Fernando. The news he received from him was part good, part bad. At last he knew that he had been right in his instinctive refusal to believe that Camilla and Chloe had gone willingly with Charles Boutet. Better still, he knew that they had escaped, but of the end of their story Dom Fernando himself was ignorant. He had learned, from his agents, of their near capture by the French, but at that point his information failed. They must hope, he said, that since there was no further news of them, they had succeeded in making contact with the frigate and were now safely in England. 'I only hope your son survived the voyage.'

'My son?'

'Of course, you did not know. Doña Camilla gave birth to a fine healthy boy while she was staying in my cottage. You have an heir, senhor.' He did not, being a kindly man, add, 'I hope.'

He hurried, however, to assure Lavenham that his wife and sister had the best possible guide in the shape of 'Mr. Smith', a British agent of whose daring and ingenuity he had heard amazing stories. 'If anyone could get them home safe, he would. But now we must think of you. Lisbon is no place for you these days. The French tyranny grows worse every day; they know that a British landing is imminent and are trying to terrorise us out of joining them. They are wasting their efforts,' he went on proudly, 'I can tell you that when your countrymen land the Portuguese will rise to a man. There are rumours, which the French strenuously deny, that Oporto is in a state of revolt already, and we only await the opportunity to follow their example. The Spaniards are not the only ones with courage to resist a tyrant. But in the meanwhile, we must think what we can do to hide you. I fear that I am the most dangerous of hosts. Monsieur Boutet is my sworn enemy and he is all in all with Junot these days—I will not dignify him with his title of Count of Abrantes.' Once more, as he had done for Camilla, Dom Fernando explained the maddening impossibility of getting a boat out to the British squadron which still blockaded Lisbon harbour. They were talking in his house which overlooked the harbour and could see the lights of the British ships as they spoke, but, Dom Fernando said, to reach them, in the teeth of the French guard, was impossible. 'No, my friend, you must await the English landing.'

And so Lavenham spent a month of infuriating inactivity working as a gardener on Dom Fernando's estate in Sintra. He had much to think about. He had a son—or had he? As so often before, he tortured his brain in a hopeless effort to remember what had really happened that night when he rode wounded and exhausted home to Camilla. That obstinately, despite everything, he loved her, he now knew . . . Could her story be true? In that moment of light-headed exhaustion could he really have forgotten his long loathing of women? Surely incredible, if so, not to remember. And yet, if not he, who was the father? Something about Dom Fernando's reception of him had almost convinced him at least that suspicions in that direction were unjustified— shameful. Apologising, in his heart, to Dom Fernando, he let his circling suspicions range once more, until, inevitably, they settled on Charles Boutet. All women were false. Suppose Chloe had been lying all the time to protect Camilla. And yet, all his instincts cried out against this explanation. In the teeth of everything, some instinct in him insisted that she was innocent. The result, after some days of intolerable thought, was a dreadful hatred of Charles Boutet. Ignorant of his true relationship to Camilla, he came finally to the conclusion that, not content with making love to Chloe, the Frenchman must have seized some unguarded moment to rape Camilla. This explanation, at last, had the ring of possibility about it. It would explain everything except Camilla's lies to him. If only (here he savagely cut away a whole swathe of baby grapes) if only she had told him the truth, he would have cared for her, protected her ... He stopped and gazed, for a moment, in astonishment at the drooping vine leaves on the ground. He had come a long way from hating women.

That night one of Dom Fernando's servants rode out with the news that the British had landed at last north of Lisbon, and been joined already by a Portuguese contingent. Helpless himself in Lisbon, Dom Fernando advised that Lavenham make his way there to join them, and, in the hope that he would succeed in doing so, sent him a packet of reports on the state of the French defences to be delivered to the British commander, Sir Arthur Wellesley. Delighted to have something to do at last, Lavenham set out at once, but found the countryside alive with French troops so that it took all his skill and knowledge of the district to avoid them through a day of arduous hill walking. By evening, he found himself on a little hill commanding a view of the British camp, but saw, to his dismay, a thin line of French outposts strung out between him and it. But there was no time to be cautious. Wellesley must have the papers tonight. He tucked them more securely into the secret pocket he had contrived in his rough peasant's jacket and started to work his way inch by inch down the hillside. He had memorised the positions of the different French pickets as best he could from his point of vantage, but as he worked his way along the winding bed of a little stream he soon found it hard to be sure exactly where he would encounter them. His progress grew slower and slower, with frequent pauses, in the gathering dusk, to look and listen for any clue as to the whereabouts of the enemy.

Just the same, he was almost upon them when a sentry's muttered curse made him shrink back among the bushes that grew along the stream. Watching and listening, he realised that the valley that had seemed so promising had, in fact, brought him directly towards French headquarters. Its sides were too precipitous to be climbed; there was not the slightest chance of going forward: he would have to retrace his steps to the head of the valley. It was dark, now, with only the promise of moonlight later, and it was lucky for him, as he felt his way back up the valley, that the attention of the French was concentrated in the other direction, towards the British lines. Otherwise, they must surely have heard him as he tore and fumbled his way, almost by touch alone, through the thick undergrowth.

Back once more on his hilltop, he had to admit to himself that the position, for the time being, was hopeless. He would have to wait for first light and make another attempt at crossing the French lines then. Having decided this, he settled himself philosophically for a few hours of uncomfortable sleep. Waking, with the first glimmerings of dawn, he was aware of a stirring of activity in the British camp. His hopes flared up at once. If they were preparing an attack, his chance of getting through to them, in the confusion of the fighting, would be enormously improved. Forcing himself to patience, he waited and watched, chewing meditatively on his last dry crust. He must know the direction of the attack, before he set out to try and get through to the advancing forces. As the light gradually strengthened, and he was able to get a better view of the British and French positions, he found himself increasingly certain of what must be the direction of the British advance. Inevitably, before they could march towards Lisbon, they must dislodge the French from the little village of Brilos which commanded the route they must take. If he stayed where he was, he would almost certainly be taken in the course of the day. He decided to stake everything on his interpretation of the British plan and set out for Brilos.

His best route, at first, took him back into the hills, and for a while the going was easy enough, with a thick screen of shrubbery masking him from the nearest French position. Both armies were awake now, and he could hear, in the clear morning air, the echoes of commands from the two camps. These sounds, with their suggestion of the comradeship of a soldier's life, intensified the loneliness and danger of his own position and he found himself, for a moment, near to despair. What was the use of going on? He was merely courting inevitable capture and death. And yet, what had he to live for? Camilla and Chloe were almost certainly dead, through his fault. How could he face England without them? He did not even want to. Strange to realise that Camilla had become the most important thing in his life. If she and her child should, by a miracle, have survived, he would forget everything and acknowledge the boy as his heir. The decision, towards which he had slowly been coming for several days, brought him an immense happiness and in its sudden glow he turned a corner too fast and walked into a French picket. Alerted by danger, he began to call furiously for an imaginary mule, pretended belatedly to see the Frenchmen, and demanded in peasant Portuguese, whether they had seen an imp of Satan, in the form of a big wall-eyed mule, pass that way. With many curses he described how the beast had escaped him and began to hope, as they showed signs of tiring of his monologue, that they would let him go without question. But one of them, more alert than the others, interrupted him; 'That is all very well,' he said in French, 'but we have orders to take in anyone we find, for questioning.'

His heart sinking, Lavenham pretended he did not understand and the man turned impatiently from him to shout to one of his companions. 'Here, you, François, you said you were cold. Here's an errand to warm you; take this cretin to Captain Boutet. It was

202

he who wanted to examine all these canaille . . . let him have them.'

For a moment, Lavenham wondered whether to make a dash for it, but decided his better chance lay in sticking to his character of an ignorant peasant and praying that the English attack would come soon. He knew this countryside pretty well, but not well enough to pose for long as a native. François tied his hands behind him and drove him ahead of him down the little path that led to headquarters. Stumbling obediently along, Lavenham had much to think about. He was being taken to Captain Boutet. Could this possibly be Chloe's and, as he now thought, Camilla's betrayer? The long bitterness boiled within him and, if he could have escaped, he would not.

The question did not arise. Five minutes' uneventful walk brought them to the little farm that served as French headquarters. Outside it, a slim figure in captain's uniform was standing drinking a beaker of coffee. Was it the same man he had seen, once, so indistinctly, in the garden of the Marvila Palace? Infuriatingly, he could not be sure, but stood, inwardly fuming, outwardly a picture of peasant stupidity, while François described his capture in rapid, vulgar French.

Captain Boutet listened impassively, then dismissed the man. He stood for a moment gazing thoughtfully at Lavenham, whose hands were still tied behind his back, then, carelessly fingering his pistol, he spoke in English: 'Welcome to our camp, my dear brother-in-law.'

Lavenham could not believe his ears. 'What?'

Boutet laughed. 'So they never told you, the dear girls. Well, to tell truth, I rather wondered whether they would. Yes, my Lord Lavenham, I am your wife's brother, and hope soon to complete our delightful relationship by becoming your sister's husband. In the meanwhile, we must consider what use to make of your not altogether opportune appearance. You are searching, I collect, for my sister—and yours. You will not find them, though I might contrive a meeting once you have given your consent to my marriage to Chloe. It is not, you understand, a matter of the slightest moment to me whether I have it or not, but we French, as you know, treat family ties with a good deal more respect than you British seem to. Chloe will be grateful to marry me on whatever basis, but I for my part would prefer to do everything gracefully and in order. So come in, my dear brother-in-law and give me your consent in writing.' Still lightly touching his pistol he gestured Lavenham ceremoniously into the main room of the little farmhouse.

Obeying in helpless silence, Lavenham thought he had never known despair before. Ever since he had talked with Dom Fernando, he had hoped against hope that Camilla and Chloe were safe home in England; now it seemed they were in Boutet's hands and Chloe dishonoured beyond repair. Anguish for her was mixed with a baffled questioning about Camilla. Boutet was her brother? Scoundrel though he clearly was, it was not possible that he was the father of the child. Tormented with new doubts—could it be Dom Fernando after all?—he hardly listened to what Boutet was saying but watched without interest as he produced paper and pen and began rapidly to write. 'There,' he said at last, 'that I think should do it.' He held up the paper for Lavenham to read. 'We shall have to unbind your hands so that you may sign, but I trust you will not attempt to take advantage of it. My men are within call, and—they do not love the British overmuch.' As he spoke, he had quickly untied the rope that held Lavenham's hands behind him and now laid the paper on the table with his left hand and stood back, covering him with the pistol.

The paper was a brief and comprehensive statement of Lavenham's entire approval of Chloe's marriage with Boutet and a guarantee of his assistance (if such should be needed) in bringing it about.

'It will be best for everyone,' said Boutet significantly, 'if you sign without delay.'

'I must see my wife and sister first.'

'Do you think so? How droll. First things first, my lord. I do not believe you would wish to see them as you might if you refused to sign.'

The threat was all the worse for being so vague. Lavenham picked up the pen. 'But how do I know you have them?' he asked, playing at once for information and for time.

'How do you know? Because I tell you so; word of a Forêt.'

'Oh?' Dryly. 'I have had some experience of your father's word.'

Boutet turned sallow with rage. 'Enough of this. You will sign at once, or you will regret it.'

'Shall I?' Lavenham took up the pen again and shifted the paper a little on the table. If only something would distract Boutet for even a second he might have a chance, now that his hands were free. 'How soon shall I see my wife and sister?'

'I said, enough of this talk!' Boutet was interrupted by the sound of shots and shouting outside. It was the distraction for which Lavenham had prayed, and in the moment when Boutet's attention shifted he swung the heavy table in his face, seized a sword from a pile of arms in the corner of the room and leapt for the door.

Boutet was after him in an instant, with a shout of 'Stop him,' but, like Lavenham, he was distracted by what he saw. The British attack had begun in earnest, and the little French detachment that had been based on the farmhouse were fighting for their lives. For the moment, Boutet's duties as commander outweighed personal thought and he was too busy shouting orders to his hard-pressed followers to spare more than a curse for Lavenham, who threw himself headlong into the thickest of the fray.

It was a risky enough action, since he wore the uniform of neither army, but his furious onslaught on the French rear did much to break their spirit. Imagining themselves surrounded, they broke and fled, leaving only Boutet and a few of his men still furiously engaged in hand to hand combat with the British. Once more, Lavenham threw himself into the little knot of fighting men, his one idea now to preserve Boutet's life. He must learn from him where Camilla and Chloe were.

Most of the British had gone in pursuit of the fleeing French but an officer and a few men were still fighting with Boutet and his followers. The result was a foregone conclusion. The French had never recovered from the first shock of surprise, and even as Lavenham ran up, all but Boutet had fallen or surrendered. The rest of the little English force were busy with the prisoners, while their officer was engaged in a furious sword fight with Boutet. Lavenham, waiting his chance to intervene, could not help admiring the Frenchman's cold skill as a swordsman. As he watched, a skilful thrust disarmed the Englishman and another would have finished him (for none of his men was near enough to come to his assistance). But this was the moment Lavenham had been waiting for. His sword flashed out and sent Boutet's flying. 'Surrender!' He spoke in English, and, quickly, to the officer, 'I am English, though I may not seem so. It is of the greatest importance that this man live.'

'Oh?' The English officer calmly retrieved his sword. 'I should be inclined to say I did not see the necessity of it, but I owe you something—my life, I rather think, and you are welcome to his —if you want it.' He gave a quick succession of orders to those of his men who had come running up. In a moment, Boutet was disarmed and bound. 'And now.' He held out his hand to Lavenham. 'Pray tell me to whom I am indebted for this most timely assistance.'

'My name is Lavenham.' He was surprised to find his hand being furiously wrung.

'The lost Lord Leominster? My dear sir, this is a happier encounter than I had dreamed. I am Weston, and more at your service than I can say. But come, I am afraid my rascals may run into trouble if they follow the French too far.'

'One moment.' Lavenham turned to Boutet. 'If you wish to live,' he said, 'tell me where my wife and sister are.'

Boutet spat. 'Why should I?'

The Duke of Weston intervened. 'Lady Leominster and Lady Chloe?' he asked. 'What has this rascal been telling you of them? It is not long since I had the pleasure of escorting them to England. If his only usefulness lies in a pretended knowledge of their whereabouts, I suggest we dispose of him at once.'

'Good God,' Lavenham looked at Boutet with loathing. But, 'No,' he said, 'favour me so far. Neither she nor I have much cause to love him, but he seems to be my wife's brother.'

Weston whistled. 'Lady Leominster's brother? How devilish inconvenient. We really do not want a brother-in-law in the hulks, do we?'

While Lavenham was digesting this startling remark, Weston gave a series of quick orders to his sergeant, and then, 'So much for that,' he said. 'Will you give me the pleasure of your company while we round up these idiots of mine before they get themselves into real trouble?'

Horses were brought up and as they mounted Lavenham asked, 'You said, "We do not want a brother-in-law in the hulks"?'

'Why yes. I have been trying to forget Lady Chloe for the last six weeks, but I begin to think it would be simpler to marry her. With your permission, of course.'

Chapter 14

In the end, Camilla and Chloe went to Brighton after all. It was much against Camilla's will, for she could not help a superstitious terror that by leaving Haverford Hall she might fail to receive some vital message from her husband. But in the country quiet that was to have refreshed her, Chloe pined so visibly from day to day that at last Camilla had to give in to old Lady Leominster's insistence that what they all needed was a touch of sea air and society. Everyone who was anyone was at Brighton courting the Prince of Wales, for who knew when his father might not plunge finally into madness and leave him master of the country?

'Not that I care two straws about that,' said the old lady robustly to Camilla, 'but frankly, I am anxious about your sister. If you ask me, she is pining for that young scapegrace of a Duke, and it seems, unfortunately, as if he had forgotten that she so much as existed. The only cure I ever found for a broken heart was another one, and I suggest we take her to Brighton and see what we can do about it.'

Having wrung reluctant agreement from Camilla and a listless acceptance of the plan from Chloe, she gave them no time to change their minds, but went to work with a will to find them a suitable house in Brighton. This was no easy matter, since all the most eligible houses had been taken long since, and Camilla had just begun to hope that they would be able to stay at home after all, when Lady Leominster announced triumphantly, one morning, that her agents had secured her a charming house on the cliff above the town and that they were all to set out next day.

It proved indeed a delightful house, and though Lady Leominster's friends muttered gloomy warnings about the chances of being held up and robbed on one's way home at night, Camilla and Chloe liked its position somewhat out of the town, and the extent of grassy hill that stretched away behind it. Nor did they find themselves entirely immune to the delights of Brighton, particularly since they were welcomed even more enthusiastically here than they had been in London. Sir Arthur Wellesley had landed in Portugal by now and society talked of nothing but his position, his chances, and, inevitably, of Portugal itself. Camilla and Chloe, who had actually been there, who had seen the country over which many a son and brother must now be marching, found themselves the objects of all attention, the centre of every conversation. So courted, so admired, so listened to, it was impossible not to enjoy themselves a little. After all, when the Prince of Wales took the trouble to cross the room and talk to them, they must, inevitably, warm to him and to life in general.

Seeing them surrounded with would-be partners for the dance, when they visited Brighton's Assembly Rooms, or listened to like oracles at one of the Prince's musical evenings at the Pavilion, Lady Leominster was almost alarmed at the success of the cure she had wrought. A superficial old creature herself, she had not the perception to realise that it was all on the surface. The only time of day when Camilla and Chloe really lived was when the mail came. Mutually aware of this, they tacitly helped each other in a thousand dodges to ensure that they were always at home at this all-important moment, and as the hot August days wore on they found themselves closer friends than ever in their silent, shared anxiety.

They were at the Pavilion for an afternoon concert when the news of Wellesley's victory of Vimiero began to be rumoured about. No one knew how the rumour had started, but as usual Camilla and Chloe found themselves the centre of an eager little crowd of enquirers. They had actually been to Vimiero? What was it like? Would the terrain favour the English forces, or the enemy? Were the French soldiers really such raw troops? Would the Portuguese come out strongly on the side of their old allies? Torn with anxieties of their own, the two girls nevertheless did their best to answer these questions, which themselves sprang from the terrors of many a mother and sister.

Presently Camilla looked about her. 'But where is the Prince?'

'He retired, hurriedly, this half hour past or more,' said one of Chloe's admirers. 'Perhaps he has received despatches at last.'

The questions continued, but Camilla and Chloe answered at random, their eyes and thoughts fixed on the entrance to the Prince's private apartments. One good lady was surprised to be told that Vimiero was a thriving city (Camilla was thinking of Lisbon) and another that Lisbon was an insignificant village (Chloe, of course, had Vimiero in mind). Both their thoughts were taken up with the same, all-important question. If the Prince had indeed retired to read the despatches describing the battle, would Lavenham — or the Duke — be mentioned? In some ways Camilla's anguish was the greater. After all Chloe knew that the Duke was in Sir Arthur's army. If he had been killed, it would certainly be reported, so that, for her, even silence would be good news. But all Camilla knew about Lavenham was that he had been landed north of Lisbon. He might have perished weeks since at the hands of the French. It was when she was thinking this that she told a particularly portentous dowager that the French were gallant allies, and the Portuguese raw troops.

The old lady raised her eyebrows and began an elaborately sardonic query, when Chloe interrupted her unceremoniously.

'Look,' she said, 'the Prince.'

The door of the private apartments had been thrown open and the Prince appeared, his plump person magnificent as usual, with, behind him, two gentlemen in travelling dress. As he paused for a moment, looking about the room, Chloe caught Camilla's hand.

'It is,' she said. And then, 'Can it be?'

Camilla was chalk white. 'Yes.'

Followed by the two dusty and unsuitably garbed gentlemen, the Prince crossed the room to where Camilla and Chloe stood, holding hands for courage.

'My dear Lady Leominster, Lady Chloe,' the Prince received their curtseys with his usual affable dignity. 'I bring you, you see, the best of news. We have won a great victory. These gentlemen have but now brought the despatches; they are covered with glory as well as with dust; you will welcome them, I know, for my sake as well as their own.'

And then, with a royal tact of which he was sometimes capable, he turned away to answer the eager questions of the crowd, leaving Camilla and Chloe face to face with Lavenham and the Duke. It was a moment of almost unbearable tension. Camilla had not seen her husband for almost a year, Chloe had not seen the Duke since she had been so rude to him on board the *Indomitable*. To make it worse, they knew themselves the target of all eyes. Camilla, who had tormented herself with imagined meetings with Lavenham, had never conceived of anything so frightful as this.

He was kissing her hand; 'At last,' he said.

The Duke was kissing Chloe's. 'If I dare?' His eyebrows rose in a grimace reminiscent of Mr. Smith. And then: 'My dear Lady Chloe, allow me to congratulate you on being once more a blonde.'

'Oh, you are impossible,' fumed Chloe. 'Camilla, everyone is staring, let us go home.'

'Yes,' said Lavenham. 'Let us indeed go home.' He urged the Duke to accompany them, but Weston refused. 'You will have much to say to each other. I will not risk Lady Chloe's further displeasure by intruding myself on your reunion. Besides, I intend to ride over this evening, to visit my mother. I will give myself the pleasure of calling upon you tomorrow morning, if I may?'

The remark was addressed equally to Camilla and to Chloe, but it was Chloe who answered. 'Tomorrow morning? Absurd! The Duchess lives clear at the other side of the county.' Then she coloured, furious with herself at having betrayed too much knowledge.

He merely bowed, took her hand in farewell and repeated; 'I shall see you, I hope, betimes in the morning. Though I can hardly hope to find you still sleeping as I did, once, on our travels.'

This reminder of the enforced intimacies of their journey at once infuriated and silenced Chloe. Colouring up to her exquisite eyebrows, she retrieved her hand, which he had somehow managed to keep, and followed Lavenham and Camilla from the room. Catching up with them, she broke into angry speech; 'I can see my grandmother was right. He is nothing but an overgrown schoolboy after all. Ride across country and back in a night indeed! I never heard of anything so ridiculous.'

'You would not have thought him ridiculous,' said Lavenham mildly, 'if you could have seen him on the field of Vimiero. He was mentioned in despatches, remember.'

'And so were you,' said Chloe, 'and with more reason, I'll be bound.' She fell silent, gazing steadfastly away towards the sea, to conceal, Camilla suspected, the tears she could not control. An oddly constrained silence fell on the three of them as they stood there, waiting for their carriage. There was so much to say, but how to begin? Normally, Chloe might have been relied on to plunge in with question and exclamation, but today even she was silent. It was a relief to all of them when their carriage appeared at last, and the little bustle of installing themselves provided a momentary slackening of the tension.

As the carriage moved forward Lavenham and Camilla both began to speak at once, then fell silent, deferring to each other. At last, Chloe laughed, 'At this rate,' she said, 'we shall arrive home without the slightest inkling of each other's adventures, and my grandmother will think us quite absurd. Come, Lee, you begin; tell us what you have been doing, racketing about in Portugal, and how you came to fall in with that braggadocio Duke of Weston.'

'Why, if you must know,' he told her gravely, 'We saved each other's lives—and from a friend of yours, too, a Monsieur Boutet.' And then, sparing her confusion, he turned to Camilla. 'My dear, why did you not tell me he was your brother?'

The endearment, the affectionate tone of the question were almost too much for Camilla. Swallowing tears, 'I . . . I did not dare,' she stammered.

'Was I so formidable a husband? Truly, I have much to answer for, and you much to forgive.'

Unable to speak, Camilla was grateful when Chloe burst in with a question. 'You encountered Charles? And saved Weston's life? But, tell me, what did you do to Charles?'

'Why, that was Weston's affair, since he was in command of the troops that rescued me and took Boutet prisoner.'

'A prisoner?' Camilla breathed. 'In England?'

'No, no,' Lavenham took her hand, 'do not distress yourself about him. I do not know exactly what instructions Weston gave his men. I can only tell you that by the time we reached the main body of the army, your brother had escaped.'

Camilla breathed a heartfelt sigh of relief, as Chloe spoke. 'Really, sometimes that Duke shows glimmerings of sense.' And then, anxiously: 'Lee, you did not tell him about Charles and me?'

'Why, no. I did not think it my business. I merely told him what Boutet himself had just told me, that he was my brother-in-law.' He smiled to himself as he recollected the Duke's reaction, and Chloe teased him in vain to find out what had amused him.

The carriage had left the town by now and was rolling up the hill towards their house. When Chloe pointed it out, Lavenham pulled the check string and told the coachman to stop. 'We have much to talk of, you and I,' he said to Camilla. 'Can I persuade you to walk the rest of the way with me?'

Panic seized her. She had counted on Lady Leominster's support at this crucial moment. But instinct answered for her, a faint, half intelligible, 'Yes.'

The carriage had stopped. Lavenham jumped lightly down, held out his hand for Camilla and apologised quickly to Chloe for leaving her. Then he gave Camilla his arm and led her away from the road to the grassy path that ran up over the cliff.

The carriage rumbled away; they were alone with the sound of the sea below and the larks above. For a little while, these were the only sounds. Lavenham walked on in silence, and her quick, anxious upward glances showed him a little pale, a little forbidding. At last he spoke.

'You have a son,' he said.

She stopped short. It was now or never. '*We* have a son.'

He looked down at her, surely more kindly than she had expected. 'That is your story still? I wish you would tell me the truth; I have tortured myself so, these long months, trying to understand, to believe . . . But how can I? Only this I do believe, you were never, purposefully, false to me. It is not in your nature. Only tell me what happened, what disaster befell you there, alone—and through my fault—in a strange land, and we'll speak no more of it. The child shall be my heir.'

Too much moved for words, Camilla clung, for a moment, silently, to his arm, searching vainly, in face of this extraordinary generosity, for the best way to tell him that the child was provably his. But, preoccupied with each other, they had approached the house without noticing, and now saw Lady Leominster and Chloe coming to greet them.

Lady Leominster took them quickly through the first greetings, her bright, observant eyes travelling, as she did so, from Lavenham to Camilla and back. Then: 'But why do we linger here? You must be impatient to see your son, Lavenham. He is asleep but

214

I told the nurse to expect visitors.' And, her bright eye fixing his: 'He has the Lavenham foot. My poor Camilla was in despair till I explained it to her.'

'I was nothing of the kind,' said Camilla, maternal feeling conquering every other anxiety. 'He is the most beautiful baby . . .' Her voice dwindled and died.

Lavenham had gone chalk white. There was a little silence, while Camilla trembled and Chloe looked, puzzled, from one to the other. At last Lavenham spoke. 'If he has his mother's looks to make up for his father's deformity I am sure he is. Come, my love, take me to see him.' And then, as they climbed the stairs, alone, for a moment together: 'You will forgive me, Camilla? Can you? Why did you not tell me?'

She pressed his hand. 'I am glad I did not. I shall never forget your goodness. Thinking as you did, you would have acknowledged him just the same. But come, see—' They were at the nursery door.

Edward was sleeping with an infant's passionate intensity. Bending over him. Lavenham smiled. 'I think I should have known him anyway.'

'Yes, I have often thought he had something of your look of determination.'

'You mean my damnable obstinacy? Well, thank God, with you for a mother, he will have a better upbringing than his father's. Do you know, I heard the other day, quite by chance, that my mother is dead.'

'Oh.' She did not know what to say.

'You will think it heartless perhaps, but I cannot tell you what a relief it is to me.' And then, in a rush, 'Oh, Camilla, give me time, and I may be some kind of a husband to you yet.'

'Of course.' But little Edward, disturbed by their voices, rolled over and gave something between a yawn and a grunt. 'Come,' she said, 'we shall wake him.'

'He sounds just like a pig,' said his father.

There was so much to be said, so many stories to be exchanged, that they all sat up till the small hours while Lavenham told of the hardships of the voyage to the Brazils ('but they were as nothing, compared to my anxiety for you,') and Camilla and Chloe, in return, described their rustication in the convent grounds and then their flight with 'Mr. Smith'.

'He seems devoted to you,' ventured Lavenham at last.

'Oh, to Camilla, yes,' answered Chloe. 'As for me, he found me an unspeakable burden from first to last, and made no secret of it. But, Lee you look dead—have you the migraine?—And as for me, I intend to be up and riding on the downs before breakfast.'

'But the Duke is to call on us,' Camilla reminded her, and then, forgetting the Duke at sight of Lavenham's pale and furrowed face: 'Chloe is right, you have the migraine, Lavenham. I can see it.'

'Yes, but at last I have my wife, too, to soothe it away with her clever hands.'

It was the signal for the party to break up. Conducting Lavenham to his room, Camilla paused for a moment at the door. 'Do you really wish me to try and soothe away your headache?'

'If you are not too tired.' There was something chilling about the formal phrase, and as she followed him into the room Camilla felt, with something like despair, that after all nothing had changed. They had slipped back, fatally, into the old intolerable position. She was still, after all that had passed, a figure in a farce, a wife and not a wife.

Lavenham closed the door behind her, removed his jacket and lay down with a sigh of relief on the wide bed. Her thoughts in a rebellious turmoil, she began the familiar task of soothing away his pain. He lay quiet for a while, yielding himself to her ministration, then, suddenly, turned over and grasped her wrists.

'Is it possible that you can still love me? After all I have done to you?'

Too late now, for pride and pretence: 'How can I help it?' she said simply.

Slowly, tenderly his hands were travelling up her arms to her bare shoulders. 'You should have let the girl undress you,' he said, 'You will find me but an awkward lady's maid, but, oh, my love, if you can truly forgive me, I mean to be a good husband.' His hands had found the fastenings of her dress now, but were indeed making but a bungled job of it.

'Let me.' As their hands touched, her impatience matched his. There was the sound of tearing cloth, a little sigh of satisfaction (from him? from her?) as her dress fell, an empty shell on the ground and he pulled her down on the bed beside him. His lips moved hungrily across her shoulder. 'To think I could have forgotten,' then, as she opened her mouth to speak, he closed it with his burning lips on hers.

.   .   .

The morning was gay with larks as Chloe rode up the downs behind the house, with only a groom in attendance. Her grandmother always breakfasted in bed and neither Camilla nor Lavenham had come down in time to prevent her escape. Now, taking breaths of cool, salt-flavoured air she set her horse to a gallop, congratulating herself on having got clean away from them all. It had been easy enough to see, last night, that Camilla and Lavenham were set for a reconciliation and domestic bliss, but how could she endure to share it? They treated her as a child—and had all of them apparently forgotten that today was her eighteenth birthday. They should be congratulating her on being grown up at last, but they were too much occupied with their own affairs. And why not? she asked herself bitterly. All she had done with her life so far was to make a fool of herself, first over the music master, then over Charles Boutet. It was no wonder her family had little patience or thought for her. And now . . . But she would not let herself think of her newest folly, the madness of loving the Duke, who cared more for his old mother than for her. She put her horse once more to the gallop, leaving her grumbling groom far behind.

Drawing up at last, breathless, on the hilltop, she found herself looking down on the house from which she had come, and saw the figure of a horseman ride out of the gate and turn up the long slope towards her.

At once she turned her horse's head away and started at a steady canter down the further slope of the hill. Absurd to imagine that the lone horseman might be the Duke, but intolerable, if it should happen to be, that he should think that she had expected him to follow her. She urged on her horse with foot and voice, but it was tiring now and responded only sluggishly to her encouragement. And suddenly, illogically, she was sure that the lone horseman was indeed the Duke come in search of her, having discovered at last to what an extent she had been compromised by that journey across Portugal. She was a romantic heroine—no doubt about that, but one, it had been gradually borne in upon her, not in the very best of taste. Camilla, overwrought with anxiety on Lavenham's account, had failed to notice the faint, delicate overtones with which society had contrived to indicate that while it was one thing for a married lady and her infant son to escape, glamorously, across Portugal with an eligible Duke, it was quite something else again for an unmarried girl about whose name some faint grey hint of scandal already clung.

Camilla had missed those slight, almost imperceptible withdrawings of rustling skirts, but Chloe had felt every one of them. Her heart sore already because of the Duke's disappearance first to Ireland and then to Portugal, she had been a helpless target for the gentlest, the subtlest and most intolerable of persecutions. The very admiration of her courage expressed by the ladies she met had contrived to carry in it a hint of shock, the suggestion—always implied, never outspoken—that they were glad that it had not happened to them, or, worse still, to their daughters; the attentions of the young men who had thronged around her had had a hint of freedom about them that she had found equally detestable and difficult to handle. This had been bad enough, but the thought that the Duke might become aware of it and feel himself in honour bound to offer her his hand was much worse. She looked back. The solitary horseman had reached the crest of the hill and caught up with her loitering groom. She saw them talk for a moment; then the groom, apparently dismissed, turned his horse back the way he had come, while the other figure, black and unrecognisable against the light, began to descend the hill towards her.

With a desperate kick of her heels, she contrived to urge her horse into an unwilling canter, and then, at last, a gallop. No use; an occasional surreptitious glance over the shoulder showed the figure behind her steadily gaining and becoming, as he drew nearer, more and more unmistakably the Duke. Absurdly, illogically, she panicked, and her horse, sensing it, wheeled suddenly and started hell-for-leather for home. Its reins were caught in a grip of iron. 'Good morning, Lady Chloe,' said the Duke politely.

Short of breath, helpless and furiously panting, she was aware that her hat had slipped to the back of her head, her cheeks were flushed, her hair, no doubt, all to pieces. His hands still held her horse's reins; helpless, she faced him. 'Good morning, Your Grace.'

'My Grace?' He raised his eyebrows. 'We are very formal all of a sudden. You did not treat Mr. Smith with such courtesy.'

'Nor did he me.'

He laughed. '*Touché*. Will you ever forgive me, I wonder, for that journey? So long as we live, I believe you will be twitting me with the fact that when we first met you were a reluctant brunette.'

'I cannot believe that it is a matter that will concern you greatly.'

'No? Not to have my wife for ever out of charity with me? You give me credit for greater fortitude than I possess.'

'What did you say?'

He laughed. 'At last I have contrived to startle you out of that society calm of yours. I said, "my wife". Surely you must know that we are beyond the social pale, you and I, if we do not marry? It is a regrettable truth, but if you do not make an honest man of me, I do not know how I am to face my devoted family – who have, by the by, been praying this age that I would die gloriously on the field of battle.'

'I wish you had,' she said furiously.

'That do not I.' Very leisurely, he reached into the deep pocket of his riding coat, produced a piece of paper and handed it to her. Her eyes huge with amazed indignation, she saw that it was a special licence for the marriage of His Grace the Duke of Weston with Lady Chloe Beatrice Sophronisba Lavenham, Spinster.

'You take things, surely, somewhat for granted,' she managed. And then, 'How did you know about the Sophronisba.'

'Your guilty secret? Your brother told me, of course, when he consented to the match.'

'Lavenham? Consented? I do not understand you, sir. My brother has said nothing to me of this.'

'Naturally, since I asked him not to. I prefer to do my own wooing. Besides, he has had his own affairs to think of. We settled it all when we first met in Portugal, and, being men, have not spoken of it since.'

'In Portugal? You knew already what would be said?'

'I knew at last that I could not live without you. My good Chloe, why do you think I went away, but to try and forget you, and why have I come back, but because I can't do it? Marriage has always been the thing of all others I meant to avoid. Do you seriously think that a little gossip would drive me into it? I shall be a deplorable husband; I shall drink and ride to hounds and probably beat you, but, I flatter myself, you will be as bad as a wife. Do you not think we might make a fine cat and dog affair of it, you and I, and snap our fingers at society?'

220

She had sat, so far frozen in her saddle, but now she could not help laughing. 'It is a most moving proposal, sir, and I am grateful to you for your efforts to spare me the knowledge of its real motives. But it is no use; I know as well as you do that only consideration for my brother drives you to it. Well, rest easy, and tear up your licence for I'd not have you if the gossip were ten times as loud.'

'No?' He took the licence readily enough, but tucked it carefully back into his pocket, from which he produced a small leather box. 'Then your birthday present is sadly wasted. Unless you wish to use it for your wedding with Monsieur Boutet.'

He handed her the box and she could not help opening it and looking for one heartwrung moment at the two rings that nestled there side by side, one a magnificent ruby, the other a plain gold band. She looked up at him. 'I . . . I do not understand.'

'You thought me a monster, did you not, to ride off so callously, yesterday, but I had to fetch these. No Duke of Weston has been married without the ruby since the Conquest – or before, for all I know – and I look on marrying you as a desperate enough venture without risking a family curse.'

She could not help laughing. 'Your proposal, sir, is grossly flattering!'

'Is it not? Shall we not have a fine quarrelsome life of it, you and I?' He took her hand. 'But it is your birthday. Let me give you joy.' He slid the ruby ring on to her engagement finger. 'If you call it joy to be engaged to a bully, which I know all too well is what you think me.'

She looked up at him. 'I . . . I do not know what to say. Are you *sure?*'

'Sure that I love you? Having fled you, from London to Ireland, and from Ireland to Portugal? I am back, my love, and you only lose time arguing for I mean to have you.' Suddenly his arms were round her, his lips found hers. For a long time, peacefully, their horses grazed, heads down to the close turf.

'Well,' he said at last, 'am I still to destroy the licence and make my cousin happy?'

She turned her flushed face up to his. 'I should be sorry to waste your trouble.'

'Well thank the Lord for that,' was his surprising reply. 'In that case, we must hurry. Mr. Fisher will have given us up long since.'

'Mr. Fisher?'

'The Reverend Mr. Fisher, vicar of Hove, who has been waiting our coming this two hours past.'

'You cannot be serious?' But she knew he was.

'Never more so. Why should society have the chance to whisper at our wedding? And why should I have to wait longer for you? Besides, I might change my mind or you yours. The risk is too great.' And he kissed her again to underline the remark.

．　　　．　　　．

Rising late with the lethargy of pure happiness, Camilla was surprised to learn that Chloe had been out riding for more than two hours, and that the Duke of Weston had called and ridden after her. When she reported this to Lavenham, he merely smiled. 'They will return, no doubt, in their own good time.'

Lady Leominster, however, when she came down, every hair and patch of rouge in place, was anxious and angry. 'That child will shame us yet,' she said. 'Mark my words, she will. To have run off again, and on her birthday, too!'

'Her birthday!' Camilla exclaimed. 'Oh, why did you not tell me?'

'I had other things to think about,' said her husband.

At that point, their first caller was announced and for the next hour they came in droves, full of congratulations, fuller still of questions. In the face of Camilla's and Lavenham's obvious happiness, spiteful questions were obviously out of order, but Chloe's absence produced a plentiful crop. 'Dear Lady Chloe . . . such a romantic story . . . such a pity the dear Duke is . . . well . . . you know . . .'

Smiling, listening, answering, Camilla began, with growing horror, to realise what Chloe must have been going through. Anxiety gnawed at her. She looked to Lavenham for reassurance, but he, too, was deep in a morass of question and compliment which seemed to grow more and more strident as time passed and still Chloe did not appear. Camilla had been through despair and back again, had found Chloe's lifeless body at the foot of the cliff, or drifting with the tide, when a red-faced footman threw open the doors of the room, cleared his throat to ensure silence, and announced in stentorian tones: 'Their Graces, the Duke and Duchess of Weston.'